T0305435

BUSINESS AND COMMUNITY IN MEDIEVAL ENGLAND

The Cambridge Hundred
Rolls Source Volume

Catherine Casson, Mark Casson,
John S. Lee and Katie Phillips

BRISTOL
UNIVERSITY
PRESS

First published in Great Britain in 2020 by

Bristol University Press
University of Bristol
1-9 Old Park Hill
Bristol
BS2 8BB
UK
t: +44 (0)117 954 5940
www.bristoluniversitypress.co.uk

North America office:
Bristol University Press
c/o The University of Chicago Press
1427 East 60th Street
Chicago, IL 60637, USA
t: +1 773 702 7700
f: +1 773-702-9756
sales@press.uchicago.edu
www.press.uchicago.edu

© Bristol University Press 2020

British Library Cataloguing in Publication Data
A catalogue record for this book is available from the British Library

Library of Congress Cataloging-in-Publication Data
A catalog record for this book has been requested

ISBN 978-1-5292-0973-0 hardcover
ISBN 978-1-5292-0975-4 ePub
ISBN 978-1-5292-0974-7 ePdf

Cover design by blu inc.
Front cover image: extract from John Hamond's map of Cambridge, 1592 (Courtesy of the Cambridgeshire Collection, Cambridge Central Library)

Printed and bound by CPI Group (UK) Ltd, Croydon, CR0 4YY

Contents

Abbreviations   v

Notes on the Authors   ix

Introduction   1

The Cambridge Hundred Rolls   7

Appendix 1: Amercements in Cambridge 1176–7: list of people,   245
many from Cambridge, who were amerced for carrying
corn by water without a licence

Appendix 2: Cambridge tallage of 1211: analysis of payments   249
1211–25

Appendix 3: Amercements of the Abbot of Ramsey and William   259
de Kantilup and their associates in Cambridge in 1219

Appendix 4: Gifts (oblata), representing fines for offences   263
made by Cambridge people in 1221

Appendix 5: Summary of information in published editions of   267
the Pipe Rolls relating to people and places in Cambridge,
1130, 1158–1224, 1230 and 1242

Appendix 6: Selected excerpts from *Rotuli Curiae Regis* I–XX,   285
relating to people and places in Cambridge

Appendix 7: Selected excerpts from *Calendar of Fine Rolls* I–III,   297
relating to people and places in Cambridge

Appendix 8: Cambridge debts: selected cases from the Exchequer   299
of the Jews, 1219–81

Appendix 9: Cambridge: Jewish records of debts by people   315
resident in or closely connected to Cambridge

Appendix 10: Feet of fines: selected cases relevant to the town   321
    of Cambridge

Appendix 11: Cambridgeshire subsidy rolls and eyres   325

Appendix 12: Mayors and bailiffs of Cambridge, 1263–1300,   333
    as listed by the antiquary William Cole

Appendix 13: Ancient places in Cambridge   337

Appendix 14: Family dynasties of property owners   343

References   365
Index   373

Abbreviations

BNM   Gray, J. Milner, *Biographical Notes on Mayors of Cambridge* (Cambridge, 1921)

BT   Bateson, Mary (ed.), *Cambridge Guild Records* (London, 1903)

CCCC   Online Catalogue of Corpus Christi Deeds https://janus.lib.cam.ac.uk/db/node.xsp?id=EAD%2FGBR%2F2938%2FCCCC09 (accessed 1 August 2017)

CCR   *Calendar of Close Rolls* (London, 1892–1972)

CPR   *Calendar of Patent Rolls* (London, 1835–1986)

EJ I   Rigg, J. M. (ed.), *Calendar of the Plea Rolls of the Exchequer of the Jews, I: Henry III, 1218–1272* (6 vols) (London, 1905)

EJ II   Rigg, J. M. (ed.), *Calendar of the Plea Rolls of the Exchequer of the Jews, II: Edward I, 1273–5* (6 vols) (Edinburgh, 1910)

EJ III   Jenkinson, H. (ed.) *Calendar of the Plea Rolls of the Exchequer of the Jews, III: Edward I, 1275–7* (6 vols) (London, 1925)

EJ IV   Richardson, H. G. (ed.), *Calendar of the Plea Rolls of the Exchequer of the Jews, IV: Henry III, 1272; Edward I, 1275–1277* (6 vols) (London, 1972)

EJ V   Cohen, S. (ed.), *Plea Rolls of the Exchequer of the Jews, V: Edward I, 1277–9* (6 vols) (London, 1992)

EJ VI   Brand, P. (ed.), *Plea Rolls of the Exchequer of the Jews, VI: Edward I, 1279–81* (6 vols) (London, 2005)

FC   Farrer, William, *Feudal Cambridgeshire* (Cambridge, 1920)

FFHR	Pipe Roll Society, *Feet of Fines of the Reign of Henry II and of the First Seven Years of the Reign of Richard I, AD 1182–1196* (London, 1894)
FFR	Pipe Roll Society, *Feet of Fines of the Tenth Year of the Reign of King Richard I and a Roll of the King's Court in the Reign of King Richard I, AD 1198–9* (London, 1900)
J	Stokes, H. P., *Studies in Anglo-Jewish History* (Edinburgh, 1913)
KC	Maitland, Frederic William (ed.), *Three Rolls of the King's Court in the Reign of King Richard I, AD 1194–5* (London, 1891)
LB	Clark, John Willis (ed.), *Liber Memorandum Ecclesie de Bernewelle* (Cambridge, 1907)
M	Maitland, Frederic William, *Township and Borough* (Cambridge, 1898)
ODNB	Cannadine, David (ed.), *Oxford Dictionary of National Biography* (Oxford, 2004), available at https://www.oxforddnb.com/ (accessed 1 July 2018)
PDC	Hunter, Joseph (ed.), *Fines, Sive, Pedes Finium: AD 1195–1214, I: Bedfordshire, Berkshire, Buckinghamshire, Cambridgeshire and Cornwall* (2 vols, 1835–44) (London, 1835)
PDH	Turner, G. J., *A Calendar of the Feet of Fines Relating to the County of Huntingdon Levied in the King's Court from the Fifth Year of Richard I to the End of the Reign of Elizabeth, 1194–1603* (Cambridge, 1913)
PDR	Rye, Walter, *Pedes Finium or Fines Relating to the County of Cambridge, Levied in the King's Court from the Seventh Year of the Reign of Richard I to the End of the Reign of Richard III* (Cambridge, 1891)
PR	*Pipe Rolls*, 98 vols (London, 1884–2016), especially the published rolls for the years 1130–1224, 1230 and 1242, vols 1–9, 11–19, 21–58, 50, 52–8, 60, 62, 64, 66, 68, 73, 75, 77, 80, 85, 86, 89, 91, 93, 94, 95, 98
S	Stevenson, W. H., *Calendar of Merton Deeds for Cambridgeshire* (n.d., Merton College Library)

StJ	Underwood, Malcolm (ed.), *Cartulary of the Hospital of St. John the Evangelist* (Cambridge, 2008)
StR	Gray, Arthur, *The Priory of St. Radegund* (Cambridge, 1898)
TNA	The National Archives, London
VCH 2 Huntingdon	Page, William (ed.), *The Victoria History of the County of Huntingdon, II* (3 vols) (London, 1932)

Notes on the Authors

Catherine Casson is Lecturer in Enterprise at Alliance Manchester Business School, University of Manchester, and a member of the Centre for Economic Cultures, University of Manchester. Her publications include a co-authored book with Mark Casson, *The Entrepreneur in History: From Medieval Merchant to Modern Business Leader* (Basingstoke, 2013), and articles in *Urban History*, *Business History Review*, *Business History* and the *Economic History Review*.

Mark Casson FBA is Professor of Economics at the University of Reading and Director of the Centre for Institutions and Economic History. He has published in *Economic History Review*, *Explorations in Economic History*, *Business History Review*, *Business History*, *Economic Journal* and other leading journals. He is the co-author (with Catherine Casson) of *The Entrepreneur in History* (Basingstoke, 2013) and co-editor (with Nigar Hashimzade) of *Large Databases in Economic History* (Abingdon, 2013).

John S. Lee is Research Associate at the Centre for Medieval Studies, University of York. He has an MA in Medieval History from the University of Durham and a PhD in History from the University of Cambridge. He teaches for the Centre for Lifelong Learning at the University of York. He has published the monographs *The Medieval Clothier* (Woodbridge, 2018) and *Cambridge and its Economic Region, 1450–1560* (Hatfield, 2005). He is co-editor, with Christian Steer, of *Commemoration in Medieval Cambridge* (Woodbridge, 2018). Book chapters include 'Crises in the Late Medieval English Cloth Trade', in A. T. Brown, Andy Burn and Rob Doherty, *Crises in Economic and Social History: A Comparative Perspective* (Woodbridge, 2015). He has also published articles in *Urban History*, *Economic History Review*, *The Local Historian*, *Yorkshire Archaeological Journal* and other journals, including 'Decline and Growth in the Late Medieval Fenland: The Examples of Outwell and Upwell', *Proceedings of the Cambridge Antiquarian Society* 104 (2015). He has recently prepared a chapter, 'Trinity in the Town', for a forthcoming multi-volume history of Trinity College, Cambridge.

Katie Phillips completed her PhD, 'The Leper and the King: The Patronage and Perception of Lepers and Leprosy by King Henry III of England and King Louis IX of France', at the University of Reading, funded by the Arts and Humanities Research Council. This work follows on from the dissertation produced for her MA(Res), an edited version of which has been published as 'The Hospital of St Mary Magdalene – The Leper-House at Reading Abbey', Berkshire Archaeological Journal 81 (2013). Further publications include 'Saint Louis, Saint Francis and the Leprous Monk at Royaumont', *The Reading Medievalist* 2 (2015) and 'Devotion by Donation: the Alms-Giving and Religious Foundations of Henry III', *Reading Medieval Studies* XLIII (2017).

Introduction

The *Rotuli Hundredorum*, better known as the Hundred Rolls, contain 1,800 pages of statistical information relating to property rents in c.1279 for King Edward I. A printed edition was published by the Record Commission in 1818, using the original medieval Latin, in a special typeface designed to replicate the abbreviated script of medieval scribes. It is this edition that has formed the basis for most (though not all) subsequent research on property holding at that time.

The geographical coverage of the rolls is incomplete, and Cambridge has better coverage than almost all other towns of similar size in England. Frederic Maitland pioneered statistical analysis of the Hundred Rolls in the appendix to his book *Township and Borough*, published in 1898. Cambridge, however, has been misunderstood. In the early 20th century its history was extensively studied by members of the Cambridge Antiquarian Society and its predecessor organizations, including distinguished scholars such as Gray and Stokes.[1] These scholars, like Maitland, were unaware that the coverage of Cambridge by the Record Commission was incomplete. The first and last rolls were included by the Commission, giving an impression of completeness, but the middle roll was omitted. This additional roll did not come to light until quite recently. This volume provides a new edition of the Hundred Rolls for Cambridge, including the previously unpublished roll. It also provides appendixes of new translations of untranslated sources that reveal the history of the properties recorded in the Hundred Rolls and the families who owned them. A companion monograph, analysing the contents of the rolls, has also been published by the authors with Bristol University Press. It is entitled *Compassionate Capitalism: Business and Community in Medieval England*.

The content of the Hundred Rolls

The Hundred Rolls are the records of government enquiries in 1255, 1274–5 and 1279–80 that were conducted across the subdivisions of English counties known as hundreds.[2] The commission of 1255 focused on royal rights, that of 1274–5 on 'liberties and the misdeeds of officials' and that of 1279–80 on liberties and landholding.[3] For each enquiry commissioners were instructed to go in person to their allocated county or counties and to 'take evidence of sworn juries of knights and freeholders in every hundred'.[4] The evidence related to four issues: domains of the king (namely fiefs, escheats, liberties and holdings), who possessed them in and in what form (domain, tenancy, service, cottage, free tenancies, woods, parks, chases, warrens, waters, rivers, freedoms and market days), from whom (tenants or others) and of which fee or other tenures of scutage. The results of these enquiries were recorded and provided to the king, but unfortunately little is known about how the information in the rolls was used.[5] The commissions of 1274–5 were examined by Cam, with a focus on the administrative procedures of the commission and the information they provided on the working of Edward I's government.[6] The report of the commission of 1279–80 was examined by Raban, who presents it as the most ambitious of all the enquiries and suggests that, although unfinished, it may have been intended to be a comprehensive survey of landholding similar to that compiled in the Domesday Book in 1086.[7]

This volume is based on material for the enquiries of 1279–80. Twenty-six teams of commissioners for the survey were appointed on 12 March 1279 and were instructed to go in person to their allocated county or counties and to 'take evidence of sworn juries of knights and freeholders in every hundred'.[8] The Cambridge borough Hundred Rolls, the focus of this book, provide a snapshot of the town in 1279 and give its history going back to c.1200.[9]

The articles setting out the scope of the inquiry into Cambridgeshire were distinctive in comparison to other counties; on the one hand they did not require investigation into the conduct of the current sheriff or escheator, but on the other they required the history of every property holding.[10]

The immunity of the sheriff suggests that he may have had exceptional influence over the local inquiry. Sir William le Moyne of Raveley, Sheriff of Cambridgeshire and Huntingdonshire, 1275–8, came from a distinguished Norman family. This family had held the manor of Raveley, Huntingdonshire since the 11th century, and was responsible for the foundation of Ramsey Abbey (the family name translates as 'the Monk'). Sir William had previously been sheriff in 1258, when he had participated in a royal inquiry into grievances in Cambridgeshire.[11] His personal interest may explain some of the distinctive features of the Cambridge rolls.

The bailiffs of Cambridge, as officials of the borough, may also have had an influence in the scope and scale of the inquiry. They certainly had an incentive to support the inquiry. They had some long-standing grievances against a previous sheriff, and they were seeking to confirm two charters of Henry II, in which they were successful. Finally, access to university scholars as well as monks may explain why the rolls were written up in such a professional manner. The choice of Cambridge in this study did not, therefore, derive from its status as a university town, which was largely nascent at this time, but simply from the unprecedented scope of its records. Our interpretation of the contents has been strengthened by the use of additional documents produced by royal officials and religious institutions, and by deeds archived in various colleges.

While comprehensive coverage of England was apparently the intention of the 1279–80 enquiries, in practice the coverage was uneven. Some counties were covered very well, such as Cambridgeshire and Huntingdonshire, while others were covered only partially or not at all. In 1812–18 the Record Commission printed an edition of the rolls, known at the time as *Rotuli Hundredorum*.[12] The rolls were transcribed but not translated, and printed in archaic script. Since then new rolls have come to light; the definitive list is online in The National Archives Discovery catalogue.[13] The rolls can be inspected at The National Archives in Kew. There are three rolls, but only two were published by the Record Commission because the third had not been discovered at the time. These two rolls were analysed statistically by Maitland in the appendix to *Township and Borough*, and have formed the basis of all Cambridge local history since then.[14] The existence of the third roll was noted by Raban, but it remained neglected.[15] This roll transforms our knowledge of Cambridge because it contains important information on several parishes whose properties were largely omitted from the first two rolls, giving a false impression that their population and density of building was very small.

The numbering of the rolls in the Discovery catalogue reflects the order in which they were identified, and not the sequence in which they were prepared in 1279. One reason why the existence of a missing roll was not recognized earlier is that the first roll contains the heading and the second roll has a space at the end, giving the impression that they are complete. It is only when the third roll was examined that it became clear that it is actually second in the sequence. Previous Cambridge antiquarians, such as Gray and Stokes, noted apparent inconsistencies between the rolls and other sources, but did not pursue the issue.[16] For this volume a new edition of the Hundred Rolls has been prepared, with a full translation of all three rolls in their original order, and with additional material on the Barnwell suburb too.

The county of Cambridge is also covered well by the Hundred Rolls. The county has played a prominent part in large-scale studies of medieval landholding and peasant agriculture.[17] The most ambitious study of peasant landholding in Cambridgeshire based on the Hundred Rolls was undertaken by Cicely A. H. Howell. Howell's study was never completed, but an archive of research materials relating to published and unpublished work on peasant landholding and to unfinished research using the Cambridgeshire Hundred Rolls has survived.[18]

Additional sources

A range of additional sources were consulted with the aim of obtaining additional information on the families and institutions discussed in the Hundred Rolls.[19] In some cases the text was transcribed and translated from original documents, but in many cases it was translated from a published or unpublished Latin transcript. In a few instances, cases relating to Cambridge have been abstracted from a longer list that has already been translated.

Royal records

Contextual information on Cambridge before the time of the Hundred Rolls is provided in the Domesday Book.[20] The visits of the royal itinerant justices to Cambridge in 1247, 1261, 1268, 1272, 1286 and 1299 provide some additional context to life in the town around the time of the Hundred Rolls.[21] Eyres were usually held at seven-year intervals, and dealt with civil pleas (between individuals on subjects such as recovery of land and debt) and crown pleas (including deaths caused criminally; felonies and non-violent issues concerning the king's proprietary and prerogative rights).[22]

Financial records of the Pipe Rolls (the Crown's annual income and expenditure records), tallage accounts (inhabitants liable for tax) and subsidy rolls (records of occasional taxes on personal property) provide information on levels of wealth of individuals that is helpful for the composition of the family biographies.[23] The tallage rolls also allow us to directly engage with Maitland's work as he printed the tallage of Cambridge for 1219 as part of his investigation into the presence of a burgess class in Cambridge. We have produced an analysis of payments in the Pipe Rolls of 1211–25 and the tallage of 1225, which corrects Maitland by showing that there was no tallage in 1219. It also analyses the proportion of tallage paid by different individuals.[24]

Members of family dynasties often sought to protect or enhance their holdings through legal process. They may also have been involved in other cases pertaining to their careers and political activities. The activities of some family members appear in the records of the Curia Regis sedentary court (known after c.1250 as the Court of Common Pleas) with a remit ranging from trespass cases involving violence to actions for the recovery of moveable property, the enforcement of contracts, and the standard of service provided by professionals and craftspeople.[25] We have translated extracts from the Latin transcription of cases involving individuals from the families in Cambridge at the time of the Hundred Rolls.[26]

Acquisition, transfer and disposal of land are recorded in four royal sources. The Patent Rolls and Close Rolls contain letters and instructions issued by the Crown. They are useful for tracing transfers of land as they record rights or land granted to an individual as well as permission to sell land (sometimes called a 'licence to alienate').[27] The records of the Exchequer of the Jews detailed the civil and criminal jurisdiction of the Justices of the Jews over transactions between Christians and Jews, including loans for which property was security.[28] Feet of fines reveal disputes over property, often stemming from land transfers, held in the king's court.[29]

Civic, religious and educational institutional records

Cambridge has few surviving urban records. The mayors and bailiffs of Cambridge, 1263–1300, were listed by the antiquary Reverend William Cole (1714–82) and can be supplemented by some information from the Curia Regis Rolls and the Merton College deeds.[30] An edition of the guild records was produced by Bateson.[31] This information was useful for the family biographies in Chapter 4 and for Chapter 7 of the accompanying volume. Additional information on the history and topography of Cambridge was derived from the collections of copies of manuscript documents and observations deposited in Cambridge University Library by the Reverend Thomas Baker (d. 1740) and Cole's additional papers in the British Library.[32]

Records of religious institutions contain information on the operation of the Cambridge property market that can supplement the Hundred Rolls. For Barnwell, *Liber Memorandum Ecclesie de Bernewelle* was probably compiled in the late 13th century and, among other material, contains a rental of 1295.[33] The Prior of Barnwell's register also survives in the

Gough manuscripts at the Bodleian and provides panel data of a property portfolio on a yearly basis.[34] Jesus College archives contain the surviving charters and accounts of St Radegund's, many of which were published by Gray.[35] Deeds recording rents and donations of property also survive in the Jesus archives and inform on the support the priory received from many leading families of Cambridge, which was particularly strong during the 12th and 13th centuries. The cartulary of the hospital of St John the Evangelist is incomplete but informs on its urban and rural estate during the period c.1220–c.1280.[36] It survives in the collections of St John's College, University of Cambridge, and was recently edited by Underwood and used by Rubin in her monograph.[37]

Some college archives inform on the acquisition and disposal of property by leading Cambridge families. Merton College archives, University of Oxford, contain information about the Dunning family, whose properties were acquired by the college's founder.[38] Corpus Christi College, University of Cambridge, acquired many gifts of property from tradesmen, each of which came with its record of previous ownership, as recorded in the college deeds.[39] Peterhouse Treasury, Peterhouse College, University of Cambridge, contains deeds of relevance to the family biographies, as it was the first college to be founded.[40]

University archives also provide some information on its interactions with the property market. A compilation of statutes and ordinances dating to c.1250 exists in the Angelica Library in Rome and was edited by Father M. B. Hackett.[41] It contains a chapter detailing processes by which scholars could find lodgings and masters hire schools in Cambridge at reasonable rents.

The Cambridge Hundred Rolls

This volume provides a translation from the original of the Hundred Rolls for Cambridge, TNA SC5/CAMBS/TOWER/1, Parts 1–3 and Barnwell SC5/CAMBS/TOWER/2. Each part corresponds to a particular roll. The rolls are in reasonably good condition, although some of the text is darkened and a few small portions of text (indicated in the translation by a row of dots) are missing.

The transcriptions from which the translation was made were checked against the Record Commission edition, with the exception of Cambridge part 3, which was not available to the Commission. The sequencing of the responses to the enquiry makes it clear that part 3 actually follows part 1 and precedes part 2. However, we have retained the sequence used by TNA to avoid confusion and to maintain correspondence with the Record Commission edition. The fact that it was the middle roll rather than the final roll that was missing probably explains why the omission was not recognized until fairly recently.

Each item (or paragraph) has been given a reference number. The use of reference numbers simplifies the referencing of the rolls in the main text of the book, and it should be of value to future researchers. Some numbers are prefaced by a letter. No letter signifies an individual property or a pair of linked properties (e.g. a messuage with land attached, or a pair of adjacent messuages). A preface R indicates a stream of rental income; P indicates a portfolio of properties where only the total rent is given and individual rents are difficult to impute; A indicates that there is no information on either location or rent; and F indicates contextual information that is not directly relevant to specific properties. Numbering is sequential within each category. All items prefaced R, P and A are excluded from the regression analysis of rents in Chapter 2 'Dynamics of the Property Market' in *Compassionate Capitalism: Business and Community in Medieval England*; they are examined elsewhere in the main text.[42] For items with no letter the reference number corresponds to a row in an Excel spreadsheet of rental payments; because the Excel spreadsheet has headings in row 1, the numbering begins at 2.[43]

All remarks that appear in square brackets have been added by the editors to clarify the structure and interpretation of the rolls.

Some pairs of letters are often interchanged in the original rolls; for example, 'y' for 'i' and 'e' for 'a'. The original spellings have been followed except for commonly occurring names (e.g. 'Dunning' and 'Dunnyng' both become 'Dunning' and 'Berton' and 'Barton' both become 'Barton'). It is often difficult to distinguish 'c' from 't' in medieval handwriting, or between 'n' and 'u', and the Hundred Rolls is no exception; context often clarifies the issue but not invariably so.

In this translation place names have been literally transcribed except for frequently occurring places whose names have been standardized (e.g. Cambridge, Newnham, Howes). Owing to variations in spelling, sometimes within the same entry, many place names, although they might be guessed at, cannot be absolutely confirmed. For this reason, the variations have been transcribed as they have been written in the manuscript.

Where an individual is described as being from a particular place, the 'de' has been left and interpreted as a toponymical surname, other than in the case where the place name is preceded by a personal name and a surname, and also in the case of some commonly cited places (e.g. St Edmund's or Barton).

If a place has a standardized name then 'de' may be replaced by 'of' in personal names (e.g. Ambrose of Newnham). Several variants of the same personal or family names often appear in the rolls, and some examples are given below. Other examples are given in Chapter 4 of the accompanying volume. Names that do not occur frequently are not normally standardized between entries, but may be standardized within individual entries to avoid confusing the history of the property. Where a person has a frequently occurring surname indicating an occupation 'le' may be replaced by 'the' (e.g. Herbert the carter). This does not apply to other names, however (e.g. 'William le Rus' is preferred to 'William the Red').

Where the name of an occupation immediately follows a personal name, it has been interpreted as a surname, and capitalized as such. A few common occupations have been translated into modern day English where they equate to common surnames (e.g. Fabro/Smith, Cissor/Tailor, Pistor/Baker, Aurifaber/Goldsmith). Where the occupation is preceded by 'le', the 'le' has been maintained and again interpreted as a surname. In a number of instances, the occupation follows a personal name and surname, and in these cases the occupation has been translated as a description and not a name.

Some variants of family names: Achelard/Adelhard/Athelard; Alvechild/Aluethild/Alwewethild; Ampe/Hampe; Andre/Andrew; Astin/Astines;

Attegate/Ategate; Bole/Bolle; Briitlod/Britlof; Elesheved/Eleveshod/
Heleshewed; Forward/Forreward/Fereward; Longis/Lungis; Puch/Punch;
Spartegrave/Spertegrave; Torbelville/Turbelvile/Turbelvill/Turblevile/
Trubelvile; Vivien/Fiyien/Fiyion/Fithion/Siyion; Whitesmith/
Witemith/Witemyth/Withemyth/Wyteswith

Some variants of place names: Abington/Abinton; Eversden/Euresdon;
Hauxton/Hoketon/Hogiton/Houghton; Hockley/Hokele; Wilbraham/
Wilburham/Wilberrham; Wimpole/Winepol/Wynepol/Wenepol.

[INTRODUCTION]

COUNTY OF CAMBRIDGE

[F1]   Inquiries obtained on behalf of the Lord King in the county of
         Cambridgeshire from the seventh year of King Edward I, both
         of the demesnes of the Lord King and the fiefs, escheats and
         liberties of the vassals and all items of fiefs and holdings affecting
         the Lord King and other things whatever they may be, and who
         holds them in demesne as in demesne, in tenancy as in tenancy,
         in service as in service, in cottage tenure as in cottage tenure, and
         subsequently in free tenancies as in free tenancies, and in woods
         and in parks, in chases, and in warrens, and in lakes, in rivers
         and all freedoms and markets and other holdings whatever and
         wherever they may be, and by which, either from the tenants,
         or from others and which fee and other tenures of scutage are
         accustomed to be given and should be given and how much of
         feudal honour no matter what, and which fee they hold, in what
         manner, in which way and for what time.

[JURORS]

[F2]   The sworn statement of the jurors of the town of Cambridge
         written in the text above, evidently by Bartholomew son of
         Michael, Nicholas Mort … [Morice], Robert Weymond, Henry
         Tuylet, Gerald de Wyvard, William Seman, Richard Bateman
         senior, Geoffrey le Ferun, Richard Bateman junior, Robert
         de Madingley, Richard Goldring, John of St Edmunds, Radulph
         de Teversham and Hugh de Brunner.[44]

[KING'S POSSESSIONS: CASTLE]

[F3]   Which and how many manors the Lord King has in his
         possession in the counties of Cambridge and Huntingdon both
         from ancestry of the lords of the Crown and from escheats and
         purchases.

Item it is said in his oath above that the Lord King has the Castle of Cambridge in his possession with the county, and this was given by his sheriff who now is.

Item it is said and that the predecessors of the Lord King held the said castle with the said county in the above-mentioned manner.

[RENTS]

[2]   Item it is said that Mabilia heir of Henry Hyrp owns a certain piece of land in the fee of the castle for which she pays per annum to the bailiffs of Cambridge 4d.

[3]   Item Leon Dunning holds 1 messuage with its appurtenances in the same fee which he bought from Nicholas, heir of Nicholas Waryn, for which he pays per annum to the said sheriff 4d.

[4]   Item Leon holds a certain piece of land in the same fee for which he pays per annum, to the said sheriff, 6d.

[5]   Item Robert heir of Robert Seman holds a certain piece of land in the same fee for which he pays per annum, to the said sheriff, 12d.

[SOCAGE: see also below]

[F4]   Item if any free tenant in socage or bondage tenant from the ancient domain of another tenant in socage or any free tenant or other bondage tenant from land or ...[45] should be sold or in any other way alienated etcetera, no one knows.

[F5]   Item it is inquired for each hundred how much any archbishop, bishop, abbot, prior, count, baron, knight, free man or burgess holds ...[46] in the county, burgh and market town or all other towns and hamlets held as in the castle protected by forts and lands in the knight's fee, etcetera.

[THE BURGESSES]

[F6]   Item it is said that the burgesses of Cambridge hold the town of Cambridge with all its appurtenances in fee farm from the Lord King as tenant-in-chief, in meadows, pastures, mills, waters, lakes with all their liberties and customary liberties pertaining to the said town of Cambridge by charters which they have by predecessors of the Lord King, namely lord John, father of Lord King Henry. And from Lord King Henry, his son, father of Lord Edward who is now king. And they pay per annum for the aforesaid town and its appurtenances as is stated above 11 blanched pounds. And 20 new pounds and 100s. newly paid by increment and for the farm of the house of Benjamin, 1 mark. And for the land of Lord Simon de Insula and Aunger 5s. 4d. to the Lady Queen, mother of the Lord King, who holds the said town of Cambridge with its appurtenances in dower by concession of the lord Edward, her son, who is now King.

[THE BISHOP OF ELY]

[F7]   Item it is said that the Bishop of Ely holds a water-mill and a meadow pertaining to the said mill and 10s. paid annually in the said town of Cambridge. Which same mill, meadow and annual income are worth 10 pounds per annum. In which manner and by which way and from what time this warrant the said Bishop holds the said mill, meadow and income they do not know.

[BARNWELL PRIORY POSSESSIONS]

[F8]   Item the prior and canons of Barnwell hold a certain place near the wells of Barnwell where their conventual church was founded. And it consists of 13 acres of land and they have more land that Pagan Peverel, knight, gave to them, who was their founder and patron in perpetual alms, and extended it by a great extent in dry land and marshland towards the river of Cambridge.

[F9]   King Henry senior gave the place to the aforesaid Pagan Peverel for the house of the aforesaid canons.

[F10]   Item the said prior and canons have within and outside the town of Cambridge 3 carucates of land and more, and 10 pounds of income, for which they pay each year to the tenant-in-chief of the lord's fee through service owed and accustomed as is stated below. And to the bailiffs of the Lord King of Cambridge who hold the said town in fee farm from the Lord King for hawgable and landgable, 57s. at hockday, for which land and income they have in large part by gift of many people in perpetual alms and other parts by purchase and acquisition, in the same way as other parts from the community. Whereof Count David gave to them 2 acres of land lying before the gate of their church for 4d. per annum. And Countess Matilda gave them 2 acres of land in perpetual alms.

[F11]   Item also the man named Picotus Wilicom gave to them a certain place in the town of Cambridge in perpetual alms where recently St Giles's Church was situated at the castle. And here lived the said canons for 20 years until Pagan Peverel transferred them from this place to the place in Barnwell where they presently live.

[P1]   The said canons also have by gift of Dunning, great-grandfather of Harvey Dunning and Matilda, his wife, 50 acres of land in the fields on this side of the bridge and by donation of Alketillus 50 acres of land in free alms save hawgable to the Lord King, for which they pay each year to the bailiffs of the Lord King as is thenceforth in the area above in the aforesaid script, 57s.

[P2] Item they have by gift of the same Harvey 3 messuages in Cambridge, that is 1 near the household that Robert Seman once held and 2 others which Henry Lifewos and Robert the painter held and they pay to the aforesaid bailiffs of the Lord King of Cambridge for hawgable as is stated above in the aforesaid script 57s.

[P3] Item the said canons have by gift of William son of Baldwin Blancgernun 1 messuage and 20 acres of land in fee from the prior of Ely, and they pay in respect thereof per annum to the prior 20 marks and the prior of Ely acquits them to the bailiffs of the Lord King of Cambridge for hawgable, by which warranty the prior of Ely is unaware of the receipt of the said sum.

[P4] Item they have by gift of William 72 acres of land and a whole messuage which Ranulph son of Guy held from them in *Wico Pont'* in the lane, which is towards the house of Henry Wymen and the large wharf, and they pay per annum to the bailiffs of Cambridge for hawgable, as is stated in the great summary written above, 57s.

[P5] Item the said canons have 27 acres of land in the fields of Bradmore in perpetual alms by purchase of Reginald Cyne.

[P6] Item the said canons have by gift of William Waubert 21 butts of land in Portfeld which pertain to 3 acres which he bought from John le Rus, and 4 selions which pertain to 1 acre for rent of 8d., which the said John used to pay to the prior of Barnwell.

[P7] Item the said canons have by gift of Stephen de Hauxton 7 acres of land in the fields of Cambridge, of which the same Stephen bought 2 acres from William Blancgernun and 1 acre from Gregory le Sanuner and the 4 remaining acres from Godfrey Astin, of which Luke Carter holds presently 3 acres of land in Swinecroft, which William de Henges bought from the prior of Barnwell for rent of 12d. per annum.

[P8] Item the said canons have by gift of Joel who was father of Robert, former prior of Barnwell, 1 messuage and 6 acres of land, that messuage held by Stephen de Hauxton and later Peter de Welles from the prior of Barnwell for rent of 18s. 4d. per annum, by which manner that messuage lies waste and burnt and they have nothing at that place.

[P9] Item the said canons have by gift of Thomas Toylet 24 acres of land in fee from Baldwyn Blancgernun, which he held from the prior of Barnwell by charter and for rent of 26d. per annum, and 28 acres and 1 croft which the same Thomas bought from John le Rus, and 7½ acres and a ½ rood which he bought from Geoffrey Melt, and a ½ acre which he bought from Walter Baker. And 3½ acres which he had by gift of Robert Parleben, and 2 acres which he bought from Michael son of Robert Parleben, and 1 acre which he bought from John son of Roger le Infirmarer, and 2 roods which he had by gift of Radulph, son of Henry, in exchange for another 2 roods. And 1 rood which he bought from the aforesaid Geoffrey Melt. And 15d. of income paid annually which Winfr' son of Hamo of Barnwell owed to him for ½ acre of land which he held from him in the fields of Barnwell; for this land the said canons performed to the tenants-in-chief of the lord's fee the due service, by which custom they are unaware, and provided to their almoner of Barnwell a perpetual chapel for the celebration of divine mass for his soul and for the souls of all their deceased faithful. And in respect thereof they pay per annum to Maddi de Balsham, who was wife of that Thomas, for her whole life, 6 marks.

[P10] Item the said canons have by gift of Walter de Wyshunden through the hands of the bailiffs of Cambridge 10s. of income annually which he bought from Thomas of the Wardrobe, and that Thomas from Robert son of Martin and that Robert from Richard son of William and that Richard acquired those 10s. for his service by donation of the Earl David of his third penny of Cambridge.

[A1] Item the said canons have by gift of Master Nigel 6 acres of land in exchange for another 6 acres.

[A2] Item they have by gift of Roys, son of Reginald de Marshall in his frank marriage in perpetual alms 2 acres of land.

[A3] Item they have by gift of Isabella de Nedigworye 1 acre in perpetual alms.

[A4] Item they have by gift of Eustace de Nedham a ½ acre of land in perpetual alms.

[P11] The canons have by gift of Brother Atius 3 messuages in the town of Cambridge, that is 1 which Simon son of Ailede held from him and 1 that Adam Stars held and 1 which is adjacent to the stone gate with all rent pertaining to the said messuages.

[P12] Item they have by donation of the aforesaid Brother Atius the whole holding which Reginald of Abington held from him in the parish of St Mary's, with 22s. of annual income and other income of 12d., which Robert son of Richard Colt owed to him for 1 messuage before the stone gate.

[P13] They have also by gift of the aforesaid Atius 6 acres of land in fee of Baldwin Blancgernun for rent of 12d. annum for the said land, and for the payments coming to the said canons, a permanent secular chapel for celebrating divine mass for the soul of Brother Atius and for the souls of all the deceased faithful in the alms of Barnwell, and make to the tenant-in-chief of the lord's fee for service owed and by custom of which they are unaware. And to the bailiffs of the Lord King of Cambridge as is stated in the aforesaid text above, 57s.

[A5] Item they have by gift of John le Kaleys and Basilia, his wife, 40 acres of land with appurtenances in the fields of Cambridge according to that contained in a certain chirograph composed between them in the court of the Lord King. And also all rent of Master Henry de Nuttele, Master Reginald le Blund of Welles, Master Bartholomew son of Radulph de Fordham, brother of the hospital of Stourbridge Common, Osbert King, William Melo, Denis son of William Smith, John Mason, Walter son of Peter Hunte, Robert Wulward, William de Abiton, Alicia de Waleden, William Prickenie', Simon ad Aquam, Richard Sadelbowe, John Sittertis, Everard of Trumpington, brother of St John's Hospital, Cambridge, of all lands and holdings which they held previously from the aforesaid John and Basilia in Cambridge and Barnwell.

[P14] For this certain land and income conceded to the canons in the court of the Lord King by the aforesaid John and Basilia, for the whole of both of their lives, 2 corrodies of 2 canons and 1 free servant and 14s. sterling each year in 2 instalments for the provision of their clothing and suitable housing in the town of Barnwell, and 5,000 turfs for burning and 3 cartloads of straw at the feast of St Martin. And if Richard le Kaleys, son of this Basilia, and Matilda, sister of this Richard, outlive the aforesaid John and Basilia, the said prior and canons will pay to one or the other of them each year for all of their lives 8s. and the corrodies of 2[47] canons. And further the said prior concedes to the said John and Basilia for all his life 3 acres of land. Such that after the death of all the aforesaid should be quit of all matters to the said canons, forever in perpetuity. And they pay in respect thereof per annum to the heirs of the lord Baldwin Dakeney 12d., and to Robert son of Quentin Neuport 4s. 5d.

[P15]   The canons have also by gift of Thomas Plote 1 messuage in
          the town of Cambridge next to Segrimmeslane which messuage
          the same Thomas bought from various men by the means of
          small parts, one namely the piece from Robert son of Andrew
          Budday and another piece from Arnold le Hunte and another
          piece from Richard le Savunur, that messuage they released …[48]
          of the canons to Ethelred Plote until the end of his life for rent
          of 2s. per annum and this in their name he makes to the tenant-
          in-chief of the lord fee for rent owed …[49] and the custom namely
          to the bailiffs of the Lord King of Cambridge who hold the said
          town in fee farm etcetera for hawgable 4d.

[P16]   They have also by gift of Thomas Plote 5 roods of land, of which
          he bought ½ acre from Eustace Selede for rent of ½d. per annum,
          and another 3 roods he bought from Alexander de Granger, and
          that Alexander from Richard Bateman son of John Selede for
          rent of ½d., and to the heirs of John le Rus 1½d.

[P17]   The said canons have also from 2 fees which Richard Bateman,
          son of John Selede held, 12s. of annual income and for hawgable
          4d. anew, a mark of silver which they gave to the aforesaid
          Richard Bateman for quitting himself from Judaism.

[A6]   The said canons also have 2 acres of land in perpetual alms by
          gift of Bartholomew Gogging.

[P18]   Item they have 2 messuages by gift of William de Preston,
          chaplain, which same William received from them until the end
          of his life, by the acts of the bailiffs of the Lord King Cambridge
          to whom they belong and the tenant-in-chief of the lord's fee
          by service owed and by custom.

[A7]   Item the Canons have by gift of Nicholas de Hemingford who
          was the son and heir of Lord William de Hemingford 3 acres of
          land lying before the gate of Barnwell in perpetual alms.

[P19]   Item they have by gift of William, cleric, son of John Mason,
          a certain messuage and croft in Barnwell, which Robert Cook
          formerly held from him and another messuage which Robert
          de Brunner formerly held from him with homage and money-
          rent to the same Robert, namely of 16d. and 2 capons per
          annum, and a ½ acre which the same Robert held from him
          with money-rent of 5d. per annum and 1 acre which Andrew
          son of Hugh Leusene and Alicia, daughter of Richard at the
          head of the town, held from him with homage and money-rent
          of the aforesaid Andrew and Alicia namely 10d. and of 2 capons
          per annum in free and perpetual alms.

[P20] Item they have by gift of Adam Weriel son of Walter, and that Adam by inheritance of Agnes, his mother, and that Agnes through the succession of her father Adam Weriel senior, a certain messuage in Cambridge in the parish of Holy Sepulchre and another messuage opposite St John's Hospital and a croft which lies in the suburbs of Cambridge opposite the nuns of St Radegund's, made to the tenant-in-chief of the lord's fee for service owed and by which custom they are unaware. And to the bailiffs of Cambridge who hold the said town in fee farm from the Lord King as is stated for hawgable in the summary, 57s.

[A8] Item they have by gift of Jeremy of Barnwell, and that Jeremy by parental succession, namely from Hugh de Camera, a certain messuage which Oliver le Porter presently holds from them for money-rent of 3s. per annum.

[P21] Item they have by gift of Geoffrey of Barnwell, chaplain, a certain messuage in Barnwell and 5 acres of land in the fields of the same town, which messuage the same Geoffrey bought from Walter, son of Master Geoffrey of Barnwell, for money-rent of 8d. per annum, and a ½ acre of land bought from Richard son of Ivo for money-rent of 2d. per annum, and from Alan Godeman a ½ acre for rent of 3d. per annum. And from William Smith and Agnes, his wife, 2 acres with income of 18d., with a certain messuage for money-rent of 18d. per annum. And from Andrew son of Edria 1 acre of land for money-rent of 8d. This land and messuage William Paie and Isabella, his wife, received from Prior Laurence for homage and money-rent of 1 mark per annum paid to the Lord of the almonry of Barnwell. And they are unaware of the service and customs owed in payment to the tenant-in-chief of the lord's fee.

[A9] Item the said canons have by gift of Richard de Stanesfeld a certain messuage in Barnwell, which messuage the same Richard bought from Warin le Mason, and the same Warin from John son of Geoffrey; this messuage he presently holds from Radulph Cook for rent of 12d. per annum.

[A10] Item they have by gift of Geoffrey Smith ½ acre of land in exchange for 2 selions which lie next to the land of Walter Potion.

[R1] Item they have by gift of Master Robert Aunger 8d. of income received annually from the messuage which was formerly of Walter Werret, in exchange for quitclaim of 8d., from a certain messuage in Cambridge which the Friars Minor enclosed inside their walls next to the Lord King's dike.

[A11] Item they have by gift of Henry Melt 3 acres of land in perpetual alms save the service to the Lord King, namely to the bailiffs of the Lord King of Cambridge for hawgable 3d. as is stated above.

[P22] Item they have by gift of Geoffrey Melt for 15 marks, which they gave to him for his quittance from Judaism, a certain messuage in the town of Barnwell and 1 acre and 1 rood of land in the fields, and quitclaim of 1 messuage which he held from them in Barnwell, quit from all secular service save for service to the Lord King, namely 1d. which they pay each year to the bailiffs of the Lord King who hold the said town in fee farm from the Lord King as is stated above.

[F12] Item the prior and canons have a fair at Barnwell each year at the feast of the Nativity of St John the Baptist of the duration of four days, by gift and concession of King John, and in respect thereof they have confirmation from King Henry, and for the preservation of indemnities of the market of Cambridge they give each year to the bailiffs of the Lord King of Cambridge who hold the town of Cambridge in fee farm from the Lord King, ½ mark of silver for the aforesaid fair.

[F13] Item the prior and canons have common pasture with the goodwill of the whole town of Cambridge and they have nothing outside the dividing walls but that goodwill in the common pasture of the said town, with the goodwill of the whole town at their pleasure.

[F14] They have also 2 windmills which they caused to be erected above their own land for the milling of their grain and other grains which they wish to mill at the same place. No one however can be restricted to the mill there nor to their own possessions.

[F15] They have also the advowson of their church in Barnwell [through] Lord Gilbert Peche, through the descent of the heir in heirdom from the time of Pagan Peverel, who was the founder of the church and patron as is stated.

[RENTS]

[6] Item Leon Dunning holds 1 messuage with appurtenances in the parish of St Giles, Cambridge, which same messuage descended to him by hereditary right through the death of Adam Dunning, his father, which same Adam bought that messuage from Nicholas Weriel and the said Nicholas acquired that by ancient succession of his ancestors, and in respect thereof he pays per annum to the prior of Barnwell 18d. by assignment of the said Nicholas.

[7]   Item Leon holds a horse mill in the town of Cambridge which descended to him by hereditary right through the death of Adam Dunning, his father, which same Adam formerly held the said mill from Walter of St Edmunds and in respect thereof he pays per annum to the heirs of the said Walter, namely Luke of St Edmunds, 6d.

[R2]   Item Radulph, chaplain of the parish of St Clement's has 5 marks paid annually which he receives from certain messuages and incomes in the same parish by gift of Master Robert Aunger, which same Master Robert gave to the same the said aforesaid income for the celebration of mass of the Blessed Virgin Mary in the aforesaid church of St Clement's, and the same Master Robert acquired the aforesaid income by hereditary right through the descent of Aunger le Rus, his father, which same Aunger acquired the said income by ancient purchase.

[ST RADEGUND'S PRIORY]

[A12]   The prioress and nuns of St Radegund's, Cambridge, hold a certain place near Grenecroft in which they live and where their conventual church was founded, and it includes 10 acres of land, which same place they have by gift of Malcolm, former king of Scotland. Which same Malcolm gave the same aforesaid land in pure and perpetual alms for the foundation of their church in the same, it is not known by what manner the said King Malcolm came by the aforesaid land.

[A13]   Item the aforesaid prioress and nuns hold 4 acres of land lying near the aforesaid land, which same land they have by gift of Nigel, Bishop of Ely, which same Nigel gave to them in pure and perpetual alms. B. former prior of Ely and the convent of the church of Ely conceded and confirmed the said donation made to the same nuns.

[A14]   Item the aforesaid prioress and nuns hold 5 acres of land lying between the monastery and Grenecroft which they have by gift of Eustace former bishop of Ely, which same Eustace gave to the same the said land in pure and perpetual alms. And John, former bishop of Ely, and Roger, former prior of Ely and the chapter of the church of Ely conceded and confirmed the said donation made to them.

[A15]   Item the aforesaid prioress and nuns hold 2½ acres of land which they have by gift of Lord Reginald de Argentein, and the same Reginald bought the said land from Hugh Pylet, which same Hugh acquired the said land through ancient descent of his ancestors, which same land the said Lord Reginald gave to them in perpetual alms and they pay per annum to St Giles's Church of Barnwell 2s. by assignment of the aforesaid Reginald.

[A16]   Item the aforesaid prioress and nuns hold 2½ acres of land which they have by gift of Richard son of Laurence de Litleber', which same Richard acquired the said land by inheritance through the descent of the said Laurence, his father, and the said Laurence acquired that by ancient descent of his ancestors. And the aforesaid Richard gave to them the aforesaid land in perpetual alms in exchange for 2½ acres of land.

[A17]   Item the prioress and nuns hold 3 acres of land and 1 rood in the fields of Cambridge which they have by gift of Philip son of Adam de Girton, which same Philip gave them the said land in pure and perpetual alms and the said Philip formerly held that land from Baldwin son of Acelin.

[A18]   Item the aforesaid prioress and nuns hold 15 acres of land which they have by gift of Harvey son of Eustace, which same Harvey gave the said land to them in pure and perpetual alms and the said Harvey acquired that through the descent of the said Eustace, his father, which same Eustace acquired the said land by inheritance through the descent of Dunning, his father, which same Dunning acquired that by ancient succession of his ancestors.

[A19]   Item the aforesaid prioress and nuns hold 6 acres of land in the aforesaid fields which they have by gift of Hugh son of Aspelon, which same Hugh gave that to them in pure and perpetual alms, and the said Hugh acquired that land by inheritance through the death of Aspelon, his father, which same Aspelon acquired that land through the descent of his ancestors.

[A20]   Item the said prioress and nuns hold 1 acre of land in the aforesaid fields which they have by gift of Philip de Hoketon, which same Philip gave the said land to the same in pure and perpetual alms, and the said Philip acquired the aforesaid land through the descent of his ancestors.

[A21]   Item they hold 2½ acres of land which Margaret Fiyien gave to them, which same Margaret formerly bought the said land from John, son of Jordan, which same John acquired the aforesaid land through the descent of Jordan, his father, which same Jordan acquired the said land through the descent of his ancestors, and they pay in respect thereof per annum to the heirs of the said Margaret 3d. for the aforesaid land.

[A22]   Item they hold 10 acres of land which they have by gift of Margaret, former wife of Radulph Parson in the fields of

Cambridge, which same Margaret acquired the said land by ancient succession of her ancestors by inheritance and gave the said land to them in pure and perpetual alms.

[A23] Item they have 4 acres of land by gift of Jordan son of Radulph de Brecet in the fields of Cambridge, which the said Jordan gave to them in pure and perpetual alms and the same Jordan acquired the said land by hereditary right through the ancient descent of his ancestors.

[A24] Item they hold 5 acres of land and 3 roods which they have by gift of Stephen, son of Alneva, which same Stephen gave the said land to them in pure and perpetual alms and the said Alneva acquired the said land by hereditary right through the death of Athelina, her mother, which same donation, Hugh son of the said Stephen, his father, confirmed.

[A25] Item they hold 1 acre of land in the said fields which they have in pure and perpetual alms by gift of Matilda, former wife of Simon Bagge, which same Matilda acquired the said land by gift of Robert Bagge, her father, which same Robert acquired the said land by hereditary right through the death of William Bagge, his father, which same William acquired the said land by inheritance through the ancient descent of his ancestors, and Walter son of the said Matilda Bagge confirmed the established donation to the said nuns as is stated.

[A26] Item they hold 1½ acres of land which they have by gift of John son of William in the aforesaid fields, which same John acquired the said land by purchase from Robert, his brother, which same Robert acquired the said land by inheritance through the death of William, his father, which same William acquired the said land through the death of his ancestors, and they pay in respect thereof per annum to All Saints Church next to the hospital of Cambridge, 1½d. by assignment of the said John son of William.

[A27] Item they hold 2 acres of land in the aforesaid fields which they have in pure and perpetual alms by gift of Warin Grim, which same Warin acquired the said land through the death of John Grim, his father, which same John acquired the said land by hereditary right through the death of his ancestors.

[A28] Item they have 1 acre of land in the same fields which they hold in pure and perpetual alms which they have by gift of John Grim, which same established donation to them, Warin Grim, son of John, ratified and confirmed.

[A29] Item they hold 1 messuage in their parish of St Radegund's, which same messuage they have by gift of Walter de Noncius, which same Walter bought that from Randulph Bolle, which same Randulph bought that from Nicholas Sarand, which same Nicholas acquired that by ancient succession, and they pay in respect thereof per annum to the bailiffs of Cambridge who hold the said town in fee farm etcetera for hawgable 3d.

[A30] Item they hold 4 messuages and 1 piece of vacant land which they have by gift of Robert Crocheman and Cassandria, his wife, in the parish of St Andrew's, which same Robert and Cassandria acquired the said messuage by ancient succession of their ancestors, for which messuage and piece of land the said prioress and nuns pay to a certain chaplain in perpetuity for celebrating the divine mass in the aforesaid St Andrew's Church for the souls of the aforesaid Robert and Cassandria, and for the souls of all the deceased faithful, and to the tenant-in-chief of the lord's fee for service and custom they pay annually.

[A31] Item they hold another messuage in the same parish which they have by gift of William Sweteye, which same William bought that from the said Radulph Bole[50], and the said Radulph bought that from Nicholas Sarand, and the said Nicholas acquired that by inheritance through the death of his ancestors, and in respect thereof pays per annum to the bailiffs of Cambridge who hold the said town in fee farm etcetera for hawgable 1d.

[8] Item Geoffrey de Donewitch holds 2 messuages opposite St Radegund's, which he bought from Agnes le Dene, which same Agnes bought that from the prioress and nuns of St Radegund's, which same prioress and nuns acquired the said messuages by gift of Nicholas Sarand, which same Nicholas acquired those by ancient hereditary succession and in respect thereof he pays per annum to the said prioress and nuns 8s.

[A32] The aforesaid prioress and nuns receive from the aforesaid messuages and other incomes in the town of Cambridge 10 pounds paid annually, and more which they have by purchase and by gift of others, which said incomes they gave to them for their sustenance in perpetual alms, for which messuages and incomes they pay to the tenant-in-chief of the lord's fee for service owed and custom of which they are unaware, and to the bailiffs of Cambridge who hold the said town in fee farm etcetera for hawgable 14[51].

[F16] Item the aforesaid prioress and nuns have a certain fair at the feast of the Assumption of the Blessed Mary for the duration of 2 days, namely on the eve of the Assumption of the Blessed Mary with the following day, which certain fair they have by concession of

Stephen, former king of England, by charter which they have from the aforesaid king.

[ST JOHN'S HOSPITAL]

[P23]   The Master and brothers of St John's Hospital, Cambridge, hold 2 carucates of land in the fields of Cambridge, for which they pay each year to the tenant-in-chief of the lord's fee for service owed by custom as is stated below. And 6 pounds income in the town of Cambridge.

[P24]   The Master and brothers of St John's Hospital, Cambridge, hold 1 carucate of land in the territory of Cambridge by gift of Robert de Mortimer in pure and perpetual alms, which the same Robert acquired by gift of the Lord King John, and they pay each year to the bailiffs of Cambridge who hold the town of Cambridge in fee farm from the Lord King 20s. in terms established as per the original charter, which testifies that the said Robert de Mortimer acquired that from the said Lord King John.

[9]   The same Master and brothers hold 2 acres of land with appurtenances by gift of Anthony, chaplain of Stocton, lying in the fields of Cambridge, which same Anthony bought from Baldwin son of Baldwin Blancgernun for rent of 2d. annually.

[10]   The same master and brothers hold a certain messuage outside the ditch of Cambridge in the parish of St Giles, lying near the way which leads towards St Neot's, by gift of Geoffrey Blancgernun, which same Baldwin Blancgernun gave to the same Geoffrey and granted by charter for rent of 4d. per annum.

[A33]   Item they hold 8 acres of land in the fields of Cambridge which Baldwin Blancgernun gave for his soul and for the souls of his ancestors in pure and perpetual alms.

[A34]   Item they hold from the same Baldwin 1 acre of land in Binnebroc in pure and perpetual alms.

[11]   Item they hold from Geoffrey Prat of Ely 1½ acres of land in the fields of Cambridge, which same land the said Geoffrey bought from Baldwin son of Baldwin Blancgernun for rent of 1½d. paid annually.

[12]   Item they hold 1 acre of land beneath Barnwell by gift of the said Geoffrey Prat of Ely for money-rent of 2d. and 1 pair of gloves per annum.

[A35]   Item they hold 2 acres of land in the fields of Cambridge which they have by gift of Nicholas de Hemingford in pure and perpetual alms.

[A36] Item they hold 15 acres of land in the fields of Cambridge by gift of Maurice Ruff in pure and perpetual alms.

[A37] Item they hold 1 acre of land for the maintenance of a lamp by night before the sick by gift of Harvey son of Eustace Dunning in pure and perpetual alms.

[A38] Item they hold by gift of William Toylet 14 acres of land in the fields of Cambridge in pure and perpetual alms.

[13] Item they hold 2 houses from the same William in the parish of Holy Sepulchre, paying in respect thereof annually to the prior of Barnwell 6s.

[14] Item they hold 2 houses in the parish of St Botolph's by gift of Bartholomew, deacon. They pay in respect thereof annually to the bailiffs of Cambridge who hold the said town in fee farm etcetera for hawgable 1½d.

[F17] Item they hold St Peter's Church outside Trumpington Gate by gift of Henry son of Sigar' for their own use for the sustenance of the poor and sick in pure and perpetual alms.

[A39] Item they hold 1 shop in the marketplace of Cambridge by gift of Eustace de Winepol in pure and perpetual alms.

[A40] Item they hold 8 acres of land in the fields of Cambridge by gift of Michael, cleric of Huntingdon, which he acquired by gift of Master Robert de Huntingdon, his uncle, in pure and perpetual alms.

[15] Item they hold 2½ acres of land in the fields of Cambridge by gift of Eustace son of Harvey, for money-rent of 2d. per annum.

[16] Item they hold 3 acres of land in Newnham by gift of Peter son of Richard of Newnham, chaplain, for money-rent of 1d. per annum.

[17] Item they hold a ½ acre of land in the croft of Newnham by gift of Gilbert Baker, which Adam son of Eustace of Cambridge gave and confirmed by charter to the same Gilbert Baker, for money-rent of 2d. per annum.

[F18] Item the aforesaid master and brothers of St John the Evangelist's Hospital, Cambridge, have a certain area of land in the fee of the Lord King in which the aforesaid hospital with chapel of the same hospital was founded, which same area of land a certain burgess of Cambridge, namely Henry Frost, formerly gave to the town of Cambridge for the building and establishing in the same place of that hospital for the use of the poor and the sick. To which burgesses the presentation of the master of the same place is accustomed and is due by right. Which same burgesses holding the said town in fee farm from the Lord King as tenant-in-chief, were unjustly alienated, however, by the presentation of the master of the said hospital of the said burgesses by Lord Hugh of Northwold, former bishop of Ely, and by his successors, who according to their will appointed the masters abiding in the said hospital in disinheritance of the Lord King and of the aforesaid burgesses of Cambridge, with grave harm, who hold the said town in fee farm from the Lord King. And this was indicated many times to the Lord King Henry, father of the Lord Edward who is now king, and to his council and also both before the itinerant justices and before the escheators and inquisitors of the Lord King who came to Cambridge. And of this, nothing was corrected by the Lord King. And it is known that this presentation was alienated within thirty years of the time of King Henry, father of Lord Edward who is now King.

[F19] Item they said that the advowson and donation to the hospital of lepers at Stourbridge Common was accustomed to and by law should belong to the burgesses of Cambridge who hold the town of Cambridge with its appurtenances in fee farm from the Lord King. The presentation of the said hospital was unjustly alienated from the said burgesses, however, by the said Lord Hugh of Northwold, former bishop of Ely, and through his successors who according to their will gave the said chaplains abiding in the hospital in disinheritance of the Lord King and the aforesaid burgesses of Cambridge, with grave harm, who hold the said town in fee farm from the Lord King. And this was advised many times to the Lord King Henry, father of the Lord King who now is, and to his council and also both before the itinerant justices and before the escheators and inquisitors of the Lord King who came to Cambridge. And of this, nothing was corrected by the Lord King. And it is known that this presentation was alienated within thirty years of the time of King Henry father of King Edward who now is.

[F20] Item the custodians of the hospital of Stourbridge Common hold 24½ acres of land in the fields of Cambridge which they have by the gifts of many who gave the said land to the said hospital for the sustenance in the same place of lepers, in perpetual alms. And they pay per annum to the tenant-in-chief of the lord's fee by money-rent owed and by custom relating to the said lands, which same money-rent, nor to which lords the money-rent is owed, they are unaware. It is said also that the said custodians do not sustain in the same place any lepers as they should by law and is accustomed. Item they said that a certain fair is granted to the said hospital at the feast of the Exaltation of the Holy Cross, which lasts from the eve of the Feast of the Holy Cross with the following day of the Feast of the Exaltation of the Holy Cross, within the enclosure of the court belonging to the said hospital, which certain fair the Lord King John, predecessor to the Lord King who now is, conceded to the lepers abiding in the said hospital for their maintenance.

[ANGLESEY PRIORY]

[P25]   Item the prior and convent of Anglesey hold 1 messuage in the parish of St Michael's, Cambridge, which same messuage they hold by gift of Robert son of Robert Huberd, and a piece of vacant land in the same parish which they hold by gift of this Robert. And a certain granary and a certain other piece of vacant land which they hold by gift of the same Robert, and a piece of vacant land in the parish of St John's and 1 messuage in the parish of St Peter's outside Trumpington Gate. And 8 acres of land in the fields of Barnwell. And an annual income of 5s. received from 1 messuage which was formerly of Peter son of Ivo. And 4s. of annual income which they receive from Richard Bateman. And 6s. of annual income which they receive from Harvey Butcher, which they have by gift of the said Robert, son of Robert Huberd, which same Robert acquired that by ancient succession of his ancestors. And they pay for the said messuage, land and income to St John the Evangelist's Hospital 2d., and to the bailiffs of Cambridge who hold the said town in fee farm from the Lord King for hawgable 11d.

[A41]   Item the said prior and convent hold 1 shop in the marketplace of Cambridge which same they hold by gift of Harvey son of Seleda in free and pure and perpetual alms.

[A42]   Item they hold 1 messuage in the parish of St Peter's outside Trumpington Gate, which same they hold by gift of Eustace son of Radulph, which same messuage Stephen Ace formerly held in free and pure and perpetual alms, by which warranty the said prior holds the said messuage they are unaware.

[R3]   Item they hold income of 2s. by gift of Simon Chamberlain, formerly bishop of Ely in pure and perpetual alms.

[R4]   Item they have annual income of 3s. by gift of John de Ry, former rector of St Edmunds chapel, received from a certain messuage outside Trumpington Gate in the parish of St Peter's, which same messuage the said John de Ry acquired by gift of Laurence son of Alan of Blatchams, which same Laurence acquired that by gift of John son of Arnold of Cambridge.

[CALDWELL PRIORY]

[R5]   The prior and canons of Caldwell hold in the town of Cambridge 70s. of annual income by gift of Richard son of William through the hands of the bailiffs of the same town, which for a time were those same payments the same Richard had for his service by donation of Count David from his third penny of Cambridge.

[R6]   Item they have in the same town of Cambridge 100s. of annual income by gift of Roger de Anstey through the hands of the said bailiffs of Cambridge, which same Roger bought from Simon of St Luke's, whose ancestors acquired the said 100s. by donation of the said Count David from his third penny for his service in the same town and the said Count David acquired by donation of the Lord King as is said.

[SCHOLARS OF MERTON]

[P26]   Item the scholars of Merton hold 1 messuage with 45 acres of land and 50s. of annual income in the town and in the fields of Cambridge, which they bought from William de Manefeld, which same William acquired that by hereditary right through the death of Master John of Barnard Castle, which same Master John acquired that by hereditary right through the death of Master Guy of Barnard Castle, and the said Master Guy bought that from Eustace Dunning, which same Eustace acquired that through the death of Harvey Dunning, his father, and the said Harvey acquired that by ancient succession of his ancestors, and in respect thereof they pay per annum to the said William 1d., and to the bailiffs of Cambridge who hold the said town in fee farm as is stated above for hawgable and landgable 4s. 10d.

[P27]   Item they hold 15 acres of land and 10s. 2d. of annual income which they bought from the said William de Manefeld, which same William acquired that by the same hereditary succession of heirs in heirdom as is stated above, up to the said Harvey father of Eustace Dunning, which same land and 10s. 2d. of income used to be held from the Earl of Leicester and so in this manner they hold it from Lord Edmund, brother of the Lord King, and they pay in respect thereof per annum to the said Lord Edmund 3s. 10d. and scutage, more for more and less for less, to the aforesaid Lord Edmund whenever scutage occurs.

[ABBOT OF ST EDMUNDS]

[R7]   Item the abbot of St Edmunds receives 21s. income annually from certain houses in the aforesaid town of Cambridge by ancient purchase. By which manner and by which warranty he came to the said income it is not known.

[PRIOR OF ELY]

[P28]   Item the Prior of Ely holds a granary in the parish of St Michael's and 2 messuages in the parish of St John's. And 40s. annual income in the same town of Cambridge for which he pays per annum to the bailiffs of Cambridge who hold the said town in fee farm etcetera for hawgable 5s. 7½d. and 1 farthing. By which manner he came to the said messuage and rent it is not known.

[WILLIAM DE NOVACURT]

[P29]   Item William de Novacurt holds 60 acres of land in the fields of Cambridge and 20s. of annual income in the same town, which same land and income he owns by hereditary right through the death of William de Novacurt, his father, which same William acquired that through the death of Robert de Novacurt, his uncle, which same Robert acquired that by[52] inheritance of his ancestors and in respect thereof pays per annum to the bailiffs of Cambridge who hold the said town in fee farm for hawgable and landgable 13s. 3½d. And to the tenant-in-chief of the fee, namely the heirs of the lord Radulph de Cokefeld, 1 sparrow-hawk.

[PRIOR OF KENILWORTH]

[R8]   Item the prior of Kenilworth receives annually 20s. of annual income from the town of Cambridge through the hands of the bailiffs of the town. By which manner and by which warranty they do not know.

[PRIORY OF SWAFFHAM]

[P30]   The prioress and nuns of Swaffham hold a certain shop in the parish of St Mary's, Cambridge, which same shop they hold by gift of William Herre, which same William acquired that by paternal inheritance through the death of his ancestors. They have also 30s. of annual income in the same town, which aforesaid income they have by gift of many people, for which shop and incomes they pay per annum to the bailiffs of Cambridge who hold the said town in fee farm etcetera for hawgable 20½d.

[HOSPITAL OF ST JOHN OF JERUSALEM]

[P31]   Item the prior and brothers of the Hospital of Jerusalem in England hold 1 messuage in the parish of St John's, Cambridge, which same messuage they bought from Master Bartholomew de Lardario, which same Master Bartholomew acquired that by gift of Master Stephen de Lardario, his father, which same Master Stephen acquired that by ancient acquisition. Item they have another messuage in the parish of St Mary's which they bought from the aforesaid Master Bartholomew, and which same Master Bartholomew acquired that by gift of the aforesaid Master Stephen, his father, what moreover they pay per annum in respect thereof they do not know.

[GUY DE MORTIMER]

[18]   Item Guy de Mortimer, rector of the church of Kingeston holds 1 messuage in the parish of St John's, Cambridge, which he bought from Lord Robert de Greyle, which same Robert acquired that through the death of his ancestors, and in respect thereof he pays per annum to the tenant-in-chief of the lord's fee by money-rent and custom owed, namely to lord Robert de Greyle 10s., and to the heirs of John le Rus 1d.

[FRIARS PREACHER]

[P32]   Item the Friars Preacher residing in the town of Cambridge have a certain place where they live and where their church was founded. Which same place includes 8 acres of land and more in length and width, in which certain place there used to be various measures of land in which many people lived, which used to be subject to geld and feudal aid. The said friars have and hold this place in the aforesaid town in perpetual alms by purchase and by gifts of many people. From which people however they have the aforesaid place and whether or not they have confirmation from the ancestors of the Lord King or not, they do not know.

[FRIARS MINOR]

[P33]   Item the Friars Minor residing in the town of Cambridge similarly have a certain place where they live and where their church was founded, which certain place includes 6 acres of land and more in length and width, in which place there used to be various measures of land in which many people lived, which used to be subject to geld and feudal aid to the aforesaid town. The said friars have and hold this place in perpetual alms by purchase and by gifts of many people. From which people however they have the aforesaid place and whether or not they have confirmation from the ancestors of the Lord King or not, they do not know.

[FRIARS OF THE SACK]

[A43]   Item the Friars of the Sack hold a certain place where they live and where their church was founded, of this place a certain part they have by gift of Richard of Heke Lingham in perpetual alms and another part by purchase and by gift of many people. And it contains in it 3 acres of land and more, and they have confirmation of the said place from Lord King Henry, father of the Lord King who now is.

[CARMELITE FRIARS]

[A44]   Item the Carmelite Friars have a certain place where they live and where their church was founded in Newnham, of this place a certain part they have by gift of Michael Malerbe in perpetual alms, and another part by purchase and by gift of many people, and it contains in it 3 acres of land and more, and whether moreover they have confirmation from the Lord King or not they do not know.

[CRUTCHED FRIARS]

[A45]   Item the Crutched Friars residing in the town of Cambridge have and hold 1 messuage in which they live and where their chapel in which they celebrate the divine service was founded, which same messuage they bought from Henry of Barton, for which messuage they pay per annum to the said Henry of Barton 12d., and the said Henry acquits the said friars to the bailiffs of Cambridge of 4d. for hawgable to the Lord King.

[RENTS CONTINUED]

[19]   Item Luke son of Simon Roy holds 1 messuage with a certain shop and its appurtenances in the parish of St Edward's, Cambridge, which same messuage with shop descended to the same by inheritance through the death of the said Simon, his father, which same Simon bought from Milesencia, prioress of St Radegund's, for which messuage and shop he pays the said prioress 6s. per annum, by which warranty they receive the said income they are unaware. And to the heirs of Alicia Seman 2d., and to the bailiffs of Cambridge who hold the same town to fee farm etcetera in hawgable 6d.

[20]   Item the same Luke holds 1 messuage with appurtenances pertaining to the said messuage in the parish of St Mary's which certain messuage with appurtenances descended to the said Luke by inheritance through the death of the said Simon, his father, which messuage the said Simon formerly bought from the Lord Richard de Frevile of Little Shelford, and in respect thereof he pays per annum to the said Lord Richard 2s.

[21]   Item the said Luke holds a piece of empty land in the parish of Saint Benedict's which same descended to him by inheritance through the death of Lova his mother, daughter of John le Paumer and the said Lova held that by inheritance through the death of the said John le Paumer, her father, and in respect thereof he pays per annum to Nicolas Morice 4[53]s.

[A46]   Item the Chancellor and Masters of the University of Cambridge hold 3 messuages in the town of Cambridge, of which 2 messuages they have by gift of Nicolas de Hedon, cleric ...[54] messuages they have by gift of John de Thriplow, chaplain. What they pay moreover for the said messuages they are unaware nor anyone else can know.

[22]   Item Robert, son of William le Longe holds 1 messuage in the same parish in fief, which same messuage descended to the same Robert by hereditary right through the death of the said William, his father. Which same William held that by gift from Sabine Huberd. And the said Sabina bought that from Geva, daughter of Aspelon Koy. And that messuage descended to the same Geva by inheritance through the death of the said Aspelon, her father, for which messuage he pays per annum 1d. to the said Sabina. And to the nuns of Markyate 9d., by which warranty the said nuns are unaware of any claim to the said income.

[23]   Item Reginald le Bercher holds 1 messuage in fief in the same parish, which he bought from William of Barton, and the said William held that messuage by gift of William le Lomb, and the said William le Lomb held that from the nuns of St Radegund's, and he pays in respect thereof per annum to the said nuns 6d., and to the said William of Barton and his heirs ½d. for the aforesaid messuage.

[24]   Item Thomas son of Walter de Berdefeld and Isabella, daughter of Hugh le Bercher, hold in fief 1 messuage in the same parish, which same messuage descended to the same by hereditary right through the death of Letia, their mother. And said Letia held that by hereditary succession through the death of her parents,

for which they pay Master Robert Aunger 6d. per annum, just as the said nuns are unaware of any claim to the said income.

[25] Walter de Berdefeld holds 1 messuage in the parish of St Giles in fee farm to the end of his life from Robert of Hinton, which messuage descended to the same Robert by hereditary right, through the death of Robert of Hinton, his father, for which he pays per annum the said Robert and his heirs 4s. 1d.

[26] Walter son of Reginald le Bercher holds in fief 1 messuage in the same parish which he bought from Clement Fisher. And the said Clement bought that messuage from Walter le Blake. And the said Walter le Blake bought that messuage from Stephen Barat, which same messuage is in fief from Leon Dunning, and for which same messuage he pays 25d. per annum to the heirs of the said Clement.

[27] Margaret daughter of Radulph Norman holds in fief 1 messuage in the same parish in the chapter of the nuns of St Radegund's, for which she pays the said nuns 2s. per annum, by which warranty the said nuns are unaware of any claim to the said income for the messuage.

[28] William Norman holds in fief 1 messuage in the same parish which he bought from Hugh, son of Henry, shepherd. Which same Hugh held that by hereditary succession through the death of Henry, his father. And he pays thence per annum to the heirs of the said Hugh for the said messuage 12d. And to the bailiffs of the Lord King who hold the town of Cambridge in fee farm from the Lord King and his ancestors, to their farm ½d. for hawgable.

[29] William of Barton and Cecilia his wife hold in fief 1 messuage in the same parish, which same messuage descended to the said Cecilia by inheritance through the death of Walter Glaseneye, her father, which same messuage the said Walter bought from Roger Waryn, for which they pay to the heirs of the said Roger 18d., and to the bailiffs of the Lord King who hold the town of Cambridge in fee farm from the Lord King and his ancestors, to their farm, ½d. for hawgable.

[30] The said William and Cecilia his wife hold in fief a certain piece of empty land in the same parish. Which same piece of land descended to the said Cecilia by inheritance through the death of Walter Glaseneye her father. And the said Walter bought that from Pelagia daughter of Peter, son of Radulph. And that piece of land descended to the said Pelagia by hereditary right through

the death of the said Peter her father, for which they pay 1d. per annum to the said Pelagia and her heirs.

[31]   Item Simon son of Henry of Barton, chaplain, holds in fief 1 house in the same parish which he has by gift of Eleanor de Gurnay. And the said Eleanor bought that from Richard Ampe. Which same house descended to the said Richard by hereditary succession through the death of John Hamund, his father, for which he pays the said bailiffs of the Lord King who hold the town of Cambridge in fee farm as said above, to their farm in hawgable ½d.

[32]   Item William Botte holds 1 house in said parish in fief which same house descended to the said William by hereditary right through the death of William Botte, his father, which same William bought from Baldwin Blancgernun, which same Baldwyn acquired that by ancient succession of his parents, for which he pays per annum to the heirs of John Segyn 12d. by assignment of the heirs of the said Baldwin Blancgernun, and to the bailiffs of the Lord King who hold the town of Cambridge in fee farm just as is stated, to their farm in hawgable 2d.

[33]   Item Amicia Dunnyng holds 1 messuage in the said parish, which messuage Robert Dunnyng former husband of the same Amicia bought from Absolon in the Ditch, which same Absolon bought and held that from Baldwyn Blancgernun, for which she pays per annum to Master Robert Auger 6d. by assignment of the said Baldwyn. And to the bailiffs of the Lord King who hold the town of Cambridge in fee farm as is stated, to their farm in hawgable 3d.

[34]   Item the said Amicia holds 1 messuage in the same parish which she has by gift of Roger Warin her father, which said Roger acquired it by gift of Radulph son of Emme ate Wal, which said Radulph had and held it from Baldwyn Blancgernun for which she pays per annum to the heirs of John son of Michael Goggyng by assignment of the said Baldwin 4d.

[35]   Item the said Amicia holds 1 messuage in the same parish which she has by gift of Roger Waryn, her father. And the said Roger acquired this by gift of Radulph son of Emma. Which same Radulph bought it from William Colon. And the said William acquired it by ancient ancestral succession, for which she pays per annum to the bailiffs of Cambridge who hold the town of Cambridge in fee farm as is stated to their farm 1d.

[36]   Item the said Amicia holds 1 messuage in the same parish which she has by gift of Robert Dunnyng and the said Robert bought

that from William le Moun', which same William bought from Juliana, daughter of Thomas Longys, which same Thomas acquired that by ancient hereditary succession, for which she pays per annum to Alicia daughter of Norman le Cuner 6d.

[37]   Item Geoffrey Andre holds in fief 1 messuage with its appurtenances in the same parish, which messuage descended to the same Geoffrey by inheritance through the death of John Andre his father, which same John bought that from Robert Fynch, which messuage descended from the said Robert by inheritance through the death of his ancestors, for which he pays per annum to the said bailiffs of the Lord King who hold the town of Cambridge in fee farm as is stated, to their farm in hawgable 1d.

[38]   Item the said Geoffrey holds 1 house in the same parish which same house descended to Geoffrey by inheritance through the death of John Andre, his father. And the said John bought that from Alicia, daughter of Radulph. And the said Alicia held that by hereditary right through the death of the said Radulph, her father. And the said Radulph acquired that by ancient purchase, for which he pays per annum to the heirs of Hugh le Bercher ½d. And to the said bailiffs of the Lord King who hold the town of Cambridge in fee farm as is stated, to their farm in hawgable ½d.

[39]   Item the said Geoffrey holds 1 messuage with its appurtenances in the same parish in which he lives, which same messuage descended to him by hereditary right through the death of John Andre, his father. And the said messuage descended to the said John, by inheritance through the death of Aldred his father, which messuage descended to the said Aldred by inheritance through the death of Richard de Histon, his father, for which he pays per annum to the said bailiffs of the Lord King who hold the said town of Cambridge in fee farm as is stated, to their farm in hawgable 1d.

[40]   Item the said Geoffrey holds 1 messuage with its appurtenances in the same parish, which messuage descended to him through the death of the said John Andre his father. And the said John bought that from Emma, daughter of Ketel. Which same Emma acquired that from hereditary succession through the death of her father, Ketel. And he pays per annum for the said messuage to the heirs of Robert Huberd 12d. And to the bailiffs of the Lord King who hold the town of Cambridge in fee farm as is stated, to their farm in hawgable 1½d.

[41]   Item the said Geoffrey holds 1 messuage with its appurtenances in the same parish, which messuage descended to the same by inheritance through the death of the said John Andre, his father. And the said John bought that from John Frost junior, which same messuage descended to the said John Frost through the death of Cus, his nephew, by inheritance. And the said Cus acquired this by gift of John Frost, chaplain. And the said John Frost, chaplain, had this and held it by hereditary right by ancient succession of his parents, for which he pays per annum to the said bailiffs of the Lord King who hold the town of Cambridge in fee farm as is stated, to their farm ½d. in hawgable.

[42]   Item the said Geoffrey holds 1 piece of vacant land in the same parish which descended to him by inheritance through the death of John Andre, his father. And the said John bought that from William de Manefeld, which said piece of land descended to the said William by inheritance through the death of Master Guy of Barnard Castle. And the said Guy bought that from Eustace Dunnyng, which said piece of land descended to the said Eustace by inheritance through the death of Harvey Dunnyng, his father. And the said Harvey held that by ancient acquisition, for which he pays per annum to the scholars of Merton 1d.

[43]   Item said Geoffrey holds a vacant piece of land in same parish which descended to the same Geoffrey by inheritance through the death of John Andre, his father. And the said John bought that from Radulph Bolle and the nuns of Markyate, for which he pays per annum to the said Radulph and his heirs ½d. And to the said nuns 9d., by which warranty the said nuns are unaware of any claim.

[44]   Item the said Geoffrey holds 1 messuage in the same parish which he bought from William of Barton. And the said William bought that from William le Lomb and from the sisters of William Arnold. And the said William Lomb and Agnes Dere and Margaret, the sisters of the said William Arnold, bought the said messuage from the nuns of St Radegund's, for which same messuage he pays per annum to the said William of Barton and his heirs 1 rose. And to the said nuns of St Radegund's 2s., by which warranty the said nuns are unaware of any claim to the said income.

[45]   Item the said Geoffrey holds 1 messuage in the same parish which he bought from Alan, son of Roger de Howes. And that messuage descended to the said Alan by inheritance through the death of the aforesaid Roger, his father. And the said Roger

bought that messuage from John Portehors. And the said John Portehors bought that from John Frost, chaplain. And the said John Frost, chaplain, acquired that by ancient acquisition as by purchase, for which he pays per annum to the said Alan and his heirs 1 rose. And to John Portehors and his heirs 2d.

[46]   Item the said Geoffrey holds 1 messuage in parish of Holy Sepulchre, Cambridge, which messuage descended to him by inheritance through the death of John Andre, his father, which messuage the said John at one time bought from Leon Dunnyng, for which he pays per annum, by assignment of the said Leon, to Nicholas Morice and his heirs 3s. And to the nuns of St Mary de Pré 3s., by which warranty the said nuns are unaware of any claim to the said income.

[47]   Item the said Geoffrey holds 2 acres of land with appurtenances in the fields of Cambridge, which descended to him by inheritance through the death of his father John Andre. And the said John bought that from Leon Dunnyng, for which he pays per annum to the said Leon and his heirs 2d.

[48]   Item Nicholas Andre holds 1 messuage in the parish of All Saints Cambridge at the Castle, which messuage he holds by gift of John Andre his father, which messuage the said John bought from Robert Bunt, for which he pays per annum to the heirs of the said John 1 clove gillyflower. And to the bailiffs of the Lord King who hold the town of Cambridge in fee farm as is stated to their farm in hawgable 3½d.

[49]   Item Henry Blancgernun holds 1 messuage in the same parish which same descended to him by inheritance through the death of Walter Blancgernun his father. And the said Walter acquired that messuage by gift of Baldwin Blancgernun, for which he[55] pays per annum, by assignment of the said Baldwyn, to the nuns of St Radegund's 2s.

[50]   Item said Henry holds a piece of vacant land in same parish which descended to the same Henry by inheritance through the death of Walter Blancgernun his father. And the said Walter bought that from Master Robert Aunger, which same descended to the said Master Robert by inheritance through the death of Aunger, his father, for which he pays per annum to the said Master Robert and his heirs, 12d.

[51]   Item the said Henry holds 1 messuage with appurtenances in same parish, which messuage descended to the same Henry by inheritance through the death of Walter Blancgernun his father. And the said Walter bought that messuage from Albert Carter.

And that messuage descended to the said Albert by inheritance through the death of his parents, for which he pays per annum, by assignment of the said Albert, to the bailiffs of the Lord King who hold the town of Cambridge in fee farm as is stated, to their farm by hawgable 1d.

[52]   Item the said Henry holds 1½ acres and 1 rood of land lying in the fields of Cambridge, which same descended to him by inheritance through the death of Walter Blancgernun, his father. And the said Walter bought that from Juliana, daughter of Thomas Longis. Which same descended to the said Juliana by inheritance through the death of the said Thomas, her father. And the said Thomas acquired that and held it from the prior and convent of Barnwell, for which he pays per annum to the heirs of the said Juliana 6½d.

[53]   Item the said Henry holds a certain house with a piece of vacant land, which same descended to him by inheritance through the death of the said Walter, his father. And the said Walter bought that from Juliana daughter of Thomas Longys, which same descended to the said Juliana by inheritance through the death of the said Thomas, her father. And the said Thomas acquired that by ancient succession of his parents, for which he pays per annum to the heirs of the said Juliana 1d. And to the bailiffs of the Lord King who hold the town of Cambridge in fee farm as is stated to their farm in hawgable 1d.

[54]   Item the said Henry holds 2 acres of land lying in the fields of Cambridge, which descended to him by inheritance through the death of the said Walter Blancgernun, his father. And the said Walter bought that from Juliana, daughter of Thomas Longis, which same descended to the same Juliana by inheritance through the death of her father Thomas. And the said Thomas had and held that from the prior and convent of Barnwell, for which he pays per annum to the heirs of the said Juliana 6d. and 1 farthing. And to the bailiffs of the Lord King who hold the town of Cambridge in fee farm as is stated, to their farm in hawgable 1 farthing.

[55]   Item the said Henry holds 1 rood lying in the fields of Cambridge, which descended to him by inheritance through the death of Walter Blancgernun his father. And the said Walter held and bought that from Juliana daughter of Thomas Longys, which same descended to the said Juliana by inheritance through the death of the said Thomas, her father, for which he pays per annum to the heirs of the said Juliana 1 rose. And to the bailiffs

of the Lord King who hold the town of Cambridge in fee farm from the Lord King and his ancestors as is stated, to their farm by hawgable 1 farthing.

[56] Item the said Henry holds a ½ acre of land lying in the fields of Cambridge, which descended to Henry by inheritance through the death of Walter Blancgernun, his father, which said Walter bought from Thomas, son of Robert Cante'. And the said Thomas had and held that from Richard Karloc. And the said Richard acquired that by acquisition, for which he pays per annum to the heirs of the said Thomas 1 rose. And to the heirs of Richard Karloc 1 root of ginger. And to the said bailiffs of the Lord King who hold the town of Cambridge in fee farm as is stated, to their farm in hawgable ½d.

[57] Item Thomas de Impington and Roysya his wife hold 1 messuage with its appurtenances in the said parish, which messuage William of St Edmunds gave to the said Thomas in frank marriage with his daughter Roysia, wife of the said Thomas. And the said William acquired that messuage by gift of John Andre in frank marriage with Margaret, daughter of the same John. And the said John acquired that messuage by ancient purchase, for which they pay per annum to the heirs of the said John Andre 15d.

[58] Item the said Thomas and Roysia his wife hold 1 shop in the marketplace of Cambridge in the parish of Saint Mary, which same shop William of St Edmunds gave to the said Thomas in frank marriage with Roysia his wife, daughter of the same William. And the said William acquired that by gift of John Andre in frank marriage with Margaret, daughter of the same John. And the said John acquired that by ancient purchase, for which he pays per annum to the heirs of the said John Andrew 9d.

[59] Item William le Plowritte of Madingley holds 1 messuage with its appurtenances in the parish of Saint Peter at the Castle, which messuage he bought from William le Plowritte of Stanton. And the said William le Plowritte of Staunton bought that from Leon le Horsemonger. And the said Leo le Horsemonger bought that from Eustace Dunnyng. And the said Eustace acquired that by hereditary succession through the death of Harvey Dunnyng his father, for which [he pays] per annum to the scholars of Merton 8s.

[60] Item the said William le Plowritte of Madingley holds 1 messuage with its appurtenances in the said parish of Saint Peter, which messuage he bought from William le Plowritte of Stanton. And

the said William le Plowritte of Stanton bought that from Leon le Horsemonger. And the said Leon from Eustace Dunnyng. And the same descended to the said Eustace by inheritance through the death of Harvey Dunnyng his father, for which he pays per annum to the scholars of Merton 12d. And, by assignment of the said Eustace Dunnyng, to the prior and convent of Barnwell 4s., by which warranty the said prior is unaware of any claim to the said income.

[61]   Alan de Howes holds 1 messuage and a certain croft lying in the hamlet of Howes with its appurtenances, belonging to the town of Cambridge in the said parish of Saint Peter, which messuage with said croft descended to the same Alan by inheritance through the death of his father, Richard de Howes. And the said Richard held that messuage with croft from Eustace Dunning. And that messuage with croft descended to the said Eustace by inheritance through the death of Harvey Dunning his father, for which he pays per annum, by assignment of the said Eustace, to the scholars of Merton 2s.

[62]   Item the said Alan holds a ½ acre of land lying in the fields of Cambridge, which land descended to the same Alan by inheritance through the death of Richard de Howes, his father. And the said Richard bought that from Leon Dunning, which same land descended to the said Leon by inheritance through the death of Adam Dunning his father, for which he pays per annum to the said Leon and his heirs 4d.

[63]   Item the said Alan holds 1 messuage in Cambridge in the said parish, which messuage he bought from Katherina and Elena, daughters of Robert le Chaluner, which messuage descended to the said Katherina and Elena by inheritance through the death of the said Robert, their father. And the said Robert bought that from the prior of Spinney. And the said prior and convent of Spinney acquired that messuage by gift of Robert, former vicar of St Edward's Church. And the said Robert bought that messuage from William Casteleyn. And that messuage descended to the said William by inheritance through the death of Godfrey Godeman, his father, for which he pays per annum to the said prior and convent of Spinney ½ mark. And to the said bailiffs of the Lord King who hold the town of Cambridge in fee farm as is stated to their farm in hawgable ½d.

[64]   Item the said Alan holds 1 messuage in the same parish which messuage he bought from William le Plowritte of Madingley. And the said William of Stanton bought that from Adam Scot.

And the said Adam that from John de Mounz. And the said John bought that from William Castelyn. And the said messuage descended to the said William by inheritance through the death of Godfrey Godeman his father, for which he pays per annum to the said William le Plowritte of Madingley 1 clove gillyflower. And to the said Adam Scot ½d. And to William Casteleyn ½d. And to the said bailiffs of the Lord King who hold the town of Cambridge in fee farm as is stated, to their farm in hawgable ½d.

[65]   Robert Wimund holds 1 messuage in fief in the parish of Saint Peter's at the Castle which same messuage he has by gift of Richard Laurence, which same Richard acquired that by succession from his mother Isabella, which same Isabella acquired that in frank marriage by gift of her father Robert Seman. And that Robert acquired that by ancient hereditary succession of his ancestors, and he pays in respect thereof per annum to the said Richard 4s. for the aforesaid messuage.

[66]   The same Robert holds 1 messuage in the parish of Saint Peter's at the Castle, which he holds from the prioress and convent of St Radegund's, which same prioress and convent have by gift from John Frere, which same John acquired that by heritage through the death of Warin le Tailor, his uncle, and pays in respect thereof per annum to the aforesaid prioress and convent 12d.[56]

[67]   Item the same Robert holds 1 messuage in the parish of Saint Giles which same messuage he bought from Denis son of William Elesheved, which same Dennis acquired that by hereditary succession through the death of William Elesheved his father, which same William acquired that by hereditary right through the death of his mother, Elena, and pays in respect thereof per annum to the heirs of Robert Seman 4d. who are tenants-in-chief of the lord's fief.[57]

[68]   Item the same Robert holds in fief 1 rood of land in the fields of Cambridge which he bought from William Tuylet, which same William bought from Leon Dunning, and he pays in respect thereof per annum to the heirs of the said William 1d.

[69]   Item the same Robert holds 1 rood of land in fief in the same fields which he bought from John of St Edmunds, which same John acquired that by hereditary right through the succession of Robert, his father, and he pays in respect thereof per annum to the said John ½d.

[70]   Item the same Robert holds in fief 2 roods of land in the same fields by gift of Luke of St Edmunds, which same Luke held that

by hereditary right through the death of his brother Thomas, and he pays in respect thereof per annum to the said Luke 1 pair of white gloves at the price of 1d.

[71] Item the same Robert holds in fief 2 roods of land in the same fields which he bought from Eustace Dunning, which same Eustace acquired that by hereditary right by succession of Harvey Dunning, his father, and in respect thereof he pays per annum to the heirs of the said Eustace 1 peppercorn for the said land.

[72] Margaret daughter of Robert Wimund holds 1 messuage in the parish of St Giles, Cambridge, which she bought from Geoffrey of Caldecote, which same Geoffrey acquired that by hereditary succession through the death of his father, Peter de Len, which same Peter acquired that from Richard, son of Ivo, which same Richard acquired that by hereditary succession through the death of Ivo, his father, which same Ivo acquired that by ancient hereditary succession of his ancestors, and she pays in respect thereof per annum to the said Geoffrey 1 rose and to the heirs of the said Richard son of Ivo, that is to William Eliot and his wife Alexandria, 4s. for the said messuage.

[73] The same Margaret holds a piece of vacant land in the parish of Saint John which same piece of land she has by gift from Thomas Wimund, her uncle, which same Thomas acquired that by hereditary succession through the death of Walter Wimund his father, which same Walter acquired that by gift of Robert Seman his brother, and she pays in respect thereof per annum to the said Robert Seman 2s. for the said piece of land.

[74] Matilda daughter of Robert Wimund holds 1 messuage in the parish of St Giles which same messuage she bought from Jordan le Nacter', which same Jordan acquired that by purchase from Richard son of Ivo, which same Richard acquired that by ancient hereditary succession through the death of his father Ivo, and she pays in respect thereof per annum to the heirs of the said Richard Ivo 4s. for the said messuage.

[75] Richard son of Simon Brenhand of Howes holds 1 messuage with a certain croft by hereditary right from the succession of the said Simon, his father, which same messuage with croft he bought from Atius, brother of Cambridge and he pays in respect thereof per annum to the prior of Barnwell 3s. 6d. by assignment of the said Atius.

[76] John son of Walter de Howes holds 1 messuage with croft by hereditary right in Howes, which same messuage with croft the said Walter, his father, bought from Eustace Dunning, and the

same Eustace acquired that by inheritance from Harvey his father, and in respect thereof he pays per annum by assignment of the said Eustace, to the clerics of Merton, 12d.

[77] Robert Rie of Howes holds 1 messuage with croft in the said hamlet of Howes by hereditary succession, which same messuage the said Alan, father of the said Robert, bought from Eustace Dunning and he pays in respect thereof per annum by assignment of the said Eustace, to the clerics of Merton 2s.

[78] John Attegrene of Howes holds 1 messuage with croft and 3 acres of land in the fields of Cambridge which same messuage with croft and with the said land he bought from the Lady Felicia de Queie, which same Felicia acquired that by gift of William de Torbelville and pays in respect thereof per annum to the said Felicia 3s.

[79] The same John holds ½ acre of land in the said fields by hereditary succession through the death of his father Alan, which same Alan bought from William Wisman, which same William gave to the same William in frank marriage with Alicia Clai, and pays in respect thereof per annum to Mabilia Clai de Berton 3d. and 1 farthing.

[80] Item John Attegrene holds ½ acre of land in the same fields by hereditary right, which Alan his father bought from Henry Clai de Berton, and he pays the same Henry per annum 1d., and the said Henry holds that land from Roger Rumbold of Cotes.

[81] The same John holds 3 roods of land in the said fields from the heirs of Thomas Lungis of Cambridge, which same Thomas held from the prior of Barnwell, and he pays in respect thereof per annum to Henry Smith and Alicia his wife, 4d. by assignment of the said heirs.

[82] Norman le Cooper holds 1 messuage in the parish of St Giles Cambridge which he bought from John Hittie, which same John bought that from Matilda daughter of Nigel Haring, and he pays in respect thereof per annum to John Porthors ½ mark. And the same John pays in respect thereof per annum to the prior of Ely 12d., by which warranty the said prior is unaware of any claim to the said income.

[83] The same Norman holds 1 messuage in the same parish which he bought from the prior of Barnwell, and he pays in respect thereof per annum to the prior 3s. as tenant-in-chief of the lord's fief, by which warranty the said prior has no claim on the said messuage.

[84] The same Norman holds ½ acre of land in the fields of Cambridge which he bought from Simon le Clayere of Chesterton, and the

same Simon bought that from Richard le Marchant. And that Richard bought that from Juliana Lungis. Which same Juliana acquired that by hereditary succession through the death of her father Thomas, and in respect thereof he pays per annum to the said Simon ½d.

[85] Sarra daughter of Norman le Cooper holds 1 messuage in the parish of St Giles Cambridge which said Norman bought from William de Cotes, which same William acquired that by hereditary succession through the death of Radulph, chaplain of Cotes, and the same Radulph bought that from William son of Aunger. And that William held that from the brothers of St John's Hospital, and in respect thereof she pays per annum to the said William ½d., and to the said brothers of the hospital 4s. for the said messuage. By which warranty the said brothers are unaware of any claim to the said income.

[86] John le Mire holds 1 messuage in the town of Cambridge in the parish of St Giles which he bought from Laurence Seman, which same Laurence bought that from Adam Puttoc. And the same Adam held that from Robert de Houghton. And the same Robert held that by inheritance through the death of his father Robert, and in respect thereof he pays per annum to the said Laurence ½d., and to the said Robert de Houghton 6s. 3½d.

[87] Item Agnes daughter of Philip le Tailor holds 1 messuage in the parish of St Peter's Cambridge, which descended to the same by hereditary right through the death of the said Philip, her father, which same Philip held that from the scholars of Merton, and in respect thereof she pays per annum to the said scholars 6s., and to the prior of Anglesey 2s. for the said messuage, by which warranty the said prior is unaware of any claim to the said income.

[88] Item Robert Lauman of Histon holds 1 messuage in the parish of St Giles which he bought from Geoffrey de Histon, cleric, which same Geoffrey bought that from Richard Dunning, which same Richard bought that from Henry son of Elias Hoppecrane, which same Henry held that by hereditary succession through the death of the said Elias, his father, and he pays in respect thereof per annum to Robert de Houghton 8s. 6d., as tenant-in-chief of the lord's fief.

[89] William son of Walter Norman holds 1 messuage in the parish of St Giles Cambridge, from Robert de Houghton, and the same Robert held that from inheritance through the death of his father Robert, and in respect thereof he pays per annum to the said Robert 3s. 4d. as tenant-in-chief of the lord's fief.

[90]   The same William holds 1 piece of land in the parish of All
        Saints at the Castle which Walter his father held by ancient
        purchase, and he pays in respect thereof per annum to the bailiffs
        of Cambridge who hold the said town in fee farm from the
        Lord King, to their farm in hawgable 2d.

[91]   Item Amicia daughter of Albert le Sivir holds 1 house in the
        parish of St Giles from hereditary succession through the death
        of her father Albert, which said Albert held that from Robert
        de Houghton, and in respect thereof she pays per annum to the
        said Robert 3s. as tenant-in-chief of the lord's fief.

[92]   Adam Scot holds 1 messuage in the parish of St Giles which same
        messuage he bought from Robert de Houghton, and the same
        Robert held that by inheritance from Robert his father, and in
        respect thereof he pays per annum to the said Robert and his
        heirs 10s. 4½d. as tenant-in-chief of the lord's fief.

[93]   Maurice le Tailor holds 1 messuage in the parish of St Giles
        which same messuage he bought from Richard Ampe, which
        same Richard held that by inheritance through the death of his
        father John Hamon, and in respect thereof he pays per annum
        to the heirs of the said Richard 4s.

[94]   The same Maurice holds 1 messuage in the parish of St Peter's
        which he bought from Richard son of Gregory, which same
        messuage descended to the said Richard by inheritance through
        the death of his father Gregory, and in respect thereof he pays
        per annum to John son of the said Richard 2s.

[95]   The same Maurice holds 1 messuage in the parish of All Saints at
        the Castle which he bought from Matilda daughter of Roger, cleric
        of Stanton, which same messuage descended to the said Matilda by
        inheritance through the death of her father Roger, and in respect
        thereof he pays per annum to the said Matilda and her heirs 3s.

[96]   William son of Jordan holds 1 messuage in the parish of
        St Giles which same messuage descended to the said William by
        inheritance through the death of his father Jordan, which same
        Jordan held that in marriage with Christiana daughter of Richard
        Bulling, and in respect thereof he pays per annum to the heirs of
        Robert Seman 4d. as tenant-in-chief of the lord's fief.

[97]   John Warin holds 1 messuage in the parish of St Peter's which he
        bought from Richard Ledwi which same Richard held that from
        ancestral succession through the death of his father Harvey, and in
        respect thereof he pays per annum to the nuns of St Radegund's
        for the said messuage 3s. as tenant-in-chief of the lord's fief, by
        which warranty they are unaware.

[98]   The same John holds 1 messuage in the same parish which he bought from Lord Philip le Coleville, which same messuage Philip held by hereditary succession through the death of his father Henry. And in respect thereof he pays per annum to the said Philip 5s.

[99]   Matilda daughter of Thomas de Froyslake holds in fief 1 messuage by gift of her brother Thomas, which same Thomas held that by hereditary succession through the death of his father Thomas, and in respect thereof she pays per annum to Lord Philip de Coleville 20d., and to Lady Alicia, former wife of Lord William of Buckworth, knight, 6d.

[100]   Isabella daughter of Thomas de Froyslake holds in fief 1 messuage by gift of her brother Thomas, which same Thomas held that through paternal succession through the death of his father Thomas, and in respect thereof she pays per annum to Lady Alicia, former wife of William of Buckworth, knight, 6d., and to Lord Philipe de Coleville as tenant-in-chief of the lord's fief 20d.

[101]   The same Isabella daughter of the said Thomas holds in fief half part of 1 messuage in the parish of St Giles, which same she bought from John de Froyslake her brother, and she pays in respect thereof per annum by assignment of the said John, to the abbot of St Edmund's 15d., and to the bailiffs of Cambridge who hold the said town in fee farm as is stated to their farm in hawgable ½d.

[102]   Alicia wife of William le Barbur holds in fief 1 shop in the parish of St Peter's which descended to her by hereditary right through the death of her uncle Simon Fisher, which same Simon held that from the prior of Barnwell, and in respect thereof she pays per annum to the said prior 3s. 6d., and to the bailiffs of Cambridge who hold the same town in fee farm as is stated, to their farm in hawgable 1d., by which warranty the prior and convent are unaware of any claim to the said income.

[103]   Item Michael Wulward holds in fief 1 messuage in the parish of St Peter's at the Castle by hereditary right through the death of Peter Wulward his father. Which same Peter held that by inheritance through the death of Robert Wulward, his father. Which same Robert held that by inheritance through the death of his father Wulward, and in respect thereof he pays per annum to the prior of Chicksands 7s. And to Lord Peter de Chavent as tenant-in-chief of the lord's fief 3s. By which warranty the said prior is unaware of any claim to the said income.

[104]   The same Michael holds in fief a certain house which he held
         by gift of Sabina Huberd, which same Sabina bought that from
         Richard de Aldreth, which same Richard held that by hereditary
         succession through the death of Reginald de Aldreth, his father,
         and in respect thereof he pays per annum to the said Sabina
         1 rose.

[105]   The same Michael holds in fief a certain messuage in the parish
         of Cambridge which he bought from Peter, his father, and from
         Matilda, his mother, which same Peter and Matilda held that by
         gift of Margaret, mother of the said Matilda, in frank marriage,
         and in respect thereof he pays per annum to Catherine daughter
         of John Seman of Newport 3s. for the said messuage.

[106]   Item the same Michael holds in fief a certain piece of land in
         the parish of St Giles by hereditary succession through the death
         of his father Peter, which same Peter held that from the prior
         of Barnwell, and in respect thereof he pays per annum to the
         said prior 6d., by which warranty the said prior and convent are
         unaware of any claim to the said income.

[107]   John Dunning holds 1 messuage in the parish of St Giles which
         descended to him by hereditary right through the death of
         Thomas Dunning, his father. Which same Thomas bought that
         from Eustace Dunning, his brother. Which same Eustace held
         that by inheritance through the death of his father Harvey. And
         in respect thereof he pays per annum to John Porthors 8d., which
         rent of 8d. the said John bought from Richard, son and heir of
         the said Eustace Dunning.

[108]   The same John holds ½ acre of land in the fields of Cambridge
         which descended to him by inheritance through the death of his
         father Thomas, which same Thomas bought that from Eustace
         his brother, and in respect thereof he pays per annum to the
         scholars of Merton ½d., by assignment of the said Richard son
         and heir of the said Eustace.

[109]   The same John holds in the fields of Cambridge ½ acre of land
         which descended to him by inheritance through the death of his
         father Thomas, which same Thomas bought that from Radulph
         le Eir of Grantchester, and that Radulph held that by inheritance
         through the death of his father Robert and in respect thereof he
         pays per annum to the said Radulph ½d.

[110]   The same John holds 1 messuage in the parish of St John's
         Cambridge which descended to the said John by inheritance
         through the death of his father Thomas, which same Thomas
         held that by gift of Leon Dunning, and the same Leon that by

gift of Robert of St Edmunds in frank marriage with Matilda, daughter of the said Robert, and the same Robert held that by ancient acquisition, and in respect thereof he pays per annum to the said Leon 10s. for the said messuage.

[111]   Roger de Wethersfield holds 1 messuage with appurtenances in the parish of St Giles until the end of his life which he has by gift of William Seman and that William[58] held that by gift of Agnes Fisher. Which same Agnes held that from the master and brothers of St John's Hospital, Cambridge, and he pays in respect thereof per annum to the said[59] brothers 4s., by which warranty the said brothers are unaware of any claim to the said income, and to the bailiffs of Cambridge who hold the said land of William in fee farm as is stated, to their farm in hawgable 2[60]d.

[112/13] Geoffrey de Spertegrave and Agnes his wife hold 1 messuage and 12 acres of land until the end of their lives in the town and in the[61] fields of Cambridge, which messuage and said land they hold from Richard son of Robert Fithion, which same Robert held the said messuage and land by inheritance[62] through the death of Henry Fithion his father, which same Henry held that by ancient purchase and they pay in respect thereof to the prioress of St Radegund's[63] for the said messuage 8s., and to Leon Dunning for the said land 22d., by which warranty the said prioress is unaware of any claim to the said income.

[114]   The same Geoffrey and Agnes his wife hold from the said Richard 1 messuage until the[64] end of their lives, which same Richard held that by inheritance through the death of Robert Fithion, his father, and the same Robert held that by inheritance through the death of his father Henry, and the same Henry held that by ancient acquisition, and they pay in respect thereof per annum to the prioress of St Radegund's 5s., and to the abbot of St Edmunds 12d., by which warranty the said abbot and the said prioress are unaware of any claim to the said income.

[115]   Item Geoffrey and Agnes his wife hold 1 messuage in the parish of All Saints at the Castle until the end of their lives which they hold by gift from the said Richard, and the same Richard holds that by inheritance through the death of his father Robert, which same Robert held by inheritance through the death of his father Henry, and the same Henry held that by ancient acquisition, and in respect thereof they pay per annum to the said church of All Saints for the said messuage 2d.

[116]   Item Geoffrey and Agnes his wife hold 1 messuage in the parish of St Peter's at the Castle which they bought from Semannius of

Ely, which same Semannius held that by hereditary succession through the death of his father Semannius, and that Semannuis held that by ancient acquisition, and in respect thereof they pay per annum to the heirs of Robert Seman 1 mark.

[R9]   Item Geoffrey and Agnes his wife receive 9s. per annum from Gilbert Bernard, paid annually for various messuages. Which same income they acquired by gift from Isabella Wombe. Which same Isabella acquired the income by gift from Michael Bernard her father, and in respect thereof they pay per annum to St Mary's Church, Cambridge, 8d.

[117/18] Geoffrey and Agnes his wife receive per annum 3s. paid annually from John of Gaisham and from his wife Sabina for 1 messuage outside Trumpington Gate, and from Agnes de Madingley 16d. for a certain messuage in the marketplace of Cambridge, which same income they acquired by gift from the said Isabella Wombe, which same Isabella acquired the said income at one time by gift from her father Michael Bernard.

[R10]   The same Geoffrey and Agnes his wife receive per annum until the end of their lives ½ mark paid annually from Laurence Seman and his wife Agnes for their messuages and land that they hold in fief in the town and the fields of Cambridge.

[119]   Roger son of Richard Hampe holds 1 piece of vacant land in the parish of All Saints at the Castle by hereditary succession through the death of his father Richard, which same Richard acquired that by hereditary right through the death of John Hampe his father, which same John bought that from the prior and convent of Barnwell, and he pays in respect thereof per annum to the said prior and convent for the said land 2s., by which warranty the said prior is unaware of any claim to the said land.

[120]   The same Roger holds in fief 1 messuage in the parish of St Giles which descended to him by inheritance through the death of his father Richard Ampe which same Richard held that by inheritance through the death of Alicia daughter of Henry Kankelia, and the said Alicia bought that from the prior and convent of Barnwell, and in respect thereof he pays per annum to the said prior and convent 12s., by which warranty the said prior is unaware of any claim to the said messuage.

[121]   Item Roger holds 1 messuage in the same parish by hereditary succession through the death of his father Richard Ampe, which same Richard held that by inheritance from his father John Hampe, and the same John acquired that through the death of his father Reginald Kankelia, and the same Reginald bought that

from Andrew son of Peter of Cambridge, and in respect thereof he pays per annum to the abbot of St Edmunds 3s. 2d. for the said messuage, by which warranty the said abbot is unaware of any claim to the said income.

[122] The same Roger holds a piece of vacant land in the parish of St Clement's by hereditary succession through the death of the said Richard Ampe his father, and the said Richard held that through the death of his father John, which same John bought that from Geoffrey Wulward and in respect thereof he pays per annum to Robert de Houghton 2d., and to St Clement's Church 4d.

[123] Henry Smith and his wife Alicia hold 1 messuage in the parish of All Saints at the Castle which same messuage the said Henry and the said Alicia held by gift from Norman le Cooper, and the said Norman held that by gift from Juliana, daughter of Thomas Longis. Which same Juliana acquired that by paternal succession through the death of her father Thomas, which same Thomas held that from the prior and convent of Barnwell, and in respect thereof they pay per annum to the said prior and convent 2s., by which warranty the said prior is unaware of any claim to the said income.

[124] Item Henry and his wife Alicia hold in fief 2 acres of land in the fields of Cambridge, which said Henry holds by gift of the said Norman in frank marriage with Alicia, daughter of the said Norman, and the same Norman held that by gift from Juliana daughter of Thomas Longis. Which same Juliana held that through the death of the said Thomas, her father, and the same Thomas held that from the prior and convent of Barnwell, and in respect thereof they pay per annum to the said Norman 1 pair of white gloves at the price of ½d., and to the said prior and convent 5s., by which warranty the prior is unaware of any claim, and to the bailiffs of Cambridge who hold the said town in fee farm as is stated, to their farm in hawgable 2½d.

[125] William de Standon and his wife Mabilia hold in fief 1 messuage in the parish of All Saints at the Castle which descended to the said Mabilia by inheritance through the death of her father Henry Hirp. And the said Henry bought that from the Lord Henry de Coleville, which same Henry held that by ancient acquisition, and in respect thereof they pay per annum to the heirs of the said Lord Henry 12d.

[126] Item William and his wife Mabilia hold 3 half acres in the fields of Cambridge which descended to the said Mabilia by inheritance

48

through the death of her father Henry. And the same Henry bought that from Leon Dunning, and they pay in respect thereof per annum to the said Leon and his heirs for the said land 5½d.

[127] Item Margaret Warin holds 1 messuage in the parish of All Saints at the Castle and 5 acres of land in the fields of Cambridge which same messuage and the said land she has by gift and feoffment from her brother John Warin, which same John held the said messuage with the said land by inheritance through the death of his father Roger Warin, which same Roger acquired that by ancient purchase, and in respect thereof she pays per annum for the said messuage and for the said land to the prior of Barnwell 4s., and to Leon Dunning 2d., by which warranty the said prior is unaware of any claim to the said income.

[128] Item the same Margaret holds 4 shops in the same parish which she holds by gift of her brother John, which same John held by hereditary right through the death of the said Roger, his father, which same Roger held by ancient purchase, and in respect thereof she pays per annum to Simon Prat ½d., and to the bailiffs of Cambridge who hold the said town in fee farm etcetera for hawgable ½d.

[129] Item the same Margaret holds 1 messuage in the parish of Holy Trinity which she holds by gift from William Cobon, which same William held by gift from Abraham le Chapeler, which same Abraham bought that from Alberich Butcher, and from Isabella his wife, and from Roger Eim and his wife Agnes, which same Alberich and Roger held by inheritance from the said Isabella and Agnes and in respect thereof she pays per annum to the heirs of the said Isabella and Agnes 10s.

[130] Item Agnes daughter of Hugh of Barton holds 1 messuage in the parish of Holy Trinity which descended to her by inheritance through the death of the said Hugh, her father, which same Hugh held by gift from his father John of Barton, which same John held by ancient inheritance of his parents, and in respect thereof she pays per annum to Simon le Spicer 7d.

[131] Item Alicia daughter of Abraham le Chapeler holds 1 messuage in the parish of Holy Trinity which she has by gift from her father Abraham, and the said Abraham bought that from Hugh le Cordewener and his wife Mabilia, which same Hugh and Mabilia acquired that by acquisition, and in respect thereof she pays per annum to the heirs of Hugh and Mabilia 1d.

[132] Item Robert son of Robert Seman holds 1 messuage in the parish of St Giles Cambridge which descended to him by hereditary

right through the death of the said Robert, his father, which same Robert held through the death of Asspelon, his uncle, which same Asspelon held by ancient succession of his parents, and in respect thereof he pays per annum to Lady Alicia, widow of Lord William of Buckworth, 5s., and to the bailiffs of Cambridge who hold the same town in fee farm etcetera 1d.

[133] The same Robert holds 1 messuage in the parish of St Peter's at the Castle which descended to him by inheritance through the death of his father Robert Seman, which same Robert held by hereditary right through the death of his father Robert, and the said Robert held that through the death of his grandfather, and the said Semmanius acquired that by succession of his parents, and in respect thereof he pays per annum to the abbot of St Edmunds 3s., by which warranty the said abbot is unaware of any claim to the said income.

[134] The same Robert holds 11 acres of land in the fields of Cambridge which descended to him by inheritance through the death of his father, the said Robert Seman, which same Robert held through the death of his father Robert, and the same Robert acquired that through the death of Walter Wimund, his father, and the said Walter acquired that by ancient purchase, and in respect thereof he pays per annum to the bailiffs of Cambridge who hold the said town in fee farm etcetera 13d.

[135] Item Eva daughter of Christian de Huntingdon holds 1 messuage in the parish of All Saints at the Castle, which she has by gift of John de Huntingdon, former rector of St Peter's Church at the Castle, which same John bought that from Juliana Ace, which same Juliana acquired by gift of Brother Atius atte Wal, which same Brother Atius acquired by ancient purchase, and in respect thereof she pays per annum to the prior of Barnwell 6d., by which warranty the said prior is unaware of any claim to the said income. Moreover the said Eva and her heirs will sustain a candle in St Peter's Church for the soul of the said John de Huntingdon in perpetuity.

[136] Item Laurence Seman and his wife Agnes hold 1 messuage and 4 acres of land in the parish of St Peter's at the Castle which same messuage with the said land they have by gift of Richard Fiyion, brother of the said Agnes, which same Richard acquired the said messuage and the said land by hereditary right through the death of his father Robert, which same Robert held that by hereditary right through the death of his father Henry Fiyion, which same Henry acquired by ancient purchase, and in respect thereof they

pay per annum to Thomas le Heyr 1d., and to the said Richard 12d.

[137]   Item Laurence and Agnes hold 1 messuage in the parish of St John which they have by gift of Geoffrey de Spertegrave and his wife Agnes, which same Agnes has by gift of Michael Bernard, her father, which same Michael bought from Etha, sister of Nicholas the priest, and the same Etha acquired that through the inheritance of her ancestors, and in respect thereof they pay per annum to the prioress of St Radegund's 4d., by which warranty the said prioress is unaware of any claim to the said income.

[138]   Item Laurence and Agnes hold 1 acre of land in the fields of Cambridge which they have by gift from Geoffrey de Spertegrave, which same Geoffrey bought that from Isabella daughter of Michael Bernard, and the said Isabella acquired that by gift from Michael Bernard her father, and in respect thereof they pay per annum to Lady Alicia Kiriel 8d.

[139]   Item Laurence holds half of 1 messuage in parish of St Giles which he bought from Isabella de Froyslake, which same Isabella acquired by purchase from John, her brother, which same John acquired that by inheritance through the death of his brother Thomas de Froyslake, and in respect thereof he pays per annum to the abbot of St Edmunds 15d., and to the bailiffs of Cambridge who hold the said town in fee farm etcetera in hawgable 1 farthing, by which warranty the said abbot is unaware of any claim to the said income.

[140]   Item Walter de Howes holds 1 messuage and 1 acre of land belonging to the said messuage in from Radulph de Queye in the hamlet of Howes, which messuage and said acre of land descended to the said Walter by inheritance through the death of Henry de Howes, his father, and the said Henry acquired those by inheritance through the death of his father, Henry de Howes, and the same Henry acquired those by ancient purchase, and in respect thereof he pays per annum to Radulph de Queye 14d.

[141]   Item Walter holds 2 acres of land and a ½ acre in the fields of Cambridge which descended to him by hereditary right through the death of his father Henry, which same Henry acquired by inheritance through the death of his uncle Albin, and he pays per annum to Robert de Houghton 2s. 6d.

[142]   The same Walter holds 3½ acres of land in fief from the prior of Barnwell which descended to him by inheritance through the death of his father Henry de Howes, and that Henry acquired

those by hereditary right through the death of his uncle Albin, and in respect thereof he pays per annum to the said prior of Barnwell 3s., by which warranty the said prior is unaware of any claim to the said income.

[143]   Henry le Cutler holds in fief 1 messuage in the parish of St Clement's which he bought from Margeria Curteis. Which same Margeria bought that from Sabina Huberd, which same Sabina acquired by gift from Peter Curteis, which same Peter acquired through the death of his father Robert Curteis, which same Robert acquired by ancient hereditary succession of his ancestors, and in respect thereof he pays per annum to the said Margeria and her heirs ½d., and to the bailiffs of Cambridge who hold the said town in fee farm as is stated, to their farm in hawgable 1d.

[144]   Richard Laurence holds in fief 1 messuage in capital by hereditary right through the death of his father Laurence, which same Laurence held from the prior and convent of Ely and in respect thereof pays per annum to the said prior and convent 4s. for the said messuage, by which warranty the said prior and convent are [not] aware of any claim to the said income.

[145]   The same Richard holds 1 messuage in Holme by inheritance from his father Laurence, which same Laurence held from the prior and convent of Barnwell, and he pays in respect thereof per annum to the said prior and convent 14d., by which warranty the said prior is not aware, and to the bailiffs who have the said town in fee farm etcetera, to their farm in hawgable 1½d.

[146]   The same Richard holds in fief 1 messuage in the parish of Holy Trinity which descended to him by inheritance through the death of his father Laurence, which same Laurence bought from Robert Seman, which same Robert acquired that by ancient heritage of his ancestors, and in respect thereof he pays per annum to the bailiffs of Cambridge who hold the said town in fee farm, to their farm in hawgable 1d.

[147]   The same Richard holds 1 messuage in the same parish which he holds from Walter Pikerel, and the same Walter acquired that by ancient hereditary succession of his ancestors, and in respect thereof he pays per annum to Holy Trinity Church 16d.

[148]   The same Richard holds in fief half of 1 messuage in the parish of St Edward's through his wife Sabina, and that Sabina acquired that by hereditary right through the death of her brother John, and the same John acquired that by disseisin of Richard Ategate, his father, and in respect thereof he pays per annum to the almoner of Ely 27d.

[149] The same Richard holds 2½ acres of land in the fields of Cambridge, which same Richard has by gift and feoffment from the prioress of St Radegund's for so much land in exchange.

[150] The same Richard holds 1 acre of land in the fields of Cambridge which he bought from Matilda de Stowe and from her sister Margaret, which said acre of land descended to them by hereditary right through the death of their father Richard who exists in memory, and he pays in respect thereof per annum to the same 1d.

[151] The same Richard holds a certain meadow in the same fields which he bought from John Frost, and the same John acquired that by hereditary succession through the death of his father, and in respect thereof he pays per annum to the heirs of the said John 1 rose.

[152] The same Richard son of Richard Laurence holds in fief a ½ acre of land in the fields of Cambridge which he has by gift of Luke of St Edmunds, and the same Luke acquired that by inheritance through the death of his brother Thomas, and the same Thomas acquired that by hereditary succession, and in respect thereof he pays per annum to the said Luke 1 pair of white gloves at the price of 2d.

[153] The same Richard holds ½ acre of land in the same fields which his father Richard gave to him, and the same Richard acquired that by gift from Eustace Dunning, and same Eustace acquired that by inheritance through the death of his father Harvey, and in respect thereof he pays per annum to the said Richard his father 1 rose.

[154] Thomas le Marshall holds 1 messuage in the parish of St Clement's which descended to him by hereditary right through the death of Peter Marshall his father, which same Peter bought that from Nicholas Childman, which same Nicholas held that by inheritance through the death of his father, Childman, and in respect thereof he pays per annum to the heirs of Robert le Franc of Chesterton, by assignment of the said Nicholas, 8s.

[155] The same Thomas holds 1 shop in the same parish which he has by hereditary right through the death of his father Peter, which same Peter bought that from Childman, and the same Childman acquired that by ancient heritage of his ancestors, and in respect thereof he pays per annum to the heirs of the said Childman 8s.

[156] Item John Porthors holds in fief 1 messuage in the parish of St Clement's which he bought from Peter Wulward, which same Peter held that by hereditary succession through the death

of his father Robert, and the same Robert held that through the death of his father Wulward, and in respect thereof he pays per annum to the heirs of the said Peter 1d., and to St John's Hospital, Cambridge, 10s., by which warranty the said brothers are unaware of any claim to the said income.

[157] The same John holds 1 messuage in fief in the parish of Holy Trinity which same messuage descended to him by inheritance through the death of his brother Thomas, and the same Thomas acquired that by gift of his father, John of Barton, for which he pays per annum to the heirs of the said John 1 rose.

[158] The same John holds 1 house in the parish of All Saints at the Castle which he bought from John Frost, chaplain, which same John acquired that from ancient hereditary succession, and in respect thereof he pays per annum to the heirs of the said John 1 rose.

[159] The same John holds a piece of land in the parish of St Giles upon which his grange was built, which same he bought from Peter Wulward, and the same Peter acquired that by inheritance through the death of his father Robert, and the same Robert acquired that through the death of his father Wulward, and in respect thereof he pays per annum to the heirs of the said Peter 6d.

[R11] The same John has 6s. 8d. paid annually which he receives by gift from Norman le Cooper, which same income he bought from John Hitti, and in respect thereof he pays per annum for the said income of 6s. 8d., to the prior of Ely 12d., by which warranty the said prior is unaware of any claim to the said income.

[R12] The same John receives per annum 8d. in capital of the messuage of John Dunning that he bought from Richard, son of Eustace Dunning, and the same Richard acquired that by inheritance through the death of Eustace Dunning, and in respect thereof he pays per annum to the heirs of the said Richard 1 rose.

[160] The same John receives per annum 13d. paid annually from the house of John Waubert in the parish of All Saints next to St John's Hospital, which he bought from William de Manefeld, for which he pays per annum to the said William 1 rose.

[161] The same John receives per annum 1 mark paid annually from the house of the Archdeacon of Ely in the parish of Holy Trinity, which he has by gift of John of Barton, his father, for which he pays per annum to the heirs of the said John 1 rose.

[162] The same John holds 18 acres of land in the fields of Cambridge in fief from Eustace Dunning which he bought from William

de Manefeld, which same William held that by hereditary right through the death of Guy of Barnard Castle, his uncle. And the same Guy bought that from Eustace Dunning, and the same Eustace acquired that by inheritance of Harvey, his father, and he pays in respect thereof per annum to the scholars of Merton 1d. by assignment of the said William.

[163] Robert son of Aunger le Rus of Cambridge holds in the fields of Cambridge 40 acres of land and 1 acre in fief from Baldwin Blancgernun, which descended to him by inheritance through the death of Aunger le Rus, his father. And the same Aunger bought that from the said Baldwin, and in respect thereof he pays per annum to the heirs of the said Baldwin 12d.

[164] The same Robert holds in fief 1½ acres of land from the said fief which descended to him by inheritance through the death of his father Aunger, and the same Aunger bought that from the said Baldwin, and in respect thereof he pays per annum to the heirs of the said Baldwin 3d.

[A47] The same Robert holds in fief 1 messuage and other small payments paid at the value of 40s. by hereditary succession of his father Aunger, which same Aunger bought the said messuage and the said income of 40s. from the said Baldwin, and in respect thereof he pays per annum to the heirs of the said Baldwin 12d.

[165] The same Robert holds in fief 22 acres of land in the fields of Cambridge which descended to him by inheritance through the death of his father Aunger, and the same Aunger bought those from William de Dagenhale, and the same William acquired those by inheritance through the death of Henry de Dagenhale, his brother, and the same Henry acquired those by ancient hereditary succession, and in respect thereof he pays per annum on behalf of the heirs of the said William, namely to the bailiffs of Cambridge who hold the said [town] in fee farm as is stated, to their farm in landgable 11d.

[166] The same Robert holds in fief 4 acres of land until the end of his life in the said fields which he has by gift from the prior and convent of Barnwell, and in respect thereof he pays per annum to the said prior and convent 8d., by which warranty the said prior and convent are unaware of any claim to the said income.

[167] The same Robert holds 3 shops and 2 acres of meadowland which he bought from Nicholas, son of Nicholas Childman, and the same Nicholas acquired those by inheritance through the death of his father Nicholas, and in respect thereof he pays per annum to the said Nicholas son of the said Nicholas 1d.

[168]   The same Robert holds 1 shop with a certain curtilage in the parish of St Clement's which he bought from Peter Wulward, which same Peter acquired that by inheritance through the death of his father Robert, and the same Robert acquired that by inheritance through the death of his father Wulward, and in respect thereof he pays per annum to the heirs of the said Peter ½d.

[169]   Robert de Lunden holds 1 messuage in fief in the parish of St Clement's which same descended to the said Robert by inheritance through the death of Radulph le Cordewener, his father, and the same Radulph bought that from Baldwin Blancgernun, and in respect thereof he pays per annum to William son of Robert Trig 7s. 6d.

[170]   John But holds 1 messuage in fief in the parish of St Clement's which he bought from Thomas de Mervilus, which same Thomas bought that from John, son of Gilbert le Rus, which same John acquired that by hereditary succession through the death of John le Rus, his uncle, and in respect thereof he pays per annum to the said Thomas 1 crown of roses, and to the abbot of St Edmunds 3s. 6d., by which warranty the said abbot is unaware of any claim to the said income.

[171]   The same John holds in fief 1 messuage in the same parish which he bought from Matilda Corde. Which same Matilda held that by hereditary succession through the death of Walter Corde, her father, for which he pays per annum to the said Matilda 4d.

[172]   The same John holds in fief 2 acres of land in the fields of Cambridge which he bought from Matilda Corde, which same Matilda held that by inheritance through the death of her father, Walter Corde, and in respect thereof he pays per annum to the said Matilda 5d.

[173]   Richard Prest and his wife Alicia hold 1 shop in the town of Cambridge in the parish of St Clement's which they bought from Richard, son of Robert de Harston, which same Richard acquired that by inheritance through the death of Alicia de Harston, his mother. Which same Alicia acquired that by gift of Radulph Wombe, her father, and in respect thereof they pay per annum to the said Richard and his heirs 1 lb. of cumin, and to the bailiffs of Cambridge who hold the said town in fee farm as is stated, in hawgable 1 farthing.

[174]   Item Helewisa Plumbe holds 1 messuage in the parish of St Clement's which same she holds by inheritance through the death of her father Walter Plumbe, and that Walter acquired that

by ancient acquisition as from purchase, and in respect thereof she pays per annum to the abbot of St Edmunds 6s., and to Master Robert Aunger 3s., and to the bailiffs of Cambridge who hold the said town in fee farm as is stated in hawgable 1d., by which warranty the said abbot is unaware of any claim to the said income.

[175]   Item Richard de Parham holds 1 messuage in the parish of St Clement's to the end of his life from William of Pickering, and the said William acquired that by gift of Eustace Eldcorin, which same Eustace acquired that through the death of his father, Hugh Eldcorn, and in respect thereof he pays per annum to the said William 18s.

[176]   Margaret of St Albans holds in fief 1 messuage in the parish of St Clement's from the prior of Barnwell, for which she pays per annum to the said prior 1 mark, by which warranty the said prior holds no claim to the said messuage.

[177]   Item Cecilia daughter of Agnes Plumbe holds 1 messuage in the parish of St Clement's which same she held by gift of Alicia Plumbe, which same Alicia held by gift of Walter Plumbe, for which she pays per annum to St John's Hospital, Cambridge, 8s., by which warranty the said brothers are unaware of any claim to the said income.

[178]   Item Richard Aldgod, chaplain, holds 1 messuage in fief in the parish of St Clement's which descended to him by inheritance through the death of his father Henry, which same Henry held through the death of his father Robert Algold, and in respect thereof he pays per annum to the bailiffs of Cambridge who hold the said town in fee farm as is stated, in hawgable 1½d.

[179]   Item Stephen Baker, holds a grange in the parish of All Saints at the Castle which he bought from Robert Shevenehod, son of John, chaplain of Ditton, which said Robert held by gift of his father John, and the same John held by purchase from Robert Colt, and in respect thereof he pays per annum to the prior of Barnwell 4s. 6d., by which warranty the said prior has no claim to the said income, and to the said Robert ½d., and to the bailiffs of Cambridge who hold the said town in fee farm as is stated, in hawgable 2d.

[180]   Item Stephen holds 1 messuage in the parish of St Clement's which same messuage he has from Juliana, wife of Humphrey de Clopton, which same Juliana acquired by gift of Aunger le Rus, her father, for which he pays per annum to the said Juliana 20s.

[181]   Item Stephen holds ½ acre of land in the fields of Cambridge which he bought from Agnes Fisher, which same she held by purchase from William, son of Aunger Fisher, and that William held by inheritance through the death of his father Aunger, and in respect thereof he pays per annum to the said Agnes ½d.

[182]   Item Stephen Toli holds 1 messuage in the parish of St Clement's which he bought from Nicholas son of John Bernard, which same Nicholas acquired by gift of Queen Eleanor, mother of Edward, King of England who now is, until the end of the life of the said Eleanor, which same came to the said Queen in escheat by reason of the exile of the Jews, in which house they lived, for which he pays per annum to the bailiffs of Cambridge to their farm in hawgable 2d.

[183]   Item Robert son of William Toylet holds 1 messuage in the parish of St Clement's which he bought from Henry Toylet, his brother, which same Henry acquired by inheritance through the death of his brother William, which same William bought that from Nicholas son of Nicholas Childman, and in respect thereof he pays per annum to the said Henry and his heirs 1d., and to the bailiffs of Cambridge who hold the said town in fee farm as is stated, in hawgable ½d.

[184]   Item Robert holds a grange in the parish of All Saints next to St John's Hospital in fief from Leon Dunning at Dame Nichol's Hythe which he bought from his brother Henry, which same Henry held by hereditary right through the death of his brother William, and in respect thereof he pays per annum to the said Henry and his heirs ½d., and to Leon Dunning 1d. as tenant-in-chief of the lord's fief.

[185]   Item Robert holds 1 messuage in the parish of Holy Trinity which he acquired by gift of his father William, and the said William bought that from Thomas, son of Richard Burs, and that Thomas acquired that by gift of Nicholas son of John Alvewechild, and in respect thereof he pays per annum to the heirs of said William 1d., and to William de Novacurt and his heirs 18d.

[186]   Item Robert holds 1 acre of land in Cambridge which he bought from his brother Henry, which Henry acquired by inheritance through the death of his brother William, and in respect thereof he pays per annum to the said Henry 1d., and to the bailiffs of Cambridge who hold the said town in fee farm as is stated, in landgable 1d. and 1 farthing.

[187]   Item Richard son of William Seman holds 1 messuage in which he dwells in the parish of St Clement's, which same he acquired by gift of his father William and his mother Cecilia, and the said William and Cecilia bought that from Nicholas son of Everard de Wenepol, which same Nicholas bought that from the prior and convent of Barnwell, and in respect thereof he pays per annum to the heirs of the William and Cecilia 1 rose, and to the prior and convent 12d., and to the bailiffs of Cambridge who hold the said town in fee farm as is stated in hawgable 1d. and 1 farthing, by which warranty the said prior and convent are unaware of any claim to the said income.

[188]   Item Nicholas son of William Seman holds in fief 1 messuage in the parish of St Clement's which he acquired by gift of his father William and his mother Cecilia, and the said William and Cecilia bought that from Nicholas son of Everard de Wenepol, and the same Nicholas bought that from the prior and convent of Barnwell, and in respect thereof he pays per annum to the heirs of the said William and Cecilia 1 rose, and to the bailiffs of Cambridge who hold the said town in fee farm etcetera in hawgable 1d. and 1 farthing.

[189]   Item Nicholas holds 1 messuage in the parish of St Clement's which he acquired by gift of his father William and his mother Cecilia, and the said William and Cecilia bought that from William son of William Swanek, and the same William acquired that by hereditary right through the death of John Swaneke his father, and the same John held that by hereditary right through the death of William Swaneke his father, and in respect thereof he pays per annum to the heirs of the said William and Cecilia 1 rose and to the prior and convent of Barnwell 5s. 2d., by which warranty the said prior and convent are unaware of any claim to the said incomes.

[190]   Item Sabina Huberd holds her capital messuage in which she dwells in the parish of St Clement's until the end of her life, which same she has by gift of Bartholomew Gogging, her brother, which same Bartholomew acquired by gift and feoffment of Robert Huberd, former husband of the said Sabina, and that Robert acquired that by ancient purchase. And in respect thereof she pays per annum to the brothers of St John's Hospital, Cambridge, 4s., and to the abbess of Chateriss 7s., and to the said Bartholomew until the end of his life 1 rose, by which warranty the said brothers and abbess are unaware of any claim to the said income.

[191]   Item the same Sabina holds a grange in the parish of All Saints at the Castle to the end of her life which she acquired by gift from the said Bartholomew and that Bartholomew acquired by gift from the said Robert Huberd, and the same Robert bought that from Eustace Dunning, and in respect thereof pays per annum to the heirs of the said Eustace 1 pair of white gloves at the price of ½d.

[192]   Item the same Sabina holds 1 messuage in fief in the same parish which she has by gift of Robert son of Robert Huberd, which same Robert acquired by hereditary succession through the death of his father Hubert, and in respect thereof pays per annum to the prioress of St Radegund's 4s., by which warranty the said prioress is unaware of any claim to the said income.

[193]   Item the same Sabina holds 1 shop in the same parish which she bought from Elena daughter of Radulph Wombe, which Elena acquired by gift from Nicola Wombe, her mother, and the same Nicola acquired by ancient hereditary succession of her ancestors, and in respect thereof she pays per annum to the bailiffs of Cambridge who hold the said town in fee farm etcetera in hawgable 1 farthing.

[194]   Item the same Sabina holds 1 shop in the same parish which she bought from John Joachim, which same John acquired by ancient succession through the death of his father Joachim, and in respect thereof she pays per annum to the bailiffs of Cambridge who hold the said town in fee farm etcetera in hawgable ½d.

[195]   The same Sabina holds 1 messuage in the same parish which she bought from Martin of Winepol, and that Martin acquired by hereditary succession through the death of his father Everard de Wenepol, and in respect thereof she pays per annum to Lady Amica de Insula and her heirs 3s., and to the heirs of Bartholomew Wombe 15d.

[196]   The same Sabina holds 9 acres of land until the end of her life from the prior and canons of Anglesey, and in respect thereof she pays per annum to the said canons 9s. for the said land.

[197]   Item the same Sabina holds 9 acres of land in the fields of Cambridge which she acquired by gift of her son John, which same John acquired by gift of his father Robert, which same Robert formerly bought from Leon Dunnnig, and she pays in respect thereof per annum to the said Leon for the said land 5s. 6d.

[198]   Margaret de Aula holds 1 messuage in fief in the parish of St Clement's which she acquired by gift of Sabina Hubert. Which said Sabina acquired by gift of her son John, and the said

John acquired by gift formerly of Margaret Stoke, and in respect thereof she pays per annum to the said Sabina 1 pair of gloves, and to the prior of Barnwell 14d., by which warranty the said prior is unaware of any claim to the said income.

[199] Item Thomas Godeman holds in fief 1 messuage in which he lives above the water in the parish of St Clement's which same he bought from Master Robert Aunger, which same Robert acquired by inheritance through the death of his father Aunger, and the said Aunger bought from Robert Curtess, and in respect thereof he pays per annum to the said Master Robert and his heirs 11s. 6d.

[200] The same Thomas holds 1 messuage in the parish of St Andrew's which he bought from Walter Squalle and the same Walter bought at one time from the prioress of St Radegund's, and in respect thereof he pays per annum to the said prioress and convent of the same place 6s., by which warranty the prioress is unaware of any claim to the said income.

[201] The same Thomas holds 1 messuage in the parish of St Peter's at the Castle which he acquired by gift of Michael Pilat, which same Michael acquired by purchase from Dennis, son of William Elesheved, and the same Dennis acquired by inheritance through the death of his father William, and the same William acquired by inheritance through the death of Elena Ampe, and in respect thereof he pays per annum to the said Michael and his heirs 1 rose, and to Margaret, widow of Radulph Capmaker, and her heirs ½ mark, and to the heirs of Robert Seman 1 lb. of pepper, and to the bailiffs of Cambridge who hold the said town in fee farm etcetera in hawgable 2½d.

[202] The same Thomas holds 3 half acres of land in the fields of Cambridge which he acquired by gift of Michael Pilet, and that Michael acquired by purchase from Luke of St Edmunds, which same Luke acquired by inheritance through the death of Master Thomas, his brother, and that Thomas acquired by gift of his father Walter, and in respect thereof he pays per annum to the said Michael and his heirs 2d.

[203] Item the same Thomas holds ½ acre of land in the fields of Cambridge which he acquired by gift of Michael Pilet, and the same Michael acquired by inheritance through the death of his father Reginald, and in respect thereof he pays per annum to the said Michael 1d.

[204] The same Thomas holds in fief a piece of vacant land in the parish of St John's Cambridge which he bought from John Hitti, and

the said John acquired that by gift of his sister Basilia. Which same Basilia bought from Basilia, daughter of Warin Astines, and the same Basilia acquired by inheritance through the death of her father Warin Astin, and in respect thereof he pays per annum to Warin Astin 1d., and to the said John 1 rose.

[205] The same Thomas holds a piece of land in fief in the parish of St Andrews Cambridge which he bought from Master Thomas de Tid, and the same Thomas bought from Henry de Crissale, and in respect thereof he pays per annum on behalf of the heirs of the said Master Thomas namely to the heirs of Nicholas Malerbe ½d.

[206] The same Thomas holds in fief a ½ acre of land in the fields of Cambridge which he bought from Henry the linen-seller, and the same Henry acquired by ancient hereditary succession, and in respect thereof he pays per annum, on behalf of the heirs of the said Henry, namely to the bailiffs of Cambridge who hold the said town in fee farm etcetera, in hawgable ½d.

[207] The same Thomas holds in the fields of Cambridge 4 acres of land which he bought from John Porthors, and the same John bought from Richard, son of Eustace Dunning, and the same Richard acquired by inheritance through the death of his father Eustace, and in respect thereof he pays per annum to the said John and his heirs 6d.

[208] The same Thomas holds in the fields of Cambridge 6 acres of land with appurtenances which he bought from John Porthos, and the same John acquired by gift of the prior and convent of Barnwell, and in respect thereof he pays per annum to the said John 9d.

[209] William of Holme and his wife Catherine hold 1 messuage in the parish of St Clement's which same messuage descended to the said Catherine by hereditary right through the death of Emma de Walsokie, mother of the said Catherine, and the same Emma acquired that by inheritance through the death of Radulph son of Geoffrey, her uncle, and the same Geoffrey bought that from Baldwin Blancgernun, and in respect thereof they pay per annum to Master Robert Aunger 8s. for the said messuage.

[210] The same William and Catherine hold 1 messuage in the same parish which descended to the said Catherine by inheritance through the death of Emma, mother of the said Catherine, and the same Emma acquired that through the death of Radulph son of her uncle Geoffrey, and the same Geoffrey bought that from Baldwin Blancgernun, and in respect thereof they pay per

annum to the prior and Barnwell 4s. for the said messuage, by which warranty the said prior is unaware of any claim to the said income.

[211] Geoffrey le Cooper holds 1 messuage in the parish of St Clement's until the end of his life, which he took possession of in frank marriage with his wife, daughter of William de Reche, and that William held that from Robert Seman, and in respect thereof he pays per annum to the nuns of Chatteris ½ mark, by assignment of the said Robert Seman.

[212] William de Pickering holds 1 messuage until the end of his life in the parish of St Clement's which he acquired by gift of Eustace Eldcorn with his wife Letia, daughter of the said Eustace, in frank marriage, and the same Eustace acquired that by hereditary right through the death of Holdeburna his friend. Which same Holdeburna acquired by ancient purchase, and in respect thereof he pays per annum to the nuns of St Radegund's 6d., and to the bailiffs of Cambridge who hold the said town in fee farm etcetera in hawgable 2d.

[213] The same William holds 1 messuage in the same parish until the end of his life which he acquired with his wife Letia and the same Letia acquired by inheritance through the death of her father Eustace, and the same Eustace acquired that by inheritance through the death of his father Hugh Eldcorn, and in respect thereof he pays per annum to the prior of Barnwell and the convent 3s. and 1 lb. of cumin, by which warranty the said prior and convent are unaware of a claim to the said income.

[214] The same William holds 1 messuage in the same parish which descended to the said Letia, his wife, by inheritance through the death of her father Eustace, and the same Eustace acquired that by inheritance through the death of Hugh Eldcorn, his father, and that Hugh bought from the prioress and convent of Swaffham, and in respect thereof he pays per annum to the said prioress and convent ½ mark, by which warranty the said prioress is unaware of a claim to the said income.

[215] The same William holds 1 messuage in the parish of All Saints at the Castle which descended to Letia, his wife, by inheritance through the death of her father Eustace Eldcorn, and the same Eustace bought that from the brothers of St John's Hospital, Cambridge, which is in the fief of Baldwin Blancgernun, and he pays in respect thereof per annum to the said brothers of the hospital 4s., which by warranty the said brothers are unaware of a claim to the said income.

[216][Item William Seman holds 1 messuage with its appurtenances in the parish of St Clement's Cambridge, which messuage descended to the said William by inheritance through the death of his mother Cecilia, which same messuage Nicholas, son of Everard de Wynepol formerly gave to the said Cecilia, and that messuage the said Nicholas at one time bought from John, son of Richard de Wynepol, and the said John acquired that by hereditary right through the death of the said Richard, his father, for which he pays per annum to the heirs of the said John 1d., and to the bailiffs of Cambridge who hold the same town of Cambridge in fee farm from the Lord King as is stated above, and in hawgable 2d.

[217] Item the said William holds another messuage with its appurtenances above the water in the said parish of St Clement's, which messuage descended to the said William by inheritance through the death of the said Cecilia, his mother, and that messuage Martin, son of Everard de Wynepol, with its appurtenances formerly gave and granted by charter to the said Cecilia, which same messuage descended to the said Martin by inheritance through the death of the said Everard, his father, for which he pays per annum to Richard Wombe and his heirs 2s., and to the bailiffs of Cambridge who hold the same town of Cambridge in fee farm from the Lord King etcetera in hawgable 2d.

[218] The same William holds 1 shop with its appurtenances in the parish of All Saints Cambridge next to St John the Evangelist's Hospital, which same shop descended to the same William by inheritance through the death of the said Cecilia, his mother, which same shop descended to the said Cecilia by inheritance through the death of Nicholas, son of Andrew de Wynepol, for which he pays per annum to the abbot and convent of Ramsey 6d., by which warranty the said abbot is unaware of any claim to the said income.

[219] Item the said William holds 1 messuage with appurtenances in Mill Lane in the parish of St John the Baptist Cambridge, which same messuage descended to Margaret, his wife, by inheritance through the death of Walter Em, her father, and the said Walter bought that from William Elyoth, for which he pays per annum to the said William Elyoth 3d., and to St Mary's Church, Cambridge, 12d., and to the prior and convent of Barnwell 2s., by which warranty the said prior is unaware of any claim to the said income.

[220]   Item the said William holds 1 messuage with appurtenances in Straw Lane in the said parish of St John, which same messuage descended to the said Margaret, his wife, by inheritance through the death of her father Walter Em. And Walter bought that formerly from John at the water of Len, and the said John formerly bought that from Richard Billing of Chesterton, and he pays in respect thereof per annum to the said John 1 pair of gloves at the price of ½d., and to the prior of Barnwell 12d., and to the bailiffs of Cambridge who hold the same town etcetera in hawgable ½d.

[221]   Item the same William holds 1 messuage with its appurtenances in Straw Lane above the water in the said parish, which same messuage descended to the said Margaret, his wife, by inheritance through the death of the said Walter Em, her father, and the said Walter bought that messuage at one time from Elena, daughter of Algar le Savener, and the said Elena bought that from Peter, son of Serlon, for which he pays per annum, on behalf of the heirs of the said Elena, to the heirs of the said Peter 1d., and to the bailiffs of Cambridge who hold the same town of Cambridge in fee farm from the Lord King as is stated etcetera in hawgable ½d.

[222]   Item the same William holds 1 messuage with appurtenances in Milne Street in the parish of St John, which same messuage descended to the said Margaret, his wife, by inheritance through the death of Walter Em, her father, and the said Walter at one time bought that from the master and brothers of St John the Evangelist's Hospital, Cambridge, for which he pays per annum, on behalf of the said master and brothers of the said St John's Hospital, to the bailiffs of the Lord King who hold the town of Cambridge in fee farm from the Lord King etcetera, in hawgable 1d.

[223]   Item the said William holds 1 messuage with appurtenances in the parish of St Benedict's Cambridge in Segrimmeslane, which said messuage descended to the said Margaret, his wife, by inheritance through the death of Walter Em, her father, and the said messuage descended to the said Walter by inheritance through the death of his father, Robert Em, for which he pays per annum to St Benedict's Church for the sustenance of a certain lantern, 1 quarter of oil at Christmas. And to the bailiffs of Cambridge who hold the same town etcetera in hawgable 1 farthing.

[224]   Item the said William holds a granary at Dame Nichol's Hythe with appurtenances in the parish of All Saints Cambridge next to the hospital of Cambridge, which said granary descended to

the said Margaret, his wife, by inheritance through the death of Walter Em, her father, and the said Walter at one time bought that granary from Leon Dunning, which same granary descended to the said Leon through the death of Adam Dunning, his father, and he pays in respect thereof per annum to the said Leon and his heirs 1d.

[225] Item the same William holds a certain small part of empty land in the parish of St Botolph's, which same land descended to the said Margaret, his wife, by inheritance through the death of the said Walter Em, her father and the said Walter bought that from Simon Furri, for which he pays per annum to the heirs of the said Simon 1d., and to the bailiffs of Cambridge who hold the same town of Cambridge in fee farm from the Lord King etcetera in hawgable ½d.

[226] Item the same William holds 2 acres and 1 rood of land with appurtenances in the fields of Cambridge which he bought from Luke of St Edmunds, which same descended to the said Luke by inheritance through the death of Master Thomas of St Edmunds, his brother, which same Thomas acquired that by inheritance through the death of Walter of St Edmunds, his father, and he pays in respect thereof per annum to the said Luke and his heirs 5d.

[227] Item the said William holds 3½ acres in the fields of Cambridge, which same land descended to the said Margaret, his wife, by inheritance through the death of the oft-mentioned Walter Em, her father, and the said Walter bought that land from John Frost, for which he pays per annum to the heirs of the said John 3½d.

[228] Item the same William holds 3 acres of land in the same fields, which same land descended to the said Margaret, his wife, by inheritance through the death of Walter Em, her father, and the said Walter bought those from Nicolas Childman, and the said Nicholas acquired those by inheritance through the death of Childman, his father, for which he pays per annum to the heirs of the said Nicholas 1½d.

[229] Item the same William holds ½ acre of land in the fields of Barnwell, which same land descended to the said Margaret, his wife, by inheritance through the death of Walter Em, her father, and the said Walter bought that land from Jacob de Len and Elena Ace, his wife, for which he pays per annum to the heirs of the said Elena ½d.

[230] Item the same William holds ½ acre of land in the fields of Cambridge, which land descended to the said Margaret, his wife,

by inheritance through the death of Walter Em, her father, and the said Walter at one time bought that from Henry Clay of Howes, for which he pays per annum to the said Henry and his heirs ½d.

[231] Item the said William holds 2 acres of land in the fields of Cambridge which land descended to the said Margaret, his wife, by inheritance through the death of Walter Em, her father, and the said Walter bought that from Alicia, daughter of Thomas Longys, which same descended to the said Alicia by inheritance of the said Thomas, her father, and he pays in respect thereof per annum to the said Alicia and her heirs 4d., and to the bailiffs of Cambridge who hold the same town of Cambridge etcetera in hawgable ½d.

[232] Item the said William holds 1 acre of land with appurtenances in the same fields, which same land descended to the said Margaret, his wife, by inheritance through the death of Walter Em, her father, and the said Walter bought that from John Porthors, for which he pays per annum to the said John and his heirs 1d.

[233] Item the same William holds a ½ acre and 1 rood in the same fields of Cambridge with appurtenances, which same descended to the said Margaret, his wife, by inheritance through the death of Walter Em, her father, and the said Walter bought that from William, son of Ivo, for which he pays per annum to the heirs of the said William 1½d.

[234] Item the same William holds ½ acre of land with appurtenances in the same [fields of][65] Cambridge which same land descended to his wife Margaret by inheritance through the death of Walter Em, her father, and the said Walter bought that from Eustace, son of Harvey Dunning and the said Eustace acquired that by hereditary right through the death of the said Harvey, his father, for which he pays per annum to the heirs of the said Eustace ½d.

[235] Item the said William holds 1 rood of land with appurtenances in the fields of Cambridge which same descended to the said Margaret, his wife, by inheritance through the death of Walter Em, her father, which same Walter bought that from Henry Nado, and the said Henry acquired that by ancient purchase and he pays in respect thereof per annum to the heirs of the said Henry Nado ½d.

[236] Item the said William Seman holds 2 acres of land in the same fields, which same land descended to the said Margaret by inheritance through the death of Walter Em, her father, which same 2 acres of land descended to the said Walter by inheritance

through the death of Robert Em, his father, and the said Robert acquired those by ancient purchase, and he pays per annum to the heirs of Petronilla de Cotes 2d.

[237] Giles son of John of Barton holds 1 messuage with its appurtenances situated in the parish of St Clement's, Cambridge, which messuage he bought from Andrew, son of William son of Ivo, and the said messuage descended to the said Andrew by inheritance through the death of Katherine, his mother, which messuage the said William and Katherine, his wife, acquired by gift of Margaret Wulward in frank marriage, for which he pays per annum to the said Andrew and his heirs 1 pair of gloves at the price of ½d. And to the nuns of Goring 3s. And to the bailiffs of the Lord King who hold the town of Cambridge in fee farm from the Lord King and from his ancestors as tenant-in-chief in fee farm for hawgable 1d.

[238] Item the said Giles holds 1 acre of land situated in the fields of Cambridge towards Barnwell, which he bought from the said Andrew, son of said William, son of Ivo, which same land descended to the said Andrew by inheritance through the death of William son of Ivo, his father. And the said William bought that from John, son of Master Henry of Hinton. And that descended to the said John by inheritance through the death of the said Master Henry, his father, for which he pays per annum to the said Andrew and his heirs 1d.

[239] Item the said Giles holds 7½ acres of land situated in the fields of Cambridge which he acquired by gift of John of Barton, his father. And the said John bought that from Geoffrey le Fitter, which descended to the same said Geoffrey by inheritance through the death of his parents, for which he pays per annum, on behalf of the heirs of the said John de Barton, to the heirs of Geoffrey the fitter, 1 pair of gloves at the price of ½d. And to the bailiffs of the Lord King who hold the town of Cambridge in fee farm from the Lord King and his ancestors as tenant-in chief to their farm in landgable 1½d.

[240] Item the said Giles holds 1½ acres of land with its appurtenances situated in the fields of Cambridge which he acquired by gift of John of Barton, his father. And the said John bought that from Harvey Parleben. And the said Harvey acquired that by gift of Mabilia Parleben, his mother, which same land descended to the said Mabilia by inheritance through the death of her ancestors, for which he pays per annum to the heirs of the said John 1 rose. And on behalf of the heirs of the said John and Harvey to the

bailiffs of the Lord King who hold the town of Cambridge in fee farm from the Lord King and his ancestors as tenant-in-chief to their farm for landgable 1½d.

[241] Item the said Giles holds 1½ acres of land situated in the fields of Cambridge which he acquired by gift of John of Barton, his father. And the said John bought that from Harvey Parlebyen, which same descended to the said Harvey by inheritance through the death of Roger Parlebyen, his father. And the said Roger acquired that by ancient purchase, for which he pays per annum to the heirs of the said Harvey, on behalf of the heirs of the said John, 1d.

[242] Item the said Giles holds 1½ roods of land with its appurtenances situated in the fields of Cambridge which he acquired by gift of John of Barton, his father. And the said John acquired that by gift of Simon at the water. And the said Simon acquired that by ancient acquisition, for which he pays per annum, on behalf of the heirs of the said John, to the heirs of the said Simon 1 rose.

[243] Item the said Giles holds 1 rood of land situated in the fields of Cambridge in Portefeld at Lyttlemor, which he acquired by gift of John of Barton, his father. And the said John bought that from Roger, son of Gilbert Baker. And that descended to the said Roger by inheritance through the death of the said Gilbert, his father, for which he pays per annum, on behalf of the heirs of the said John, to the heirs of the said Roger, 1 clove gillyflower.

[244] Item the said Giles holds 1 acre of land situated in Swinecroft in the fields of Cambridge towards Barnwell, which he acquired by gift of John of Barton, his father. And the said John bought that from Warin Grym, which same descended to the said Warin by inheritance through the death of Aspelon, his father. And the said Aspelon acquired that by ancient acquisition, for which he pays per annum, on behalf of the heirs of the said John, to the heirs of the said Warin 1 pair of gloves at the price of ½d. And to the bailiffs of the Lord King who hold the town of Cambridge in fee farm from the Lord King and his ancestors as tenant-in-chief to their farm for landgable 1d.

[245] Item the said Giles holds ½ acre of land with its appurtenances situated in the fields of Cambridge which he acquired by gift of John of Barton, his father. And the said John bought that from Leon Dunning, which same land descended to the said Leon by inheritance through the death of Adam Dunning, his father, for which he pays per annum to the heirs of the said John 1 rose. And

on behalf of the said Leon and his heirs, to the heirs of Robert Fereward, 1 pair of gloves at the price of ½d.

[246]   Item the said Giles holds 1 acre of land situated in the fields of Cambridge which he acquired by gift of John of Barton, his father. And the said John bought that from Alan Edward and Matilda and Richard Moryn and Ediva and Geoffrey le Haneper and Radegund their wives, for which he pays per annum, on behalf of the heirs of the said John, to the heirs of the said Alana and Matilda, Richard Moryn and Ediva and Geoffrey and Radegund ½d.

[247]   Item the said Giles holds 1½ acres of land situated in the fields of Cambridge towards Barnwell, which he acquired by gift of John of Barton, his father. And the said John held that from Henry of Barton. And the said Henry bought that from Nicholas Malerbe. And the said Nicholas acquired that by ancient acquisition, for which he pays per annum to the heirs of the said John 1 rose. And on behalf of the heirs of the said John and Henry, to the heirs of Nicholas Malerbe 1d.

[248]   Item said Giles holds 3 acres of land situated in the fields of Cambridge which he acquired by gift of John of Barton, his father. And the said John bought that from Simon, son of Bartholomew Forreward, which same descended to the said Simon by inheritance through the death of the said Bartholomew, his father, for which he pays per annum, on behalf of the heirs of the said John, to the heirs of the said Simon 2d.

[249]   Item Agnes de Barton holds 7½ acres of land with its appurtenances situated in the fields of Cambridge which she acquired by gift of the Lord Prior and the convent of Barnwell, for which she pays per annum to the said prior and convent and their successors 1 clove gillyflower.

[250]   Item the said Agnes holds 3 acres of land with its appurtenances situated in the fields of Cambridge which she bought from William de Manefeld, which same descended to the said William by inheritance through the death of John of Barnard Castle. And that descended to the said John by inheritance through the death of Master Guy of Barnard Castle. And the said Master Guy bought that from Eustace Dunning, which same descended to the said Eustace by inheritance through the death of Harvey Dunning, his father, for which she pays per annum to the said William and his heirs 1d.

[251]   Item the said Agnes holds 2½ acres and 1 rood of land with their appurtenances situated in the fields of Cambridge which she

bought from Jacob le Mariner and Elena Ace, his wife, which same descended to the said Elena by inheritance through the death of Richard, son of Ivo, her father. And those descended by inheritance to the said Richard through the death of Ivo, his father. And the said Ivo acquired those by acquisition, for which she pays per annum to the heirs of the said Jacob and Elena, his wife, ½d.

[252]   Item the said Agnes holds 1½ acres of land situated in the fields of Cambridge, which she bought from Richard, son and heir of Hugh Butcher, which same descended to the said Richard by inheritance through the death of the said Hugh, his father. And the said Hugh bought that from Gilbert, son of Gilbert Goldsmith. And that descended to the said Gilbert by inheritance through the death of the said Gilbert, his father, for which she pays per annum to the said Richard and his heirs 1 rose. And by assignment of the said Richard, Harvey Parlebyen, his heirs, Margaret his wife, to the lords in chief of the same fief, 8d.

[253]   Item said Agnes holds 1 acre of land with its appurtenances situated in the fields of Cambridge, which she acquired by gift of Henry of Barton, her son. And the said Henry acquired that by gift of Richard Laurence in frank marriage with Cecilia, his wife. And the said Richard bought that from Eustace Dunning, which same descended to the same Eustace by inheritance through the death of Harvey Dunning, his father, for which she pays per annum to the said Henry and his heirs 1d.

[254]   Henry of Barton holds 1 messuage with its appurtenances situated in the parish of St Clement's in which he lives, which messuage he acquired by gift of John of Barton, his father, which messuage the said John bought from Warin, son of Aspelon. And that messuage descended to the said Warin by inheritance through the death of the said Aspelon, his father. And the said Aspelon acquired that messuage by gift of Alan, former preceptor of the brothers of Jerusalem in England, for which same messuage he pays per annum to the heirs of the said John 1 rose. And to the Preceptor and brothers of Shingay, ½ mark and for a certain piece of land in the rear part of the said messuage above the water of the Lord King, to the bailiffs of the Lord King who hold the town of Cambridge in fee farm from the Lord King and his ancestors as tenant-in-chief to their farm for hawgable ½d.

[255]   Item said Henry and Cecilia his wife hold a certain piece of land with a certain house being above in the said parish of St Clement's which said Cecilia acquired by gift of Wade, her

uncle, for which she pays per annum to the heirs of the said Wade 1 clove gillyflower.

[256] Item the said Henry holds 1 house in the parish of St Benedict's, Cambridge, which he acquired by gift of Henry of Barton, his uncle, and the said Henry bought that from Radulph le Cuver. And the said Radulph acquired that by gift of the nuns of Swaffham, for which he pays per annum to the heirs of the said Henry 1 rose. And to the heirs of the said Radulph 1 clove gillyflower. And to the nuns of Swaffham 2s. And to the bailiffs of the Lord King who hold the town of Cambridge in fee farm from the Lord King and his ancestors as tenants-in-chief to their farm for hawgable ½d.

[257] Item said Henry and Cecilia his wife hold 1 messuage with its appurtenances situated in the said parish of St Benedict's, which messuage the said Henry acquired by gift of Richard Lawrence and his wife Sabina. And that messuage descended to the said Sabina by inheritance through the death of John Ategate, her brother, which messuage descended to the said John by inheritance through the death of Richard Ategate, his brother, for which they pay per annum to the said Richard and his heirs 1 rose. And to the bailiffs of the Lord King who hold the town of Cambridge in fee farm from the Lord King and his ancestors as tenants-in-chief, to their farm for hawgable 1d.

[258] Item the said Henry and Cecilia his wife hold 1 messuage situated in the parish of St Botolph's Cambridge, which messuage the said Henry acquired with the said Cecilia, his wife, in frank marriage by gift of Richard Lawrence, and the said Richard acquired that messuage with his wife Sabina in frank marriage by gift of Richard Ategate, for which they pay per annum to the said Richard Lawrence and his heirs 1 rose. And to the heirs of the said Richard Ategate 1 peppercorn. And to Lecia Stowelle of Newnham and her heirs 1d., and to the bailiffs of Cambridge who hold the said town in fee farm etcetera in hawgable ½d. and 1 farthing.

[259] Item the said Henry and Cecilia his wife hold 7 acres of land situated in the fields of Cambridge which the said Henry acquired with the said Cecilia, his wife, in frank marriage by gift of Richard Lawrence. And the said Richard bought that from John Frost, for which they pay per annum to the said Richard and his heirs 1 rose. And to the heirs of the said John 1 root of ginger.

[260] Item the same Henry and Cecilia his wife hold 1½ acres of land situated in the fields of Cambridge which the said Henry

acquired with his wife Cecilia in frank marriage by gift of Richard Lawrence, which said Richard bought from Eustace Dunning, which same descended to the said Eustace by inheritance through the death of Harvey Dunning, his father, for which he pays per annum to the said Richard and his heirs ½d. And to the heirs of the said Eustace 1½d.

[261] Item John de Waltham holds 1 house in the parish of St Clement's, which same messuage he acquired by gift of Sabina Huberd, which same Sabina acquired that by gift of Bartholomew Gogging, her brother, which same Bartholomew acquired that by gift of Robert Hubert and the said Robert bought that from William Heleshewed, which same William acquired that by ancient hereditary succession, and in respect thereof he pays per annum to Margaret, daughter of Robert Wimund ½d., and to William Seman 6d., and to the brothers of St John's Hospital, Cambridge, 4s., by which warranty they are unaware of any claim to the said income.

[262] The same John and Elena his wife hold 1 messuage in the parish of St Botolph's which they acquired by gift of the said Sabina Huberd in frank marriage, and the said Sabina acquired that by gift of Margaret, wife of Michael Gogging, in frank marriage, and the said Margaret acquired that by gift of Richard Attegate, her father, and the said Richard acquired that by ancient succession of his ancestors, and they pay in respect thereof per annum for the sustenance of the said St Botolph's Church 4d.

[263] Item Richard Laurence holds a certain house in the parish of All Saints at the Castle, which same he bought from John Frost junior, and the said John acquired that by hereditary right through the death of John Frost, chaplain, his uncle. And he pays in respect thereof per annum to the said John and his heirs 1d.

[264] Item the same Richard holds a certain piece of land next to the court of St Radegund's, which same he bought from John Adhelard, clerk, and the same John acquired that by inheritance through the death of Adhelard, his father, and he pays in respect thereof per annum to the nuns of Ickleton 12s., whereby the said nuns are unaware of any claim to the said income.

[265] Item Margaret daughter of Edmund de Stewincton holds 1 messuage in the parish of St Clement's, which same messuage descended to the same by inheritance through the death of the said Edmund, her father, which same Edmund bought that from Humphrey de Clopton and Geliona, his wife, and in respect thereof she pays per annum to the heirs of the said

Humphrey ½d., and to the nuns of Goring 3s., and to the bailiffs of Cambridge who hold the said town in fee farm etcetera 1d., by which warranty the said nuns are unaware of any claim to the said income.

[266] Item Alicia de Pinchestre holds 1 messuage in the parish of St Clement's, which she bought from Radulph le Chapeler and his wife Margaret, and in respect thereof she pays per annum to the heirs of the said Radulph and Margaret 4s., and to the almoner of Ely 4s., by which warranty they are unaware of any claim to the said income.

[267] Item Henry de Ho son and heir of Thomas de Ho holds 1 messuage with appurtenances in the parish of St Peter's outside Trumpington Gate, which he acquired by hereditary right through the death of Thomas de Ho, his father, which same Thomas bought that from Matilda, daughter of John Cant', clerk, which same Matilda acquired that by hereditary right through the death of the said John, her father, and the same John acquired that by ancient purchase, and in respect thereof he pays per annum to the said Matilda and her heirs 1d., and to Luke of St Edmunds 4s. as tenant-in chief of the lord's fief.

[268] The same Henry holds a croft with appurtenances in the said parish, which descended to him by hereditary right through the death of the said Thomas, his father, which same Thomas bought that from Alan Baseli of Cambridge, and in respect thereof he pays per annum to the said Alan and his heirs 1d.

[269] The same Henry holds a piece of land in the said parish which descended to him by inheritance through the death of the said Thomas, his father, which same Thomas bought that from Hugh le Rus, and the said Hugh acquired that by ancient hereditary succession and in respect thereof he pays per annum to the said Hugh 1 farthing.

[270] The same Henry holds ½ rood of land in the said parish which descended to him by inheritance through the death of the said Thomas, his father, which same Thomas bought that from Margaret, daughter of Roger, clerk of Cambridge, and the said Margaret acquired that by inheritance through the death of the said Roger, her father, and the said Roger acquired that by ancient inheritance of his ancestors, and in respect thereof he pays per annum to the bailiffs of Cambridge who hold the said town in fee farm etcetera for hawgable ½d.

[271] Item William de Sawston, chaplain, holds 1 messuage in the parish of St Peter's outside the gate which he acquired by gift of

Matilda Sephare, which same Matilda acquired that by hereditary right through the death of her ancestors, and in respect thereof he pays per annum to the heirs of the said Matilda 1 rose and to Luke of St Edmunds 2s.

[272] Item William le Tanner holds 1 messuage in Newnham in the parish of St Peter's outside the gate which he acquired in frank marriage with Avicia his wife, by gift of Thomas le Mouner, father of the said Avicia, which same Thomas bought that from John, son of Deacon, and in respect thereof he pays per annum to the said John and his heirs 2s.

[273] Item Alan Bainard holds 1 messuage in Newnham in the said parish which descended to him by hereditary right through the death of William Bainard, his father, and the said William bought that from Walter Attewelle, son of Aspelon, and in respect thereof he pays per annum to the said Walter and his heirs ½d., and to the brothers of St John's Hospital, Cambridge, 8d.

[274] Item John Perin holds 1 messuage in the said parish which he bought from the abbot and convent of Lavenden, which same abbot and convent acquired that by gift of Cecilia Godso, which same Cecilia acquired that by hereditary right through the death of her ancestors, and in respect thereof he pays per annum to the said abbot and convent 12d., and to the bailiffs of Cambridge who hold the said town in fee farm etcetera for hawgable 1½d.

[275] The same John holds 1 messuage in the said parish which he acquired by gift of Peter de Welles, his brother, which same Peter bought that from John de Histon, which same John bought that from Simon Fot, and the said Simon acquired that by hereditary right through the death of his ancestors, and in respect thereof he pays per annum to the heirs of the said Peter 1d., and to Luke of St Edmunds 8d.

[276] Item John de Aylesham and his wife Sabina hold 1 messuage in the parish of St Peter's outside the gate, which same said Sabina bought from Eustace Selede, which same Eustace acquired that by inheritance through the death of Simon Selede, his brother, which same Simon acquired that by ancient succession of his parents and in respect thereof he pays per annum to the prior of Barnwell 8d., by which manner the prior is unaware of any claim to the said income.

[277] Item John and his wife Sabina hold 1 messuage in the same parish which the said Sabina bought from Thomas de Ho, and the said Thomas bought that from Harvey, son of Michael, which same Harvey bought that from the prioress and convent

of St Radegund's, by which manner the prioress and convent are unaware of any claim to the said messuage, and in respect thereof they pay per annum to the heirs of the said Thomas de Ho ½ ounce of cumin, and to the said prioress and convent 3s.

[278] Item John and Sabina hold 1 messuage in the same parish, which same said Sabina formerly bought from the prioress and convent of St Radegund's and in respect thereof they pay per annum to the said prioress and convent 3s. In which manner the said prioress and convent are unaware of any claim to the said messuage.

[279] Item John and his wife Sabina hold 1 messuage in the said parish which they bought from Richard, son of Richard Burs, which same Richard acquired that by hereditary right through the death of Richard Burs, his father, and the same Richard acquired that through the death of his ancestors, and in respect thereof they pay per annum to the said Richard ½d., and to the prioress and convent of St Radegund's 12d., in which manner the said prioress and convent are unaware of any claim to the said income.

[280] The same John holds 1 messuage in the same parish which he bought from Thomas de Cottenham, which same Thomas bought that from Richard Herward, which same Richard acquired that by hereditary succession of his ancestors, and in respect thereof he pays per annum to the said Thomas 1 clove gillyflower and to Geoffrey of Spartegrave 3s.

[281] Item John holds 1 messuage in the said parish which he bought from John Pikerel, which same John acquired that by hereditary right through the death of Henry Pikerel, his father, which same Henry acquired that in frank marriage by gift of Richard Skin, and in respect thereof he pays per annum to John Pikerel 1 rose, and to the prioress of St Radegund's 2s., in which manner the said prioress is unaware of any claim to the said income.

[282] The same John holds 1 messuage in the said parish which he bought from Hugh de Reche, and from Alicia his wife, which same messuage the said Hugh and Alicia acquired by gift from Henry Pikerel, father of the said Alicia, which same Henry acquired that by gift of Richard Skin in frank marriage with Rosa his daughter, and in respect thereof he pays per annum to Gilbert Bernard 1 pair of gloves at the price of ½d., and to the bailiffs of Cambridge who hold the said town in fee farm, etcetera, for hawgable ½d.

[283] The same John holds 1 messuage outside Trumpington Gate which he bought from John le Redere, which same John bought

that from Simon Selede, which same Simon acquired that from ancient heritage of his ancestors, and in respect thereof he pays per annum to the heirs of the said Simon 1 clove gillyflower, and to the prior of Barnwell 3s., in which manner the prior is unaware of any claim to the said income.

[284] The same John holds 1 messuage outside the said gate which he bought from Simon of Trumpington, which same Simon bought that from Eustace Selede, and in respect thereof he pays per annum to the heirs of the said Eustace 1 rose.

[285] The same John holds 1 acre of land in the fields of Cambridge which he bought from Eustace Selede, which same Eustace acquired that through the death of his brother Simon, which same Simon acquired that through the death of the said Selede, his father, and the same Selede acquired that from ancient heritage of his ancestors, and in respect thereof he pays per annum to the prior and convent of Barnwell 4d., in which manner the said prior and convent are unaware of any claim to the said income.

[286] Item John and his wife Sabina hold 3 roods of land in the fields of Cambridge which the said Sabina formerly bought from John Wombe, which same John held those by inheritance through the death of Nicholas Wombe, his father, which same Nicholas bought that from William Wisman of Newnham, and in respect thereof they pay per annum to the almoner of Barnwell 2d.

[287] Item John holds 1 rood of land in the same fields which he bought from Johanna, daughter of William, son of Ivo, which same Johanna acquired that by gift of the said William, her father, which same William acquired that by ancient purchase, and in respect thereof he pays per annum to the said John 1 clove gillyflower, and to the bailiffs of Cambridge who hold the said town in fee farm etcetera in landgable 1 farthing.

[288] The same John holds 1 acre in the said fields which he bought from John Martin, which same John bought that from William son of William …[66] that William held that from Luke of St Edmunds, and in respect thereof he pays per annum to the said John ½d., and to the said Luke 2d.

[289] Item John and his wife Sabina hold 1 acre of land in the said fields which said Sabina acquired by gift of Martin Brithnor', her father …[67] bought that from Harvey Brithnor', his brother, and the same Harvey acquired that by ancient heritage through the death of his ancestors, and in respect thereof they pay per annum to the heirs of the said Martin ½d.

[290]   Item John and Sabina hold ½ acre in the same fields which the same said Sabina acquired by gift of the said Martin, her father, which same Martin bought that from Geoffrey Doy, and in respect thereof they pay per annum to the heirs of the said Martin ½d.

[291]   Item John holds 4 acres of land in the fields of Cambridge which he bought from William de Manefeld, which same William acquired those by inheritance through the death of Master Guy of Barnard Castle, and the said Master Guy bought those from Eustace Dunning, and the same Eustace acquired those by inheritance of his ancestors, and in respect thereof he pays per annum to the scholars of Merton 2d. by assignment of the said William.

[292]   Item John and Sabina his wife hold 2 acres of land in the said fields which the said Sabina bought from Robert de Pinecote, which same Robert bought those from Alicia de Pinecote, which same Alicia acquired those by ancient succession of her ancestors, and in respect thereof they pay per annum to the said Robert 4d.

[293]   Item John holds ½ acre of land in the same fields which he bought from John Aure, which same John acquired that by inheritance through the death of John, son of Reginald Aure, his father, and in respect thereof he pays per annum to the said John Aure 1 rose.

[294]   Ambrose son of John Godrich holds 1 messuage in Newnham which descended to him by inheritance through the death of the said John, his father, which same John held that by inheritance through the death of Thomas, his father, which same Thomas bought that from Simon, son of Reginald Attegate, which same Simon acquired that by inheritance through the death of Reginald, his father, which same Reginald acquired that by ancient purchase, and in respect thereof he pays per annum to the said Simon and his heirs 1d., and to St John's Hospital, Cambridge, 12d., by which manner they are unaware of any claim to the said income.

[295]   The same Ambrose holds 1 messuage in Newnham which descended to him by inheritance through the death of the said John, his father, which same John bought that from Robert, son of William Sewale of Newnham, and the same Robert acquired that by inheritance through the death of the said William, his father, and the same William acquired that by ancient purchase, and in respect thereof he pays per annum to the said St John's Hospital 21d., by which manner they are unaware of any claim to the said income.

[296] Item Ambrose holds 3 shops in Newnham, which descended to him by inheritance through the death of John, his father, which same John bought those from William, son of Robert Carpenter, which same William acquired those by inheritance through the death of Robert, his father, and the same Robert acquired those by ancient purchase, and in respect thereof he pays per annum to the heirs of Michael, son of John Michael 6s., and to St John's Hospital, Cambridge, 4d., by which manner they are unaware of any claim to the said income.

[297] Ambrose holds 1 acre of land in the fields of Cambridge which descended to him by inheritance through the death of John, his father, which same John bought that from Master Robert Aunger, which same Master Robert acquired that by inheritance through the death of Aunger, his father, and in respect thereof he pays per annum to the said Master Robert 12d.

[P34] Item Robert, rector of the chapel of St Edmunds, Cambridge, holds 1 messuage with appurtenances which belong to the said chapel and 12½ acres of land and 1 rood of land in the fields of Cambridge belonging to the said [chapel], which messuage with the said land he acquired by gift of Luke of St Edmunds in pure and perpetual alms, which same Luke acquired the messuage with said land by hereditary right through the death of Thomas, his brother, which same Thomas acquired that by hereditary right through the death of Walter of St Edmunds, his father, and he pays in respect thereof per annum to the bailiffs of Cambridge who hold the said town in fee farm etcetera for hawgable 4½d.

[A48] The same Robert holds 2 acres of land and 3 roods in the fields of Cambridge which he acquired from John le Rus, which same John gave that to the said chapel in pure and perpetual alms for his soul and the souls of his ancestors.

[298] The same Robert holds 1 acre of land which Lord William de Mortimer senior, which same Lord William gave that to the said chapel and in respect thereof pays per annum to Leon Dunning 2d. by assignment of the said William.

[P35] Item Luke of St Edmunds holds 1 messuage with appurtenances in the parish of St Peter's outside Trumpington Gate and a horse mill in the market-place of Cambridge with 70 acres of land in the fields of Cambridge belonging to the said messuage, which messuage with its mill and the aforesaid land were acquired by hereditary succession through the death of Master Thomas his brother, which said Master Thomas acquired it as a gift of Walter of St Edmunds his father, which same Walter acquired it by hereditary right through the death of Alice his mother and the said Alice acquired it through ancient succession of her ancestors, and in respect thereof he pays per annum to Lord Radulph Pirot and Lady Cassandria his wife 2½ marks by assignment of Giles de Argentin and to the bailiffs of Cambridge for hawgable and landgable 25s. 10¾d.

[299]   Item Alan Baseli holds 1 messuage in the parish of St Peter's outside Trumpington Gate which same he bought from Matilda, daughter of John, clerk of Cambridge, which same Matilda acquired that by gift of Master Walter, son of said John, clerk, and lord Master Walter acquired that by hereditary right through the death of the said John, his father, and the said John acquired that by ancient purchase, and he pays in respect thereof per annum to Geoffrey, son of John, 12d., and to the chaplain celebrating the mass of Holy Mary in St Mary's Church, Cambridge, 12d.

[300]   Item Robert son of Andrew Frede holds 1 messuage with appurtenances in Newnham in the parish of St Peter's outside Trumpington Gate, which same messuage descended to him by inheritance through the death of Alicia Frede, his mother, which same Alicia acquired that by gift of Robert, vicar of Soham, which same Robert bought that from Ambrose of Newnham, and the said Ambrose bought that from the brothers of St John's Hospital, Cambridge, and the said brothers acquired that by gift of Nicholas le Barkere in perpetual alms, and in respect thereof he pays per annum to the said brothers of the said hospital 4s.

[301]   Item Harvey Prippe holds 1 messuage in the parish of St Peter's outside Trumpington gate, which he bought from the prior and convent of Anglesey, and the said prior and convent acquired by gift of Robert, son of Robert Huberd, which same Robert acquired that by hereditary right through the death of Amicia Godso, his mother, which same Amicia acquired that by hereditary right of her ancestors, and in respect thereof he pays per annum to the said prior and convent 6s.

[302]   Bartholomew Gogging holds 1 messuage in fief in the parish of St Botolph's, which same messuage he acquired by gift of Margaret, his mother, which same Margaret acquired that by inheritance through the death of John, her brother, which same John acquired that by hereditary right through the death of Richard, his brother, which same Richard acquired that through the death of Richard, his father, and the said Richard acquired that by ancient acquisition, and in respect thereof he pays per

annum to the heirs of the said Margaret 1 rose, and to the bailiffs of Cambridge who hold the said town in fee farm as is stated, to their farm for hawgable 1d.

[303] Item Bartholomew holds another messuage in the same parish, which he bought from Margaret, daughter of Simon atte Gate. Which same Margaret acquired that by inheritance through the death of Reginald, her brother, which same Reginald acquired that by inheritance through the death of Simon, his father, and the said Simon acquired that by inheritance through the death of Reginald, his father, and the said Reginald acquired that by ancient acquisition of his ancestors, and in respect thereof he pays per annum to the heirs of the said Margaret 1 peppercorn, and to the bailiffs of Cambridge who hold the said town in fee farm as is stated, to their farm for hawgable 1d.

[304] The same Bartholomew holds 1 messuage in the parish of St Benedict's, which same he acquired by gift of Harvey, his brother, which same Harvey bought that from Alicia, wife of William of Kirkby. And the said Alicia acquired that by gift of Walter, son of Thomas le Mercer, and the said Walter acquired that by inheritance through the death of Simon, his brother, which same Simon acquired that by hereditary right through the death of Thomas, his brother, which same Thomas acquired that through the death of Thomas, his father.

[305] The same Bartholomew holds a certain piece of empty land in the same parish which he bought from Richard, son of Richard Laurence and from Michael, son of John son of Michael, which same Richard and Michael acquired that by hereditary right through the death of Margaret and Sabina, mothers of the said Richard and Michael. Which same Margaret and Sabina acquired that by hereditary right through the death of Seva, their sister. Which same Seva acquired that by gift of Richard atte Gate, her father, in marriage, and the same Richard acquired that of old through inquiry, and in respect thereof he pays per annum to the said Richard 1 pair of gloves at the price of ½d., and to the said Michael 1 pair of gloves at the price of ½d., and to the bailiffs of Cambridge who hold the said town in fee farm as is stated, for hawgable 2d.

[306] The same Bartholomew holds 1 stall in the marketplace of Cambridge by gift of John, his brother, and the said John acquired that by gift of Richard, his uncle, which same Richard bought that from Geoffrey Olgar, which same Geoffrey acquired that by heritage through the death of his ancestors, for which he pays per

annum to Lord Peter de Chavent 6s., and to the heirs of John, brother of the said Bartholomew 1d.

[307] The same Bartholomew holds 1 messuage in the parish of Holy Sepulchre which same he acquired by gift of Eleanor de Gurney in frank marriage with Johanna, his wife. Which same Eleanor acquired that by hereditary right through the death of Ismaina, her sister, and the said Ismaina acquired that by ancient acquisition of her ancestors, and in respect thereof he pays per annum to the heirs of Michael Parleben 6d.

[308] Item Bartholomew and his wife Johanna hold another messuage in the same parish which same said Johanna acquired by gift of Henry of Berton, her father. And the said Henry acquired that by purchase from Nicholas Malerbe, which Nicholas acquired that by hereditary right through the death of Michael, his father, and the said Michael acquired that by ancient succession of his parents. And in respect thereof he pays per annum to the bailiffs of Cambridge who hold the said town in fee farm etcetera, to their farm for hawgable 7d., and to Master Pagan de Dockinge 20s. by assignment of the said Nicholas.

[309] The same Bartholomew holds 16 acres of land in the fields of Cambridge to the end of his life which he acquired by gift and concession of Michael, son of John Michael, chancellor, which same Michael acquired those by inheritance through the death of John, his father, and that John acquired those by hereditary succession through the death of Michael, his father, and the said Michael acquired those through the death of Harvey, clerk, his father, and the said Harvey bought those from the prior and convent of Barnwell, and he pays in respect thereof per annum for the said land to the said prior and convent 10s., by which warranty the said prior and convent are unaware of any claim to the said messuage.

[310] The same Bartholomew holds 3 acres of land in the fields of Cambridge which he acquired by gift of Robert Hubert, and the same Robert acquired by gift of Robert, his son, which same Robert acquired by gift of Thomas, his uncle, which same Thomas acquired those by ancient acquisition of his ancestors, and in respect thereof he pays per annum to the heirs of the said Robert 1 clove gillyflower.

[311] The same Bartholomew holds 1 acre of land in the same fields which he bought from Nicholas, son of Nicholas Childman, which same Nicholas acquired that by hereditary right through the death of Mariota, his mother. Which same Mariota acquired

that by gift of Michael, her father, in frank marriage and the said Michael acquired that by ancient acquisition of his ancestors. And in respect thereof he pays per annum to Luke of St Edmunds 2d. as the lord of the fief.

[312] The same Bartholomew holds 1 acre of land in the same fields which he bought from John, son of Michael Gogging, and the said John acquired that through parental succession through the death of Michael, his father, which same Michael acquired that through the death of Harvey, his father. And in respect thereof he pays per annum to the heirs of the said John 1 rose.

[313] The same Bartholomew holds 1 acre of land in the same fields which he bought from John, son of Robert of St Edmunds, which same John obtained that in frank marriage with his wife Mabilia, and the said Mabilia acquired that by gift of Michael Parleben, her father, and the said Michael acquired that by ancient succession of his ancestors, and in respect thereof he pays per annum to the said John and his heirs 1d.

[314] The same Bartholomew holds 1 acre of land in the same fields which he acquired by gift of John Porthors in frank marriage with Johanna, his wife, and in respect thereof he pays per annum to the said John ½d.

[315] Item Alan Attepond holds 1 messuage in the parish of St Botolph's which he bought from the lord Alan, rector of St Benedict's Church, which same lord Alan bought that from Master Robert of Skidbrooke, and the said Robert bought that from Christiana Kidelomb, which same Christiana acquired that by gift of Martin Britlof, and the same Martin acquired that by ancient succession of his ancestors, and in respect thereof he pays per annum to the nuns of St Radegund's 26d., by which warranty they are unaware, and to the said Alan, rector of the said church ½d., and to the bailiffs of Cambridge who hold the said town in fee farm etcetera for hawgable 1½d.

[316] The same Alan holds 1 messuage in the parish of St Peter's which he bought from Alexander Atteberne. And that Alexander acquired that by gift of Simon Fot, and that Simon acquired that by ancient acquisition, and in respect thereof he pays per annum to the heirs of Peter de Welles 40d. by assignment of the said Simon.

[317] Item Gerard de Wivar' holds 1 messuage in the parish of St Botolph's, which he bought from Roger, son of Simon Furri, which same Roger acquired that by inheritance through the death of Simon, his father, which same Simon bought that from

John Aured and that John acquired that by hereditary succession through the death of Reginald Aured, his father, and in respect thereof he pays per annum to the said Roger and his heirs 1 rose and to Nicholas Morice 7s.

[318] The same Gerard holds 1 messuage in the same parish which he bought from Alicia Godeman, which same Alicia acquired that by gift of John Aured, her father, and that John acquired that through the death of Reginald, his father, and the said Reginald acquired that by ancient acquisition of his ancestors, and in respect thereof he pays per annum to the said John 12d.

[319] The same Gerard holds 1 messuage in the same parish which he bought from Christiana, daughter of Eustace Ston, which same Christiana acquired that by hereditary succession through the death of Eustace, her father, and that Eustace bought that formerly from Walter of St Edmunds and that Walter acquired that by hereditary right through the death of his ancestors, and in respect thereof he pays per annum to the said Christiana 1 rose and to Luke of St Edmunds 12d.

[320] The same Gerard holds 2 shops in the same parish which he bought from Richard Wombe, which same Richard acquired those by hereditary succession through the death of John Wombe, his brother, and the same John acquired those through the death of Radulph Wombe, his father, and the same Radulph acquired those through the death of Radulph Wombe, his father, and in respect thereof he pays per annum to the said Richard 16d., and to Luke of St Edmunds 6d.

[321] The same Gerard holds 1 messuage in the same parish which he bought from Reginald Sherewind, which same Reginald acquired that by purchase from Reginald Mullot and that Reginald acquired that by ancient succession of his ancestors, and in respect thereof he pays per annum to John of Colne 1 rose, and to the bailiffs of Cambridge who hold the said town in fee farm as is stated, to their farm for hawgable 2d.

[322] The same Gerard holds ½ acre of land in the fields of Cambridge which he bought from John Goderich of Newnham, and the same John bought that from Ambrose of Newnham, and the said Ambrose acquired that by ancient acquisition as purchase, and he pays in respect thereof per annum to St John's Hospital, Cambridge, 3d., by which warranty they are unaware.

[323] The same Gerard holds a piece of vacant land in Newnham which he bought from Alicia, daughter of Robert de Hardleston, which same Alicia bought that from Simon, son of Eustace which

same Eustace acquired that by ancient acquisition, and in respect thereof he pays per annum to Leon Dunning 5d., and to St John's Hospital, Cambridge, 12d., by which warranty they are unaware.

[324] Henry son of Thomas Hardy holds 1 messuage in the parish of St Botolph's, which descended to him by inheritance through the death of Thomas, his father, and the said Thomas acquired that by hereditary right through the death of Thomas Hardy, his father, and that Thomas acquired that by ancient acquisition, and in respect thereof he pays per annum to Sabina de Belthesham 2d., and to the prioress of Markgate 12d., by which warranty they are unaware.

[325] Item Thomas of Hogiton holds 1 messuage in the parish of St Botolph's which is in fief from Christian War', which same acquired that in frank marriage with Mabilia, his wife, by gift of Henry Martin of Cotes, which same Henry bought that from Gilbert of Berden, chaplain, which same Gilbert acquired that by ancient acquisition, and in respect thereof he pays per annum to the prior and convent of Berden 2s., by which warranty they are unaware and to Lord Roger, nephew and heir of Master Nigel 20d.

[326] Item Walter son of Henry of Chesterton holds in fief 1 messuage in the parish of St Botolph's which descended to him by hereditary right through the death of Henry, his father, which same Henry bought that from Radulph de Kingeston, and that Radulph acquired that by ancient acquisition as purchase, and in respect thereof he pays per annum on behalf of the heirs of the said Radulph to the heirs of Master Nigel 12d.

[327] The same Walter holds 1 acre of land in the fields of Cambridge, which descended to him by inheritance through the death of Henry, his father, and that Henry bought that from Juliana, daughter of Thomas Longis of Cambridge, which same Juliana acquired that by hereditary right through the death of Thomas, her father, which same Thomas held that from the prior and convent of Barnwell, and in respect thereof he pays per annum to Alicia, daughter of Norman le Cuver and his heirs 2d.

[328] Item Adam le Barbur holds half of 1 messuage in the parish of St Botolph's, which he bought from Alicia Merilond, which same Alicia acquired that by hereditary right through the death of Walter Salyworth, her father, which same Walter acquired that by ancient succession of his parents, and he pays in respect thereof per annum to the said Alicia until the end of her life 15d., and after the death of the said Alicia to her heirs 1 rose, and to

the bailiffs of Cambridge who hold the said town in fee farm etcetera, to their farm for hawgable 1½d.

[329] The same Adam holds 1 messuage in the parish of St Benedict's, which messuage formerly Henry, vicar of St Botolph's Church gave to the said Adam with his sister Avelina in frank marriage, which same Henry bought that from Simon de Cottenham, and that Simon bought that from the said Adam le Barbur, and the said Adam acquired that by hereditary right through the death of Geoffrey le Barbur, his father, and that Geoffrey acquired that through the death of Richard of Colchester, his father, and in respect thereof pays per annum to Sarra of Barnwell 2s., and to St John's Hospital, Cambridge, 20d., by which warranty they are unaware, and for a certain wall belonging to the said messuage to Nichola, widow of Roger of Wikes, 2d.

[330] Sepharus le Gaunter holds 1 messuage in fief in the parish of St Botolph's in Lorteburne Lane, which he bought from the brothers of St John's Hospital, Cambridge, and in respect thereof he pays per annum to the said brothers 4s., by which warranty the said brothers are unaware of any claim to the said messuage and the said income.

[331] The same Sepharus holds 1 messuage in the parish of St Benedict's, which he bought from Robert of St Botolph's, which same Robert acquired that through the death of Simon, his father, and that Simon acquired that by ancient succession of his parents, and in respect thereof he pays per annum to the said Robert and his heirs 1 root of ginger, and to the prioress of St Radegund's and the same convent 3s., by which warranty they are unaware.

[332] The same Sepharus holds 1 messuage in the parish of St Peter's outside Trumpington Gate, which he bought from Stephen de Cottenham, chaplain. And the said Stephen acquired that by gift of Geoffrey de Aldreth, chaplain, which same Geoffrey bought that from John, son of Stephen, and the same Stephen at one time acquired that by ancient acquisition, and in respect thereof pays per annum to the said Stephen and his heirs 1 root of ginger, and to Alicia Harvey and her heirs 12d., and for the maintenance of a lamp in Holy Sepulchre Church 3d.

[333] Alan Attepont holds 1 messuage in Newnham which he bought from Jacomin de Aysnell', and that Jacomin bought that from Geoffrey Baker, of Newnham, for which he pays per annum to the heirs of the said Geoffrey 1 clove gillyflower.

[334] Item Mariota of Barton holds 1 messuage in the parish of St Botolph's which descended to her by hereditary right through

the death of Walter Bagge, her father, which same Walter acquired that by hereditary right through the death of Simon, his father, which same Simon acquired that by ancient succession of his ancestors, and she pays in respect thereof per annum to the heirs of Roger Aucutur' ½d., and to the bailiffs of Cambridge who hold the said town in fee farm as is stated, to their farm for hawgable 1d.

[335] Item the same Mariota holds 2 messuages in the parish of St John, which descended to her by hereditary right through the death of Johanna her mother, which same Johanna acquired those in frank marriage by gift of Michael Malerbe, her father, which same Michael acquired those by hereditary right through the death of Michael, his father, and that Michael acquired those by ancient succession of his ancestors, and in respect thereof she pays per annum to the heirs of the said Michael 1 peppercorn, and for the maintenance of a lamp in the St John's Church 16d., and to the bailiffs of Cambridge who hold the said town in fee farm etcetera, to their farm for hawgable.

[336] Item the same Mariota holds 2 messuages in the parish of Holy Trinity Cambridge, which same messuages she acquired by gift of John, son of Richard of Barton, which same John acquired those by inheritance through the death of the said Richard, his father, which same Richard acquired those through the death of John of Barton, his father, and in respect thereof she pays per annum to the bailiffs of Cambridge who hold the said town in fee farm etcetera, 1½d.

[337] Item the same Mariota holds 12 acres of land in the fields of Cambridge which she acquired by gift of John, son of Richard of Barton, which same John acquired those by inheritance through the death of Richard, his father, which same Richard acquired those by gift of John of Barnard Castle, which same John acquired those by inheritance through the death of Guy, which same Guy bought those from Eustace Dunning, which same Eustace acquired those from ancient succession of his ancestors, and in respect thereof she pays per annum to the heirs of John of Barnard Castle 1d. for the said land.

[338] Item Peter son of the said Richard of Barton holds 6 acres of land in the fields of Cambridge, which he acquired by gift of Richard, his father, which same Richard acquired those by gift of John of Barnard Castle, which same John acquired those by inheritance through the death of the said Guy and the said Guy bought that from Eustace Dunning and the same Eustace acquired those from

ancient succession of his ancestors, and in respect thereof he pays per annum to the heirs of the said Richard 1 pair of gloves at the price of ½d.

[339]   Item Giles son of the said Richard holds 6 acres of land in the fields of Cambridge, which he acquired by gift of the said Richard, his father, which same Richard acquired those by gift of John of Barnard Castle, which same John acquired those by hereditary right through the death of Guy, and the same Guy bought that from the said Eustace, and the same Eustace acquired those by ancient succession of his ancestors, and in respect thereof he pays to the heirs of the said Richard 1 pair of gloves at the price of ½d.

[340]   Item Matilda daughter of the said Richard of Barton holds 6 acres of land in the same fields which she acquired by gift of the said Richard, her father, which same Richard acquired those by gift of John of Barnard Castle, which same John acquired those by hereditary right through the death of the said Guy, and the said Guy bought that from the said Eustace, and the said Eustace acquired those by ancient acquisition of his ancestors, and in respect thereof she pays per annum to the heirs of the said Richard 1 pair of gloves at the price of ½d.

[341]   Item the said Matilda holds 1 messuage in the parish of Holy Sepulchre which she acquired by gift of Richard, her father, which same Richard bought that from John, son of Richard le Marscal, which same John acquired that by hereditary succession through the death of Eleanor, his mother, which same Eleanor acquired that by gift in frank marriage from Michael Malerbe, her father, and the said Michael acquired that by ancient acquisition, and in respect thereof she pays per annum to the prior and convent of Barnwell 4s., by which warranty they are unaware, and to the heirs of the said Richard 1 pair of gloves at the price of ½d.

[342]   Item the aforesaid Mariota of Barton holds 3 half acres of land in the fields of Barnwell, which she acquired by gift of John, son of Richard of Barton, which same John acquired those by hereditary right through the death of Richard, his father, which same Richard bought those from Nicholas Morice, which same Nicholas bought those from John, son of John Smith, and the said John acquired those by hereditary right through the death of John Smith, his father. And in respect thereof she pays per annum to the heirs of Laurence de Brock 7d.

[343]   Ambrose son of Geoffrey Baker of Newnham, holds 1 messuage with a croft in the parish of St Botolph's, which he acquired by

inheritance through the death of Geoffrey, his father, which same Geoffrey bought that from Roger Aysline, which same Roger bought that from Leon Dunning, and he pays in respect thereof per annum to the said Leon 16d.

[344]   Item Walter Bercharius holds 1 messuage in the parish of St Botolph's, which he bought from Alicia, widow of William de Kirkby, which same Alicia acquired that by gift of Walter, son of Thomas Sabr', her uncle, which same Walter acquired that through the death of Simon, his brother, which same Simon acquired that by hereditary right through the death of the said Thomas, his father, and in respect thereof he pays per annum to the said Alicia ½ mark.

[345]   The same Walter holds 1 messuage in the parish of St Andrew's which he bought from Alan Bangel, which same Alan acquired that through the death of William Alsope, his uncle, which same William acquired that through ancient acquisition, and in respect thereof he pays per annum to Richard Wombe 2s.

[346]   Item Walter son of Henry de Howes holds 1 messuage in the parish of St Botolph's which he acquired by hereditary right through the death of Henry de Howes, his father, which same Henry bought that from Elisius, chaplain, which same Elisius acquired that by hereditary right through the death of Nicholas le Weaver, his grandfather, and in respect thereof pays per annum to the abbot of Sawtry 4s., by which warranty they are unaware, and to the bailiffs of Cambridge who hold the said town in fee farm etcetera, to their farm for hawgable 1d.

[347]   Item Stephen Hunn' holds 1 messuage in the parish of St Botolph's which he bought from Roger Borers of Kerlinge, and the said Roger acquired that through the death of Reginald, chaplain, his nephew, and the said Richard acquired that by hereditary right through the death of Frethesenta, his mother, and in respect thereof he pays per annum to the heirs of the said Roger 4d., and to the bailiffs of Cambridge who hold the said town in fee farm etcetera, to their farm for hawgable 2d.

[348]   Item Avicia daughter of William Braci holds 1 messuage in the parish of St Botolph's which she acquired by gift of William Braci, her father, and Margaret, her mother, which same messuage Margaret Siyion gave to the said William and Margaret his wife, which same Margaret acquired that by gift of Harvey, cleric, her father, and the said Harvey acquired that by ancient succession of his parents, and in respect thereof she pays per annum to Johanna daughter of William Braci 5s., and to the bailiffs of Cambridge

who hold the same town in fee farm etcetera, to their farm for hawgable 1d.

[349] Item the same Avicia holds 1 messuage in the parish of St Benedict's which she acquired by gift of William Braci, her father, which same William bought that from Roger son of Nigel le Celer, and the said Roger acquired that by hereditary right through the death of Nigel, his father, and the said Nigel acquired that by ancient succession of his ancestors, and in respect thereof she pays per annum to the heirs of the said Roger 1d., and to the bailiffs of Cambridge who hold the said town in fee farm etcetera, to their farm for hawgable 1d.

[350] Item Margaret and Johanna and Avicia and Elena, sisters and daughters of William Braci hold 1 messuage in the parish of All Saints at the Castle which same descended by hereditary right through the death of the said William Braci, their father, which same William acquired that by paternal succession through the death of Ketel Attewal, his father, and the said Ketel acquired that by ancient acquisition, and in respect thereof they pay per annum to the heirs of John Andrew 8d. by assignment of Nicholas Malerbe.

[351] Item Margaret and Johanna and Avicia and Elena sisters and daughters of the said William Braci hold 1 messuage in the said parish which they have by hereditary right through the death of William Braci, their father, which same William acquired that by hereditary right through the death of Ketel le Mercer, and in respect thereof they pay per annum to the bailiffs of Cambridge who hold the same town in fee farm etcetera, to their farm for hawgable 1d.

[352] Item John son of Ranulph holds 1 messuage in the parish of St Benedict's which descended to him by hereditary right through the death of Ranulph, his father, which same Ranulph bought that from Margaret, daughter of Simon son of Reginald Ategate, and the said Margaret acquired that through the death of Simon son of Reginald, and in respect thereof he pays per annum to the said Margaret ½d., and to Luke of St Edmunds 12d.

[353] Item Matilda wife of Ranulph Ategate holds 1 messuage in the parish of St John's which she acquired by gift of Robert, her brother, son of Robert the steersman, which same Robert acquired that by hereditary right through the death of Robert, his father, and she pays per annum to John her brother ½d., and to the nuns of Swaffham 32d., by which warranty they are unaware, and to the bailiffs of Cambridge who hold the same town in fee farm etcetera for hawgable 4d.

[354]   Item Margaret daughter of William Sot holds 1 messuage in the parish of St Benedict's which descended to her by hereditary right through the death of William Sot, her father, and the same William bought that from Roger son of Richard le Tanner, which same Richard acquired that through the death of Richard, his father, which same Richard bought that from Henry Coynard, chaplain, which same Henry acquired that by ancient succession of his ancestors, and she pays in respect thereof per annum to the said Richard and his heirs 1 rose, and to Gilbert Bernard 12d., and to the bailiffs of Cambridge who hold the said town in fee farm etcetera, for hawgable, 2d.

[355]   Item John le Palfreyman holds 1 messuage in fief in the parish of St Botolph's which he bought from Winfred Briitlod, and the same Winfred acquired that by hereditary right through the death of Harvey Briitloth, his father, which same Harvey acquired that by ancient succession of his ancestors, and in respect thereof he pays per annum to the bailiffs of Cambridge who hold the same town in fee farm etcetera for hawgable 1d.

[356]   Item Nicholas Morice holds in fief 1 messuage in the parish of St Botolph's which descended to him by hereditary right through the death of William Morice, his father, which same William acquired that by hereditary right through the death of Morice, his father, which same Morice acquired that by hereditary right through the death of his ancestors, and in respect thereof he pays per annum to the bailiffs of Cambridge who hold the same town in fee farm etcetera for hawgable 2d.

[357]   The same Nicholas holds 1 messuage in the same parish which he bought from Reginald Sherewind, which same Reginald acquired that from Reginald Mulloc, which same Reginald acquired that by ancient acquisition, and in respect thereof he pays per annum to the bailiffs of Cambridge who hold the same town in fee farm etcetera for hawgable 2d.

[358]   The same Nicholas holds 1 messuage in the same parish which he acquired by hereditary right through the death of Isabella, his mother, which same Isabella acquired that by gift of Harvey Gogging, her father, which same Harvey acquired that by ancient succession of his parents, and in respect thereof he pays per annum to the heirs of the said Harvey 1d.

[359]   The same Nicholas holds 1 messuage in the same parish which he bought from John Doi, which same John acquired that through the death of Geoffrey Doi, his father, and the said Geoffrey acquired that by hereditary right through the death of Roger

Doi, his father, and the said Roger acquired that by ancient hereditary succession of his ancestors, and in respect thereof he pays per annum to the said John ½d.

[360]   The same Nicholas holds 1 shop in the marketplace of Cambridge in the parish of St Edward's which he bought from Nicholas Childman, which same Nicholas acquired that through the death of Nicholas, his father, and the same Nicholas acquired that with Mariota, daughter of Michael Gogging, in frank marriage, which same Michael acquired that by hereditary right through the death of Harvey, his father, which same Harvey acquired that by ancient succession of his parents, and in respect thereof he pays to the bailiffs of Cambridge who hold the same town in fee farm as is stated, for hawgable 8d.

[361]   The same Nicholas holds 1 shop in the parish of St Clement's which he bought from John Porthors, which same John bought that from Paul Wombe, which same Paul acquired that by gift of Nichola, his mother, which same Nichola acquired that by hereditary right through the death of her ancestors, and in respect thereof he pays per annum to the said John 1d., and to the bailiffs of Cambridge who hold the same town in fee farm etcetera for hawgable 1 farthing.

[362]   The same Nicholas holds another shop in the same parish which he bought from Edmund de Stanhon, which same Edmund bought that from Agnes Cuncasce, and the same Agnes bought that from John Saleman, and the same John acquired that by hereditary succession through the death of Alicia Saleman, his mother, and the said Alicia acquired that by gift of her ancestors in frank marriage, and he pays in respect thereof per annum to the said Edmund 1 rose, and to the bailiffs of Cambridge who hold the same town in fee farm etcetera for hawgable 1 farthing.

[363]   The same Nicholas holds a granary in the parish of St Michael's which same he bought from Johanna daughter of William son of Ivo, which same Johanna acquired that by gift of William, her father, which same William bought that from Adam Dunning, which same Adam acquired that by ancient succession of his ancestors, and in respect thereof he pays per annum to the heirs of the said Adam ½d.

[364]   The same Nicholas holds 18 acres of land in the fields of Cambridge which he bought from William de Manefeld, which same William acquired by inheritance through the death of Master Guy of Barnard Castle, which same Master Guy bought those from Eustace Dunning, which same Eustace acquired those

by inheritance through the death of Harvey Dunning, his father, and the same Harvey acquired those by ancient succession of his parents, and in respect thereof he pays per annum to the scholars of Merton 12d. and ½ lb. of ginger by assignment of the said William.

[365]   The same Nicholas holds 7 acres of land in the same fields which he bought from John Porthors which same bought those from William de Manefeld, and the same William acquired those by hereditary right through the death of the said Master Guy, and the same Master Guy bought those from Eustace Dunning, and that Eustace acquired those through the death of Harvey, his father, and he pays in respect thereof per annum to the said John 1d.

[366]   The same Nicholas holds 6 acres of land in the same fields which he bought from Nicholas Baker, which same Nicholas acquired those by hereditary right through the death of Simon, his father, and the said Simon acquired those by purchase from Leon Dunning and the said Leon acquired those through the death of Adam, his father, and the said Adam acquired those by ancient acquisition, and he pays in respect thereof per annum to the said Leon Dunning 6d.

[367]   Item Nicholas holds 6 acres of land in the same fields and 1 half acre and 1 rood which he bought from Robert Hubert, which same Robert acquired those by gift of Robert, his son, and the said Robert acquired those by hereditary right through the death of Thomas Toylet, his grandfather, which same Thomas acquired those by ancient acquisition, and in respect thereof he pays per annum to the heirs of the said Robert 2d.

[368]   The same Nicholas holds 2 acres of land in the same fields which he bought from John Wombe, and the same John acquired those through the death of Nicholas Wombe, his father, and which same Nicholas acquired that those by ancient acquisition, and in respect thereof he pays per annum to the said John 1d.

[369]   The same Nicholas holds 2 acres of land in the same fields which he bought from John Blodles of Newnham which same John acquired those by hereditary right through the death of William, his father, which same William acquired those by ancient acquisition, and in respect thereof he pays per annum to the heirs of the said John ½d.

[370]   The same Nicholas holds 2 acres of land in the same fields which he bought from William son of Ivo, which same William acquired those from Radulph de Trubelvile, which same Radulph

acquired those by ancient succession, and in respect thereof he pays per annum to the heirs of the said William ½d.

[371]   The same Nicholas holds 1 acre of land in the same fields which descended to him by hereditary right through the death of Isabella, his mother, which same Isabella acquired that in frank marriage by gift of Harvey Gogging, her father, and the said Harvey acquired that by ancient succession of his ancestors, and in respect thereof he pays per annum to the heirs of the said Harvey ½d.

[372]   The same Nicholas holds 3 acres of land in the fields of Barnwell which he bought from Richard Wombe, which same Richard acquired those by hereditary right through the death of Bartholomew Wombe, his father, which same Bartholomew acquired those through hereditary descent, and in respect thereof he pays per annum to the said Richard 1d.

[373]   The same Nicholas holds 4 acres of land in the fields of Barnwell which he bought from Radulph de Kingeston, which same Radulph bought those from John son of Master Henry of Hinton, which same John acquired those through the death of his ancestors, and in respect thereof he pays per annum to the heirs of the said Radulph 1 rose.

[374]   The same Nicholas holds 2 acres of land in the same fields which he bought from John Parleben, which same John acquired those by hereditary right through the death of John le Marscal, his father, which same John acquired those by ancient succession of his ancestors, and in respect thereof he pays per annum to the heirs of Laurence de Brock 6d.

[375]   The same Nicholas holds 2 acres of land in the fields of Barnwell which he bought from Johanna Mariote, which same Johanna acquired those by hereditary right through the death of Alan le Kayli, her father, which same Alan acquired those by ancient succession of his ancestors, and in respect thereof he pays per annum to the said Johanna 1 rose.

[376]   The same Nicholas holds 1 acre of land in the same fields which he bought from Bozun son of John Potekin, which same Bozun acquired that by hereditary right through the death of the said John, his father, which same John acquired that by ancient succession of his parents, and in respect thereof he pays per annum to the heirs of the said Bozun 1 rose.

[377]   The same Nicholas holds 2 acres in the same fields which he bought from Lord John, soldier of Hinton, and the said Lord John acquired those from Henry at the head of the town

of Hinton, which same Henry acquired those through the death of Lord Roger, chaplain, his brother, and the said Roger bought those from Luke of St Edmunds and in respect thereof he pays per annum to the said Lord John, soldier, 1d.

[378] John Martin holds in fief 1 messuage in the parish of St Botolph's which descended to him by hereditary right through the death of Martin, his father, which same Martin held that by purchase from Alicia Segar, which same Alicia acquired that by inheritance through the death of her ancestors and held it from the prioress of St Radegund's, and in respect thereof he pays per annum to the said prioress 16d., by which warranty she is unaware.

[379] The same John holds 5 acres of land in the fields of Cambridge which he holds from the prior and convent of Barnwell, and in respect thereof he pays per annum to the said prior and convent 3s. 6d.

[380] The same John holds 1 acre of land in the same fields which he bought from Luke of St Edmunds, and the same Luke acquired that by hereditary right through the death of Thomas, his brother, which same Thomas acquired that by gift of Walter, his father, which same Walter acquired that by gift of Radulph Pirot, and in respect thereof he pays per annum to the said Luke 1 clove gillyflower.

[381] The same John holds 3 messuages with 5 acres of land in Newnham which same he bought from John son of Geoffrey le Hose, which same John acquired those by hereditary right through the death of the said Geoffrey his father, which same Geoffrey held those from the brothers of St John's Hospital, Cambridge, and in respect thereof he pays per annum to the said brothers 7d., by which warranty they are unaware.

[382] The same John and his wife Avicia hold 3 acres of land in the fields of Cambridge which they acquired in frank marriage by gift of William Toylet, which same William bought those from Leon Dunning, and the same Leon acquired those by inheritance through the death of Adam, his father, and in respect thereof they pay per annum to Henry Toylet 11d.

[383] The same John holds 1 messuage with 1 acre of land in Newnham which he bought from Leon Dunning, which same Leon acquired those by hereditary right through the death of Adam, his father, and in respect thereof he pays per annum to the said Leon and his heirs 15½d. and 1 farthing.

[384] The same John holds 1 acre of land in Newnham which he acquired by gift of Henry Toylet, which same Henry acquired

that by hereditary right through the death of William, his father, which same William acquired that by hereditary right of his ancestors, and he pays in respect thereof per annum to the said Henry 1d.

[385] William son of Alicia de Shelford holds 1 messuage in the parish of St Botolph's which he acquired by gift of the said Alicia, and the said Alicia acquired that by gift of her father, and the said father bought that from Heleyws Keit', for which he pays per annum to the prioress of Markgate 12d., by which warranty they are ignorant.

[386] Nicholas de Drayton holds 1 messuage in the parish of St Botolph's which he bought from John son of Michael Gogging, and the same John acquired that by hereditary right through the death of Michael, his father, which same Michael acquired that by ancient succession of his ancestors, and he pays in respect thereof per annum to the said John and his heirs 4d.

[387] Elena, widow of Reginald Sherewind, holds 1 messuage in the parish of St Botolph's which she has in the name of dower until the end of her life from William son of said Reginald, which same William acquired that by hereditary right through the death of Reginald, his father, and the same Reginald bought that from Ivo de Len, which same Ivo acquired that through the death of Master Martin de Len, his brother, and the said Martin acquired that by ancient acquisition, and in respect thereof she pays per annum to the heirs of the said Ivo 1d., and to the bailiffs of Cambridge who hold the said town in fee farm etcetera for hawgable 1d.

[388] Item William Smith and his wife Agnes hold 1 messuage in the parish of St Botolph's which the said Agnes and Robert Smith, former husband of the said Agnes, bought from the brothers of St John's, Cambridge, and they pay in respect thereof to the said brothers 9s., by which warranty the said brothers are unaware of any claim to the said messuage.

[389] Item William Miller of Biggleswade holds 1 messuage in the parish of St Botolph's, which he bought from Henry, vicar of St Botolph's Church, which same Henry bought from Walter Haliday, which same Walter bought that from Richard le Barbar, which same Richard bought that from the brothers of St John's Hospital, Cambridge, and in respect thereof he pays per annum to the said Henry and his heirs ½d., and to the brothers of the said Hospital 6s., in which way they are unaware of any claim to the said income.

[390]   Saer of Feering and his wife Mariota hold 1 messuage in the parish of St Botolph's, which messuage Elisius Weaver and aforesaid Mariota former wife of the said Elisius bought from Master Simon Prat, which same Master Simon acquired that by hereditary right through the death of Geoffrey Prat of Ely, his father. Which same Geoffrey acquired that by ancient purchase, for which he pays per annum, by assignment of the said Master Simon, to Margaret wife of the former chaplain, Abraham, 4s., and to Luke of St Edmunds 2s.

[391]   Item the said Saer and his wife Mariota hold 1 messuage in the said parish, which same said Mariota formerly bought from John Martin, which same John bought that from Margaret, daughter and heir of Richard Herccat, which same Richard formerly gave to Henry Mundi of Barnwell with the said Margaret his daughter in frank marriage, and the said Richard bought that from Matilda Parvus, and the said Matilda acquired that by hereditary succession of her parents, for which they pay per annum to the said John 1 lb. of cumin, and to Bartholomew Gogging 40d., and to the heirs of Thomas de Ho 20d.

[392]   Item Saer and Mariota hold 1 messuage in the said parish which messuage Isabella Morice gave to Elisius Textor in frank marriage with the said Mariota, which same messuage Harvey Clerk and Alicia his [wife] gave to William Morice in frank marriage with the said Isabella their daughter, and in respect thereof they pay per annum to Nicholas Morice ½d.

[393]   Item Saer and Mariota hold 1 messuage in the said parish which Mariota formerly bought from Isabella daughter of Matilda le Barbaresse, which same descended to the said Isabella by inheritance through the death of the said Matilda, her mother, which messuage Richard de Saxton and the said Matilda his wife bought from Johanna, daughter of John Aured, which messuage descended to the said John by inheritance through the death of John Aured his father, for which they pay per annum to the said Isabella 1 rose, and to John Aured and his heirs 2s. 6d.

[394]   Item Saer holds 1 messuage in Newnham in the parish of St Peter's, which messuage Mariota, his wife, daughter of Bernard de Scalariis bought from Thomas de Derham, baker, and the said Thomas bought that from the brothers of St John's Hospital, Cambridge, and the said brothers held that by gift of Mabilia de Haslingfield, and in respect thereof he pays per annum to the said Thomas and his heirs 1 clove gillyflower and to the said brothers of St John's Hospital 12d.

[395]   Item Saer holds a certain piece of vacant land in Newnham in the said parish which he bought from Luke Carter, and the same Luke bought that from Stephen of Newnham, son of Acelina Miller, and the said Stephen acquired that through the death of the said Acelina, his mother, and in respect thereof he pays per annum to the said Stephen 1 rose through the heirs of the said Luke, and to the brothers of St John's Hospital, Cambridge, 9d., by which warranty they are unaware of any claim to the said income.

[396]   Item Nicholas of Drayton and his wife Margarita hold 1 messuage in the parish of St John's Cambridge, which same messuage the said Margarita bought from Simon ad Aquam, and the said Simon formerly bought from Simon ad Aquam of Wimbotsham, and the said Simon bought that from Gregory Ere, and the said Gregory acquired that by ancient succession of his ancestors, and in respect thereof they pay per annum to the said Simon ½d.

[397]   Item Nicholas and his wife Margarita hold 1 messuage in the same parish which he bought from Simon ad Aquam, which same Simon bought that from Richard son of Richard le Wenet, which same Richard acquired that by inheritance through the death of the said Richard, his father, which same Richard acquired that by inheritance through the decease of Stephen Sadelbon, and the said Stephen bought that from Robert Marshall, and they pay in respect thereof per annum to the said Simon ½d., and to Robert de Brinkley 12d., and to Roger, chaplain, nephew of Master Nigel 12d.

[398]   Cecilia former wife of Peter de Welles holds a piece of vacant land destroyed a short time ago in the parish of St Benedict's, which she acquired by gift of Peter son of Peter de Welles, her son, which same Peter acquired that by hereditary right through the death of the said Peter, his father, which same Peter bought that from Master William de Beston, and the same William bought that from Stephen son of Stephen de Hauxton, and that Stephen acquired that by hereditary right through the death of Stephen, his father, which same Stephen acquired that by succession of his ancestors, and in respect thereof she pays per annum to the said Master William 4d., and to the prior and convent of Barnwell 18s., and to the bailiffs of Cambridge who hold the said town in fee farm etcetera for hawgable 1d., to the said named prior and convent who acquired the said piece of land by gift of Johel one time father of Robert, former prior of Barnwell.

[399]   Item the same Cecilia holds 1 messuage in the same parish with 4 acres of land in the fields of Cambridge, which messuage with

said land she acquired by gift of Nicholas Childman, her father, in frank marriage, which same Nicholas acquired that in frank marriage by gift of Nicholas Gogging with Mariota, daughter of the said Michael, and in respect thereof she pays per annum to the heirs of the said Nicholas 1d., and to John But and his heirs 15s.

[400]   The same Cecilia holds 1 messuage in the same parish which she acquired by gift of Peter son of Peter de Welles, which same Peter acquired that by inheritance through the death of the said Peter de Welles, his father, which same Peter bought that from Eustace Selede, and the said Eustace acquired that by ancient succession of his parents, and in respect thereof she pays per annum to the heirs of the said Eustace 3s., and to Luke of St Edmunds 12d.

[401]   Item the same Cecilia holds 2 messuages in the parish of St Mary's Cambridge, which same she acquired by gift of the said Peter son of Peter de Welles, her father, which same Peter acquired those by inheritance through the death of the said Peter, his father, and that Peter bought those from Stephen son of Stephen de Hauxton, and the said Stephen acquired those from ancient succession of his ancestors, and in respect thereof she pays per annum to the heirs of the said Stephen 2d.

[402]   Item the same Cecilia holds 1 messuage in the parish of St Botolph's which she acquired by gift of Peter son of Peter de Welles, which same Peter acquired that by hereditary right through the death of the said Peter, his father, which same Peter bought that from Thomas Mulloc, which same Thomas acquired that by inheritance through the death of Reginald Mulloc, and the said Reginald acquired that by ancient purchase, and in respect thereof she pays per annum to the heirs of the said Thomas 1d.

[A49]   Item the same Cecilia holds 20 acres of land in the fields of Cambridge which she acquired by gift of the said Peter son of Peter de Welles, and that Peter acquired those by inheritance through the death of the said Peter, his father, which same Peter acquired those from the prior and convent of Barnwell in exchange for the same amount of land in the fields of Barton.

[403]   Item the same Cecilia holds 1 acre of land in the same fields which she acquired by gift of the said Peter son of Peter de Welles and that Peter acquired that by hereditary right through the death of the said Peter de Welles, his father, which same Peter bought that from John Wombe, which same John acquired that by hereditary right through the death of Nicholas Wombe, his

father, and that Nicholas acquired that from ancient heritage of his ancestors, and in respect thereof she pays per annum to the said John 2d.

[404] Item the same Cecilia holds 3 acres of land in the fields of Cambridge which she acquired by gift of the said Peter son of the said Peter de Welles and the said Peter acquired those by inheritance through the death of the said Peter de Welles, his father, which same Peter bought those from Ambrose of Newnham, which same Ambrose acquired those from ancient purchase, and in respect thereof she pays per annum through the heirs of the said Ambrose, to Geoffrey Cynwet and Roger, chaplain of Newnham, 1d.

[405] Item John son of Harvey Gogging holds 1 messuage in the parish of St Benedict's, which same he acquired by hereditary right through the death of the said Harvey, his father, which same Harvey acquired that by inheritance through the death of John Gogging, his father, which same John acquired that by gift of Harvey, cleric, his father, and the said Harvey acquired that through the death of his ancestors, and in respect thereof he pays per annum to the heirs of the said Michael Gogging 20d.

[406] Item William de Rudham, cleric, holds 1 messuage in the parish of St Benedict's, which he bought from John, son of Harvey Gogging, which same John acquired that by hereditary right through the death of the said Harvey, his father, which same Harvey acquired that by inheritance through the death of John Gogging, his father, which same John acquired that by inheritance through the death of Harvey Gogging, cleric, his father, and the said Harvey acquired that by hereditary right through the death of his ancestors, and in respect thereof he pays per annum to the said John 1d., and to the nuns of St Radegund's 30d., by which warranty the said nuns are unaware of any claim to the said income.

[407] The same William holds 1 messuage in the same parish which he bought from the prior and convent of Barnwell, and the said prior and convent acquired that by gift of Master Thomas de Tid, which same Thomas bought that from Harvey son of John Gogging, which same Harvey bought that from John, son of Erhard of Trumpington, and in respect thereof he pays per annum to the said prior and convent 6d., and to the nuns of St Radegund's 4s., by which warranty the said nuns are unaware of any claim to the said income.

[408] The same William holds 1 messuage in the parish of All Saints next to the Hospital which he bought from Matilda, widow of

Harvey Gogging, which same Matilda acquired that by gift of Bartholomew Tailor, her father, in frank marriage, and the same Bartholomew acquired that by hereditary right of his ancestors, and in respect thereof he pays per annum to the said Matilda ½d., and to the almoner of Croyland 4s., by which warranty the said almoner is unaware of any claim to the said income.

[409]   Item Radulph de Comberton holds 1 messuage in the parish of St Benedict's which he bought from Johanna le Kayli, which messuage descended to the said Johanna by inheritance through the death of Alan le Kayli, her father and the said Alan acquired that by ancient purchase, and in respect thereof he pays per annum to St John's Hospital, Cambridge, 12d., and to the bailiffs of Cambridge who hold the said town in fee farm etcetera for hawgable ½d., by which warranty the brothers of the said hospital are unaware of any claim to the said income.

[410]   Item Radulph holds 1 messuage in the same parish which he bought from Avicia, daughter of Benedict Merchant, which same messuage descended to the said Avicia by inheritance through the death of Cassandria, her mother, and in respect thereof he pays per annum to the said Avicia and her heirs 1d., and to the nuns of St Radegund's 12s., by which warranty the said nuns are unaware of any claim to the said income.

[411]   Geva wife of Thomas Suin, cleric, holds 1 messuage in the parish of St Benedict's which same messuage descended to the said Geva by inheritance through the death of Simon Campiun, her father, and the said Simon acquired that by ancient purchase and in respect thereof she pays per annum to Luke of St Edmunds 6d.

[412]   Item Peter son of Thomas Swyn holds 1 messuage in the parish of St Peter's outside Trumpington Gate which descended to him by inheritance through the death of the said Thomas, his father, and the said Thomas acquired that through the death of Harvey Swyn, his father, and in respect thereof he pays per annum to the bailiffs of Cambridge who hold the said town in fee farm from the Lord King etcetera, for hawgable 2d.

[413]   The same Peter holds 1 messuage in the same parish which descended to him by inheritance through the death of the said Thomas, his father, which same Thomas acquired that by hereditary right through the death of Harvey Swyn, his father, and the said Harvey acquired that through the death of Alicia Wylunet, his mother, and in respect thereof he pays per annum to Luke of St Edmunds 8d.

[414] Item Robert Wulward holds 1 messuage in the parish of St Benedict's which he bought from Richard Weaver and the said Richard acquired that by inheritance through the death of his ancestors, and in respect thereof he pays per annum to the said Richard 1d., and to the prior of Barnwell 3s., by which warranty the said prior is unaware of any claim to the said income.

[415] Item Robert and his wife Sarra hold 1 shop in the parish of St Edward's which they acquired by gift of John Gogging in frank marriage, which same John acquired that by gift of Harvey, cleric, his father, and the said Harvey acquired that by ancient succession of his ancestors, and in respect thereof they pay per annum to the said John 1d., and to the brothers of St John's Hospital 3s., and to the bailiffs of Cambridge who hold the said town in fee farm etcetera for hawgable 8d., in which manner also and by which warranty the said brothers are unaware of any claim to the said income.

[416] Item Robert and Sarra hold a ½ acre of land in the fields of Cambridge which they acquired by gift of the said John Gogging in frank marriage, which same John acquired that by gift of Harvey, cleric, his father, which same Harvey acquired that by ancient succession of his ancestors, and in respect thereof they pay per annum to the said John and his heirs 1½d.

[417] The same Robert holds a ½ acre of land in the fields of Cambridge which descended to him by inheritance through the death of Martin Wulward, his father, and the same Martin bought that from Erhard Attehyl of Grantchester, and in respect thereof he pays per annum to the heirs of the said Erhard 1d.

[418] Item William Erchebaud holds 1 messuage in the parish of St Benedict's which he bought from William le Furbur of Sawston which same William bought that from Thomas Baker and the said Thomas bought that from the prioress and convent of St Radegund's and in respect thereof he pays per annum to the heirs of the said William 1 farthing, and to the said prioress and convent 12d., and to Luke of St Edmunds 2s., in which manner and by which warranty the said prioress and the said convent are unaware of any claim to the said income.

[419] Item Simon son and heir of Peter le Corder holds 1 messuage in the parish of Holy Trinity which descended to him by inheritance through the death of the said Peter, his father, which same Peter bought that from Matilda and Agnes, daughters of Richard de Rowe, baker, which same Matilda and Agnes acquired that by inheritance through the death of the said Richard, their

father, which same Richard acquired that by ancient purchase, and he pays in respect thereof per annum to William of York and Matilda, his wife, and to John and Agnes, his wife, 1 clove gillyflower, and to the heirs of Paul Wombe 1d., and to the bailiffs of Cambridge who hold the said town in fee farm etcetera for hawgable 2d.

[420]   Item William son of Benedict de Harleston holds a certain piece of a messuage in the parish of St Benedict's in Lorteburne Lane which he bought from Thomas de Wynepol, cleric, and from his wife Leticia and from Margaret, sister of the said Leticia, which same piece of land descended to the said Leticia and Margaret, her sister, by inheritance through the death of John le Paumer, father of the said Leticia and Margaret, her sister, and in respect thereof he pays per annum to the said Thomas and Leticia, his wife, and to their heirs 9d., and to the bailiffs of Cambridge who hold the said town in fee farm etcetera for hawgable ½d.

[421]   Item Richard le Herde holds 1 messuage in the parish of St Benedict's which he bought from Richard de Potton and from Thomas, his brother, which same Richard and Thomas acquired that by inheritance through the death of William, father of the said Richard and Thomas, and the said William bought that from Adam Coynterel, chaplain, and that Adam acquired that by ancient hereditary succession, and in respect thereof he pays per annum to the heirs of Richard le Wenet' 4d. by assignment of the said Richard and Thomas.

[422]   Item Osbert le Farrier and his wife Berota hold 1 messuage in the parish of St Benedict's which same messuage descended to the said Berota by inheritance through the death of William de Linton, her father, which same William acquired that by inheritance through the death of Richard de Linton, his father, which same Richard acquired that by inheritance through the death of his ancestors, and in respect thereof they pay per annum to Luke of St Edmunds 19d., and to the nuns of Swaffham 2s., by which warranty the said nuns are unaware of any claim to the said income.

[423]   Item Osbert le Farrier holds 1 messuage in the parish of St Benedict's which he bought from Robert Freman, which same Robert acquired that by hereditary right through the death of William Freman, his father, and the said William bought that from Stephen de Hauxton. And the said Stephen acquired that by ancient purchase, and in respect thereof he pays per annum to the said Robert ½d., and to Luke of St Edmunds 12d.

[424] Item Osbert holds a piece of vacant land in the said parish which he bought from Margaret and Alvana, daughters of Hawisa Thurston, which same piece of land descended to the said Margaret and Alvena by inheritance through the death of the said Hawisia, their mother, which same Hawisia acquired that by inheritance through the death of Thurston, her father, and the said Thurstan acquired that from ancient purchase, and he pays in respect thereof to the heirs of the said Margaret and Alvena ½d., and to the heirs of Stephen de Hauxton 5s., and to the bailiffs of Cambridge who hold the said town in fee farm etcetera for hawgable 1d.

[425] The same Osbert holds 1 messuage in the parish of St Edward's, Cambridge, which he bought from Alexander de Gresbi, carpenter, which same Alexander acquired that by gift of Master Laurence, his brother, which same Master Laurence bought that from Henry Elyot, which same Henry acquired that by hereditary right through the death of John Elyot, his brother, which same John acquired that from hereditary succession of his ancestors, and in respect thereof he pays per annum to the heirs of the said Alexander 1d., and to the heirs of the said Henry Elyot 1 pair of white gloves at the price of 1d. And to the bailiffs of Cambridge who hold the said town in fee farm etcetera for hawgable 1d.

[426] The same Osbert holds a piece of vacant land in the parish of St Mary's which he bought from William le Weyse and the said William bought that from Alicia daughter of John Smith, which same Alicia acquired that by hereditary right through the death of the said John, her father, and the said John acquired that by hereditary right through the death of his ancestors, and in respect thereof he pays per annum to Richard Wombe 4s., and to the heirs of Christiana Astines 2s.

[427] The same Osbert holds a piece of vacant land in the parish of St Benedict's opposite the Friars Preacher and 1½ acres of land in the fields of Barnwell, which piece of land and said land he bought from Luke of St Edmunds, which same Luke acquired that by hereditary right through the death of Thomas, his brother, which same Thomas acquired that by gift of Walter, his father, and the said Walter acquired that from ancient heritage of his ancestors, and in respect thereof he pays per annum to the said Luke and his heirs 7d.

[428] Item William Cook of Nortyivel and his wife Margaret hold 1 messuage in the parish of St Benedict's which same messuage the said Margaret acquired by gift of Osbert le Farrier, her

father, and the said Osbert bought that from John Bagge, which same John acquired that by inheritance through the death of Thomas Bagge, his father, and the said Thomas acquired that by hereditary right through the death of his ancestors, and in respect thereof he pays per annum to the heirs of the said John 1 lb. of cumin, and to St Botolph's Church 2s. 6d. And to the bailiffs of Cambridge who hold the said town in fee farm etcetera for hawgable 1d.

[429]   Item John de Wisbech holds 1 messuage in the parish of St Benedict's which he bought from John Halte, shoemaker, which same John bought that from William de Kirkby which same messuage Walter, cleric, gave to the said William and Alicia, his wife, and the said Walter acquired that by inheritance through the death of Simon, his brother. And the said Simon acquired that through the death of Thomas, his brother, and the said Thomas acquired that through the death of Thomas, his father, and in respect thereof he pays per annum to the heirs of the said William and the said Alicia 12s. 4d., and to St Benedict's Church 12d., and to the bailiffs of Cambridge who hold the said town in fee farm etcetera for hawgable 1½d.

[430]   Item Henry, chaplain, son of William le Paumer holds a certain piece of vacant land in the parish of St Benedict's which descended to him by inheritance through the death of Eleanor, his mother, which same Eleanor acquired that by gift of Lord Thomas, rector of St Benedict's Church, her father, which same Thomas bought that from Ernulph Smith, and in respect thereof he pays per annum through the heirs of the said Ernulph to Luke of St Edmunds 2d.

[431]   Item Walter de Hinton, chaplain, holds 1 messuage in the parish of St Benedict's, Cambridge, which messuage Richard, former servant to the lord Richard, rector of the church of Hinton, acquired that by gift of Robert Edward of Cambridge, and the said Robert acquired that by ancient purchase, and in respect thereof he pays per annum to the heirs of the said Robert 1 pair of gloves and to Luke of St Edmunds 6d.

[432]   Item John of Braintree holds 1 messuage in the parish of St Benedict's which he bought from John, son of Gervase Baker, and Mabilia, his wife, which same Mabilia acquired that by gift of the said John, her husband before she was betrothed, which same messuage descended to the said John by inheritance through the death of the said Gervase, his father, and the said Gervase bought that from Reginald Balifart of St Ives, and he pays in respect

thereof per annum to the said John and Mabilia and their heirs one[68] [word missing on ms] and to Luke of St Edmunds 4½d.

[433] The same John holds 1 messuage in the same parish which he bought from Thomas, son of John Warin and Margaret, his sister, which same Thomas and Margaret acquired that by gift of the said John Warin, his father, and the said John bought that from Roger Preng, for which he pays per annum to the said Thomas and Margaret ½d., and to Luke of St Edmunds[69].

[434] The same John holds a piece of vacant land in the same parish which he bought from Radulph de Comberton, and the said Radulph acquired that by gift of Gervase Baker, and the said bought that from Simon Bademan, for which he pays per annum to the said Radulph 1 rose, and for the maintenance of a candle in St Benedict's Church in front of the altar of Holy Mary 2s., and to the heirs of the said Simon 12d.

[435] The same John holds 1 messuage in the parish of St Edward's which he bought from Andrew Pruet, and the said Andrew acquired that by gift of William Pruet, his brother, for which he pays per annum to the heirs of the said Andrew ½d.

[436] The same John holds 1 shop in the parish of St Edward's, which he acquired by gift of John Aubri in frank marriage with Mabilia, his sister, and the said shop descended to the said John Aubri by inheritance through the death of Aubrey, his father and in respect thereof he pays per annum to Richard Bateman senior ½d., and to the abbess of Chatteris 6s., and to the brothers of St John's Hospital, Cambridge 4s., by which warranty the said brothers and abbess are unaware of any claim to the said incomes.

[END OF ROLL 1, BEGINNING OF ROLL 2. POSSIBLE POINT AT WHICH ROLL 3 FITS INTO THE SEQUENCE]

[437] Item John holds a piece of vacant land in the parish of St Benedict's which he acquired by gift of the said John Aubry in frank marriage with Mabilia, his wife, which same piece of land descended to the said John by inheritance through the death of Aubrey, his father, and in respect thereof he pays per annum for the maintenance of a lamp in St Mary's Church 2s.

[438] The same John holds 1 messuage in Newnham in the parish of St Peter's outside Trumpington Gate, which he acquired by gift of the said John Aubry in frank marriage with Mabilia, his wife, which same messuage descended to the said John by inheritance through the death of Aubrey, his father, and in respect thereof he

pays per annum to St John's Hospital, Cambridge, 4d., by which warranty they are unaware.

[439] Item William le Bleckestere holds 1 messuage in Lorteburne Lane in the parish of St Benedict's, which he bought from Thomas de Winepol and Leticia, his wife, and Margaret, sister of the said Leticia, which same Leticia and Margaret acquired that by hereditary right through the death of John le Paumer, and the said John acquired that by inheritance through the death of his ancestors, and in respect thereof he pays per annum to Leticia and Margaret 9d., and to the bailiffs of Cambridge who hold the said town in fee farm etcetera for hawgable ½d.

[440] Item William le Combere holds 1 messuage in the said parish which he acquired by hereditary right through the death of Radulph of Euresdon, which same Radulph bought that from Agnes Swereles, and the said Agnes acquired that by hereditary right through the death of Robert Scurri, her uncle, which same Robert acquired that by ancient purchase, and in respect thereof he pays per annum to Nicholas Morice 16d., and to Isabella daughter of Nicholas Wombe 8d.

[441] Item William le Kaleys holds 1 messuage in the parish of St Benedict's, which he bought from William of Lawshall, and the said William acquired that by gift of Simon of Lawshall, his brother, and the said Simon acquired that by gift of Cassandria Chrocheman and the said Cassandria acquired that by gift of Simon Cademan, chaplain, and the said Simon acquired that through the death of Robert Cademan, his father, and in respect thereof he pays per annum to the said William 1 clove gillyflower, and to Luke of St Edmunds 2s.

[442] Item Thomas Carpenter of Stanton holds 1 messuage in the said parish which he bought from Agnes le Hunte, which same Agnes acquired that by gift of Walter le Hunte, her brother, which same Walter acquired that by hereditary right through the death of Peter le Hunte, his father, and the said Peter that by ancient purchase, and in respect thereof he pays per annum to Roger, chaplain, heir of Master Nigel 30d., and to the said Agnes ½d.

[443] Item Basilia de Toseland holds 1 messuage in the parish of St Benedict's which she acquired by gift of Robert, former rector of Hardwick, which same Robert bought that from John Porthors and the said John bought that from Margaret Gosenol, which same Margaret acquired that by gift of Robert Gosenol, her brother, and in respect thereof she pays per annum to Robert Seman 6d., and to John, son, 1½d., and to the bailiffs

of Cambridge who hold the said town in fee farm etcetera for hawgable 1d.

[444] Item John de Fincham holds 1 messuage in the said parish which he bought from Henry de Waddon and Alicia Harvey, his wife, which same Henry and Alicia bought that from Richard, son of Gregory and the said Richard acquired that by ancient purchase, and in respect thereof he pays per annum to the said Henry and Alicia 12d., and to the bailiffs of Cambridge who hold the said town in fee farm etcetera 1d.

[445] Item Richard de Snailwell holds 1 messuage in the parish of St Benedict's which he acquired by gift of Mabilia, Matilda and Alneya, daughters of Richemann le Sauver which same messuage descended to the same by hereditary right through the death of the said Richemann, their father, which same Richemann bought that from William of St Edmunds, and the said William acquired that from ancient heritage of his ancestors, and in respect thereof he pays per annum to the heirs of the said Richemann 1d., and to the heirs of Robert Seman 6d., and to Luke of St Edmunds 4s., and to the bailiffs of Cambridge who hold the said town in fee farm etcetera for hawgable ½d.

[446] Radulph Beupain holds 1 messuage in the said parish which he bought from Richard of Barton, which same Richard acquired that by gift of John son of John Marshall, and the said John acquired that by inheritance through the death of said John, his father, for which he pays per annum to the heirs of Robert de Fulton 10s.

[447] Simon son of John de Bradele, holds 1 messuage in the parish of St John the Baptist in Cambridge, which same messuage descended to him by hereditary right through the death of Reynard, his brother, which same messuage descended to the said Reynard by inheritance through the death of John de Bradele, his father, which same John held that from the almoner of Ely, and in respect thereof he pays per annum to the said almoner 14s., in which way the said almoner is unaware of any claim to the said income.

[448] The same Simon holds 1 messuage in the said parish which he bought from Alicia, daughter of Richard de Bradele, which same Alicia acquired that by hereditary right through the death of Richard, her father, and the same Richard acquired that by ancient purchase, and in respect thereof he pays per annum to bailiffs of Cambridge who hold the said town in fee farm etcetera for hawgable 1d.

[449] The same Simon holds 1 messuage in the aforesaid parish which same messuage he acquired by gift of John de Bradele, his father, which same John bought that from Richard Laurence senior, and in respect thereof he pays per annum to the said Richard and his heirs 12d.

[450] The same Simon holds 1 messuage in the parish of St Mary's which messuage descended to him by inheritance through the death of Reynard, his brother, which same Reynard acquired that by hereditary right through the death of John de Bradele, his father, and the same John bought that from Walter son of Radulph Mun, and the same Walter acquired that by hereditary right through the death of Radulph Mun his father, and in respect thereof he pays per annum to St Mary's Church 3d., and to the heirs of the said Radulph ½d.

[451] The same Simon holds 3 half acres of land in the fields of Cambridge which descended to him by inheritance through the death of Reynard, his brother, which same Reynard acquired those by inheritance through the death of John, his father, which same John bought those from Cassandria Astines, which same Cassandria acquired those by hereditary right through the death of Godfrey, her brother, which same Godfrey acquired those by inheritance through the death of Warin Astin, his father, and in respect thereof he pays per annum to the heirs of the said Cassandria 2½d.

[452] The same Simon holds 2 acres of land in the same fields which descended to him by hereditary right through the death of Reynard, his brother, which same Reynard acquired those by inheritance through the death of John de Bradele, his father, which same John bought those from Cassandria Astin, which same Cassandria acquired those by inheritance through the death of Godfrey, her brother, and the same Godfrey acquired those by inheritance through the death of Warin Astin, his father, and in respect thereof he pays per annum to the heirs of the said Cassandria 2d.

[453] Johanna daughter of William Braci holds 1 messuage in the parish of All Saints at the Castle, which she acquired by gift of William Braci, her father, in frank marriage, which same William acquired that by gift of Cecil at the Castle, and she pays in respect thereof per annum to the scholars of Merton 12d.

[454] John son of Richard Gregory holds 1 messuage with appurtenances in the parish of St John's, Cambridge, which same messuage descended to him by hereditary right through

the death of Richard, son of Gregory, his father, which same Richard acquired that in frank marriage with Matilda, his wife, by gift of Robert of St Edmunds, father of the said Matilda, which same Robert bought that from Peter son of Radulph, which same Peter acquired that by inheritance through the death of Radulph son of Ivo, his father, which same Ivo bought that from the prioress and nuns of St Radegund's, and in respect thereof he pays per annum to the said prioress and nuns 4s. 6d., and to the heirs of Robert of St Edmunds 1d., in which way and by which warranty the said prioress and nuns are unaware of any claim to the said messuage.

[455] Adam son of William, burgess of Cambridge, holds 1 messuage in the parish of St Michael's which same messuage descended to him by hereditary right through the death of William, his father, which same William bought that from Sewell Cog, and the same Sewell acquired that by ancient purchase, and in respect thereof he pays per annum to the prior of Thremhall 3s. by assignment of John de Engayne who is tenant-in-chief of that fief who gave the said income to the said prior.

[456] The same Adam holds a piece of vacant land in the same parish which descended to him by hereditary right through the death of William, his father, which same bought that from Leon Dunning, which same Leon acquired that by hereditary right through the death of Adam Dunning, his father, and in respect thereof he pays per annum to the said Leon 2d.

[457] The same Adam holds 1 messuage with appurtenances in the parish of St Benedict's which same messuage he bought from Walter Hein, which same Walter acquired that by hereditary right through the death of Robert Eim, his father, and in respect thereof he pays per annum to the heirs of the said Walter 8d.

[458] The same Adam holds 1 acre of land in the fields of Cambridge which he bought from Master Nicholas de Totington, which same Master Nicholas bought that from Matilda, daughter of Robert of St Edmunds which same Matilda acquired that by gift of Robert, her father, and in respect thereof he pays per annum to the said Matilda and her heirs ½d.

[459] Simon son of Simon ad Aquam holds in fee 1 messuage in the parish of St John's, Cambridge, which descended to him by hereditary right through the death of the said Simon, his father, which same Simon bought that from the prioress and nuns of St Radegund's and in respect thereof he pays per annum to the said prioress and nuns 1 mark, in which way the said prioress

and convent are unaware of any claim to the said messuage and by which warranty.

[460] The same Simon holds in fee 1 messuage in the parish of St Botolph's which descended to him by inheritance through the death of the said Simon, his father, which same Simon bought that from William de Ickleton and from Margaret, his wife, which same Margaret acquired that by hereditary right through the death of Reginald Attegate, paying in respect thereof per annum to the said Reginald and Margaret and their heirs ½d., and to the prior and convent of Barnwell 12d., in which way the said prior and convent are unaware of any claim to the said income or by which warranty.

[461] The same Simon holds 1 messuage in fee in the parish of St Botolph's, which descended to him by hereditary right through the death of Simon, his father, which same Simon bought that from Richard de Shelford, chaplain, which same Richard bought that from Bartholomew son of John, and in respect thereof he pays per annum to the said Richard and his heirs 1 clove gillyflower, and to the prior of Barnwell and the convent 2s. 6d., and to the bailiffs of Cambridge who hold the said town in fee farm etcetera for hawgable 1½d., moreover the said prior and convent are unaware of any claim to the said income.

[462] The same Simon holds 2 acres of land and ½ acre and 1 rood in the fields of Cambridge which descended to him by hereditary right through the death of Simon, his father, which same Simon acquired those from Leon Dunning, which same Leon acquired those by inheritance through the death of Adam, his father, and in respect thereof he pays per annum to the said Leon 2d.

[463] The same Simon holds 2 acres of land in the same fields which descended to him by inheritance through the death of the said Simon, his father, which same Simon bought those from the said Leon, which same Leon acquired those by inheritance through the death of Adam, his father and in respect thereof he pays per annum to the said Leon 2d.

[464] The same Simon holds a ½ acre of land in the same fields which descended to him by hereditary right through the death of Simon, his father, which same Simon bought that from Robert de Houghton, which same Robert acquired that by ancient heritage of his ancestors, and in respect thereof he pays per annum to the heirs of the said Robert ½d.

[465] The same Simon holds 3 half acres of land in the same fields which descended to him by hereditary right through the death of

Simon, his father, which same Simon bought those from William son of Elena Ampe, and the same William acquired those by inheritance through the death of the said Elena, his mother, in respect thereof he pays per annum to the heirs of the said William ½d., and to the bailiffs of Cambridge who hold the said town in fee farm etcetera for landgable 1½d.

[466] The same Simon holds 2 acres of land in the same fields which descended to him by inheritance through the death of the said Simon, his father, and the same Simon bought those from Nicholas Childman, and the same Nicholas acquired those by hereditary right through the death of Childman, his father, and in respect thereof he pays per annum to the heirs of the said Nicholas 2d.

[467] The same Simon holds 2 acres of land and a ½ acre in the said fields which descended to him by hereditary right through the death of Simon, his father, which same Simon bought those from Cassandria daughter of Warin Astin, and the same Cassandria acquired those by inheritance through the death of Godfrey Astin, her brother, and in respect thereof he pays per annum to the heirs of the said Cassandria 2½d.

[468] The same Simon holds a ½ acre of land in the same fields which descended to him by hereditary right through the death of Simon, his father, which same Simon bought that from William Wisman, and the same William acquired that from ancient heritage of his ancestors, and in respect thereof he pays per annum to the heirs of the said William ½d.

[469] Richard de Hockley holds 1 messuage with appurtenances in the parish of St John's in Mill Lane which he bought from Robert Huberd and from Sabina, his wife, and the said Robert and Sabina, his wife, acquired that by gift of Robert, son of the said Robert, which same Robert acquired that by hereditary right through the death of Cecilia Godsho, and in respect thereof he pays per annum to the said Robert and Sabina, his wife, and their heirs 16s., and to the bailiffs of Cambridge who hold the said town in fee farm etcetera for hawgable 2½d.

[470] The same Richard holds 1 messuage in the parish of St Mary's which he acquired by gift of John de Bradele in frank marriage with Avicia, his wife, daughter of the said John, which same John bought that from Walter son of Radulph Mun, and the same Walter acquired that by inheritance through the death of Radulph Mun, his father, and in respect thereof he pays per annum to the heirs of the said John ½d., and to St Mary's Church 4d.

[471] The same Richard holds a granary in the parish of All Saints next to the Hospital, which William son of Ivo gave to the said Richard, his son, for his service, which same William bought that from Leon Dunning, and in respect thereof he pays per annum to the heirs of the said William ½d., and to Leon Dunning ½d.

[472] The same Richard holds 1 messuage in the parish of St John's, which he bought from John Ace, which same John acquired that by hereditary right through the death of John Ace, his father, which same John bought that from Lecia de Eltisley, and the said Lecia acquired that through the death of her ancestors, and he pays in respect thereof per annum to the heirs of John Ace ½d., and to the prioress of St Radegund's 4s., in which manner the said prioress is unaware of any claim to the said income, and by which warranty.

[473] The same Richard holds 1 messuage in the said parish which he bought from Robert de Bradele, which same Robert bought that from John ad Aquam, which same John acquired that by gift of Simon ad Aquam, his brother, and the said Simon bought that from Lecia de Eltisley, which same Lecia acquired that by hereditary right through the death of her ancestors, and in respect thereof he pays per annum to the said Lecia 3s., and to Robert of Bradley 1d., and to John ad Aquam 1d., and to the bailiffs of Cambridge who hold the said town in fee farm etcetera for hawgable 1d.

[474] The same Richard holds 1 acre of land in the fields of Cambridge which he bought from William son of Ivo, his father, which same William bought that from Eustace Dunning, and in respect thereof he pays per annum to the scholars of Merton 1d.

[475] The same Richard holds 1 acre and a ½ acre and 1 rood of land in the fields of Cambridge which he bought from Johanna, daughter of William son of Ivo, which same Johanna acquired those by gift of the said William son of Ivo, and the same William bought those from Eustace Dunning, and in respect thereof he pays per annum to the heirs of the said Johanna 2d.

[476] The same Richard holds 1 half acre of land in the same fields which he bought from Margaret daughter of Richard de Stowe, which same Margaret acquired that by gift of the said Richard de Stowe, her father, and the same Richard bought that from Eustace Dunning, and in respect thereof he pays per annum on behalf of the heirs of the said Margaret to the scholars of Merton ½d.

[477] The same Richard holds a certain piece of land of the same curtilage in the parish of St John's which he bought from

Robert Wulward, which same Robert acquired that by gift of Roger Wulward, his brother, which same Roger acquired that by hereditary right through the death of Martin Wulward, his father, and in respect thereof he pays per annum to the said Robert 1[70]d.

[478]   Item Simon son of Richard de Hockley holds 4 acres of land and a ½ acre and 1 rood in the fields of Cambridge which he acquired by gift of Richard de Hockley, his father, which same Richard bought those from John Porthors, which same John acquired those by gift of the prior and convent of Barnwell, in which manner the said prior and convent are unaware of any claim to the said land, and in respect thereof he pays per annum to the said Richard and his heirs 1 rose and to John Porthors and his heirs 1d.

[479]   Item Simon son of Richard de Hockley holds 1 messuage in the parish of St John's which he acquired by gift of the said Richard, his father, which same Richard bought that from Robert Wulward, and the same Robert acquired that by gift of Roger Wulward, his father, which same Roger bought that at one time from Martin Wulward, his father, and in respect thereof he pays per annum to the said Richard, his father and his heirs 1 rose and to Robert Wulward and his heirs 1d.

[480]   Item Robert and Simon sons of Richard de Hockley hold 2 acres of land in the fields of Cambridge which they acquired by gift of the said Richard, their father, which same Richard bought those from Luke of St Edmunds, and the same Luke acquired those by inheritance through the death of Thomas, his brother, which same Thomas acquired those by gift of Walter, his father, which same Walter acquired those from ancient heritage, and in respect thereof they pay per annum to the said Luke 4d.

[481]   Item Richard de Hockley and Eva, his wife, hold 2 acres of land in the fields of Barnwell which Thomas, labourer, and Agnes, his wife gave to the said Eva, which same Thomas and Agnes acquired by gift of Robert de Madingley, father of the said Agnes, which same Robert bought that from Leon Dunning, and in respect thereof they pay per annum to the heirs of Robert de Madingley 1 rose and to the said Leon and his heirs 4d.

[482]   Item Richard and Eva, his wife, hold 1 messuage in the parish of St Michael's, which descended to the said Eva by hereditary right through the death of Geoffrey, her brother, which same Geoffrey bought that from Bartholomew, son of Harvey Wombe, which same Bartholomew bought that from Alicia, his mother,

and in respect thereof they pay per annum to the heirs of the said Bartholomew 1d.

[483] Item Robert le Steresman holds 1 messuage in the parish of St John's which descended to him heritage through the death of Robert le Steresman, his father, and the same Robert acquired that by hereditary right through the death of Roger le Steresman, his father, which same Roger acquired that by hereditary right through the death of Alicia Thorel, and said Alicia acquired that by ancient succession of her ancestors, and in respect thereof he pays per annum to the heirs of the said Alicia Thorel 3s., and to the heirs of Reginald de St Ives 1½d., and to the heirs of Simon Godeman 12d., and to the bailiffs of Cambridge who hold the town in fee farm etcetera for hawgable 1 farthing.

[484] The same Robert holds 2 acres of land in the fields of Cambridge which he acquired by gift of Nicholas son of Simon Baker, which same Nicholas bought that from the said Simon, his father, and the same Simon bought that from Leon Dunning, and in respect thereof he pays per annum on behalf of the heirs of the said Nicholas to the said Leon 1d.

[485] Item Simon Scan and Cassandria, his wife, hold 1 messuage with appurtenances in the parish of St John's, which descended to the said Cassandria by inheritance through the death of Golde Bassat, her brother, which same Golde bought that from John, son of Matthew le Hanre, which same John held that by gift of Matthew le Hanre, his father, which same Matthew bought that from William Saphir, and in respect thereof they pay per annum to the heirs of William Saphir ½d., and to the bailiffs of Cambridge who hold the said town in fee farm etcetera for hawgable 4d.

[486] Item Simon and Cassandria, his wife, hold 1 messuage in the same parish which descended to the said Cassandria by inheritance through the death of Golde, her brother, which same Golde bought that from William son of Johanna Purdew, which same Johanna acquired that from ancient succession of her parents, and in respect thereof they pay per annum to the heirs of the said Johanna ½d., and to the bailiffs of Cambridge who hold the said town in fee farm etcetera for hawgable 1 farthing.

[487] Item Simon and Cassandria hold 1 acre of land in the fields of Cambridge which descended to the said Cassandria by inheritance through the death of the said Golde, her brother, and the same Golde bought that from Richard son of Gregory le Savener, which same Richard acquired that by inheritance

through the death of Gregory, his father, and the same Gregory bought that from Leon Dunning and the same Leon acquired that by inheritance through the death of Adam, his father, and in respect thereof they pay per annum to the heirs of the said Richard ½d., and the heirs of the said Richard pay the said ½d. to the said Leon Dunning as tenant-in-chief.

[488]   Item Simon and Cassandria, his wife, hold 1 acre of land in the fields of Barnwell which descended to the said Cassandria by inheritance through the death of the said Golde, her brother, which same Golde bought from Nicholas Malerbe, which same Nicholas acquired that by inheritance through the death of Michael Malerbe, his father, and in respect thereof they pay per annum to the heirs of Nicholas Malerbe 1d.

[489]   Item Simon and Cassandria, his wife, hold 3 half acres of land in the fields of Barnwell which descended to the said Cassandria by inheritance through the death of the said Golde, her brother, which same Golde bought those from Cassandria Astins, which same Cassandria acquired those by inheritance through the death of her ancestors, and in respect thereof they pay per annum to Roger, chaplain, nephew of Master Nigel, 1½d.

[490]   Item Simon and Cassandria, his wife, hold 1 rood in the said fields which descended to the said Cassandria by inheritance through the death of the said Golde, her brother, which same Golde bought that from Hugh Findesilver, which same Hugh acquired that by purchase from Walter de Stapelford, and in respect thereof they pay per annum on behalf of the heirs of the said Hugh and Walter to Luke of St Edmunds 3d.

[491]   Item Roger de Redlingfield, chaplain, holds 1 messuage in parish of St John's Cambridge with 26 acres of land pertaining to the said messuage which same messuage and said land he acquired by gift of Master Nigel, doctor, his uncle, and the same Master Nigel at one time bought that messuage with the said land from Cassandria, daughter of Cristiana Warin, which said Cassandria acquired that messuage and said land by hereditary right through the death of Godfrey Astin, her brother, and in respect thereof he pays per annum to Robert Quintin of Newport 4s. 5½d., and to the bailiffs who hold the said town in fee farm etcetera for hawgable 6s. 6d.

[492]   The same Roger holds 1 messuage in the same parish which he bought from the parishioners of St Clement's and it is called Dagenhale and in respect thereof he pays per annum to St Clement's Church ½d.

[493]   The same Roger holds 1 messuage in the parish of St Mary's which was formerly of the Church of the Brothers of Penitence of Jesus Christ, which same they acquired by gift of the said Master Nigel, his uncle, and the same Master Nigel bought that from Richard Carloc, and in respect thereof he pays to the bailiffs of Cambridge who hold the said town in fee farm etcetera for hawgable ½d.

[494]   Item John of Barking, chaplain, holds 1 messuage with appurtenances in the parish of St John's outside Trumpington Gate, which he bought from Alicia, daughter of William Lucke, miller, which same Alicia acquired that by hereditary right through the death of John, her brother and the said John acquired that by inheritance through the death of the said William, his father, and the said William bought that from Thomas Elyot, and the said Thomas acquired that from ancient hereditary succession, and in respect thereof he pays per annum to the said Thomas and his heirs 4s.

[495]   The same John holds 1 acre of land in the fields of Cambridge, which he bought from the said Alicia daughter of William Lucke, which same Alicia acquired that by inheritance through the death of John, her brother, which same John acquired that through the death of the said William, his father, and the said William bought that from Leon Dunning, and the said Leon acquired that from ancient heritage, and in respect thereof he pays per annum to the said Leon 1d.

[496]   Item Alicia daughter of William Lucke holds 1 messuage in Landgrythes Lane in the parish of St Botolph's, which she acquired by hereditary right through the death of the said John, her brother, which same John acquired that by inheritance through the death of the said William, his father, and the said William bought that from Jacob son of William Miller, which same Jacob acquired that by hereditary right through the descent of William, his brother, and the said William acquired that by gift of Cristiana Deudeners, and the said Cristiana bought that from Robert de Hauxton, and in respect thereof she pays per annum to the heirs of the said Robert 10s., and to the prior of Barnwell 18d., by which warranty they are unaware of any claim to the said income.

[497]   Item Master Nicholas de Totington holds 1 messuage in Straw Lane in the parish of St John's, Cambridge, which same he bought from Helewisa and Margaret, daughters of John Ace, which same they acquired by gift of Elena daughter of Richard

son of Ivo, their mother, and the said Elena acquired that by gift of the said Richard, her father, in frank marriage and in respect thereof he pays per annum to the heirs of the said Helewisa and Margaret 1d., and to the bailiffs of Cambridge who hold the town in fee farm etcetera for hawgable 1d.

[498]   The said Master Nicholas holds a piece of vacant land next to his said messuage which he bought from Simon Godeman and extended it from the granary of Walter Em to the messuage which was of Thomas Wulward, and is 10 foot in width, for which he pays per annum to the prior of Barnwell 12d., by which warranty they are unaware of any claim to the said income, and he holds the granary from the heirs of Simon Godeman and in respect thereof he pays per annum to the said heirs 1d.

[499]   The same Master Nicholas holds another messuage in the same lane which same he bought from Thomas of Samford, vicar of Waledene, which same Thomas bought that from Richard son of Ivo, and the said Richard acquired that from ancient purchase, and in respect thereof he pays per annum to the said Thomas de Sanford 1 rose and to the heirs of Richard son of Ivo 4s. 2d.

[500]   Item the Abbot of Warden holds 1 messuage in the parish of St John's Cambridge, which same messuage he bought from Nicholas of Hitchin, cleric, which same Nicholas acquired that by gift of Master Nicholas of Hitchin, his uncle, and the same Master Nicholas bought that from Master Bartholomew de Lardario, which same Master Bartholomew acquired that by gift of Master Stephen de Lardario, his father, and the same Master Stephen acquired that by ancient purchase, and in respect thereof he pays per annum to the bailiffs of Cambridge who hold the said town in fee farm by gift of the king as is stated, for hawgable 1½d.

[501]   The Abbot of Tilty holds 1 messuage in the parish of St John's which he bought from Philip le Burgelun, cleric, which same Stephen held that by inheritance through the death of William Burgelun, his brother, and the said William bought that from William Seman of Newnham, which same William acquired that by hereditary right through the death of Seman, his father, and the said Seman acquired that by ancient succession of his ancestors, and in respect thereof he pays per annum to the bailiffs of Cambridge who hold the said town in fee farm from the Lord King as is stated for hawgable 1d.

[502]   Item John Auwre holds 1 messuage with appurtenances in the parish of St John's, Cambridge, which same messuage Johanna

Potekine gave to the same John and surrendered before the justice of the Lord King at Woodstock, and the said Johanna acquired that messuage by gift of Alicia Potekyne, her mother, and the said Alicia acquired that messuage by gift of Simon Auwre, her brother, and the said Simon acquired that messuage by gift of Reginald Auwre, his father, for which he pays per annum to the bailiffs of the Lord King who hold the same town of Cambridge in fee farm etcetera for hawgable 2d.

[503]   Item the same John holds 1 messuage with appurtenances in the parish of St Botolph's, Cambridge, which same messuage descended to the said John by inheritance through the death of John Auwre, his father, which same messuage descended to the said John through the death of Reginald, his father, and the said Reginald acquired that through the death of Auwre le Draper, his father, and he pays in respect thereof per annum to the bailiffs of the Lord King who hold the said town of Cambridge in fee farm from the Lord King etcetera for hawgable 4d.

[504]   Item Master William le Blunt holds 1 messuage in the parish of St Botolph's, which same he acquired by gift of the prior of Ely, and he pays in respect thereof per annum to the heirs of Master Eustace de Shelford 28d., and to the bailiffs of Cambridge who hold the same town of Cambridge in fee farm from the Lord King etcetera for hawgable 2d.

[505]   Item Isabella Morini holds in fee 1 messuage in the parish of St Edward's, which same messuage John, chaplain, son and heir of Aubrey Butcher, gave to the said Isabella until the end of her life, which same descended to the said John by inheritance through the death of the said Aubrey, his father, which same Aubrey acquired that by hereditary right through the death of Geoffrey, son of John Selede, and in respect thereof she pays per annum on behalf of the heirs of the said John, chaplain, to the prioress of St Radegund's 2s., by which warranty the said prioress is unaware of any claim to the said income.

[506]   Item the same Isabella holds 1 messuage in the same parish which same said John, chaplain, gave to the said Isabella, which same John acquired that by hereditary right through the death of the said Aubrey, his father, and the same Aubrey acquired that from William Pruet, and the same William acquired that by acquisition, and in respect thereof she pays per annum on behalf of the said John and his heirs to the prioress of St Radegund's 4s., by which warranty the said prioress is unaware of any claim to the said income.

[507]   Item the same Isabella holds 1 messuage in the same parish which
         she acquired by gift of John, chaplain, son of the said Aubrey,
         which same John acquired that by hereditary right through the
         death of the said Aubrey, his father, which same Aubrey bought
         that from William Pruet, which same William acquired that by
         acquisition as a purchase and in respect thereof pays per annum
         on behalf of the said John and his heirs to the prior and convent
         of Barnwell 4s., by which warranty the said prior is unaware of
         any claim to the said income.

[508]   Item the same Isabella holds 1 stall in the same parish which
         descended to her by inheritance through the death of Richard
         Morin, her father, which same Richard bought that from William
         Pruet, which same William acquired that by acquisition, and
         in respect thereof she pays per annum to Saer son of William
         Dencot 4s. 4d.

[509]   Item Isabella holds 2 acres and 1 rood of land in the fields of
         Cambridge which she acquired by gift of the said John, chaplain,
         which same John acquired that through the death of Aubrey, his
         father, which same Aubrey bought that from William son of Ivo,
         for which she pays per annum to Agnes of Barton and her heirs
         7d.

[510]   Item the same Isabella holds 1 acre of land in the fields of
         Barnwell, which she acquired by gift of the said John, chaplain,
         which same John acquired that by hereditary right through the
         death of the said Aubrey, his father, and the same Aubrey bought
         that from Matilda Aleyns, which same Matilda acquired that
         through the death of her father and in respect thereof she pays
         per annum to the heirs of the said Matilda 1 pair of gloves, and to
         the bailiffs of Cambridge who hold the same town of Cambridge
         in fee farm etcetera for landgable 1d.

[511]   Item the same Isabella holds ½ acre of land in the fields of
         Cambridge which descended to her by inheritance through
         the death of Edwina, widow of Richard Morin, which same
         Edwina acquired that by ancient succession of her ancestors, and
         in respect thereof she pays per annum to the bailiffs of Cambridge
         who hold the same town of Cambridge in fee farm etcetera for
         landgable 1 farthing.

[512]   Item Alan de Snailwell holds 1 messuage in the parish of
         St Edward's which he bought from John Sadelbowe, which same
         John acquired that by gift of Mabilia de Histon, his mother,
         which same Mabilia acquired that by gift of Master John
         de Histon, cleric, and in respect thereof he pays per annum to

the heirs of the said John 1d., and to the almoner of Ely 2s., by which warranty the almoner is unaware of any claim to the said income.

[513]   The same Alan holds a piece of land with a house above being in the parish of St Benedict's, which he bought from Radulph de Comberton and from Agnes, his wife, and the said Radulph and Agnes bought that from Alicia, daughter of Benedict Merchant, which same Alicia acquired that by hereditary right through the death of Cassandria Astin, her mother, and in respect thereof he pays per annum to the said Radulph and Agnes his wife 1d.

[514]   The same Alan holds a piece of land with a house above being in the parish of St Edward's, which he bought from Richard son of Gregory le Savener, which same Richard acquired that by hereditary right through the death of Gregory, his father, and in respect thereof he pays per annum on behalf of the heirs of the said Richard to Nicholas Morice 2s.

[515]   Item John de Westwick holds 1 messuage in the parish of St Edward's which he bought from Nicholas beyond the market and from Thomas his son and heir, which same messuage descended to the said Nicholas by hereditary right through the death of William, his father, which same messuage the said William bought from Stephen le Cordewener, and in respect thereof he pays per annum to William de Comberton 3s., and to the bailiffs of Cambridge who hold the same town of Cambridge in fee farm etcetera for hawgable 1d.

[516]   Item the same John and Sabina, his wife, hold 1 messuage in the same parish which same they acquired by gift of Simon son of Nicholas beyond the market, which same Simon acquired that by gift of Nicholas, his father, and in respect thereof they pay per annum to the said Simon 10s., and to the heirs of Robert Seman 12d.

[517]   Item the same John holds 1 acre of land in the fields of Barnwell, which he bought from Nicholas beyond the market, and from Thomas his son and heir, which same land Michael Gogging gave to the said Nicholas in frank marriage with his wife, and in respect thereof he pays per annum to the heirs of the said Michael 2d.

[518]   The same John holds a piece of vacant land in the parish of St Botolph's, which he bought from Nicholas beyond the market and from Thomas his son and heir, which same land the said Nicholas acquired by gift of Michael Gogging in frank marriage

with his daughter Margaret, and in respect thereof he pays per annum to the heirs of the said Michael ½d.

[519]   Item Margaret daughter of Nicholas beyond the market holds 1 messuage in the parish of St Edward's and a ½ acre of land pertaining to the said messuage lying in Swinecroft, which same messuage with land Margaret, widow of Michael Gogging, gave and granted by charter to Margaret, daughter of the said Nicholas, which same Margaret acquired that by hereditary right through the death of Richard Attegate, her father, and in respect thereof she pays per annum to the heirs of the said Michael 1 rose and to the almoner of Ely 27d., by which warranty the almoner is unaware of any claim to the said income.

[520]   Item William Paris holds 1 messuage in the parish of St Edward's which he acquired by gift of Thomas Spileman and Margaret, his mother, which same descended to the said Thomas by inheritance through the death of Henry Spileman, his father, and in respect thereof he pays per annum to the said Margaret 1 clove gillyflower, and to Master Robert Aunger 11d., and to the heirs of Richard son of Gregory 2d., and to the almoner of Ely 2s. 6d., by which warranty the almoner is unaware of any claim to the said income.

[521]   The same William holds 1 messuage with croft in the town of Barnwell which he bought from John de Fordham, which same John bought that from Robert Cook, and in respect thereof he pays per annum to the heirs of the said John 1 rose and to the heirs of the said Robert 1 peppercorn, and to Leon Dunning 5d., and to William de Novacurt 6d.

[522]   Item Derota daughter of Nicholas beyond the market holds 1 messuage in the parish of St Edward's which she acquired by gift of Nicholas, her father, which same Nicholas bought that from Mabilia and Matilda and Alvena, daughters and heirs of Richemann le Savener, which same messuage descended to the same by hereditary right through the death of Richemann, their father, and in respect thereof she pays per annum to the heirs of the said Richemann 1 pair of gloves at the price of ½d., and to the almoner of Ely 3s., by which warranty the almoner is unaware of any claim to the said income.

[523]   Item Radulph Scutard holds 1 messuage in the parish of St Edward's which he bought from Gilbert son of Michael Bernard, which same Gilbert acquired that by inheritance through the death of Michael, his father, which same Michael bought that from Robert le Ke, butcher, and the said Robert

acquired that by ancient acquisition, and he pays in respect thereof per annum to Gilbert Bernard 7s.

[524]   The same Radulph holds 1 shop in the parish of St Mary's which he bought from Deonisia, sister of Aspelon Odierne, which same Deonisia acquired that by hereditary right through the death of her brother, and the said Aspelon bought that from the nuns of St Mary de Pré, and in respect thereof he pays per annum to the said nuns 2s., and to the bailiffs of Cambridge who hold the same town of Cambridge in fee farm for hawgable 2d., by which warranty the nuns are unaware of any claim to the said income.

[525]   Item Alan Scutard and Margaret, his wife, hold 1 shop in the parish of St Edward's which they bought from Henry of Norwich, cleric, and the same Henry acquired that by gift of Alicia daughter of Peter Makeston, which same Alicia bought that from John Makeston, her brother, and the said John acquired that through the death of Peter Makeston, his father, and the said Peter bought that from Lord William Grim, chaplain, and in respect thereof they pay per annum to the said Henry 1 pair of gloves at the price of ½d., and to the prioress of St Radegund's 6s., by which warranty the prioress is unaware of any claim to the said income.

[526]   Item Alan and Margaret hold 1 messuage in the parish of St Andrew's which descended to the said Margaret by inheritance through the death of Roger Ethun, her father, which same Roger acquired that by inheritance through the death of Eudo Glover, his father, and the same Eudo bought that from Harvey son of Eustace, which same Havey acquired that by ancient acquisition, and in respect thereof they pay per annum to Richard son of Lord John de Scalar' of Thriplow 11d.

[527]   Item William Ide holds 1 shop in the parish of St Edward's which descended to him by hereditary right through the death of Henry de Harleston, his father, which same Henry bought that from William Baker, and the same William bought that from John son of Hugh, and the same John bought that from Ysandus son of Lewyn, and in respect thereof he pays per annum to the heirs of Lewin 3s., and to the almoner of Ely 7d., by which warranty the almoner is unaware of any claim to the said income.

[528]   Item John le Franceys and Margaret, his wife, hold 1 messuage in which they live until the end of their lives in the parish of St Edward's, which they have by gift of the abbot and convent of Tilty, which same abbot and convent acquired that messuage by gift of the said John and Margaret through a deed issued in

the court of the lord, which same Margaret acquired that same messuage by hereditary right through the death of Alicia Scolice, her mother, which same Alicia acquired that by hereditary right through the death of her ancestors, and in respect thereof they pay per annum to the bailiffs of Cambridge who hold the said town in fee farm etcetera for hawgable 1d. by assignment of the abbot and convent.

[529]   Item the said John and Margaret his wife hold 1 messuage in the parish of St Mary's, Cambridge, which same messuage the said Margaret bought from Robert de Houghton, which same Robert acquired that by hereditary right through the death of Robert de Houghton, his father, which same Robert acquired that by ancient acquisition, and in respect thereof they pay per annum to the heirs of the said Robert 7s.

[530]   Item John and Margaret hold a piece of vacant land in the same parish which the said Margaret bought from Master Thomas of St Edmunds, which same he acquired by gift of Walter, his father, which same Walter acquired that by ancient hereditary succession of his ancestors, and in respect thereof they pay per annum to Luke of St Edmunds ½ mark.

[531]   Item John and Margaret hold 1 messuage in the parish of St Andrew's which descended to the said Margaret by hereditary right through the death of Alicia Scolice, her mother, which same Alicia acquired that by hereditary right through the death of Matilda Scolice, her mother, which same Matilda acquired that by ancient succession of her ancestors, and in respect thereof they pay per annum to the Bishop of Ely 18d., by which warranty the Bishop is unaware of any claim to the said income.

[532]   Item John and Margaret his wife hold 1 messuage in the parish of Holy Trinity which descended to the said Margaret by inheritance through the death of the said Alicia, her mother, which same Alicia acquired that through ancient hereditary succession of her parents, and in respect thereof they pay per annum to the heirs of Robert de Houghton 16d., and to the bailiffs of Cambridge who hold the said town in fee farm etcetera for hawgable 1d.

[533]   Item Roger de Wilburham holds 1 messuage in the parish of St Edward's until the end of his life, which same messuage descended to Agnes, his former wife, by inheritance through the death of Richard Morin, her father, which same Richard acquired that by hereditary right through the death of Geoffrey Morin, his brother, which same Geoffrey acquired that by inheritance through the death of Radulph Morin, his father,

and the said Radulph acquired that by ancient succession of his ancestors, and in respect thereof he pays per annum to Saer of Trumpington 2s. 6d., and for a light of the Holy Mary in St Mary's Church 10d., and to the bailiffs of Cambridge who hold the said town in fee farm etcetera for hawgable 2d.

[534] The same Roger holds ½ acre of land in the fields of Cambridge which descended to the said Agnes, his wife, by inheritance through the death of Richard Morin, her father, and the said Richard acquired that by hereditary right through the death of Geoffrey, his brother, which same Geoffrey acquired that through the death of Radulph Morin, his father, which same Radulph acquired that by ancient heritage of his ancestors, and in respect thereof he pays per annum to the heirs of Richard of Barton 1 lb. of cumin, and to the bailiffs of Cambridge who hold the said town in fee farm etcetera for landgable 1 farthing.

[535] Item John le Barbur and Avicia, his wife, hold 1 messuage in the parish of St Edward's until the end of their lives and of their sons that they will have, which same they acquired by gift of the brothers of St John's Hospital, Cambridge and the said brothers acquired that from Emma Scan, and the said Emma formerly acquired that from the said brothers, and in respect thereof they pay per annum to the said brothers 8s.

[536] Item Thomas, son of Edmund Miller, holds 3 shops in the market place of Cambridge in the parish of St Edward's, which he bought from William Toylet, which same William bought from Richard son of Richard of Newnham, which same Richard acquired those by inheritance through the death of Walter, cleric, his father, which same Walter acquired those by ancient purchase, and in respect thereof he pays per annum to the heirs of the said William 10s., paid annually.

[537] The same Thomas holds another shop in the same parish which he acquired by gift of Robert Wulward, which same Robert acquired that by hereditary right through the death of Martin Wulward, his father, which same Martin acquired that from ancient hereditary succession, and in respect thereof he pays per annum to the said Robert as long as he should live 9s., and to Margaret, daughter of the said Robert 12d., and to the bailiffs of Cambridge who hold the said town in fee farm etcetera for hawgable 8d.

[538] The same Thomas holds 2 shops in the said parish which he bought from John Aure, which same John acquired those by hereditary right through the death of John son of Reginald Aure,

and the said John acquired those by hereditary right through the death of the said Reginald, his father, and in respect thereof he pays per annum to the said John 2s.

[539]   Item Michael son of Julian Pageley holds 1 shop which descended to him by inheritance through the death of Juliana, his mother, which same Juliana bought that from Ernest, her brother, which same Ernest acquired that by inheritance through the death of his ancestors, and in respect thereof he pays per annum to St Mary's Church, namely for a light 34d., to the bailiffs of Cambridge who hold the said town in fee farm etcetera for hawgable 2d., and to St Edward's Church 12d.

[540]   Item the same Michael holds 1 shop in the same parish which descended to him by inheritance through the death of Juliana, his mother, which same Juliana bought that from Ernest, her brother, which same Ernest acquired that by inheritance through the death of his ancestors, and in respect thereof he pays per annum to St John's Hospital, Cambridge, 1d.

[541]   Item Thomas son of Edmund Miller, holds 1 messuage in the parish of St John's, Cambridge, which he acquired by gift of Robert Wulward with Margaret daughter of the said Robert in frank marriage, which same Robert acquired that through the death of his ancestors, and in respect thereof he pays per annum to the nuns of St Radegund's 20d. by assignment of the said Robert.

[542]   The same Thomas holds 1 messuage in the parish of St Peter's outside Trumpington Gate which he bought from Richard Timpon, which same Richard acquired that by inheritance through the death of William Timpon, his father, and the said William acquired that by ancient purchase, and in respect thereof he pays per annum to the nuns of St Radegund's 4d., and to St John's Hospital, Cambridge, 4d. by assignment of the said William father of the said Richard.

[543]   Item Robert Karun holds 1 messuage in the parish of St Edward's which same messuage descended to him by hereditary right through the death of Nichola, his mother, which same Nichola acquired the said messuage by gift of Robert Seman, her father, in frank marriage, which same Robert acquired that by inheritance through the death of Walter Wimund, his father, which same Walter acquired that by ancient purchase, and he pays in respect thereof per annum to the heirs of Robert Seman 14s. 8½d., and 2 lb. of pepper and 1 lb. of cumin for the said messuage.

[544]   Item Nicholas Goldsmith, holds in fee 1 messuage in the parish of St Mary's Cambridge, which same messuage he bought

from Henry Nado, and that Henry acquired that by hereditary succession through the death of Robert Nado, his father, and the said Robert acquired that by ancient acquisition, for which he pays per annum through the heirs of the said Henry to John de Standon and his heirs 6s., to the bailiffs of Cambridge who hold the said town in fee farm etcetera to their farm 1d.

[545] Item Nicholas holds 1 shop in the same parish which he bought from Henry Nado and that Henry acquired that by inheritance through the death of Robert, his father, and that Robert acquired that by ancient acquisition, and he pays in respect thereof to William de Novacurt and his heirs 14d.

[546] The same Nicholas holds 1 messuage in the same parish which he bought from Jordan le Skinner and from Cecilia, his wife, which messuage descended to the said Cecilia by inheritance through the death of Geoffrey Achelard, his father, and that Geoffrey acquired that by inheritance through the death of Achelard, his father from ancient succession, and in respect thereof he pays per annum to the said Jordan and Cecilia his wife ½d. and to the bailiffs of Cambridge who hold the said town in fee farm etcetera to their farm 2d.

[547] Reginald de Comberton holds 1 messuage in the parish of St Mary's which he bought from Roger de Wilburham, and that Roger acquired that by gift of Johanna daughter of Geoffrey le Hanaper, and the said Johanna acquired that by inheritance through the death of the said Geoffrey, her father, and that Geoffrey acquired that from ancient acquisition namely by purchase, and in respect thereof he pays per annum to the said Roger and his heirs 1 rose, and to the heirs of Ernest Merchant, 2s., and to St Mary's Church 12d., and to the bailiffs of Cambridge who hold the said town in fee farm etcetera for their farm 1d.

[548] The same Reginald holds 1 messuage in the same parish in fee from St Radegund's which he bought from the prioress and convent of the same place, and in respect thereof he pays per annum to the heirs of Thomas Wulward 4s. 8d., and to the said prioress and convent 6d.

[549] The same Reginald holds 1 messuage in the parish of St Andrew's which he bought from Simon son of Simon Mundi of Barnwell, and that Henry bought that from John Curteys, and that John acquired that by ancient acquisition of his ancestors, and in respect thereof he pays per annum to the said Henry and his heirs ½d., and to the prior of Barnwell 12d., by which warranty

he is unaware, and to the bailiffs of Cambridge who hold the said town in fee farm etcetera for hawgable 1d.

[550] The same Reginald holds 1 messuage in the parish of St Michael's, Cambridge, which he bought from Geoffrey de Welles, chaplain, and the same Geoffrey acquired that by inheritance through the death of Catherine, his sister, and the same Catherine acquired that from hereditary succession through the death of John de Welles, her father, and that John acquired that from ancient hereditary succession, and he pays in respect thereof per annum to the said Geoffrey and his heirs 1 clove gillyflower, and to the prior of Barnwell 12d., by which warranty they are unaware, and to the bailiffs of Cambridge who hold the said town in fee farm as is stated for their farm 2d.

[551] The same Reginald holds 3 roods of land in the fields of Barnwell which he bought from John Crul, and the same John acquired those by inheritance of his ancestors, and in respect thereof he pays per annum to the said John and his heirs 4d. and 1 farthing.

[552] The same Reginald holds 1 acre of land in the fields of Cambridge which he bought from Richard Saverei of Cotes, and that Richard acquired that from ancient heritage, and in respect thereof he pays per annum to the said Richard and his heirs 1d.

[553] The same Reginald holds 2 acres of land in the fields of Cambridge which he bought from John Porthors, and that John bought those from the prior and convent of Barnwell, and in respect thereof he pays per annum to the said John and his heirs 6½d.

[554] The same John Balle of Cambridge holds 1 messuage in the parish of St Mary's which he acquired from Thomas Godeman with Alicia, his wife, in frank marriage, and the said John bought that from Roger son and heir of the said Alicia, and that descended to the said Roger by inheritance through the death of Alicia, his mother, and in respect thereof he pays per annum for the maintenance of a lamp in St Mary's Church 6d., and to the prioress of St Radegund's 3s., by which warranty they are unaware.

[555] The same John holds 1 messuage in the parish of St Andrew's, Cambridge, which he acquired by gift of Simon Bernard, and that Simon acquired that from Simon Flinston, and that Simon acquired that by ancient acquisition of his ancestors, and in respect thereof he pays per annum to the heirs of Simon Bernard 2s., and to the said Simon Flinston 2s.

[556]   Luke Carter holds in fee in the fields of Cambridge 3 acres of land which he bought from Margaret Henges, and the said Margaret acquired that by inheritance through the death of William, her brother, and that William acquired that from paternal succession through the death of William Henges, his father, and in respect thereof pays per annum to the said Margaret ½d., and to the prior of Barnwell 12d., by which warranty the said prior is unaware of any claim to the said income.

[557]   Item Alicia, sister of Ernest Merchant, holds 1 messuage in the parish of St Mary's which descended to her by inheritance through the death of Ernest, her brother, and the same Ernest bought that from Simon son of Bartholomew Forward, and that Simon acquired that through the death of Elye le Porter, his ancestor, and in respect thereof she pays per annum to the heirs of Robert Seman 5s. 6d., to Leon Dunning and his heirs 2s. 9d.

[558]   Item the same Alicia holds 5 acres of land less 1 rood in the fields of Cambridge which descended to her by inheritance through the death of the said Ernest, her brother, and that Ernest bought those from Leon Dunning, and that Leon acquired those by inheritance through the death of Adam, his father, and in respect thereof she pays per annum 1 rose to the said Leon.

[559]   Item the same Alicia holds a grange in the parish of St Michael's which descended to her by inheritance through the death of Ernest, her brother and that Ernest bought that from Margaret daughter of Bartholomew le Tailor, which same Margaret acquired that by gift of Bartholomew, her father, and that Bartholomew bought that from the prior of Hatfield, and in respect thereof she pays per annum to the said prior 6d., by which warranty they are unaware of any claim to the said messuage and rent.

[560]   Item John Yve holds 1 messuage in the parish of St Mary's which he acquired by gift and concession of Mabilia daughter of Ivo Copin and Agnes, her sister, which same Mabilia and Agnes acquired that by inheritance through the death of Ivo Copin, their father, and the same Ivo acquired that by purchase from Nicholas the potter, and in respect thereof he pays per annum to the heirs of the said Nicholas 7d.

[561]   Item the same John holds 2 shops in the marketplace of Cambridge where he sells meat, which he has by gift of the said Mabilia and Agnes her sister, and the said Mabilia and Agnes acquired those by inheritance through the death of Ivo, their father, which same Ivo bought those from Radulph son of Henry

Wombe, and in respect thereof he pays per annum to the bailiffs of Cambridge who hold the said town in fee farm etcetera for their farm 8d.

[562] Item Thomas of Arrington holds 1 messuage in the parish of St Mary's which he bought from John le Cutler, which same John bought that from Margaret daughter of William Henges, which same Margaret acquired that by inheritance through the death of William Henges, her father, and the said William acquired that by ancient acquisition, and in respect thereof he pays per annum to the said John 1 peppercorn, and to Margaret Henges ½d., and to St John's Hospital, Cambridge, 4s., by which warranty they are unaware.

[563] Item Richard Bateman senior holds in fee 1 messuage in the parish of St Mary's which he bought from Master Adam de Lincoln, which same Master Adam bought that from John son of Reginald Aured, and that John bought that from the prioress and convent of St Radegund's, and in respect thereof he pays per annum to the said prioress and convent 10s., and to the said John Aured 2d., by which warranty the said prioress and convent are unaware of any claim to the said messuage and rent.

[564] Item Richard holds 3 acres of land in the fields of Cambridge which he bought from John Blodles, which same John acquired those by hereditary right through the death of William Blodles, his father, and that William acquired those by gift of Berenger le Moyne, and in respect thereof he pays per annum to the heirs of the said John 2d.

[565] Item Richard holds 3 acres of land in the fields of Cambridge, which he bought from John Blodles, which same John acquired those by hereditary right through the death of William Blodles, his father, and that William acquired that from Lord Berenger le Moyne, and in respect thereof he pays per annum to the heirs of the said John 2d.

[566] Item Richard holds 2 shops in the same parish namely in Carnificio which same he bought from Richard Burs which same Richard acquired those by inheritance of Roger le Riche, his uncle, and that Roger held those from ancient acquisition, and in respect thereof he pays per annum to St Edmund's Chapel in the same town 8s., and to St Mary's Church 8s., and to Alan Segin 2s. by assignment of Robert Aunger.

[567] Item Richard holds 1 shop in the parish of St Edward's, which he acquired by hereditary succession through the death of John Selede, his father, which same John acquired that by inheritance

through the death of Selede, his father, and in respect thereof he pays per annum to the prior and convent of Barnwell 4s., by which warranty they are unaware.

[568] The same Richard holds a piece of vacant land in the parish of St Mary's which he bought from Richard Burs, and the same Richard acquired that by inheritance through the death of Roger le Riche, his uncle, and he acquired that by ancient acquisition, and in respect thereof he pays per annum to the abbess of Stratford 2s., by which warranty they are unaware.

[569] Item Margaret of Abington holds 1 messuage in the parish of St Mary's in fee which she bought from the prior and convent of Barnwell, and in respect thereof she pays per annum to the said prior and convent 12s. 4d.

[570] Item the same Margaret holds 1 messuage in the same parish which descended to her by inheritance through the death of Margaret, her mother, and the same Margaret acquired that by inheritance through the death of Robert, chaplain, her father, and in respect thereof she pays per annum to Alicia Harvey and her heirs ½ mark and to William de Novacurt and his heirs 16d.

[571] Item Margaret holds 1 shop in the same parish which descended to her by inheritance through the death of Margaret of Abington, her mother, and the same Margaret acquired that by inheritance of Robert, chaplain, her father, and in respect thereof she pays per annum to St Mary's Church 4d., and to the bailiffs of Cambridge who hold the said town in fee farm etcetera for hawgable 2s.

[572] Item the said Margaret holds 1 messuage in the parish of St Benedict's outside Trumpington Gate, which descended to her by inheritance through the death of Reginald of Abington, her father, and that Reginald bought that from Walter of St Edmunds, and that Walter acquired that from hereditary succession, and in respect thereof she pays per annum to the heirs of the said Walter 12d.

[573] Item the same Margaret holds 3 acres of land in the fields of Barnwell which descended to her by inheritance through the death of Margaret, her mother, and that Margaret acquired those by inheritance through the death of Robert, chaplain, her father, and in respect thereof she pays per annum to Leon Dunning 2s.

[574] The same Margaret holds 1 acre of land in the fields of Cambridge in fee from the prior of Barnwell, which descended to her by inheritance through the death of Margaret, her mother, and the same Margaret acquired that by inheritance through the death of Robert le Chapeler, her father, and in respect thereof she pays

per annum to the said prior 12d. by which warranty they are unaware.

[575] Item Margaret holds 2 acres of land in the fields of Cambridge which descended to her by inheritance through the death of Margaret, her mother, and that Margaret acquired those by inheritance through the death of Robert le Chapeler, her father, and the same Robert acquired those by ancient acquisition, and in respect thereof she pays per annum to the bailiffs of Cambridge who hold the said town in fee farm etcetera for their farm 2d.

[576] William of Norfolk and Margaret his wife hold 1 shop in the parish of St Mary's in the marketplace which same shop the said Margaret acquired by gift of Henry Hubert, her father, which same Henry acquired that from Richard, son of Ivo, which same Richard bought that from Richard Perles, and that Richard acquired that by ancient succession of his ancestors, and in respect thereof he pays per annum to Anchorite of Trumpington 4s. 6d., and to the heirs of Ernest Merchant, 2s. 6d. by assignment of the said Richard.

[577] Item William and Margaret his wife hold 1 shop in the same parish, which said Margaret acquired by gift of Henry Hubert her father, and that Henry bought that from Robert Odierne, and the said Robert acquired that from the nuns of St Mary de Pré, and in respect thereof they pay per annum for a certain chaplain celebrating mass at the altar of St Mary in the same church 12d.

[578] Walter Wragon holds 1 shop in the parish of St Mary's which descended to him by inheritance through the death of Robert Wragon, his father, and that Robert bought that from Baldwin Blancgernun, and in respect thereof he pays per annum to St John's Hospital, Cambridge, 9s., by assignment of the said Baldwin.

[579] Item Wakelin le Barbur holds 1 messuage in the parish of St Mary's in which he lives, which he bought from Walter of Oxford serving at the University of Cambridge, and the same Walter acquired that from the nuns of St Mary de Pré, and in respect thereof he pays per annum to the said nuns 3s., and to the said Walter 1d., by which warranty the said nuns are unaware of any claim to the said income.

[580] Item Walter le Hunte holds 1 messuage in the parish of St Mary's which descended to him by inheritance through the death of Gilbert le Hunte, his father, which same Gilbert acquired that from hereditary succession through the death of Margaret, his mother, which same Margaret bought that from the prior and

convent of Ely, and in respect thereof he pays per annum to the said prior and convent 16d., by which warranty the said prior and convent are unaware of any claim to the said income.

[581] Item Walter holds 1 shop in the marketplace of Cambridge in the same parish which he bought from Walter le Hunte, his uncle, which same Walter acquired that through the death of Peter le Hunte, his father, which same Peter acquired that by ancient acquisition as from purchase, and in respect thereof he pays per annum on behalf of the said Walter le Hunte and his heirs to St Benedict's Church 1 lb. of wax, and to Master Robert Aunger 2s., and to St John's Hospital, Cambridge 12d., by which warranty they are unaware.

[582] The same Walter holds a piece of vacant land in the same parish which he bought from Walter le Plumber, which same Walter acquired that by inheritance through the death of Gilbert le Plumber, his father, which same Gilbert acquired that from ancient acquisition of his ancestors, and in respect thereof he pays per annum to the said Walter ½d., and to William Seman 20d., and to the abbot and convent of Thorney 8d. by which warranty they are unaware.

[583] The same Walter holds 1 messuage in the parish of St Benedict's which he acquired by gift and concession of Agnes le Hunte, his friend, and that Agnes acquired that by gift of Walter son of Peter le Hunte, her brother, and the said Walter acquired that from paternal succession through the death of the said Peter, his father, which same Peter acquired that by ancient acquisition as from purchase, and in respect thereof he pays per annum to William de Novacurt 16d.

[584] Geoffrey le Farrier holds in fee 1 messuage in the parish of St Mary's which he acquired by gift of Roger of Ely, which same Roger acquired that by gift of Cecilia, wife of the said Geoffrey which same Cecilia bought that from Walter Crocheman, and that Walter acquired that by gift of Richard, his brother, and in respect thereof he pays per annum to the said Walter 1d., and to the prioress of St Radegund's 8s., by which warranty they are unaware.

[585] The same Geoffrey holds 1 messuage in the same parish in which he resides, which he bought from Alan son of Radulph Scutard, which same Alan acquired that from Walter Grandin, which same Walter bought that from Deonisia, daughter and heir of Aspelon Odierne, which same Deonisia acquired that from hereditary succession through the death of the said Aspelon, her father,

which same Aspelon acquired that by ancient acquisition of his ancestors, and in respect thereof he pays per annum to the said Alan 1 rose and to the heirs of Aspelon Odierne ½d., and to the nuns of St Mary de Pré 5s., by which warranty they are unaware.

[586] The same Geoffrey holds 1 shop in the same parish in the marketplace which he bought from Radulph Scharp, and the same Radulph acquired that from hereditary succession through the death of Robert Scharp, his father, and that Robert acquired that from ancient succession of his ancestors, and in respect thereof he pays per annum to John above the market 5s., and to St John's Hospital, Cambridge, 20d., by which warranty they are unaware.

[587] The same Geoffrey holds 1 shop in the parish of St Edward's, Cambridge, which he bought from the brothers of St John's Hospital, and the said brothers held that from Eustace Selede, and that Eustace acquired that by ancient acquisition of his ancestors, and in respect thereof he pays per annum to the said brothers 2s.

[588] The same Geoffrey holds 1 shop in the same parish which he bought from Robert of St Botolph's, which same Robert acquired that by inheritance through the death of Simon of St Botolph's, his father, which same Simon acquired that from ancient acquisition, and in respect thereof he pays per annum to the almoner of Barnwell 8d. by assignment of the said Robert.

[589] Item Thomas le Cutler holds 1 messuage in fee in which he resides in the parish of St Mary's which he bought from Matilda, former wife of Bartholomew Tailor, which same Matilda acquired that by gift of Geoffrey Potekine, her father and that Geoffrey acquired that by ancient succession of his ancestors, and in respect thereof he pays per annum to Richard son of Robert Bartholomew 6d., and to Thomas Potekine 18d., and to St Mary's Church 2s., and to the prioress of St Radegund's 2s., by which warranty they are unaware.

[590] Item Robert le Witemyth holds 1 messuage in the parish of St Mary's which he acquired by inheritance through the death of William le Wyteswith', his father, which same William bought that from Adam Dunning, which same Adam acquired that from ancient acquisition by purchase and in respect thereof he pays per annum to the heirs of the said Adam, namely Leon Dunning, 2s. 3d.

[591] The same Robert holds 2 stalls in the same parish which he bought from Henry son of Barholomew, which same Henry acquired those by gift of Bartholomew, his father, and that Bartholomew

acquired those by ancient succession of his ancestors, and in respect thereof he pays per annum to Thomas Potekin ½d. by assignment of the said Henry son of Bartholomew.

[592] Robert of St Botolph's holds 1 shop in the parish of St Mary's which descended to him by inheritance through the death of Simon of St Botolph's, his father, which same Simon acquired that by ancient acquisition as by purchase, and in respect thereof he pays per annum to St John's Hospital, Cambridge, 2s., by which warranty they are unaware and to the heirs of Nicholas Childman 21d., and to Master Robert Aunger 2s.

[593] The same Robert holds 1 shop in the parish of St Edward's, which descended to him by inheritance through the death of Simon, his father, and that Simon acquired that by ancient acquisition, and in respect thereof he pays per annum to the almoner of Ely 8d., by which warranty the almoner is unaware of any claim to the said income.

[594] Item William de Tingewick holds 1 messuage in the parish of St Mary's in which he resides, which he acquired by gift of Ernest Merchant, and the same Ernest bought that from Henry Nadon, and that Henry acquired that by hereditary right through the death of Robert Nadon, his father, and in respect thereof he pays per annum to the prior and convent of Hatfield 10s., and to the heirs of the said Ernest 1 pair of gloves at the price of ½d., by which warranty the said prior is unaware of any claim to the said income.

[595] Item John Matelast holds 1 messuage in the same parish which he acquired by gift of John Matelast, his uncle, and that John bought that from Nicholas Malerbe, and that Nicholas acquired that by hereditary right through the death of Michael Malerbe, his father, and the same Michael acquired that by ancient acquisition of his ancestors, and in respect thereof he pays per annum to the heirs of William Crocheman 5s. 10d. by assignment of the said Nicholas and to St Mary's Church 12d.

[596] Item Thomas Merchant, holds 1 messuage in the parish of St Mary's which he bought from Jordan of St Radegund's and Cecilia, his wife, and from Alicia, sister of the said Cecilia, which same messuage descended to the said Cecilia and Alicia, her sister, by inheritance through the death of Geoffrey Athelard, their father, which same Geoffrey acquired that by hereditary right through the death of John Athelard, his brother, which same John acquired that by ancient succession of his ancestors, and in respect thereof he pays per annum to the said Jordan and Cecilia his wife

1 pair of gloves at the price of ½d., and to the said Alicia and her heirs ½d., and to the brothers of St John's Hospital, Cambridge, 2s. by which warranty they are unaware.

[597] Item Thomas holds 1 stall in the same parish which Robert de Madingley gave to Agnes, his daughter, wife of the said Thomas, and the said Robert bought that from Gunnilda, widow of Simon de Kirkby, which same Gunnilda acquired that from hereditary succession through the death of her ancestors, and in respect thereof he pays per annum to Henry de Wikes and his heirs 2s., and to Agnes Fichien and her heirs 16d.

[598] Item Margaret daughter of John de Flocthort holds 1 messuage in the parish of St Mary's, which she acquired by gift of John, her father, and the same John at one time bought that from Bartholomew Goldsmith, and the same Bartholomew bought that from Stephen Dreye, which same Stephen acquired that through the death of Hugh Dreye, his father, and in respect thereof she pays per annum to the heirs of the said Bartholomew 1 rose and to the said Stephen Dreye ½d., and to Master Robert Aunger 4s.

[599] Item William le Comber holds 1 messuage in fee in the parish of St Mary's which descended to him by inheritance through the death of Osbert, his father, which same Osbert bought that from Andrew de Wenepol and that Andrew acquired that through the death of Eustace de Wenepol, his brother, and that Eustace acquired that from ancient succession of his ancestors, and in respect thereof he pays per annum to Nicholas Morice 10d., and to Walter le Plumber 8d., and to Alicia, wife of William de Kirkby 3s., and to Robert son of Robert le Withemyth 2s. by assignment of Nicholas de Winepol heir of the said Andrew.

[600] Item the same William holds 1 shop in the same parish which he bought from John Porthors, which same John bought that from Walter the plumber and that Walter acquired that through the death of Gilbert le Plumber, his father, and in respect thereof pays per annum to Sabina Huberd 12d., and for the maintenance of 1 lamp in St Mary's Church 4d.

[601] The same William and Matilda his wife hold a stall in the said parish which they have by gift of Robert Witemith, father of the said Matilda, and that Robert acquired that through the death of William Witemyth, his father, and that William acquired that by ancient succession of his ancestors, and in respect thereof they pay per annum to the heirs of Nicholas Childman 6d.

[602] Item the same William holds 1 messuage in the said parish which he acquired by gift of John son of William le Coteler, which same

John acquired that through the death of William le Coteler, his father, and he pays in respect thereof per annum to the heirs of Henry Nadon 1d. by assignment of John le Coteler.

[603]   Item the same William holds 1 messuage in the said parish which he acquired by gift of Robert le Witemyth and the said Robert acquired that through the death of William le Witemith, his father, and in respect thereof he pays per annum to Nicholas Morice ½ mark by assignment of the said Robert, and to St Radegund's Church 1 gallon of oil for the maintenance of a lamp in the said church.

[604]   Item the same William holds 1 acre of land in the fields of Cambridge which he bought from Custancia, wife of Richard le Taverner, which same Custancia acquired that by gift of Richard, her son, and that Richard acquired that by purchase from Elena Alsope, and the said Elena acquired that by ancient acquisition, and in respect thereof he pays per annum to the bailiffs of Cambridge who hold the said town in fee farm etcetera for their farm 1d.

[605]   The same William holds 1 messuage in the parish of St John's, Cambridge, which he bought from John, son of Nicholas Wombe, which same John acquired that by hereditary right through the death of Amicia, his mother, and the same Amicia acquired that by gift of John, son of Reginald Aured, and in respect thereof he pays per annum to the said John son of Nicholas 1d.

[606]   Item Richard Bateman junior holds 1 messuage in fee in the parish of St Mary's which he bought from Juliana, widow of Humphrey de Clopton, and the said Humphrey and Juliana, his wife, bought that from William son of Baldwin de Stowe, and the said William acquired that by gift of Alan, cleric, his brother, and that Alan acquired that by gift of Agnes de Stowe, his mother, and the same Agnes acquired that from Adam Dunning, her father, and in respect thereof he pays per annum to the said Juliana and her heirs 1d., and to Leon Dunning 18½d.

[607]   Item Richard holds 4 shops in the same parish which he bought from Thomas de Cottenham and the same Thomas bought those from Robert son of Robert de Hauxton and the same Robert acquired those by hereditary right through the death of Robert, his father, and in respect thereof he pays per annum to the said Thomas and his heirs 1 rose, and to Robert de Madingley and his heirs 3s., and to the brothers of St John's Hospital, Cambridge, 3s., by which warranty the said brothers are unaware of any claim to the said income.

[608] The same Richard holds 3 shops in the parish of St Michael's in fee farm which he acquired by gift of the prior and convent of Anglesey and the said prior and convent acquired those by gift of Robert Hubert, and that Robert acquired those by hereditary right through the death of Cecilia Godso, his friend, which same Cecilia acquired those by ancient succession of her parents, and in respect thereof he pays per annum to the said prior and convent 5s., and to the bailiffs of Cambridge who hold the said town in fee farm as is stated for hawgable 1 farthing.

[609] The same Richard holds 1 messuage in fee in the parish of St Edward's which he acquired by gift of the said prior and convent of Anglesey, which said prior and convent acquired that by gift of Robert Hubert, and that Robert acquired that from heritage through the death of Cecilia Godso, which same Cecilia acquired that by ancient succession of her ancestors, and in respect thereof he pays per annum to the said prior and convent 6d.

[610] The same Richard holds a piece of vacant land in the parish of St Michael's, Cambridge, which he bought from Richard Bateman senior, which same Richard bought that from John Wombe, and that John acquired that from hereditary succession through the death of Nicholas Wombe, his father, and that Nicholas acquired that from ancient succession of his ancestors, for which he pays per annum to the said Richard 1 rose and for the maintenance of a lamp before the high altar in St Michael's Church 8d.

[611] The same Richard holds 1 messuage in the parish of St Mary's which he bought from Gilbert de Hardleston, his uncle, and the said Gilbert bought that from Richard Bateman senior, which same Richard acquired that through the death of John Selede, his father, for which he pays per annum to the said Gilbert 1d., and to the prior of Barnwell 10s., by which warranty they are unaware.

[612] The same Richard holds 3 half acres of land in the fields of Cambridge which he bought from John But, which same John bought those from Nicholas de Reche, and the said Nicholas acquired those through the death of Richard, his brother, and that Richard acquired those by ancient acquisition, and in respect thereof he pays per annum to the said John and his heirs 2d.

[613] The same Richard holds 3 half acres of land in the fields of Cambridge which he bought from Richard Bateman senior, his father, and the same Richard bought those at from John Blodles, which same John acquired those by inheritance through the

death of William Blodles, his father, and that William acquired those from ancient succession of his ancestors, and in respect thereof he pays per annum to the said John Blodles 1 rose and to the said Richard Bateman 1d.

[614] The same Richard holds ½ acre of land in the fields of Cambridge which he bought from John above the market, and that John bought that from Richard Laurence senior, and in respect thereof he pays per annum through the heirs of the said John to the said Richard Lawrence 1d.

[615] Walter le Plumber holds 1 messuage in the parish of St Mary's which descended to him by hereditary right through the death of Gilbert, his father, and the same Gilbert acquired that by inheritance through the death of Arnold, his father, and that Arnold acquired that by inheritance through the death of Gilbert, his father, and in respect thereof he pays per annum to St Mary's Church 3s.

[616] Item the same Walter holds 1 acre of land in the fields of Cambridge which descended to him by hereditary right through the death of Gilbert, his father, and that Gilbert acquired that by inheritance through the death of Arnold, his father, and the said Arnold acquired that through the death of Gilbert, his father, and in respect thereof he pays per annum to Leon Dunning 12d.

[617] The same Walter holds 1 messuage in the parish of St Mary's which descended to Juliana, his wife, by inheritance through the death of Thomas le Farrier, her father, and that Thomas acquired that by ancient acquisition, and in respect thereof he pays per annum to the heirs of Robert Nadon 6s.

[618] The same Walter holds a vacant piece of land in the same parish which he bought from William, chaplain of Ditton, which same William acquired that by purchase from William Penle, and that William held that from St Mary's Church, and in respect thereof he pays per annum to the said church 3d.

[619] Item William le Lorimer holds 1 messuage in the parish of St Mary's which he bought from Margaret daughter of William Henges, and that Margaret acquired that by inheritance through the death of William Henges, her father, and that William acquired that through the death of William Henges, his father, and that William acquired that through the death of Alexander, his father, and that Alexander bought that from Robert Nadon, which same Robert acquired that by ancient acquisition, and in respect thereof he pays per annum on behalf of the heirs of the said Margaret to Master Adam de Bondone 6s., and to the bailiffs

of Cambridge who hold the said town in fee farm etcetera for hawgable 2d.

[620]   The same William holds 1 shop in the said parish which he bought from Henry Nadon and that Henry acquired that by inheritance through the death of Robert Nadon, his father, which same Robert acquired that by acquisition as by purchase, and in respect thereof he pays per annum on behalf of the heirs of the said Henry to Master Adam de Bondon 6s.

[621]   Item Thomas Podipol holds a vacant piece of land in the parish of St Mary's which descended to him by inheritance through the death of Seman Podipol, his father, and the same Seman acquired that by inheritance through the death of Thomas Podipol, his father, and the same Thomas acquired that by inheritance through the death of John Podipol, his father, which same John acquired that from ancient acquisition, and in respect thereof he pays per annum to the bailiffs of Cambridge who hold the said town in fee farm for their farm for hawgable 2d.

[622]   Robert, son of Robert de Madingley, holds 1 messuage in the parish of St Mary's which same messuage descended to him through the death of the said Robert, his father, which same Robert bought that from Isabella daughter of Bartholomew Wombe, which same Isabella acquired that by gift of Custancia, her mother, which same Custancia acquired that in frank marriage by gift of Richard le Tailor, her father, and he pays per annum for the said messuage to St John's Hospital, Cambridge, ½ mark by which warranty they are unaware, and to the bailiffs of Cambridge who hold the said town from the Lord King in fee farm for hawgable 2d.

[623]   Item the said Robert holds 1 messuage in the same parish which same descended to him by hereditary right through the death of the said Robert, his father, which same Robert acquired that by gift of Thomas son of Laurence, which same Thomas bought that from Robert Carpenter, for which he pays per annum to the heirs of the said Robert Carpenter 1d., and to the bailiffs of Cambridge for their farm for hawgable ½d.

[624]   Item the said Robert holds 1 messuage in the same parish which same messuage Thomas de Tudenham and Matilda, his wife, gave to him in frank marriage with Derota, his wife, which same Thomas and Matilda bought that from John Mateley, which same John acquired that by inheritance through the death of William Matelay, his brother, which same William bought that from the prior and convent of Barnwell, and he pays in respect thereof per

annum to the heirs of the said John ½d., and to the said prior and convent 7s., by which warranty they are unaware of any claim to the said income.

[625] Item the said Robert holds 3 acres of land in Binnebroc which same descended to him through the death of the said Robert, his father, which same Robert bought those from the prior and convent of Barnwell, for which he pays per annum to the said prior and convent of Barnwell 6d.

[626] Item the said Robert holds 4 acres of land in the fields of Cambridge which same descended to him by hereditary right through the death of the said Robert, his father, which same Robert bought those from Leon son of Adam Dunning, which same Leon acquired those by inheritance through the death of the said Adam, his father, and in respect thereof he pays per annum to the said Leon and his heirs 6d.

[627] Item the said Robert holds 3 acres of land in the said fields which same descended to him by paternal succession, which same Robert bought those from Richard le Tailor and Margaret, his wife, which same Richard and Margaret bought those from Nicholas Malerbe, which same Nicholas acquired those from paternal inheritance through the death of Michael Malerbe, his father, for which he pays per annum to the heirs of the said Nicholas 3d.

[628] Item the said Robert holds 1 acre of land in Binnebroc which same descended to him through the death of Robert, his father, which same Robert acquired that from the prior and convent of Barnwell in exchange for the same amount of land in the fields of Madingley, for which he pays per annum to the said prior and convent 2½d.

[629] Item the said Robert holds 3 roods of land in the same field which same descended to him through the death of the said Robert, which same Robert bought those from William Waubert, which same William acquired those through the death of John, his father, which same John acquired those by ancient heritage of his ancestors, for which he pays per annum to the said William and his heirs 1d.

[630] Item the said Robert holds 1 rood of land in the crofts of Newnham which descended to him through the death of Robert, his father, which same Robert bought that from Henry Nadon, which same Henry acquired that by hereditary right through the death of Robert Nadon, his father, for which he pays per annum to the heirs of the said Henry ½d.

[631]   Item the said Robert holds 1 rood of land in the same field which
         he acquired by gift of Thomas de Tudenham and Matilda, his
         wife, which same Thomas bought that from Nicholas Goldsmith,
         which same Nicholas acquired that from Ernest Merchant, which
         same Ernest bought that from Andrea le Neve, for which he pays
         per annum to Andrea le Neve ½d.

[R13]   Item the said Robert receives per annum in the parish of
         St Mary's 3s. paid annually with brooms, which were of Robert
         de Hauxton, which same descended to him by hereditary right
         through the death of Robert, his father, which same Robert
         bought those from Robert son of Robert de Hauxton, which
         same descended to him through the death of Robert, his father,
         for which he pays per annum to the same Robert 1 rose.

[632]   Item Margaret daughter of Robert de Madingley holds 2 acres
         of land in the fields of Cambridge which she acquired by gift of
         Matilda daughter of Ysantus, which same Matilda bought those
         from Isabella daughter of Michael Bernard, which same Isabella
         acquired those by gift of Nicholas, her son, which same Nicholas
         acquired those by gift of Michael Bernard, which same Michael
         bought those from Gilbert Baker, which same Gilbert bought
         those from William of St Edmunds with the agreement and will
         of Walter, his son, for which she pays per annum to the said
         Isabella 1 clove gillyflower, and to the heirs of the said William
         of St Edmunds annually 2d.

[633]   Matilda daughter of Ysantus holds 1 messuage in the parish of
         St Mary's which same messuage descended to her by hereditary
         right through the death of Alfred, her brother, which same Alfred
         acquired that by paternal succession through the death of Ysantus,
         his father, which same Ysantus acquired that same by succession
         through the death of Alicia, his mother, which same Alicia acquired
         that through the death of Ivo Pipestraw, her father, for which she
         pays per annum to the nuns of St Radegund's 12d., by which
         warranty the said nuns are unaware of any claim to the said income.

[634]   Item the same Matilda holds 1 messuage in the parish of
         St Edward's which same messuage descended to her through the
         death of Alfred, her brother, which same Alfred acquired that
         through the death of Ysantus, his father, which same Ysantus
         bought that from Peter son of Serl, for which she pays per annum
         to the bailiffs of Cambridge who holds the same town in fee farm
         from the Lord King for hawgable 1d.

[635]   Item the said Matilda holds 1 messuage in the parish of St Mary's,
         which same messuage she acquired by gift of John Atewald,

which same messuage the said John bought from Master Walter of Tyrington, which same Walter bought that from Laurence Ligator', which same Laurence bought that from William Herre, butcher, for which she pays per annum to St Edmund's Chapel 6d.

[636] Item the said Matilda holds 1 messuage with 2 acres of land in the parish of St John's which same messuage with said land descended to her through Robert son of Robert Hubert, canon of Anglesey, which same Robert acquired that through the death of Amicia, daughter of Thomas Tulicht, which same Amicia acquired the said messuage with the said land from hereditary succession through the death of Cecilia Godso, her mother, which same Cecilia held that through the descent of John le Hoft, her brother, for which same messuage she pays per annum to St Mary's Church 4d., and to Roger, nephew of Master Nigel 4d., and for the aforesaid land to the bailiffs of Cambridge for their farm as is stated for hawgable 2d.

[637] Item the said Matilda holds 1 house in Straw Lane which same messuage descended to her through the death of Alfred, her brother, which same Alfred acquired that through the death of Ysantus, his father, which same Ysantus bought that from John Ace, for which he pays per annum to the bailiffs of Cambridge for their farm as is stated for hawgable ½d.

[638] Item the said Matilda holds 1 messuage in the parish of St Michael's with the advowson of the said church, which same messuage with the said advowson descended to her by hereditary right through the death of Alfred, her brother, which same Alfred acquired the said messuage with advowson by hereditary right through the death of Ysantus, his father, which same Ysantus held the said messuage with same aforesaid advowson by hereditary succession through the death of Alice, his mother, which same descended to the said Alice by inheritance through the death of Ivo Pipestraw, her father, which same descended to the said Ivo through the death of Reginald Pipestraw, his father, which same Reginald held the said messuage with the said advowson by hereditary right through the descent of his ancestors in the time of Henry, king of England, grandfather of King Henry, father of Edward, who is now king of England, for which messuage she pays per annum to the bailiffs of Cambridge for their farm as is stated 2d.

[R14] Item the said Matilda receives 3s. paid annually from the house of William Yde, which same she acquired by inheritance through the death of Alfred, her brother, which same Alfred acquired those through the death of Ysantus, his father, which same Ysantus acquired those through the death of Alicia, his mother, which same Alicia acquired those through the descent of her ancestors.

[R15] Item the said Matilda receives 5s. paid annually from the house of Simon de Potton in the parish of St Mary's, which same the said Matilda and Thomas de Todenham, her husband, bought from Catherine, daughter of William Herre, which same Catherine acquired that by hereditary right through the death of William Herre, her father, which same William acquired that through the descent of his ancestors, for which she pays per annum to the said Catherine 1 pair of white gloves at the price of ½d.

[639] Item the said Matilda holds 7 roods of land which the same Matilda and Thomas, her husband, bought from Philip Alsope, which same Philip acquired those by gift of Elena Alsope in frank marriage with Sarra, his wife, which same Elena and William, her husband, bought from Walter Haliday, for which she pays per annum to Philip and his heirs ½d., and to the almoner of Barnwell 2d. per annum.

[640] Item the said Matilda holds 1 acre of land in the aforesaid fields which same descended to her by hereditary right through the death of Isabella Golde, which same Isabella and Gold, her husband, bought from Harvey Gogging, which same Harvey acquired that by hereditary right through the death of his father, for which she pays per annum to the heirs of the said Harvey 1d.

[641] Item the said Matilda holds a piece of vacant land in the parish of St Mary's which said piece of land the said Matilda and Thomas, her husband, bought from John of Barton, goldsmith, which same John acquired that.

[642] Simon of Potton holds 1 messuage in the parish of St Mary's in the market-place of Cambridge which he bought from Agnes of Barton, which same Agnes bought that from Robert son of Robert de Hauxton, which same Robert acquired that by hereditary right through the death of Robert, his father, for which he pays per annum to the said Agnes 1d., and to St Benedict's Church 2s., which Dera Gibelot at one time gave to the said church in perpetual alms for her soul and the souls of her ancestors.

[643] Item the said Simon holds 1 messuage in the same parish which he bought from Nicholas son of Richard de Wilberham, which same Nicholas acquired that by hereditary right through the

death of Richard de Wilberham, his father, for which he pays per annum to the said Nicholas 1 clove gillyflower and to Matilda daughter of Ysantus 5s.

[644]   Item Simon and Margaret, his wife, hold 1 messuage in Trumpington Street which same descended to them through the death of John Paternoster, husband of the said Margaret, which same John acquired that by gift of Simon le Carter in frank marriage with the said Margaret, his daughter, which same Simon bought that from John le Rus, for which he pays per annum to the almoner of Barnwell 2s., by which warranty the said almoner is unaware of any claim to the said income.

[645]   Item Sabina daughter of John Paternoster holds 1 messuage in the parish of St Peter's outside the gate, which same messuage she acquired by gift of John Paternoster, her father, which same John bought that from Thomas son of William le Weaver, for which she pays per annum to the said William and his heirs 1 clove gillyflower.

[646]   Item the said Simon holds 1 acre of land in the fields of Cambridge which he bought from Luke of St Edmunds, which same Luke acquired that by hereditary right through the death of Walter, his brother[71] which same Walter acquired that by hereditary right through the death of William, his father, for which he pays per annum to the said Luke of St Edmunds 2d.

[647]   Item the said Simon holds 3 acres of land which he bought from Amicia de Torp, which same Amicia acquired those by gift of Richard, her father, for which he pays per annum to the same Luke 3 farthings.

[648]   Item the said Simon holds 1 shop in the parish of St Mary's, which same shop the said Simon bought from Jordan, brother of Master Martin of St Radegund's, for which he pays per annum to the Lord Peter de Chavent 6s.

[649]   John of Rockland holds 1 messuage with appurtenances in the parish of St Mary's, which same messuage he bought from Nicholas Carun, which same Nicholas bought that from the executors of Roger de Wykis, for which he pays per annum to the bailiffs of Cambridge who hold the same town from the Lord King in fee farm for hawgable 1½d.

[650]   Thomas Blome and Matilda, his wife, hold 2 shops in the parish of St Mary's which they acquired by gift and feoffment of Gilbert son of Godfrey de Kediton, which same Gilbert bought that from Richard son of Robert son of Bartholomew, which same Robert held that by hereditary right through the death of Bartholomew,

his father, and they pay in respect thereof per annum to the said Gilbert 1 clove gillyflower and to the said Richard son of Robert Bartholomew 9d.

[651] Warin de Teversham holds 1 shop in the parish of St Mary's in the marketplace which same Warin bought that from John Gerund and Elena, his wife, which same shop descended to the said Elena through the death of William Braci, her father, and he pays in respect thereof per annum to the said John and Elena 5s.

[652] Geoffrey le Farrier holds 1[72] and a half of land in the fields of Barnwell, which same he acquired by gift of Dionisia, his mother, which same Dionisia acquired that by inheritance through the death of her father William Kenewy, and the said William acquired that by ancient purchase, and he pays in respect thereof per annum to the said Dionisia and her heirs 6d.

[653] Item William Castelein holds 1 shop in the parish of St Mary's which same he bought from Richard Purs, which same Richard bought that from Richard Purs, his father, which same Richard acquired that by ancient purchase, and in respect thereof he pays per annum through the said Richard and his heirs to the almoner of Barnwell 8s.

[654] Simon Prat son of Geoffrey of Ely holds a piece of vacant land in the parish of St Mary's which same piece of land descended to him through the death of Geoffrey his father by hereditary right, which same Geoffrey bought that from Geoffrey son of Orgar, which same Geoffrey acquired that by inheritance through the death of Orgar, his father, and he pays in respect thereof per annum to William Elyhot 2½d. and 1 lb. of cumin.

[655] The same Simon holds 1 messuage in the parish of St Edward's which same messuage he bought from John son of Geoffrey Morin, which same John acquired that said messuage by inheritance through the death of Geoffrey Morin, his father, which same Geoffrey acquired that in frank marriage with Matilda, his wife, and he pays in respect thereof per annum for the said messuage to the said John and his heirs 6d.

[656] Item Richard Wombe holds in fee 1 messuage in the parish of St Michael's, Cambridge, which same Richard acquired that by hereditary succession through the death of John Wombe, his brother, which same John acquired that by hereditary right through the death of Bartholomew Wombe, his father, which same Bartholomew acquired that through the death of Radulph Wombe, his father, which same Radulph acquired that by hereditary succession through the death of his ancestors, and

in respect thereof he pays per annum to the heirs of Harvey Parleben 1d., and to the heirs of Thomas de la Bruere 1 pair of gloves at the price of ½d.

[657] The same Richard holds 1 shop in the parish of St Mary's which descended to him by inheritance through the death of John, his brother, which same John acquired that by hereditary right through the death of Bartholomew Wombe, his father, and the said Bartholomew acquired that by inheritance through the death of Radulph Wombe, his father, and the said Radulph acquired that by ancient purchase from John Copin, and the said John acquired that by inheritance through the death of Harvey Copin, his father, which same Harvey acquired that by ancient purchase, and in respect thereof he pays per annum to the heirs of the said John Copin ½d., and to the bailiffs of Cambridge who hold the said town in fee farm etcetera for hawgable 8d.

[658] Item Richard holds 1 messuage in the parish of St Botolph's which he acquired by inheritance through the death of John Wombe, his brother, which same John acquired that through the death of Bartholomew Wombe, his father, and the said Bartholomew acquired that through the death of Michael Wombe, his brother, and the said Michael acquired that by gift of Radulph Wombe, his father, and the said Radulph bought that from Michael Malerbe, and the said Michael acquired that by ancient purchase, and in respect thereof he pays per annum to the heirs of the said Michael Malerbe 1d., and to the bailiffs of Cambridge who hold the said town in fee farm etcetera for hawgable 3d.

[659] The same Richard holds a piece of vacant land in the parish of All Saints next to the Hospital which descended to him by inheritance through the death of John Wombe, his brother, which same John acquired that by hereditary right through the death of Bartholomew, his father, and the said Bartholomew acquired that by inheritance through the death of Radulph Wombe, his father, which same Radulph bought that from Thomas de la Bruere and the said Thomas acquired that through the death of Robert de la Bruere, his father, and the said Robert acquired that by ancient succession of his parents, and in respect thereof he pays per annum to the heirs of the said Thomas 1d.

[660] The same Richard holds 20 acres of land in the fields of Cambridge which he acquired through the death of John, his brother, which same John acquired those through the death of Bartholomew, his father, which same Bartholomew acquired

those through the death of Radulph Wombe, his father, and the same Radulph bought those from Master Walter de Histon, and the said Master Walter bought those from John le Rus, which same John acquired those through the death of Maurice le Rus, his father, which same Maurice acquired those by ancient succession of his parents, and in respect thereof he pays per annum to the heirs of the said John 3s.

[661] The same Richard holds 5 acres of land in the same fields which he acquired by hereditary right through the death of the said John, his brother, which same John acquired those through the death of Bartholomew, his father, which same Bartholomew acquired those by hereditary right through the death of Radulph Wombe, his father, and the said Radulph bought those from Radulph de Gernon and the said acquired those by ancient purchase, and he pays in respect thereof per annum to the heirs of the said Radulph 18d., and to the bailiffs of Cambridge who hold the said town in fee farm etcetera for their farm 5d.

[662] The same Richard holds 3 selions in the same fields from the aforesaid hereditary succession of the heirs to Radulph Wombe, which same Radulph bought those from Richard son of Lota and the same Richard acquired those by inheritance through the death of Lota, his mother, and the said Lota acquired those by hereditary succession of her ancestors, and in respect thereof he pays per annum to the heirs of the said Richard son of Lota 3d., and to the bailiffs of Cambridge who hold the said town in fee farm etcetera for landgable 1d.

[663] Item Richard holds 1 rood of land in the fields of Cambridge which he acquired by inheritance through the death of John, his brother, which same John acquired that through the death of Bartholomew, his father, and the said Bartholomew acquired that through the death of Radulph, his father, and the said Radulph bought that from William Seman, and the said William acquired that by ancient succession of his parents, and in respect thereof he pays per annum to the heirs of the said William 1 farthing, and to the bailiffs of Cambridge who hold the said town in fee farm etcetera for landgable 1 farthing.

[664] The same Richard holds 1 acre of land in the fields of Cambridge which same Richard acquired that from the aforesaid hereditary succession to the heirs to Radulph Wombe, which same Radulph bought that from Andrew Pateware, and the same Andrew acquired that by ancient purchase, and in respect thereof he pays per annum to the heirs of the said Andrew 3d.

[665] The same Richard holds 3 half acres of land in the same fields from the aforesaid hereditary succession of the heirs to Radulph Wombe, and the said Radulph bought those from Adam son of Eustace, and the said Adam acquired those by hereditary right through the death of Eustace, his father, and the said Eustace acquired those by ancient inheritance of his ancestors, and in respect thereof he pays per annum to the said Adam 3d.

[666] The same Richard holds 3 half acres of land in the same fields which descended to him from the said hereditary succession in inheritance to the heirs of the said Radulph Wombe, which same Radulph bought those from Walter le Child of Wilburham, and the said Walter acquired those by ancient purchase, and he pays in respect thereof per annum to the heirs of the said Walter 10d.

[667] The same Richard holds 2 acres of land in the fields of Cambridge which he acquired from the same hereditary succession as is stated above to Radulph Wombe, which same Radulph bought those from John of the Infirmary, and the said John acquired those through the death of Roger of the Infirmary, his father, which same Roger acquired those by ancient purchase, and in respect thereof he pays per annum to the heirs of the said John 2d.

[668] The same Richard holds 1 acre of land in the same fields which he acquired by inheritance through the death of John, his brother, which same John acquired that by inheritance through the death of Bartholomew Wombe, his father, which same Bartholomew acquired that through the death of Radulph, his father, and the said Radulph acquired that by purchase from Adam son of Eustace, and the said Adam acquired that by inheritance through the death of the said Eustace, his father, and in respect thereof he pays per annum to the heirs of the said Adam 3d.

[669] The same Richard holds 1 acre of land in the same fields which descended to him by inheritance through the death of John, his brother, which same John acquired that by hereditary right through the death of Bartholomew Wombe, his father, which same Bartholomew acquired that by inheritance through the death of Radulph Wombe, his father, which same Radulph bought that from Jordan de Marins, which same Jordan acquired that by ancient inheritance of his parents, and in respect thereof he pays per annum to the heirs of the said Jordan 2d.

[670] The same Richard holds ½ acre of land in the aforesaid fields which he acquired from the aforesaid hereditary succession to the heirs as is stated above to Radulph Wombe, which same Radulph

bought that from Mabilia Melt, which same Mabilia acquired that by inheritance through the death of Henry Melt, her father, and the said Henry acquired that by ancient inheritance of his ancestors, and in respect thereof he pays per annum to the heirs of the said Mabilia 1d.

[671] Item Henry Toylet holds in fee 1 messuage in the parish of St Michael's which he has by gift of William Toylet, his father, which same William bought that from John son of Hugh Findesilver, which same John acquired that through the death of the said Hugh, his father, which same Hugh acquired that by ancient purchase, and in respect thereof he pays per annum to the prior of Barnwell 12d., by which warranty the said prior is unaware of any claim to the said income.

[672] The same Henry holds a piece of land above which his grange is situated in the parish of All Saints at the Castle, which he has by gift of the said William, his father, and the said William acquired that by ancient purchase, and in respect thereof he pays per annum to the prior and convent of Barnwell 12d., by which warranty the said prior is unaware of any claim to the said income.

[673] The same Henry holds 1 messuage in the parish of Holy Sepulchre which he has by hereditary right through the death of William Toylet, his father, which same William bought that from Matilda Miriel and from Margaret, daughter of the said Matilda, which same they acquired by ancient succession of their ancestors, and in respect thereof he pays per annum to Lord Roger of the Exchequer 2s., and to the[73] nuns of Swaffham 3s., by which warranty the said nuns are unaware of any claim to the said income.

[674] The same Henry holds a granary in the parish of All Saints next to the hospital of Cambridge, which he has by hereditary right through the death of the said William Toylet, his father, which same William bought that from Leon Dunning, which same Leon acquired that by inheritance through the death of his ancestors, and in respect thereof he pays per annum to the aforesaid Leon 2d.

[675] The same Henry holds 29 acres of land in the fields of Cambridge which descended to him by inheritance through the death of William Toylet, his father, which same William bought those from Leon Dunning, which same Leon acquired those by inheritance through the death of Adam, his father, and the said Adam acquired those by ancient purchase, and in respect thereof

he pays per annum to the said Leon and his heirs 7d. and 1 lb. of cumin.

[676]   The same Henry holds ½ acre of land in the same fields which he bought from Alan de Howes, and the said Alan acquired that by hereditary right through the death of Richard de Howes, his father, and in respect thereof he pays per annum to the said Alan 1d.

[677]   The same Henry holds 1 acre of land in the same fields which descended to him by inheritance through the death of William Toylet, his father, which same William bought that from Matilda de Wimbotsham, which same Matilda acquired that by inheritance through the death of her ancestors, and in respect thereof he pays per annum to the heirs of the said Matilda 2d.

[678]   The same Henry holds 3 half acres of land in the fields of Cambridge which he acquired by hereditary right through the death of William, his father, which same William bought those from Richard son of Walter of Newnham, cleric, which same Richard acquired those by inheritance through the death of the said Walter, his father, and in respect thereof he pays per annum to the heirs of the said Richard ½d.

[679]   The same Henry holds 3 roods of land in the aforesaid fields which he has by hereditary right through the death of the said William, his father, which same William bought those from Thomas Godeman, which same Thomas acquired those by inheritance through the death of Hugh Godeman, his father, which same Hugh acquired those by ancient purchase, and in respect thereof he pays per annum to the said Thomas 1½d.

[680]   The same Henry holds 2 acres of land in the aforesaid fields which he has by hereditary right through the death of the aforesaid William, his father, which same William bought those from John Gogging, which same John acquired those by hereditary succession through the death of Michael Gogging, his father, and in respect thereof he pays per annum to the heirs of John Gogging 2d.

[681]   The same Henry holds 6 selions in the fields of Cambridge which he has by inheritance through the death of the said William, his father, which same William bought those from John Waubert of Newnham, which same John acquired those by hereditary succession through the death of William Waubert, his father, which same William acquired those by ancient succession of his parents, and in respect thereof he pays per annum to heirs of the said John Waubert 1d.

[682]   The same Henry holds ½ acre of land in the aforesaid fields which he bought from Matilda daughter of Richard de Stowe, and the said Matilda acquired that by hereditary right through the death of the said Richard Baker, her father, and in respect thereof he pays per annum to the heirs of the said Matilda 1d.

[683]   The same Henry holds 7 acres of land and a ½ acre in the fields of Cambridge which he has by hereditary right through the death of William, his brother, which same William bought from Nicholas son of Nicholas Childman, which same Nicholas acquired those by hereditary right through the death of the said Nicholas, his father, and the said Nicholas acquired those through the death of Childman, his father, and the said Childman acquired those by ancient hereditary succession of his parents, and in respect thereof he pays per annum to the bailiffs of Cambridge who hold the said town in fee farm etcetera for hawgable 10d.

[684]   Item William Crocheman holds 1 messuage in the parish of St Michael's, which he has by gift of Master Richard Crocheman, his father, which same Master Richard acquired that by exchange from Walter Crocheman, his brother, for a certain other messuage which the same Walter acquired by hereditary right through the death of Fulk, his father, and the said Fulk acquired that by ancient succession of his parents, and in respect thereof he pays per annum to the bailiffs of Cambridge who hold the said town in fee farm etcetera for hawgable 4d.

[685]   The same William holds a piece of vacant land at the top of the aforesaid messuage towards the east and in respect thereof he pays per annum to Lord Simon de Furneus 6d., and to the nuns of St Radegund's 1 pair of gloves at the price of ½d., and to the heirs of the aforesaid Richard Crocheman 1 pair of gloves at the price of ½d.

[686]   The same William holds 1 messuage in the parish of St Mary's which he has by gift of John Goldring, which same John acquired that by inheritance through the death of William Goldring, his father, which same William bought that from Alexander Bozun, which same Alexander acquired that by inheritance through the death of John Potekin, his father, and in respect thereof he pays per annum to Agnes of Barton 10s., and to the nuns of St Radegund's 6s. 8d., by which warranty they are unaware of any claim to the said income, and to the bailiffs of Cambridge who hold the said town in fee farm etcetera for hawgable 1d.

[687]   Item Adam de le Grene of Walpol, chaplain, and Thomas of Moulton hold a certain messuage in the parish of St Michael's

which they bought from John son of Paul Wombe, which same John acquired that by inheritance through the death of Paul Wombe, his father, which same Paul acquired that by gift of Radulph Wombe, his father, which same Radulph acquired that by ancient purchase, and in respect thereof they pay per annum to the said John 1d., and to the nuns of St Radegund's 2s. by which warranty they are unaware of any claim to the said income.

[688] Item Margaret daughter of Fulk of Barnwell holds 1 messuage in the parish of St Michael's which descended to her by hereditary right through the death of the said Fulk, her father, which same Fulk acquired that by hereditary right through the death of Peter of Barnwell, his father, and the said Peter acquired that by ancient succession of his ancestors, and in respect thereof she pays per annum to the scholars of Merton 6d.

[689] Item the same Margaret holds 1 messuage in the parish of St Benedict's which descended to her by inheritance through the death of the aforesaid Fulk, her father, which same Fulk acquired that by ancient succession of his ancestors, and in respect thereof she pays per annum to William de Novacurt and his heirs 12d.

[690] Item Richard le Der holds 1 messuage in the parish of St Michael's which he bought from William de Huntingdon, which same William bought that Gilbert Yep, which same Gilbert acquired that by ancient purchase, and in respect thereof he pays per annum to the prior of Thremhall 3s. 1d. by assignment of John de Engayne, who gave the said income to the aforesaid prior.

[691] Item Master William de Beston holds 1 messuage in the parish of St Michael's which he bought from Ermina de Hardwick, which same Ermina acquired that by gift of Master Alexander of St Edmunds, and the said Alexander acquired that by ancient purchase, and in respect thereof he pays per annum to the Templars of Deneye ½ mark by which warranty they are unaware of any claim to the said income.

[692] Item Master Adam de Boudon holds 1 messuage in the parish of St Michael's which same he holds from the master and brothers of St John's Hospital, Cambridge, which same master and brothers acquired the said messuage by concession and quitclaim of Thomas Toylet, and the said Thomas acquired that by ancient purchase, and in respect thereof he pays per annum to the said master and brothers 2s. by assignment of the aforesaid Thomas, and to the nuns of St Radegund's 2s., by which warranty they are unaware of any claim to the said income.

[693]   Item Master Stephen de Aseligfeld, rector of St Michael's Church holds 1 messuage in the same parish which same messuage Johanna de Benwick gave to the said church in pure and perpetual alms, and the said Johanna acquired that by gift of Master Adam de Boudon, and the said Master Adam bought that from Thomas Arinvene, the upholder, and the said Thomas bought that from William de la Bruere, chaplain, and the said William acquired that by hereditary right through the death of Thomas de la Bruere, his father, which same Thomas acquired that by ancient purchase, and in respect thereof he pays per annum to the said lord William de la Bruere, chaplain, and his heirs [274] and to the prior and convent of Anglesey 12d., by which warranty the said prior and convent are unaware of any claim to the said income, and to the bailiffs of Cambridge who hold the said town in fee farm etcetera for hawgable 2d.

[694]   Item Lord Simon Constable, knight of Holderness, and Johanna, his wife, hold 1 messuage in the parish of St Michael's which descended to the aforesaid Johanna by inheritance through the death of Thomas de Stanton, her father, and the said Thomas acquired that by ancient purchase, and in respect thereof they pay per annum to the prioress and convent of St Radegund's 3s., by which warranty they are unaware of any claim to the said income.

[695]   Item the said Simon and Johanna his wife hold 2 shops in the parish of All Saints next to the hospital, which same shops descended to the said Johanna by hereditary right through the death of Thomas, cleric, her father, and the said Thomas acquired those by ancient purchase, and in respect thereof they pay per annum to Richard Wombe 2s., and to the almoner of Ely 6s. by which warranty the almoner is unaware of any claim to the said income.

[696]   Item William de la Bruere, chaplain, holds 1 messuage in the parish of St Michael's which he has by hereditary right through the death of Thomas de la Bruere, his father, which same Thomas acquired that through the death of Robert, his father, and the said Robert bought that from Henry and Herbert, sons of Segar' of Cambridge, and in respect thereof he pays per annum to the bailiffs of Cambridge who hold the said town in fee farm etcetera for hawgable 4d.

[697]   Item Master Andrew de Gisleham holds 1 messuage in the parish of St Michael's which he bought from Master Nicholas de Totington and the said master acquired that by gift of Robert, former rector of the church of Willingham, which same Robert

bought that from Master Adam de Boudon, which same Master
Adam bought that from John Seliman, and the said John acquired
that by inheritance through the death of Saleman, his father, and
in respect thereof he pays per annum to Master Adam 12d., and
to the prior of Barnwell 4s., by which warranty the said prior
is unaware of any claim to the said income, and to the bailiffs
of Cambridge who hold the said town in fee farm etcetera for
hawgable 2d.

[698] Master Radulph de Walepol, archdeacon of Ely, holds 1 messuage
with appurtenances in the parish of St Michael's, which same he
has by gift of the venerable father Nicholas, Bishop of Winchester,
which same bishop bought that from Thomas Toylet and gave,
for the help in maintaining a certain chaplain celebrating divine
service for the soul of the venerable Father Hugh, former Bishop
of Ely, 20s. every year.

[699] Simon son and heir of Simon Godeman holds 1 messuage with
appurtenances in the parish of St Michael's, Cambridge, which
descended to him by inheritance through the death of the said
Simon, his father, and the said Simon bought that from John,
son of Bartholomew Wombe, which same John acquired that
by hereditary right through the death of the said Bartholomew,
his father, which same Bartholomew acquired that by hereditary
right through the death of Radulph Wombe, his father, and the
said Radulph acquired that by ancient purchase, and in respect
thereof he pays per annum to Richard Wombe and his heirs 6d.

[700] The same Simon holds 7 acres of land in the fields of Cambridge
and Barnwell which same descended to him by inheritance
through the death of Simon Godeman, father, which same Simon
bought those from John Aure, which same John acquired those
by inheritance through the death of John Aure, his father, and
the said John acquired those through the death of Reginald, his
father, which same Reginald acquired that by purchase from
William son of Master Geoffrey, for which he pays per annum
to John Aure and his heirs ½d., and to Luke of St Edmunds 3s.

[701] The said Simon holds 5½ acres of land lying in the fields of
Cambridge which descended to him by inheritance through the
death of the said Simon, his father, which same Simon bought
those from William son of Ivo, and the said William bought those
from Leon Dunning, and the said Leon acquired those through
the death of Adam Dunning, his father, and in respect thereof
he pays per annum to the heirs of the said William 2 roses, and
to the said Leon 4d.

[702]   Item the said Simon holds 2 acres of land lying in Swinecroft which descended to him by inheritance through the death of the said Simon, his father, which same Simon bought those from John Aure, and the said John acquired those by hereditary right through the death of John Aure, his father, which same John acquired those by inheritance through the death of Reginald Aure, his father, and the said Reginald bought those from the prioress and convent of St Radegund's, and the said prioress and convent acquired those by gift of Harvey son of Eustace, and in respect thereof he pays per annum to the said John and his heirs 1d., and to the heirs of Robert Seman 1d., and to the heirs of John le Rus 1 lb. of cumin, and to the prioress and convent of St Radegund's 12d.

[703]   The same Simon holds 1 half acre of land in the fields of Barnwell which descended to him by inheritance through the death of the aforesaid Simon, his father, which same Simon bought that from Richard Burs and Margaret, his wife, and in respect thereof he pays per annum to the said Richard and Margaret and their heirs 1 clove gillyflower and to the heirs of Radulph le Chapeler 1d.

[704]   The same Simon holds 3 roods of land in the fields of Barnwell which descended to him by inheritance through the death of the said Simon, his father, which same Simon bought those from Richard Burs and William Castelein, which same Richard and William acquired those by inheritance through the death of their ancestors, and in respect thereof he pays per annum to the said Richard and William and their heirs 2 roses.

[705]   Item the said Simon holds 1 rood and a half of land in the fields of Cambridge which descended to him by inheritance through the death of Simon, his father, which same Simon bought that from Eustace Dunning, and the said Eustace acquired that by inheritance through the death of Harvey Dunning, his father, and in respect thereof he pays per annum to the scholars of Merton ½d.

[706]   Item Avicia daughter of Simon Godeman holds 1 messuage with appurtenances in the parish of All Saints which she has by gift of the said Simon, her father, which same Simon bought that from John de Brampton, which same John acquired that through the death of Robert de Brampton, his father, and the said Robert acquired that by inheritance through the death of Radulph de Brampton, which same Radulph bought that from Robert de la Bruere, and in respect thereof she pays per annum on behalf of the heirs of the Simon to the brothers of Thremhall

2s., and to the heirs of the said Robert de la Bruere 1 rose, by which way and by which warranty the said brothers are unaware of any claim to the said income.

[707] Item the same Avicia holds 6 acres and 3 roods of land in the fields of Cambridge which she has by gift of the said Simon, her father, which same Simon bought those from John Aure, which same John acquired those by hereditary right through the death of John, his father, and in respect thereof she pays per annum on behalf of the heirs of the said Simon to the said John and his heirs 7d., and to the heirs of Stephen de Hauxton 4d., and to the heirs of John le Rus 2d.

[708] Item the same Avicia holds 2 acres of land in the same fields which she has by gift of the aforesaid Simon, her father, and the said Simon bought those from John Porthors, and in respect thereof she pays per annum on behalf of the heirs of the said Simon to the said John 2d.

[709] Item the same Avicia holds 1 acre and a half in the aforesaid fields which she has by gift of the said Simon, her father, which same Simon bought those from William son of Ivo, and in respect thereof she pays per annum on behalf of the heirs of the said Simon to the said William and his heirs 2d.

[710] Item the said Avicia holds ½ acre of land in the fields of Cambridge which she has by gift of the said Simon, her father, which same Simon bought that from Humphrey Brucnot and in respect thereof she pays per annum on behalf of the heirs of the said Simon to the heirs of the said Humphrey 1 rose, and to the heirs of Thomas Longis 2d., and to the heirs of the said Simon for the aforesaid messuage and the aforesaid land ½d.

[711] Item Alicia daughter of Simon Godeman holds 1 messuage in the parish of St John's, Cambridge, which she has by gift of Simon Godeman, her father, which same Simon bought that from Thomas Plote, and the said Thomas that from Walter de Huntingdon. And the said Thomas bought a certain part of that messuage from Richard son of Ivo, and in respect thereof she pays per annum on behalf of the heirs of the said Simon to the heirs of Thomas Plote 1d., and for the part of land to the heirs of the said Richard 2d., and to the heirs of Walter de Huntingdon ½d.

[712] Item the same Alicia holds a piece of land with a house situated above in the parish of All Saints above the water at Dame Nichol's Hythe which she has by gift of the said Simon, her father, and the said Simon bought that from Andrew, son of William son

of Ivo, which same piece of land descended to the said Andrew by inheritance through the death of the said William, his father, and the said William bought that from Richard son of Ivo, his brother, which same Richard acquired that by inheritance through the death of Ivo, his father, and in respect thereof she pays per annum on behalf of the heirs of the said Simon to the heirs of the said Andrew ½d., and to William Eliot and his heirs ½d., and to the heirs of the said Richard 12d.

[713] Item the same Alicia holds a certain shop in the parish of All Saints which she has by gift of the said Simon, her father, which same Simon bought that from Henry de Waddon and the said Henry acquired that by gift of Henry Nadon, and the said Henry bought that from the said Henry de Waddon and Alicia Harvey, his wife, and the said Alicia acquired that by gift of Bartholomew Wombe, her son, and the said Bartholomew acquired that by inheritance through the death of Harvey Wombe, his father and in respect thereof she pays per annum on behalf of the heirs of the said Simon to the heirs of Henry de Waddon 1 rose and to the heirs of Richard son of John Em of Grantchester 1 rose.

[714] Item the same Alicia holds 8 acres of land and a half in the fields of Cambridge which she has by gift of the said Simon, her father, and the said Simon bought those from John Porthors, for which she pays per annum to the said John and his heirs 6d.

[715] Item the said Alicia holds 2 acres and a half of land in the fields of Cambridge which she has by gift of the said Simon, her father, and the said Simon bought those from William son of Ivo, and the said William acquired those by ancient purchase, for which she pays per annum to the heirs of the said William 6d.

[P36] John de Fulton holds 1 messuage and 6 acres of land and a half and 10s. of annual income in the town and fields of Cambridge, which same messuage and land and income he has by hereditary right through the death of Robert de Fulton, his father, which same Robert acquired those by gift of Henry, rector of the church of Barrington, which same Henry bought those from Peter de Welles, which same Peter bought those from Robert of St Edmunds, and in respect thereof he pays per annum to the prior and convent of Barnwell 18d., by which warranty they are unaware of any claim to the said income.

[716] Item Agnes de Huntingdon holds 2 messuages in the parish of All Saints next to St John's Hospital which same messuages she has by gift of Master Simon de Huntingdon, which same Master Simon bought those from John son of Nicholas Wombe, which same

John acquired those by inheritance through the death of the said Nicholas Wombe, his father, and the said Nicholas acquired those by gift of Radulph Wombe, his father, which same Radulph acquired those by ancient purchase, and in respect thereof she pays per annum to the said John ½d., and to the prioress of St Radegund's 8s., by which warranty they are unaware of any claim to the said income, and to the bailiffs of Cambridge who hold the said town in fee farm etcetera for hawgable ½d.

[717]   Item the same Agnes holds 1 messuage in fee in the parish of St Radegund's which she bought from John, former vicar of All Saints Church next to the Hospital, which same John bought that from William Cook which same William acquired that by hereditary succession through the death of Geoffrey Cook, his father, which same Geoffrey bought that from Nicholas Sorand, and the said Nicholas acquired that by ancient purchase, and in respect thereof she pays per annum to the prioress of St Radegund's 4s., by which warranty they are unaware of any claim to the said income.

[718]   Item Walter Pylat holds 1 messuage in the parish of All Saints next to the hospital which he bought from the master and brothers of St John's Hospital, Cambridge, and in respect thereof he pays per annum to the said master and brothers 5s., in which way and by which warranty the master and brothers are unaware of any claim to the said income and to the said messuage.

[719]   Item John son of William Waubert holds 1 messuage in the parish of All Saints next to St John's Hospital, Cambridge, which he has by gift of John Torel, his nephew, which messuage descended to the said John by inheritance through the death of Alan Torel, his father, and the said Alan acquired that through the death of his ancestors, and in respect thereof he pays per annum to Radulph son of Felicia de Queye 28d., and to John Porthors and his heirs 13d., and to Master Robert Aunger 8d., and to the prior of Anglesey 1d., by which warranty the said prior is unaware of any claim to the said income.

[720]   Item John holds 1 acre of land in Newnham which descended to him by inheritance through the death of William Waubert, his father, which same William bought that from John Waubert, his brother, and the said John acquired that through the death of Walter Waubert, his father, and the said Walter acquired that by ancient purchase, and in respect thereof he pays per annum to the prior of Barnwell 18d., by which warranty the said prior is unaware of any claim to the said income.

[721] Item Lucia who was wife of William Toylet holds 1 messuage in the parish of All Saints next to the hospital which she bought from William of St Edmunds, chaplain, which same William acquired that by gift of Robert of St Edmunds, his father, which same Robert bought that from Andrew de Winepol, which same Andrew acquired that by ancient succession of his ancestors, and in respect thereof she pays per annum to the chancellor of the University of Cambridge 3s., and to St John's Hospital, Cambridge, 12d.

[722] Item Richard Crocheman holds 1 messuage in the parish of All Saints next to the hospital which descended to him by inheritance through the death of Walter Crocheman, his father, which same Walter acquired that by hereditary right through the death of Catherine, his sister, which same Catherine bought that from Robert le Surgeon, which same Robert acquired that by ancient succession of his ancestors, and in respect thereof he pays per annum to the prioress of St Radegund's 6d., by which warranty they are unaware of any claim to the said income, and to the bailiffs of Cambridge who hold the said town in fee farm etcetera for hawgable 1½d.

[723] Item Richard holds 1 messuage in the parish of St Michael's which he has by gift of Henry Nadon, which same Henry bought that from Margaret daughter of Fulk of Barnwell, which same Margaret acquired that by gift of the aforesaid Fulk, her father, which same Fulk acquired that by ancient succession of his ancestors, and in respect thereof he pays per annum to the aforesaid Margaret 4d.

[724] Item Richard holds 1 acre of land in Cambridge which he has by gift of the said Henry Nadon, which same Henry bought that from Richard Wombe, which same Richard acquired that by inheritance through the death of John, his brother, which same John acquired that by inheritance through the death of Bartholomew Wombe, his father, and in respect thereof he pays per annum to the prior of Barnwell 12d.

[725] Item William de Billigford holds 1 messuage in the parish of All Saints next to the hospital which he has by gift of Cristiana de Norton, which same Cristiana acquired that by gift of John de Norton, chaplain, and the said John bought that from Geoffrey de Histon, and the said Geoffrey bought that from Michael Pylet, which same Michael acquired that by hereditary succession through the death of Mabilia, his friend, and the said Mabilia acquired that by ancient succession of her ancestors,

and in respect thereof he pays per annum to the said Michael 1 lb. of cumin, and to the said Cristiana 1 pair of gloves at the price of 1d., and to Alan Segin 12d., and to St John's Hospital, Cambridge, 12d., and the to the nuns of St Radegund's ½ mark, in which way and by which warranty the aforesaid brothers of St John's Hospital and the said nuns are unaware of any claim to the said income.

[RENTS WITH MISSING LOCATION INFORMATION]

[A50]   Item Henry de Waddon and Alicia, his wife, hold 1 messuage in Cambridge by gift of Master Robert Aunger le Rus for service of 1d. and pay to the prior of Barnwell 8d.

[A51]   Item the same Henry and Alicia hold 2 messuages from Nicholas, son of Andrew de Winepol for service of ½d.

[A52]   Item they hold 1 messuage from Thomas Godeman for service of ½d. and pay to Lord John de Engayne 3s.

[A53]   Item they hold 1 messuage from the heirs of William Achelard for service of 1 clove gillyflower and pay to the prioress of St Radegund's 4s. per annum.

[A54]   Item they hold 1 messuage from the heirs of Henry Eveske for service of 12d.

[A55]   Item they hold a small piece of land from William of St Edmunds for service of ½d.

[A56]   Item they hold 1 shop from Walter le Hunte for service of ½ lb. of cumin.

[A57]   Item they hold 1 shop from the heirs of the aforesaid Philip de Hengham for service of 1 clove gillyflower.

[A58]   Item they hold 1 shop from Richard Bateman for service of ½d.

[A59]   Item they hold 4 acres of land from the heirs of William son of Ivo for service of 1 clove gillyflower.

[A60]   Item they hold 4 acres of land from the heirs of Robert of St Edmunds for service of 1 rose.

[A61]   Item they have from fixed rents 6s. 8d. from the heirs of Nicholas Jochim for the same service.

[A62]   Item they have from Bartholomew son of Harvey Wombe 8s. ½d. paid annually.

[NO INFORMATION ON CHURCH FREEHOLD]

[F21]   Item it is inquired how much any archbishop, bishop, etcetera has in freehold, as in freehold in demesne as in demesne.

It is said that at this time no one responds in any other way as they responded in the previous clause.

[SCUTAGE OBLIGATIONS]

[F22]   Item it is inquired from which fiefs and other tenures scutage should be given and should become accustomed etcetera.

It is said that the prior and canons of Huntingdon hold 60 acres of land in knight's fee which they have by gift of Lord Radulph de Turbelvill and Alicia, his wife, and they owe scutage when it should occur. Which same prior and convent have a charter of confirmation from lord Reginald le Grey which acquits them from scutage and all other service.

[P37]   Item Sabina Hubert holds 16 acres of land in the fields of Cambridge in knight's fee from the ancestors of lord Reginald le Grey, namely from Lady Emma de la Leye, and she pays per annum for the aforesaid land to lord Reginald le Grey 1 lb. of pepper, and gives for scutage 10s. to the said lord Reginald le Grey when it should occur, namely as much as pertains to a quarter part of 1 knight's fee.

[P38]   Item Leon Dunning holds in the town and in the fields of Cambridge half a knight's fee and 4 pounds paid annually and 1 water-mill pertaining to the said half fee, which descended to him by inheritance through the death of Adam Dunning, his father, which same Adam held that from Lord Robert de Mortimer, and that Lord Robert held that from lord Robert de Brus, and he pays per annum for the aforesaid half knight's fee and the aforesaid 4 pounds paid annually and the mill to Lord William de Mortimer, son of the said Lord Robert, 32 marks, and the said lord William owes the ewerer, the aforesaid Leon, for scutage when it should occur and from all other things pertaining to the said half fee.

[P39]   Item Radulph de Queye holds in the town and fields of Cambridge, in Newnham and in Barnwell 1 messuage and 38 acres of land and 2 acres of meadow by gift and feoffment of Felicia, widow of William de Queye, his mother, which same Felicia had and held the aforesaid messuage of land and meadow by gift of Alicia de Turbelvill, and he pays in respect thereof per annum to the heirs of lord Radulph de Trubelvile 1 lb. of pepper, and gives scutage when it should occur for a quarter part of 1 knight's fee.

[P40]   Item the scholars of Merton hold 15 acres of land and 10s. 2d. paid annually in fief of the county of Leicester, and they pay in respect thereof per annum to Lord Edmund, brother of the Lord King, 3s. 10d., and give scutage when it should occur, more for more and less for less, just as is written above.

[VARIOUS ISSUES ON WHICH THERE IS NO INFORMATION]

[F23]   Item it is inquired how much land or holdings any free men, tenants or cottagers hold in the market town or other towns or hamlets, etcetera.

It is said that this clause does not affect the town of Cambridge.

[F24]   Item it is inquired who holds the communal fishery or a separate one in waters or river of the Lord King etcetera.

It is said that the townspeople of Cambridge have a communal fishery in its waters of the county belonging to the town of Cambridge, which same waters have by demise and concession of the ancestors of the Lord King through charters that they hold in respect thereof as is stated above, by this clause how much by any archbishop, bishop, etcetera.

[F25]   Item if anyone holding from the Lord King as tenant-in-chief, through baronial tenure or grand or petty serjeanty, has sold their lands or holdings to anyone, or alienated them in any way, etcetera.

It is said that nothing is known regarding this clause.

[F26]   Item it is inquired who claims to have liberties, what kind and in which manner and which liberties have been made use of until now, whether by charters of the predecessors of the king or by their own power or authority or by favour or permission of the bailiffs or sheriffs or ministers of the Lord King, should they have these liberties or not. Item if anyone besides the Lord King or any other person superior or inferior should have encroached on or appropriated those liberties for themselves etcetera.

[ENCROACHMENTS BY THE UNIVERSITY]

[F27]   It is said that the Chancellor and Master of the University of Cambridge, by their own authority have encroached upon and appropriated greater liberties than are contained in the charters which they have from the predecessors of the Lord King, by their own authority as is stated, compelling the sheriffs of the Lord King of Cambridge with sentences of excommunication to vouch for with a corporal oath regarding those which relate to the Lord King and to the office of the sheriffs of the aforesaid Lord King in clear prejudice to the Lord King, since in the charters that they have from the predecessors of the Lord King, it is not contained that the aforesaid sheriffs of the Lord King should vouch for the same Chancellor and Master by corporal oath as is aforesaid.

[RIGHTS OF THE GUILD OF MERCHANTS]

[F28]   Item it is said that the towns-people of Cambridge have a guild of
merchants and that none of them should plead outside the walls
of the town of Cambridge regarding any plea except pleas of
external tenures, and that none of them should engage in duels,
and that writs relating to the Crown can be deraigned according
to the ancient custom of the town, and that they should be quit
of tolls of passage, export, bridges, stallage inside and outside
the marketplace, and in the sea-ports of England and through
all lands of the Lord King on this side of the sea and overseas,
and they that they have the return of all writs in the vill of
Cambridge liberties relating to them, and that through their own
hands the correspondence from the Exchequer of all demands
and summonses relating to the same Exchequer, and that in the
aforesaid town they can judge all pleas relating to the said town,
both from prevention of distress and from other pleas that can
be judged without a justiciar, and that from those they can elect
and appoint a coroner in the aforesaid town for the performing
in emergency the attachment in crown pleas of the Lord King in
the aforesaid town of Cambridge. These liberties moreover the
townspeople have and claim to have through charters which they
have from the predecessors of the above-mentioned Lord King.

[NO INFORMATION ON ENCROACHMENTS ON MARKET
PRIVILEGES]

[F29]   Item it is inquired who has a gallows, tumbrel, pillory and other
items that are associated with the execution of justice, the assize
of bread, and profit from ship wreck, returns of writ or other
items relating to the king.

It is said that the towns-people of Cambridge have gallows,
tumbrel, pillory and the other items which are included in this
clause, except from ship wreck by ancient habit of customs and
pertaining to the said town of Cambridge, and also by demise
and concession of the kings, predecessors of the above-mentioned
Lord King.

[NO INFORMATION ON ENCROACHMENTS ON CHASES
AND WARRENS]

[F30]   Item who from ancient liberties has chases and warrens by
concession of the Lord King and his predecessors. Item who has
newly appropriated these for themselves.

It is said that nothing is known regarding this clause.

[FAIRS AND MARKETS]

[F31] Item it is inquired who has chases and warrens, fairs, markets or other liberties which relate to the Lord King, etcetera.

It is said that the townspeople of Cambridge who have a certain market in the town of Cambridge in Rogation week, and a market in the same town pertaining to the borough of Cambridge by ancient custom by demise and concession of the kings, predecessors to the Lord King, through charters which they have from the predecessors of the above-mentioned Lord King.

[PURPRESTURE BY THE BISHOP OF ELY]

[F32] Item it is inquired if anyone or their ancestors should cause any purpresture besides the Lord King or other royal dignitary, etcetera.

It is said that the lord bishop of Ely caused a certain purpresture above the common pasture belonging to the town and county of Cambridge in *Meldich*, erecting a certain ditch the length of 8 perches to the great prejudice and damage of the whole county of Cambridge.

[MORE ISSUES ON WHICH THERE IS NO INFORMATION]

[F33] Item if any man of religion holds any church for his own use, any advowsons that should by law belong to the Lord King, etcetera.

It is said that nothing is known regarding this clause.

[F34] Item it is inquired if any land or holdings which should be escheated to the Lord King or in his custody should be in their possession or in the possession of others, etcetera.

It is said that nothing is known regarding this clause.

[F35] Item it is inquired of whatever knight's fee, fee of land or other holding has been given or sold to men of religion or others in prejudice of the Lord King, where the Lord King loses ownership, or by marriage or inheritance, etcetera.

It is said that nothing is known regarding this clause.

[F36] Item it is inquired of the breaking of ancient customs of service and other things having been taken away from the Lord King and his ancestors, etcetera.

It is said that nothing is known regarding this clause.

[F37] Item it is inquired of the fiefs and vassals of the Lord King and their holdings who in any way hold from themselves as tenant-in-chief, etcetera.

It is said that nothing is known regarding this clause.

[F38]   Item it is inquired how many hundreds and wapentakes should be in the possession of the Lord King and how many in the possession of others, etcetera.

It is said that nothing is known regarding this clause which does not touch upon the aforesaid town of Cambridge.

[F39]   Item it is inquired if the heirs of any tenants of the Lord King as tenant-in-chief, of any ownership and marriage relating to the King and should be taken away from the Lord King or cancelled, and anyone married without licence of the Lord King etcetera. Item if any woman or girl should be freely married through the Lord King to anyone who should be given in marriage without licence of the king or was seized and married against their will by whom, etcetera.

It is said that nothing is known regarding this clause.

[F40]   Item it is inquired if any land or holdings which should be escheated to the Lord King should be concealed and in whose possession they would appear to be, etcetera.

It is said that nothing is known regarding this clause.

[F41]   Item if anything from the fief of the Lord King or his barons, serjeants, magnates or lesser men should have been sold or in any other way alienated, etcetera.

It is said that there is nothing to know regarding this clause.

[F42]   Item who are those who are held as guards or for the making the defences of the castle of the Lord King, etcetera.

It is said that nothing is known regarding this clause.

[WATERMILLS]

[F43]   Item it is inquired if anyone should have diverted the course of the waters of the rivers of the Lord King and raised lake or weir mills, etcetera.

It is said that Leon Dunning holds a water mill pertaining to his tenement which he holds from Lord William de Mortimer, which mill-lake is divided from the lake of the Lord King, which same lake belongs to the burgesses of Cambridge who hold the town of Cambridge in fee farm from the Lord King as is stated, in which manner and by which warranty the said lake had been divided they do not know.

[ADVOWSONS OF HOSPITALS: for churches see below]

[F44]   Item who are the patrons of the abbeys, priories, high offices, prebends, wardens of the hospital and the liberties of the chapel of the Lord King which from antiquity belong to the crown of the King, and which should be in his possession and which are not, etcetera.

It is said that the advowson and donations to St John the Evangelist's Hospital, Cambridge, and the hospital of lepers of Stourbridge Common by law should belong to the burgesses of Cambridge who hold the said town of Cambridge in fee farm from the Lord King as is stated above, and as is fully written above in that clause 'How much each archbishop, bishop' etcetera.

[ESCHEATS OF CRIMINALS' PROPERTY TO THE KING]

[F45]   Item it is inquired of the land of the Normans of felons, fugitives and others who are and should be escheated to the Lord King, etcetera.

It is said that Bonenfaunt Judeus who had been recently hung for clipping coins had a certain piece of vacant land in the town of Cambridge which should be escheated to the Lord King.

[ENCROACHMENTS ON THE KING'S DIKE]

[F46]   Item which and how many town plots and vacant pieces of land the King has in the towns, borough, market town and other towns and hamlets, etcetera.

It is said that the Lord King, that is Lord Henry, father of King Edward who now is, in the time of the troubles in the kingdom of England caused to be constructed certain dikes which surround the town of Cambridge from one part with a certain border pertaining to the said dike, which same dike with adjacent border remains empty and no one carries out completion, to the great danger and damage of all men having courtyards abutting the aforesaid border, nevertheless it is said that Richard Laurence planted certain trees underneath the Lord King's dike opposite his courtyard for the maintenance and repair of the said dike but no right or ownership was claimed for him with regard to the ground or to the trees.

[F47]   Item the same Richard built a certain bridge crossing over the said dike so that he could have entrance and exit for his beasts and his cattle to his common pasture of Grenecroft, as the said Richard and his ancestors were accustomed to have in the time of peace, from time immemorial.

[F48]   Item they say that Thomas de Clopton appropriated for himself, from the border pertaining to the aforesaid dike of the Lord King, a certain piece of land adjacent to the dike at the end of his courtyard, of a length of 50 feet and width of 8 feet, between the top of the dike and his courtyard.

[F49]   Item Stephen, chaplain, appropriated to himself similarly a certain piece of land lying next to the dike at the end of his courtyard, of the length of 36 feet and width between the top of the dike and his court of 8 feet.

[MORE ISSUES ON WHICH THERE IS NO INFORMATION]

[F50]   Item of the holdings of the farm of the Lord King, citizens of the town or in other manors of the Lord King in fee farm, who by interference to the said farm take escheats and are alienated by them, or retained in which manner they thereupon converted them to their own use.

It is said that nothing is known regarding this clause.

[F51]   Item if any man of religion has intruded into the fief of the Lord King completely or at a time where the Lord King lost ownership and the marriage of heirs, by which manner and in which way and at what time.

It is said that nothing is known regarding this clause.

[F52]   Item it is inquired how much anyone holds of assarts inside the forests of the Lord King, and how much the land and those holdings are worth per annum, and how much the King receives from those assarts per annum, in customary income of service and others. And if anyone else in respect thereof should have anything that they have taken that pertains to that, etcetera.

It is said that nothing is known regarding this clause, which is not affecting the town of Cambridge.

[GREAT BRIDGE OF CAMBRIDGE]

[F53]   Item what bridges and causeways which should be and are accustomed to being royal and comital highways, and who has been accustomed to repairing these, and those allowing the delay to these.

It is said that the repair and maintenance of the Great Bridge of Cambridge belongs to the county of Cambridge, and somebody from the aforesaid county holding land subject to geld who should maintain the bridge as long as the bridge requires repair and maintenance. It is said also that the aforesaid bridge is damaged and weakened, such that large carts and others making the crossing at the same place fall into the water, such that so many men crossing with horses are causing great danger and damage there.

[ADVOWSONS OF CHURCHES]

Of advowsons of churches and who are the true patrons of the churches sited in the town of Cambridge.

[F54]   It is said that the advowson and donation of St Mary's Church, Cambridge, belongs to the Lord King, who is the true patron of the aforesaid church.

[F55]   Item it is said that the advowson and donation of St Michael's Church, Cambridge, belongs de Matilda de Walda, who is the true patron of the aforesaid church and by law the patronage belongs to her through hereditary right through the death of her ancestors as is stated in the great roll.

[F56]   Item it is said that the advowson and donation of St Benedict's Church, Cambridge, belongs to lord Giles de Argenteyim who is the true patron of the aforesaid church, the patronage belonging to him through hereditary right through the death of his ancestors as is stated.

[F57]   Item it is said that the prior and convent of Barnwell have in their own use All Saints' Church, and St Peter's Church, and St Giles's Church at the Castle, and Holy Sepulchre Church in the Jewry, and St Edward's Church, and St Joseph's Church, and St Botolph's Church of which they were rightly made protector, and the true patron of the aforesaid churches, by which manner and in which way and by which warranty they obtained the aforesaid churches it is not known, because they have held the aforesaid churches for such a long time that no memory remains.

[F58]   Item the prioress and nuns of St Radegund's hold St Clement's Church and All Saints' Church in the Jewry for their own use, who were rightly made protector, and the true patron of the aforesaid churches by which manner and in which way and by which warranty they obtained the aforesaid churches it is not known, because they have held the aforesaid churches for such a long time that no memory remains.

[F59]   Item it is said that the abbot and convent of Derham hold Holy Trinity Church for their own use, who were rightly made protector and the true patron of the aforesaid church, by which manner and in which way and by which warranty they obtained the aforesaid churches it is not known.

[F60]   Item it is said that the prior and convent of Ely hold St Andrew's Church outside the gate of Barnwell, for their own use, of which they were rightly made patron and protector of the aforesaid churches by which manner and in which way and by which warranty they obtained the aforesaid churches it is not known, because they have held the aforesaid churches for such a long time that no memory remains.

[F61]   Item it is said that the advowson and donation of St Edmund's Chapel belongs to Luke of St Edmunds, who is rightly the patron of the aforesaid chapel and by law the patronage belongs to him by hereditary right through the death of his ancestors.

[F62]   Item it is said that the Master and brothers of St John the Evangelist's Hospital, Cambridge hold St Peter's Church outside Trumpington Gate for their own use, which they were rightly made patron and protector of the said church, by which manner and in which way and by which warranty they obtained the aforesaid churches it is not known, because they have held the aforesaid churches for such a long time that no memory remains.

[BEGINNING OF PART 3: POSSIBLE END OF THE ROLL IF PART 3 FITTED IN WHERE INDICATED EARLIER]

[726]   John of Orwell and Helewisa, his wife, hold 1 messuage in the parish of Holy Sepulchre for the term of their lives, which messuage Thomas le Rus father of Helewisa bought from Leon Dunning, and the same Leon Dunning inherited it through the death of Adam, his father, who held it through ancient succession of his ancestors, and he pays per annum to the said Leon ¼d.

[727]   The same John and Helewisa, his wife, hold a ½ acre of land in Cambridge for the term of their lives, which the aforesaid Thomas le Rus, father of Helewisa, bought from Leon Dunning, who acquired it by inheritance through the death of Adam, his father, which Adam held it through ancient succession, and he pays per annum to the aforesaid Leon 1d.

[728]   John of St Edmunds holds in fee 1 messuage in the parish of Holy Sepulchre for the term of his life, which was once held by Mabilia his wife in free marriage, and the said Mabilia acquired it by inheritance through the death of William, the son of Michael Parleben, his father, and the aforesaid William acquired it through succession on the death of the aforesaid Michael Parleben, his father, and he pays per annum to the nuns of St Radegund's 5s., regarding claims of which they have no knowledge.

[729]   William son of John of St Edmunds holds in fee 1 acre of land in the fields of Cambridge which he holds as the gift of William, chaplain, son of Robert of St Edmunds, his uncle, and the said William acquired it by purchase from Bartholomew Wombe, and the same Bartholomew bought it from Matilda who was the wife

of Richard le Wange, and he pays per annum to the said William 1 rose and to the aforesaid Bartholomew 1 needle with thread.

[730] Robert de Wadford holds 1 messuage in fee in the parish of St Clement's in which he lives, and which he bought from Nicholas Pistree, and the same Nicholas held it by succession through the death of Simon, his father, and he pays per annum to the aforesaid Nicholas and his heirs 1 rose and to the almoner of Barnwell 13d. By which warranty they receive the income the almoner is unaware.

[731] The same Robert holds 1 messuage in the parish of St Andrew's which he bought from Master William de Salop, and the same Master William bought it from William the cleric of Ely, and the same William bought it from Nicholas de Hauxton, and the same acquired it from Simon de Hauxton, his brother, and the same Simon acquired it through the death of Henry, his father, and he pays per annum to the aforesaid William 1 rose, and to the bailiffs of Cambridge who hold the town at fee farm 2d.

[732] The same Robert holds 1 messuage in the parish of St Michael's which he bought from the prior and convent of Barnwell, and the aforesaid prior and convent acquired it by the gift of Thomas Toylet, and the same Thomas acquired it through ancient purchase, and he pays per annum to the prior and convent 6d.

[733] Michael Pilat holds a certain piece of land in the parish of All Saints by the Castle where his grange is situated, which he bought from Henry son of Elias Hoppecrane, and that Henry inherited it through the death of Elias, his father, and the said Elias held it from the nuns of St Radegund's and he pays per annum to the aforesaid nuns 6d., regarding claims on which they are ignorant.

[734] The same Michael holds 1 messuage in the parish of St Clement's which he bought from Thomas Godeman, which Thomas acquired by gift of Margaret Sagat, his niece, and the said Margaret acquired it through the death of Peter, her father, and the said Peter bought it from Lord Radulph Pirot and Master Robert Aunger, and he pays per annum to the aforesaid Radulph Pirot 8s., and for a chaplain to celebrate the mass of the Blessed Virgin Mary in the church of St Clement's 6d., and to the aforesaid Thomas 1 rose, and to the bailiffs of Cambridge for hawgable 2½d.

[735] The same Michael holds 2 messuages in fee in the parish of All Saints near St John's Hospital which he inherited through the death of Reginald de Fordham, his father, and the same Reginald inherited them through the death of Reginald, his father, and

he pays per annum to Robert, chaplain of Thorndon, 2s. by assignment of the heirs of Warin Astin.

[736] The same Michael holds 1 piece of vacant land in the parish of All Saints near the Hospital which he inherited through the death of Margaret, his mother, which she acquired through the death of Mabilia, her mother, which Mabilia bought from Alice, daughter of Thomas le Carpenter, which she held by succession through the death of the aforesaid Thomas, and he pays per annum to the aforesaid Alice 1 rose.

[R16] The same Michael holds 4s. of income per annum which same he acquired through the death of Margaret, his mother, which same Margaret acquired that by inheritance through the death of William Pilat, her father, and the said William acquired that through ancient purchase.

[737] Henry Pilat and Sarah, his wife, hold 1 messuage with appurtenances in the parish of Holy Sepulchre, Cambridge, which they bought from Geoffrey de Aldreth, chaplain, and the said Geoffrey bought it from John, son of Stephen le Cupere, and the same John held that by inheritance through the death of Agnes of Colchester, his mother, and the same Agnes acquired that through the death of her father. And in respect thereof they pay per annum to the prior and convent of Barnwell 8s. and 1 lb. of pepper, and on behalf of Geoffrey the chaplain and his heirs for sustaining a lamp in the church of Holy Sepulchre 3d., by which warranty they are unaware.

[738] Thomas de Len holds 1 messuage in the parish of Holy Sepulchre which he bought from the prior and convent of Barnwell, which same messuage Walter le Heimoggere, his father, gave and resigned to the aforesaid prior and convent, and he pays in respect thereof to the aforesaid prior and convent 11s.

[739] Master Thomas Toylet holds in fee 1 messuage in the parish of Holy Sepulchre, which he holds by gift and concession from William Toylet, his father, and the same William bought this from Lord Roger of the Exchequer, and the same Roger bought this same from Moses the Jew of Clare, and in respect thereof he pays per annum to the heirs of Roger of the Exchequer 1 lb. of cumin, and to the nuns of St Mary de Pré ½ mark, and to Leon Dunning 7d., and to the heirs of William Toylet ½d., and Amicia the mother of Thomas Toylet holds the said for the term of her life by demise and concession of the aforesaid Thomas and the nuns know of no claim on their income.

[740]   The same Master Thomas holds 1 messuage in fee in the parish of St Clement's which he has by gift of William Toylet, his father, which same William bought that from Simon, son of Harvey Dunning, and he pays per annum to the heirs of the said Simon 22d., and to the heirs of said William 1 pair of gloves, and to the nuns of St Radegund's 4s., and in what manner and by which warranty they receive this income they are unaware.

[741]   The same Thomas holds 1 messuage in the parish of St Clement's by gift of William, his father, and that William bought it from the brothers of St John's Hospital, Cambridge, and Hamo Tailor, and the aforesaid Hamo held half of the aforesaid messuage from the brothers of the aforesaid hospital, and in respect thereof he pays to the aforesaid brothers 4s., and to John Aured 4s., and to the heirs of the aforesaid William 1 pair of gloves for the aforesaid messuage, and by which warranty the brothers have the aforesaid income and messuage they are unaware.

[742]   The same Thomas holds 1 messuage in the parish of All Saints by the Castle by gift of William, his father, and the said William held that by gift of William Brat' and that William held that by inheritance through the death of Ketel le Draper, his father, and he pays per annum to the heirs of the said William 1 rose, and to the heirs of William his father 12d.

[743]   The same Thomas holds 1 granary in the parish of All Saints near the Hospital by the gift of Thomas Toylet, his uncle, and that Thomas bought that from Leon Dunning, and that Leon held that by inheritance through the death of Adam, his father, and in respect thereof he pays per annum to the heirs of Thomas Toylet ½d., and to Leon Dunning 6d.

[744]   Johanna, former wife of William le Mire, holds 1 messuage in the parish of All Saints near the Hospital from the prior of Fordham, which prior bought the said messuage from Ernest Merchant, which Ernest bought it from John Porthors, and the same John bought it from Agnes of Barton, his mother, and that Agnes bought it from Meyndale, and in respect thereof she pays per annum to the aforesaid prior 20s.

[745]   William Carpenter holds 1 messuage in fee which he acquired by hereditary right through the death of Adam, his father, and that Adam bought that from the prioress of St Radegund's, and in respect thereof he pays per annum to the prioress 3s. By which warranty received the said messuage and the said income the prioress is unaware.

[746] Hubert, son of Geoffrey Cook, and Emma his wife hold
1 messuage in the parish of St Radegund's, which they hold by
the gift of Matilda le Cu and the said Matilda bought that from
the prioress of St Radegund's, and in respect thereof they pay
per annum to the aforesaid prioress 3s. In what manner and by
which warranty they receive the said income they are unaware.

[747] Alexander le Mason holds in fee 1 messuage in the parish of
St Radegund's which descended to him through the death of
Robert de Coggeshall, his father, and the said Robert bought
that from the prioress of St Radegund's, and in respect thereof
he pays per annum to Eve de Madingley 4s.

[748] Alice, former wife of Hamo le Tailor, holds 1 vacant piece of land
in the same parish [St Radegund's] which she bought from Jordan
le Skinner, and that Jordan bought that from Alice Athelard, and
the said Alice acquired it by ancient inheritance, and in respect
thereof she pays per annum to Lord Peter de Chavent 6d.

[749] Benedict le Merchant holds 1 messuage in the parish of All
Saints, which same messuage Roger Baker gave to Cassandria
his daughter, wife of Benedict, and the said Roger acquired that
by gift of Anketin Baker, and that Anketin bought that messuage
from Andrew de Winepol, for which he pays per annum to the
heirs of the said Andrew 2s. 6d.

[750] Adam de Hauxton and Ismaina his wife hold a half of 1 messuage
in the parish of Holy Sepulchre, which the said Ismaina acquired
through by hereditary right through the death of Thomas Get,
her father, which the said Thomas bought from Radulph Paris,
and in respect thereof he pays per annum to the prior of Barnwell
6d. by assignment of the said Radulph, and to Michael Pilat 6d.

[751] Edmund de Hauxton and Alicia his wife hold a half of 1 messuage
which descended to the said Alice by inheritance through the
death of Thomas Geth, her father, and the same Thomas bought
it from Radulph Paris, and in respect thereof they pay to the
prior of Barnwell 6d. by assignment of the aforesaid Radulph,
and to Michael Pilat 6d.

[752] William son of Robert Trig holds 1 messuage in the parish of
St Clement's which same he acquired by hereditary right through
the death of the said Robert, his father, and the same Robert
bought from Thomas Yerild, and the said Thomas acquired that
by ancient purchase, and in respect thereof he pays per annum
to the heirs of Master Bartholomew Wombe 10s.

[R17] The same William holds 7s. 6d. annual income by gift of Robert
le Lond', by hereditary right through the death of the said

Robert, his father, which same Robert bought that from Master Simon Prat of Ely, and the said Simon held that annual income by hereditary right through the death of his ancestors.

[753/4] Richard Goldring holds 1 messuage in the parish of Holy Trinity in which he lives, of this messuage he bought half from Alice, daughter of Roger le Barbur, which same Roger bought that said half messuage from John of Barton, and the same John acquired that half through ancient succession from his ancestors. The other half of the said messuage he bought from William Elyot, and the said William acquired that half by gift of Henry, his father, and that Henry acquired that part by ancient succession of his ancestors, and he pays in respect thereof per annum to the heirs of John of Barton 11s. 6d., and to William Elyot 1 ounce of ginger for the aforesaid messuage.

[755] The same Richard holds 1 messuage in the parish of St Mary's which he bought from John Matelashe, which same messuage the said John bought from Walter de Welles, and the said Walter bought that messuage from Master William de Beston, and the said Master William bought that from William le Parchmenter, and the said William acquired that through ancient purchase and he pays in respect thereof per annum to the said John 1 clove gillyflower, and to Alice daughter of Harvey 1 pair of gloves worth ½d.

[756] Nicholas son of Geoffrey Potecar holds 1 shop in the parish of Holy Trinity, which shop he acquired by hereditary succession through the death of Geoffrey, his father, which same Geoffrey bought that from John de Wytsond, and the said John bought that from Richard Tailor, and the said Richard acquired that in feoffment from John of Barton, and the said John acquired that by ancient succession through the death of his ancestors, and he pays in respect thereof to the aforesaid John de Wytsond 1d., and to the heirs of John of Barton 6s.

[757] The same Nicholas holds 1 messuage in the parish of St Benedict's, which same messuage he acquired through the succession of his paternal and maternal heirs, through the death of Geoffrey his father and Matilda his mother, and the aforesaid Geoffrey and Matilda acquired that by gift from Roger de Fulbourne, the father of the aforesaid Matilda, and the said Roger bought that from Hugo son of Arnold Baker, and the aforesaid Hugo acquired it by ancient succession of the aforesaid Arnold his father, and he pays in respect thereof per annum to Richard son of Laur' 4s. 6d., and to Robert son of Hugo 1d.

[758]   The same Nicholas and John son of Richard Goldring hold a certain messuage in the parish of St Mary's, which they have by gift and feoffment by Roger de Fulbourne, and the said Roger bought the said messuage from John Potekyne, and the said John acquired that by paternal succession through the death of Geoffrey, his father, which same Geoffrey acquired that by ancient succession of his ancestors, and they pay in respect thereof to the bailiffs of Cambridge who hold the said town in fee farm from the Lord King as is stated above, to their farm for hawgable 1d.

[759]   Fulk le Turner holds in fee 1 messuage in the parish of Holy Trinity which he bought from Peter the triumvir, which same Peter bought that from Jordan le Skinner, and the said Jordan acquired from Kus de Histon, his mother, which same Kus acquired by gift of Master Martin of St Radegund's and the said Master Martin acquired that through ancient purchase and he pays in respect thereof per annum to the said Peter 1 clove gillyflower, and to the prior and convent of Barnwell 8s. for the aforesaid messuage, by which warranty the prior and convent receive the said income they are unaware.

[760]   Roger Goldsmith holds 1 messuage in the same parish which same he bought from John Golde, and the said John acquired that by hereditary right through the death of Master William Golde, his brother, and the said William acquired that by hereditary descent through the death of William de Theford, his father, which same William bought it from Harvey, father of Eustace Dunning, and he pays in respect thereof per annum to the said John 1 rose, and to the abbot and convent of Ramsey 16d., by which warranty they are unaware.

[761]   Alice le Chapeler holds 1 messuage in the same parish in which she lives, which same she holds by paternal succession through the death of Henry, her father, and the said Henry acquired that by gift and enfeoffment of Alexander of Banns and Elycia his wife and William of Dagenhale and Cecilia his wife, which said Elycia and Cecilia acquired the said messuage by paternal right, and she pays in respect thereof per annum to the aforesaid Alexander and his heirs and to William Manguane and his heirs 2s., and to the prior of Barnwell 6d. By which warranty the prior receives the said income they are unaware.

[762]   Alexander of Brackley holds 1 messuage in the same parish which same he bought from Margaret, daughter of John Berner, and that messuage descended to the said Margaret by paternal right

through the death of the said John, her father, and the said John bought that from Radulph de Gernon, for which messuage he pays per annum to the aforesaid Margaret and her heirs 1d., and to the heirs of Henry de Hawile 26d., and to the bailiffs of the Lord King who hold the town of Cambridge in fee farm from the Lord King as is stated above, to their farm for hawgable 1¼d.

[763] John son of Hugo Potecar holds 1 seld in the parish of Holy Trinity, which same seld descended to the said John by paternal right through the death of the said Hugo, his father, and the said Hugo at one time bought that seld from Gilbert Potecar, and the said Gilbert acquired that through hereditary descent through the death of Walter Goldsmith, his uncle, for which he pays per annum to the heirs of Richard, son of John of Barton, 10s.

[764] The same John holds 1 shop in the same parish which descended to him by paternal right through the death of Hugo, his father, which same Hugo bought that from Gilbert Potecar, and the said Gilbert bought that at one time from Simon Godelot, and the said Simon bought that from Michael Mote, which same shop descended to the said Michael by inheritance through the death of Henry Mote, his brother, which same Henry at one time bought that from John of Barton, for which he pays per annum to the heirs of Richard son of John of Barton 6s.

[765] The same John holds in fee 1 messuage in the same parish which same descended to the said John by paternal right through the death of Hugo, his father, and the said Hugo bought that from Alan Langil and the said Alan acquired that by hereditary succession through the death of Walter Haliday, his father, and the said Walter acquired that by gift of William Alsope, his brother, and the said William bought that from William, chaplain of St Radegund's, for which he pays per annum to the aforesaid Alan and his heirs 1 rose, and to the prioress and convent of St Radegund's 6d. By which warranty the prioress and convent receive the said income they are unaware.

[766] The same John holds 1 messuage in the same parish which descended to him by paternal right through the death of the aforesaid Hugo his father, which same Hugo bought that from William Yde and the said William bought that from, Johanna daughter of Alan Kayly, which messuage descended to the said Johanna by paternal right through the death of the said Alan Kayly, her father, and the said Alan acquired that by ancient acquisition, and he pays in respect thereof per annum to the said William Yde and his heirs 2s.

[767]   Nicholas Golde holds 1 messuage in the same parish which he bought from John, his brother, which same John bought that from the brothers of the St John's Hospital, Cambridge, which same brothers had and held that from John son of the Dean, and the said John acquired the aforesaid messuage from the church of Holy Trinity, and he pays in respect thereof per annum to the said John 1 rose, and to the said brothers 6s. 6d., and the said brothers of the hospital pay per annum to the Holy Trinity Church 2s. for the aforesaid messuage.

[768]   Nicholas in le Dike holds 1 messuage in fee in the same parish which same he bought from John of Hardwick and Matilda his wife, and the said John and Matilda bought that messuage from Roger at the cross, and the aforesaid Roger bought that from the prioress and convent of St Radegund's, for which he pays per annum to the said John and Matilda 1 clove gillyflower, and to the aforesaid prioress and convent 10d. By which warranty the said prioress and convent receive the said income they are unaware.

[769]   The same Nicholas holds 1 messuage in the same parish which he bought from Reginald, son of Gregory son of Baker de Fulbourne, which same Reginald acquired that by hereditary descent through the death of Mabilia, wife of John le Blinde, and the said John and Mabilia his wife bought that from Richard le Gras, which Richard bought that at one time from Matilda Aleyns, and he pays in respect thereof per annum to the heirs of the said Reginald 1 clove gillyflower, and to Richard Wombe and his heirs 2s.

[770]   Simon le Mustarder and Alice his wife hold 1 messuage in the parish of Holy Trinity which same messuage Baldwin le Monner and the said Alice his wife bought at one time from Walter son of Robert Edward, which same descended to the said Robert by inheritance through the death of Peter Punch, for which he pays per annum to the said aforesaid Walter 1 rose, and to Robert de Houton 16d.

[771]   Simon, brother, holds 1 messuage in fee in the same parish which he bought from the sisters of the house of St Mary of Longstowe, which same sisters held the said messuage by gift and enfeoffment of John of Barton, which same John acquired by ancient hereditary succession, and he pays in respect thereof per annum to the heirs of the said John 8s. 1d., and to the aforesaid sisters 1d.

[772]   Henry Page holds in fee 1 messuage in the same parish in which he lives, which he bought from Richard Bateman junior, which

same Richard acquired by hereditary succession through the death of Wade his uncle and he pays in respect thereof per annum to the aforesaid Richard 1 pair of gloves worth 1d., and to the nuns of Swaffham 3s., and the to the prioress of St Radegund's 1d. By which warranty the said nuns receive the said income they are unaware.

[773] The same Henry holds 2 shops in the same parish which he bought from Matilda Aleyn in her free widowhood, and said Matilda held the aforesaid 2 shops by gift and enfeoffment of William le Fittere, her father, and he pays for the aforesaid shops per annum to the almoner of Tilty 4s., and to Isabella widow of Albrin Butcher, 1d., and to the prioress of St Radegund's 3s. By which warranty the said almoner said the said prioress receive the said income they are unaware.

[774] The same Henry holds 1 messuage in the parish of St Radegund's which he bought from Roger son of Eustace Carter, which same Roger held that from his inheritance through the death of Eustace, his father, for which he pays per annum to the aforesaid Roger 1 rose, and to the prioress of St Radegund's 3s., by which warranty she is unaware.

[775] The same Henry holds 1 shop in the marketplace of Cambridge which he bought from Simon Prat, and the said Simon held the said shop by hereditary succession through the death of Geoffrey, his father, which same Geoffrey acquired that by ancient purchase, and he pays in respect thereof per annum to the said Simon ½d., and to the sacristan of Ely 5s. By which warranty the said sacristan receives the said income he is unaware.

[776] Robert, chaplain, holds a certain messuage in the parish of Holy Trinity which same he bought from Matilda, widow of Alan Edward, and the said Matilda held it as a gift and enfeoffment from William le Fitter, her father, and the said William acquired that by ancient purchase and he pays in respect thereof per annum to the said Matilda 1d., and to the almoner of Ely 4s. By which warranty the said almoner receives the said income he is unaware.

[777] The same Robert holds 1 messuage in the same parish which he bought from William son of William le Fitter which William acquired that by paternal right through the death of William le Feuterer, his father, which same William acquired that by ancient purchase and he pays in respect thereof per annum to the Holy Trinity Church 6d. by assignment of the said William.

[778] The same Robert holds a certain vacant piece of land [parish not stated – Holy Trinity assumed] which he bought from the

prioress of St Radegund's, and the said prioress acquired that as a result of omission and quitclaim of Radulph, chaplain, who acquired that by paternal right through the death of Radulph, his father, which same Radulph acquired that through ancient acquisition, and he pays in respect thereof per annum to the aforesaid Radulph 1 rose, and to the aforesaid prioress of St Radegund's 3s.

[779] Sewall Tailor holds 1 messuage in the same parish which he bought from Gunilda and Margaret and Alice, the heirs of Roger Clay, which same Gunilda, Margaret and Alice inherited the said messuage by paternal right through the death of Roger, their father, and the said Roger acquired that by ancient hereditary succession of his ancestors, and he pays in respect thereof per annum to Henry de Wykys and Agnes his wife 28d.

[780] The same Sewall holds 1 vacant piece of land in the same parish which he bought from Saer, son of Adam de Ditton, which same Saer acquired that by hereditary succession through the death of the said Adam, his father, which same Adam acquired that through the death of Walter Arnothyze, which same Walter held that from William de Novacurt, and he pays in respect thereof per annum to the heirs of the said William 16d.

[781] The same Sewall holds 1 shop in the parish of St Mary's, Cambridge, which he bought from Bartholomew le Noble and Matilda his wife, which same shop Geoffrey Potekyn at one time gave to the aforesaid Bartholomew with Matilda, his daughter, in free marriage, which same shop the said Geoffrey held from the master and brothers of St John's Hospital, Cambridge, and he pays in respect thereof per annum to the said brothers 28d. By which warranty the said brothers receive the said income they are unaware.

[782] The same Sewall holds 1 acre of land in the fields of Barnwell which he bought from Robert, chaplain, which same Robert bought that from Peter Punch and Robert Edward, which same Peter and Robert held that from Margaret Kyriel of Hinton, and he pays in respect thereof per annum to the said Margaret and her heirs 4d., and to Lord John, son of John de Cadin', 2d.

[783] William le Stereman holds in fee 1 messuage in the same parish by paternal right through the death of Geoffrey Tailor, his father, which same Geoffrey bought that from Richard of Barton and that Richard acquired that by hereditary right through the death of John of Barton, his father, which same John acquired that by ancient acquisition of his ancestors, and he pays in respect

thereof per annum to the heirs of the said Richard 2s. for the said messuage.

[784] The same William and Rosa, his wife, hold ½ a shop in the marketplace of Cambridge in the parish of St Mary's, which same half shop William acquired by gift of Avicia Dunning with the said Rosa her daughter in frank marriage, which same said Avicia acquired that by hereditary descent through the death of John, her brother, which same John acquired that by hereditary right through the death of Roger Warin, his father, which same Roger acquired it through ancient purchase, and they pay in respect thereof per annum to Leonard Dunning as lord of the fee 3d.

[785] The same William and Rosa hold 1 messuage with a certain croft in Newnham which same said Rosa acquired by paternal right through the death of Robert Dunning, her father, and that Robert held that from Leonard Dunning, who is lord of the fee, and they pay in respect thereof per annum to the aforesaid Leonard 14d. for the aforesaid messuage and croft.

[786] The same William and Rosa hold a ½ acre of land in the fields of Cambridge by hereditary right through the death of Robert Dunning, her father, which same Robert bought that from John de Huntingdon, chaplain, and the same John bought that from the prior and convent of Barnwell, and he pays in respect thereof per annum to the said John ½d., and to the bailiffs of Cambridge who hold the town of Cambridge in fee farm from the lord King, for hawgable 1d.

[787] Simon Potecar holds in fee 1 messuage in the parish of Holy Trinity, which same he bought from Master John de Histon, which same John bought that from Thomas of the Infirmary, which same Thomas acquired it by hereditary right through the death of his grandfather Walter Goldsmith, and he pays in respect thereof per annum to the heirs of the said Master John 3s., and to the heirs of John of Barton 10s. as tenant-in-chief of the aforesaid fee, and to the bailiffs of Cambridge who hold the town of Cambridge in fee farm from the lord King, to their farm for hawgable 1d.

[788] The same Simon holds 1 building in fee in the same parish which he bought from William Wardeben, which same William acquired that by gift of Master John de Histon with his daughter in marriage, and the said John bought that from the said Thomas of the Infirmary, which same Thomas acquired that through descent of the said Walter Goldsmith, and he pays in respect thereof per annum to the said William and his heirs 10s.

[789]   The same Simon holds a third part of 1 messuage in the same
parish which he bought from Mabilia, daughter of John Reyner,
which Mabilia acquired that by hereditary right through the
death of John, her father, and the said John held that from Henry
de Hainule, and he pays in respect thereof per annum on behalf
of him and his heirs to the tenants-in-chief of the aforesaid fee,
that is the aforesaid Henry de Hainule and his heirs, a third part
of 40d., and to the bailiffs of Cambridge who hold the town of
Cambridge in fee farm from the lord King as is stated above, for
hawgable a third part of 3d.

[790]   The same Simon holds a certain parcel of vacant land in the
parish of St Michael's, which same piece descended to Mariota,
his former wife, through the death of John de Lincoln, her father,
which same John acquired that through ancient succession of his
ancestors, and he pays in respect thereof per annum to William
de la Bruere, chaplain, 6d., and the same William owes service
to the aforesaid Simon and his heirs of 1^{75} and to the bailiffs of
Cambridge who hold the town of Cambridge in fee farm from
the lord King as is stated above, to their farm 2d.

[791]   Cecilia daughter of Simon Potecar holds a certain piece of land
in the parish of St Michael's by gift of Simon, her father, and
Mariota, her mother, which same piece Simon acquired in
marriage with the aforesaid Mariota, his wife, by gift of John
de Lincoln, which same John acquired that through ancient
purchase, and she pays in respect thereof per annum to the
heirs of the said Simon 1 rose, and to the and to the bailiffs of
Cambridge who hold the town of Cambridge in fee farm from
the lord King, to their farm for hawgable ½d.

[792]   Eleanora, daughter of the said Simon, holds a certain piece of vacant
land by gift of Simon, her father, which same Simon acquired
that in frank marriage with Mariota, his wife, by gift of the said
John de Lincoln, which same John acquired that through ancient
purchase, and she pays in respect thereof per annum to the high
altar at St Michael's Church 3s., by assignment of the said Simon
and Mariota, and to the bailiffs of Cambridge who hold the town
of Cambridge as is stated above, to their farm for hawgable ½d.

[793]   Samson Goldsmith holds in fee 1 messuage in the parish of Holy
Trinity, which messuage he bought from John le Cordewener,
which same John bought that from Alice, daughter of Henry
le Chapeler, which same Alice acquired that by hereditary
succession through the death of Henry, her father, and the
said Henry bought that at one time from William of Banns

and Alexander Mangaunt, which same William and Alexander acquired that through ancient succession of their ancestors, and he pays in respect thereof per annum to the same John 1 rose, and to the said Alice 12d., and to the said William and Alexander and their heirs 4s.

[794]   Robert Mathefray and Margaret his wife hold 6 shops in the parish of St Clement's, which same shops the said Margaret holds by hereditary succession through the death of Robert, her brother, which same Robert held those by hereditary right through the death of John, his father, which same acquired those through ancient purchase, and they pay in respect thereof per annum to Robert son of Robert de Hauxton 4d.

[795]   The same Robert and Margaret hold 1 messuage in the parish of Holy Trinity in which they live, which same messuage they acquired by demise of Robert son of Radulph, chaplain, which messuage they hold for the life of the aforesaid Margaret, his mother, and the said Robert acquired the said messuage by paternal right through the death of Radulph, his father, which same Radulph bought the said messuage from John Tws, which same John held that by gift of Richard Bateman senior, his brother, and they pay per annum to Holy Trinity Church 3s., and to the said Richard 1d.

[796]   John le Centerer holds 1 messuage in the parish of Holy Trinity which is towards Barnwell, which same messuage he bought from Isabella, daughter of Geoffrey le Chapeler, which same Isabella held the aforesaid messuage by hereditary succession through the death of the said Geoffrey le Chapeler, which same Geoffrey acquired that by ancient succession of his ancestors and he pays in respect thereof per annum to Margaret, widow of Abraham le Chapeler, 3s., and to the bailiffs of Cambridge who hold the town of Cambridge from the lord King in fee farm, to their farm for hawgable 1d.

[797]   The aforesaid Robert and Margaret his wife hold 1 acre of land in the fields of Barnwell, which same acre the said Margaret acquired by gift and feoffment of the aforesaid brothers in exchange for some land adjacent in the courtyard of the said brothers, which same brothers held this acre by gift and feoffment of Stephen de Hauxton, which same Stephen acquired the said land by hereditary right, and they pay in respect thereof per annum 1 clove gillyflower.

[798]   The same Robert and Margaret hold a ½ acre of land in the same fields, which Radulph le Chapeler and the aforesaid Margaret

bought from William Brodeye, and the said William acquired the same ½ acre by purchase, and they pay in respect thereof per annum to the aforesaid William 4d.

[799] Richard of St Edmund's holds 1 messuage with appurtenances in the parish of Holy Trinity which same messuage he acquired by hereditary right through the death of Humphrey, his father, and the same Humphrey bought that messuage from Jordan Skinner at St Radegund's, and the same Jordan acquired that by ancient purchase, and he pays in respect thereof per annum to the prior of Barnwell 7s. 4d., and to the said Jordan ½d. By which warranty the said prior receives the said income he is unaware.

[800] Walter de Hildirele and Elena his wife hold 1 messuage in the parish of Holy Trinity, which same messuage was held by Richard, son of Humphrey of St Edmund's, for the duration of the life of Elena named above, which same messuage the said Richard acquired by paternal right through the death of Humphrey, his father, which same messuage the said Humphrey bought from Thomas of Barton and Agnes, his mother, and the aforesaid Thomas bought the said messuage from John Markys, and they pay in respect thereof per annum to the aforesaid Thomas and Agnes and their heirs 4s.

[801] Geoffrey de Waledene holds 1 messuage in the parish of Holy Trinity which same messuage he bought from Eva de Madingley, which same Eva acquired that by hereditary right through the death of Geoffrey, her brother, which same Geoffrey bought that from Thomas son of the priest and Agnes his wife, which same Agnes acquired that by gift of Robert of Madingley, her father, which same Robert bought that from Hugo Newcome, and the same Hugo acquired that by ancient purchase, and he pays in respect thereof per annum to the abbess of Chatteris 5s., and to Leonard Dunning 10d., and to John Golde 4d., and to the said Eva and her heirs 1d. By which warranty the said abbess receives the said income she is unaware.

[802] Lord Roger of Trumpington, knight, holds 1 messuage in the same parish, which he holds by hereditary right through the death of Lord Robert, his father, which same Lord Robert acquired that by hereditary right through the death of Lord Everard of Trumpington, his father, and he pays in respect thereof per annum to the bailiffs of Cambridge who hold the same town from the lord King in fee farm, to their farm for hawgable 4d.

[803] Robert Kokyn holds 1 messuage in the aforesaid parish which he bought from Alan de Howes, which same Alan bought that

from Thomas Hernwene, and the said Thomas bought that from Hugo of Barton, and he pays in respect thereof per annum to the heirs of the said Hugo 7s., and to Lord Peter de Chavent 6d.

[804]   Thomas de Clopton holds 1 messuage in the same parish, which same Thomas acquired that by gift of Master Radulph Tullel in frank marriage with Alice, daughter of the said Radulph, which same Radulph bought that from William Hertheband and Alice his wife, and the said Alice acquired that by hereditary succession through the death of Hugo Newcome, her father, and the said Hugo bought that from Walter de Histon, and the said Walter acquired it by gift of Master John de Histon, and the said Master John bought that from Geoffrey le Fittere, and he pays in respect thereof per annum 29d.

[805]   The same Thomas holds 1 messuage in the same parish by gift of Master Radulph in frank marriage with Alice his daughter, which same Radulph bought that from Thomas de Cottenham and Margaret his wife, by chirograph in the court of Lord Roger Lenatu, which same descended to the said Margaret by inheritance through the death of Hugo Newcome, her father, and the said Hugo bought that from Walter de Histon, which same Walter acquired that by gift of Master John de Histon, and the said Master John bought that from Geoffrey le Fittere, and he pays in respect thereof per annum 1d.[76]

[806]   Robert de Hale holds 1 messuage in the parish of Holy Trinity which he has by gift of Master Nicholas of St Quentin's, and the said Master Nicholas bought that from John Aluethild, and the said John acquired that through ancient succession, and he pays in respect thereof per annum to heirs of the said John Alwewethild 1d.

[807]   John Golde holds in the same parish 1 messuage, which same messuage he has by hereditary right through the death of William, son of William, his brother, and the said William bought that from Martin Goto, and the said Martin acquired that through ancient purchase, and he pays per in respect thereof per annum to the heirs of Radulph, chaplain, 1 rose.

[808]   Stephen, son of William le Cu, holds 1 messuage in the parish of Holy Trinity which same he has by hereditary right through the death of William, his father, and the said William acquired that by hereditary right through the death of Geoffrey le Cu, his father, and the same Geoffrey acquired that by ancient purchase, and he pays in respect thereof per annum to the nuns of St Radegund's 2s. By which warranty the nuns receive the said income they are

unaware. And to the bailiffs of Cambridge who hold the said town in fee farm etcetera for hawgable 2d.

[809] John Godsone holds 1 messuage in the parish of St Andrew's which he bought from William Godsone, and the said William bought that from Henry son of Hugo, and the said Henry bought that from Herbert le Carter and the said Herbert acquired that messuage by ancient purchase, and he pays in respect thereof per annum on behalf of the heirs of the aforesaid William Godsone to the heirs of Henry son of Hugo 40d., and for sustaining 4 lamps in St Andrew's Church, 40d.

[810] The same John holds 1 piece of vacant land in the same parish which he bought from Simon de Lanselle, and the said Simon acquired that by gift of Cassandria Crocheman, and the said Cassandria bought that from Robert de Lanselle, her brother, and the said Robert acquired that by hereditary succession through the death of his ancestors, and he pays in respect thereof per annum to the said Simon and his heirs 1 pair of gloves at the price of ½d., and to the nuns of Swaffham 18d., and to the prior of Barnwell 6d., by which warranty they are unaware.

[811] The same John holds 1 piece of land with a certain house already existing in the same parish, which same he acquired by gift of William Godsone, and the said William bought that from the nuns of St Radegund's, for which he pays per annum on behalf of the heirs of the aforesaid William to the aforesaid nuns 18d.

[812] The same John and Amicia, his wife, hold 1 messuage with appurtenances in the parish of Holy Trinity, which same messuage William Carpenter gave to the said John with the said Amicia, his daughter, in frank marriage, and the said William bought that from Alan Edward, and the said Alan acquired that with Matilda, his wife, in frank marriage by gift of her father, and they pay in respect thereof per annum to the prioress of St Radegund's 1 lb. of cumin.

[813] John of Biggleswade holds 1 messuage in the parish of St Andrew's, which same he bought from Henry of Morden, which same Henry acquired and held that from the prioress and nuns of St Radegund's, and he pays in respect thereof per annum to the said Henry 1 rose, and to the said nuns ½ mark by assignment of the said Henry.

[814] The Master and Brothers St John's Hospital, Cambridge hold 1 messuage in the same parish which same messuage Robert, chaplain of Ely, gave to the same in perpetual alms for the salvation of his soul and of his ancestors, and the aforesaid Robert

bought that from Jacob Chirothecar of Cambridge, and he pays in respect thereof per annum to the bailiffs of Cambridge who hold the same town in fee farm, for hawgable 2d.

[815] William de Wilburham, chaplain, holds 1 messuage in the parish of St Andrew's, Cambridge, which same messuage descended to the said William by hereditary right through the death of Peter de Wilburham, his brother, and the said Peter acquired that by paternal right through the death of Walter de Wilburham, their father, which same Walter bought that from the prioress and nuns of St Radegund's, for which he pays per annum to the prioress and convent 10s. and 1 lb. of pepper as tenant-in-chief of the lord's fee.

[816] The same William holds 1 messuage in the parish of St Benedict's in the fee of Luke of St Edmund's, which same descended to the said William through the death of the said Peter, his brother, and the same Peter acquired that by hereditary right through the death of Walter, his father, for which he pays per annum to the said Luke 2s. 8d.

[817] The same William holds 1 messuage in the parish of St Edward's which he acquired by gift of Roger de Wilburham, his brother, and the same Roger bought that from John Mariote and Johanna, his wife, daughter of Alan Kayly, and he pays in respect thereof per annum to the prior and convent of Barnwell 20d. by which warranty they are unaware, and to John Yve and his heirs 2d.

[818] The same William holds 1 messuage in the same parish by gift of Roger, his brother, and he bought that from Thomas, son of Robert, vicar of St Edward's, which same Robert bought that from John Mariote and Johanna his wife, daughter of Alan Kayly, for which he pays per annum to the prioress and nuns of Markyate 8d. by assignment of the said John.

[819] The same William holds 4½ acres of land in the fields of Cambridge in fee from Luke of St Edmund's, which descended to him through the death of Peter de Wilburham, his brother, which same Peter acquired that by hereditary right through the death of Walter de Wilburham, his father, for which he pays per annum to the said Luke and his heirs 20d.

[820] The same William holds a ½ acre of land in the fields of Cambridge which descended to him by hereditary right through the death of the said Peter, his brother, which same Peter acquired that by hereditary right through the death of the aforesaid Walter, his father, for which he pays per annum to William Elyot and his heirs 2d.

[821]   The same William holds 2 acres of land in the same fields which he acquired by gift of Roger de Wilburham, his brother, which same Roger bought those from John Anvre, and that John acquired those by hereditary right through the death of John, son of Reginald, his father, for which he pays per annum to the said Roger 1 rose, and to the aforesaid John Andre and his heirs 1 pair of gloves at the price of ½d.

[822]   William Elyhot holds 1 capital messuage in the parish of St Andrew's which descended to him by hereditary right through the death of Master Thomas Elyhot, his brother, which same Master Thomas acquired that by hereditary right through the death of Sabina, his mother, which same Sabina acquired that from Simon, her nephew, which same Simon acquired that by hereditary right through the death of Geoffrey Oregar, which same Geoffrey acquired that by paternal right after the death of Orgar, his father, for which he pays per annum to the bailiffs of Cambridge who hold the same town in fee farm from the lord King, for hawgable 4d.

[823]   The same William holds 2 curtilages with 1 house and 2½ acres in the same parish, which descended to the same William by inheritance through the death of Master Thomas Elyhot, his brother, which same Master Thomas acquired those by hereditary right after the death of Sabina, his mother, which same Sabina acquired those at one time from Simon, her nephew, for which curtilages and house and 2½ acres of land he pays per annum to the bailiffs of Cambridge as is stated above for hawgable 2½d.

[824]   The same William holds 1 curtilage in the same parish which descended to the same William by hereditary right after the death of Master Thomas, his brother, which same Master Thomas acquired that by hereditary right after the death of Nicholas, former son of Henry son of Hugo, which same Nicholas acquired that by hereditary right after the death of Henry son of Hugo, his father, for which he pays per annum to the bailiffs of Cambridge who hold the same town from the lord King in fee farm, for hawgable ½d.

[825]   The same William holds a certain messuage in the parish of St Mary's which Henry Elyhot gave to him, which same Henry acquired that by hereditary right after the death of Robert his former nephew, the son of John, brother of Henry, which same Robert acquired through that by hereditary right after the death of John Elyhot, his father, for which he pays per annum to Willam de Novacurt 18d.

[826] The same William holds a certain messuage in the marketplace in the same parish [St Mary's] which descended to him by inheritance after the death of Master Thomas, his brother, which Master Thomas acquired that by hereditary right after the death of Sabina, his mother, which same Sabina acquired that by purchase from Geoffrey Oregar, her brother, for which pays to the bailiffs of Cambridge who hold the same town in fee farm from the lord King for hawgable ¾d.

[827] The same William holds a certain messuage in the same parish which he bought from Richard son of Hugo le Rus, which same Richard acquired that by hereditary right through the death of Margaret, his mother, which same Margaret acquired that by paternal right after the death of Louis, her father, for which he pays to the bailiffs of Cambridge who hold etcetera for hawgable ½d.

[828] The same William holds some messuage in Mill Lane in the parish of St John's which descended to him by inheritance through the death of Master Thomas, his brother, which same Master Thomas acquired it by paternal right through the death of Henry Elyhot, his father, which same Henry acquired that through ancient acquisition, and he pays in respect thereof per annum to the prioress of St Radegund's and the convent 20d., by which warranty they do not know.

[829] The same William holds 1 house and 1 curtilage in the same parish which descended to the same William by inheritance through the death of Master Thomas, his brother, which same Master Thomas acquired that by hereditary right after the death of Henry Elyhot, his father, which same Henry acquired that through ancient succession of his ancestors, for which he pays per annum to the bailiffs of Cambridge who hold the same town in fee farm from the lord King for hawgable ½d.

[830/1] The same William holds 2 houses in the same parish which descended to the same William by inheritance after the death of Master Thomas, his brother, which same Thomas acquired those by hereditary right after the death of Henry, his father, which same Henry bought one from Maurice le Rus and the other from Richard Bonney, for which he pays per annum to the prioress of Swaffham 28d. by which warranty they do not know.

[832] The same William and Alexandria, his wife, hold a certain messuage in the parish of St Michael's, which Richard son of Simon gave to Alexandria, his daughter, in marriage, which same Richard at one time bought from Peter son of Richard of

Barnwell, which same Peter at one time bought from the Prior of Barnwell, for which he pays per annum to the Prior of Barnwell 23d. as tenant-in chief.

[833] The same William and Alexandria his wife hold 1 messuage in the parish of St John's which messuage John son of Ivo gave to them in marriage, which same John bought from Isondia, which same Isondia acquired that by hereditary right after the death of her father, for which they pay per annum to Katherine daughter of Michael Bernard 5s.

[834] The same William holds 1½ acres of land which descended to him by hereditary right after the death of his brother Master Thomas, his brother, which same Thomas acquired that by hereditary right after the death of Sabina, his mother, which same Sabina acquired that at one time from Simon, her nephew, and he pays in respect thereof per annum to the bailiffs of Cambridge who hold the same town in fee farm from the lord King for hawgable 1½d.

[835] The same William holds 3 acres of land which descended to him by inheritance after the death of Master Thomas, his brother, which same Thomas acquired those by hereditary right after the death of Sabina, his mother, which same Sabina acquired those at one time from Simon, her nephew, for which he pays per annum to the bailiffs of Cambridge as is stated above for hawgable 1½d.

[836] The same William and Alexandria his wife hold 5 acres and ½ rood of land which descended to the aforesaid William and Alexandria his wife by hereditary right through the death of Richard son of Ivo, which same Richard acquired those by hereditary right after the death of Ivo, his father, which same Ivo acquired those through ancient succession of his ancestors, for which he pays per annum to Luke of St Edmund's 2s.

[837] The same William and Alexandria his wife hold 5 acres of land in the fields of Cambridge which descended to the aforesaid William and Alexandria his wife by inheritance after the death of Richard son of Ivo, which same Richard acquired those by hereditary right after the death of Ivo, his father, which same Ivo acquired those by ancient succession of his ancestors, for which he pays per annum to Leon Dunning 2s.

[838] The same William holds 3 acres in the same fields which he bought from Eustace Dunning, which same Eustace acquired those by hereditary right after the death of Harvey, his father, which same Harvey acquired those by hereditary right after the death of Dunning, his father, for which he pays per annum to the clerks of Merton 2d.

[839] The same William holds 1½ acres in the same fields which descended to the same William by inheritance after the death of Master Thomas, his brother, which same Master Thomas acquired those by hereditary right after the death of Sabina, his mother, which same Sabina acquired those at one time from Simon, her nephew, and he pays in respect thereof per annum to the bailiffs of Cambridge who hold the same town in fee farm from the lord King for hawgable 1½d.

[840] The same William holds 1½ acres in the same fields which he bought from Simon Scan and Cassandria his wife, which same Simon and Cassandria his wife acquired those by hereditary right after the death of Godwin, brother of the aforesaid Cassandria, which same Godwin acquired those by ancient succession of his ancestors, and he pays in respect thereof per annum to the said Simon and Cassandria 10d.

[841] The same William holds a ½ acre of land which he acquired by purchase from Luke of St Edmund's which same Luke acquired that by succession through the death of Master Thomas, his brother, and which same Thomas acquired that by hereditary right through the death of Walter, his father, and he pays per annum to the aforesaid Luke 2d.

[842] Thomas son of Maurice de Fulbourne holds 1 messuage in the parish of St Andrew's which same messuage the said Thomas bought from Mabilia, daughter of Radulph of Scotton, which same Mabilia acquired that by gift of the said Radulph, her father, which same Radulph bought that from Henry of Crishall, clerk, which same Henry bought that from John Parleben, and the said John acquired that by hereditary right through the death of John Smith, his father, and the said John acquired that by ancient acquisition, and he pays per annum to the bailiffs of Cambridge who hold the same town in fee farm from the lord King for hawgable ¾d.

[843] John Flori of Scotton holds 1 messuage in the same parish which he acquired by gift of Radulph Flori, chaplain, which same Radulph bought that from Henry, clerk of Crishall, and the said Henry bought that from John Parleben, which same John acquired that through hereditary succession through the death of John Smith, his father, and the said John acquired that by ancient succession of his parents, and he pays in respect thereof per annum to the bailiffs of Cambridge who hold it as is stated above for hawgable ¾d.

[844] William de Lodis holds ½ messuage in the same parish, which same William bought that from Jacob son of William Miller,

and the same Jacob acquired that by the descent of William, his brother, and the said William acquired that by parental right through the death of William, his father, which same William bought that from Matilda Punch, and the said Matilda acquired that by ancient hereditary succession through the death of her ancestors, and he pays in respect thereof per annum to St Andrew's Church 26d., and to the bailiffs of Cambridge who hold the same town in fee farm from the lord King, to their farm for hawgable ½d.

[845] Master Radulph de Walepol, Archdeacon of Ely, holds 1 messuage in the parish of St Andrew's, which same messuage he bought from Master William de la Lade, which same Master William bought that from Master Richard de Gedney, which same Master Richard bought that from Master Thomas de Hingolphorp, and the said Thomas bought that from Peter Warener, which same Peter acquired that by gift of Master Warener, and the said Warener bought that from John of Barton, which same John acquired it by ancient succession of his parents, and he pays in respect thereof to the heirs of the said John of Barton 1 mark, and for hawgable to the lord King ½d.

[846] Master Andrew de Middilton holds a certain house in the parish of St Andrew's which he bought from Henry de Duxford and Alice his wife, which same Henry and Alice held the said house from Walter de Bottisham and Cristiana his wife, and he pays in respect thereof per annum by assignment of Henry and Alice his wife to St Andrew's Church 15d.

[847] The same Andrew holds in the parish of Holy Sepulchre 1 messuage with appurtenances, which same messuage he bought from Agnes Wakelyn and Mabilia her sister for the duration of his life, which same Agnes and Matilda inherited the said messuage by hereditary right through the death of Walter Pago, their brother, and the said Walter acquired that by gift of Michael Malerbe, which same Michael acquired that by ancient acquisition, and he pays in respect thereof per annum to Master Robert Anger 3s., and to the aforesaid Agnes and Mabilia 2s.

[848] William of Astota holds 1 messuage in the parish of St Andrew's which he bought from Simon Flinston, which same messuage the same William gave in pure and perpetual alms to the prior and convent of Barnwell, and the aforesaid prior and convent subsequently gave and conceded that messuage to the aforesaid William of Aston for the duration of his life, for which he pays per annum to the said Simon and his heirs 1d., and to the prior

and convent of Anglesey 12d., and to the bailiffs of Cambridge who hold the same town in fee farm from the lord King, for their farm for hawgable 1d.

[849]   The same William holds 1 messuage with its appurtenances in the same parish which he bought from Walter son of Robert Edward, which same Walter acquired that by ancestral right after the death of Robert Edward, his father, which same Robert acquired that by hereditary right after the death of William Edward, his father, which same William acquired it by ancient acquisition, and he pays in respect thereof per annum to the said William and his heirs 1 rose, and to the almoner of Barnwell 2s., by which warranty they are unaware.

[850]   The same William holds 1 messuage in the parish of St Edward's which was formerly of Juliana Pageles, which same Juliana held the said messuage from the prior and convent of Ely, which same messuage the said William acquired by gift of the said prior and convent, and he pays in respect thereof per annum to the said prior and convent 18d.

[851]   The same William as tenant-in-chief of the lord's fee holds a certain part of land of a certain messuage in the same parish which he bought from Richard son of Richard de Wytewell, which same Richard acquired that by ancestral right through the death of Richard de Wytewell, his father, which same Richard acquired that through ancient acquisition, and he pays in respect thereof per annum to the said Richard 1d., and to the almoner of Ely 6s., by which warranty they do not know.

[852]   Simon Flinston holds 1 messuage in the parish of St Andrew's which he bought from Nicholas Chilman, and the said Nicholas bought the said messuage from the heirs of Hamo Kyriel, which same Hamo acquired that through ancient acquisition, and he pays in respect thereof per annum to Eleanor, former wife of the aforesaid Nicholas in the name of dower ½ mark, and for a lamp for the Blessed Mary in St Andrew's Church 6d.

[853]   Nicholas de Impington and Juliana his sister hold 1 messuage with appurtenances in the aforesaid parish, which same messuage they acquired by gift of Godfrey, chaplain of Impington, which same Godfrey bought that from Radulph Flori de Stonton, and the said Radulph bought that from Robert Edward, and the said Robert acquired that by hereditary right through the death of William Edward his father, and the said William acquired it through ancient succession of his ancestors, and he pays in respect thereof per annum to the bailiffs of Cambridge who hold

the same town in fee farm from the lord King to their farm for hawgable 2½d.

[854] Sarah Alsope holds a certain messuage in the parish of St Andrew's which she has by gift of Eleanor Alsope, which same messuage William Alsope and the aforesaid Eleanor his wife bought from John Potekine, which same John acquired the said messuage by ancient succession through his parents, and he pays in respect thereof per annum to the aforesaid John and his heirs ½d.

[855] The same Sarah holds a certain messuage in the same parish which she acquired by gift from Juliana sister of the said Elena, and the said Juliana bought that from Roger de Lirlington, which same Roger acquired the said messuage by ancient acquisition, and she pays in respect thereof per annum to[77] son of Simon of Hawkiston 2s. by assignment of the said Roger.

[856] John Golde holds 1 messuage in the parish of St Andrew's which same messuage he acquired by hereditary right through the death of William Golde, his brother, which William acquired that by succession from Golde, his mother, which same Golde acquired that through ancient purchase, and he pays in respect thereof per annum to the heirs of Alan Puch 1 pair of white gloves worth 1d., and for hawgable 2d.

[857] John le Coteler holds 1 messuage in the parish of St Andrew's, Cambridge, from Beatrice Bely, which same descended to the said Beatrice by hereditary right through the death of John Kyn, her brother, and the said John bought that from Walter Stereman of Derneford, and the said Walter acquired that by ancient succession of his parents, for which he pays per annum to the heirs of the said Beatrice ½d., and to the heirs of the said Walter 3d., and to Alice Herin and her heirs 2s., and to sustain a candle in St Andrew's Church 12d., and to sustain another candle in Holy Trinity Church 12d., and to the Bishop of Ely 4½d., by which warranty the said bishop receives the income they are unaware.

[858] The same John holds in fee 1 vacant plot in the same parish, which same plot of land he acquired by gift of John his son, which same plot descended to the said John, son of John le Coteler, through the death of William Godsone, and the said William bought that from the nuns of St Radegund's, for which he pays per annum to the said nuns 18d. as tenant-in-chief of the fee.

[859] The same John and Juliana, his wife, hold 1 messuage with appurtenances in the parish of St Mary's, which the said Juliana acquired by gift of John de Bradley, her father, and the said John

bought that certain messuage from Richard de Bradley, which same Richard acquired that through ancient succession of his parents, for which they pay per annum to the heirs of the said John ½d., and to St Mary's Church, Cambridge 4d.

[860] Wymerus le Gaunter holds 1 messuage in the parish of St Andrew's, which same he bought from John Curteys, which same John acquired that by hereditary right through the death of Matilda, daughter of Adam le Gaunter, which same Matilda acquired that by gift of Adam le Gaunter, her father, in frank marriage, which same Adam acquired that through ancient acquisition, and he pays in respect thereof per annum to the aforesaid John 1 pair of white gloves worth 1d., and to the master and brothers of St John's Hospital, Cambridge, 2s. By which warranty the said brothers they receive the said income they are unaware.

[861] Master William of Norwich holds 1 messuage in the same parish which he bought from Master William, doctor, of Barsham, which same Master William bought that from Roger the chaplain, and the said Roger acquired it through ancient acquisition, for which he pays per annum to the heirs of the said Master William 1 root of ginger, and to the prioress and convent of St Radegund's 18d., and to the bailiffs of Cambridge who hold the same town in fee farm from the lord King as is stated above for their farm for hawgable 1¾d., by which warranty the said nuns receive the said income they are unaware.

[862] The same Master William of Norwich holds 1 small piece of vacant land in the same parish which he acquired from Thomas Prentice and Agnes his wife and Matilda Plote, daughters and heirs of Thomas Plote, which same plot descended to the aforesaid Agnes and Matilda by hereditary right through the death of Thomas Plote, their father, and he pays in respect thereof per annum to John Prentice and his heirs ½d., and to the said Matilda 1 rose.

[863] William of St Edmunds holds 1 messuage in the same parish which he bought from Walter Edward, which same Walter acquired that by succession of his parents through the death of Robert Edward, his father, which same messuage the said Robert acquired by hereditary right through the death of William, his father, and the said William acquired that by ancient acquisition of his ancestors, and he pays in respect thereof per annum to the said Walter ½d., and to Leon Dunning 12d., and to John Godsone 2s., and 3d. for sustaining a lamp in St Andrew's Church.

[864] Winfrid de Costessey holds 1 messuage in the same parish [St Andrew's] which she acquired by gift of Matilda, widow of Thomas Servient' of the University of Cambridge, which same said Thomas and Matilda bought that messuage from Walter Hardwyne, which same Walter bought that from Henry son of Gerald le Gaunter, and the aforesaid Gerald acquired that by ancient succession of his ancestors, and he pays in respect thereof per annum to the said Matilda and her heirs 1lb. cumin, and to the almoner of St Edmund's 6d., and to the bailiffs of Cambridge who hold the same town in fee farm from the lord King as is written above to their farm for hawgable 1d., by which warranty the almoner receives the said income they are unaware.

[865] William Markys holds in fee 1 messuage in the same parish which same messuage he bought from Robert de Scelford, which same Robert acquired that by gift and enfeoffment of the prioress of St Radegund's, which same prioress acquired by the gift of Simon Godelot, which same Simon acquired by ancient acquisition, and he pays in respect thereof per annum to the said Robert 1 rose, and to the aforesaid prioress 14s. 7d. as tenant-in-chief of the aforesaid fee.

[866] Henry le Fener holds 1 messuage in the same parish which he bought from Robert of Ely, chaplain, and the said Robert bought the that messuage from Lord John de Stalar, knight, which same messuage descended to the said Lord John through the death of Margaret, daughter of Alan Alwyne, which same messuage she held for the life of the said John, and he pays in respect thereof per annum for sustaining a lamp in St Andrew's Church 6d., and to Richard, son of the aforesaid John, and his heirs 18d. by assignment of the said Lord John.

[867] Alan of Hinton holds 1 messuage in the same parish which he bought from Sarah Alsope, which same Sarah held by gift of Elena Alsope, which same Elena bought that from Jacob Chirothecar, which same Jacob acquired that through ancient succession of his ancestors, and he pays in respect thereof per annum to the prioress of St Radegund's 3s., and to the said Sarah 1 rose, by which warranty the said nuns receive the said income they are unaware.

[868] Walter de Hauxton, clerk, holds a certain messuage in the same parish which same messuage he bought from William ate Broke, and the aforesaid William bought that from William son of William le Miller, and the same William acquired that by hereditary descent through the death of William his father,

which same said William acquired that by gift and enfeoffment of Simon Prat, and the said Simon acquired that by parental succession through the death of Geoffrey Prat his father, which same Geoffrey acquired that by gift of the prior of Ely, and he pays in respect thereof per annum to the almoner of Ely 3s., and to the aforesaid William 1 clove gillyflower. By which warranty the almoner receives the said income they are unaware.

[869]   The same Walter holds 1 vacant plot in the parish of Holy Trinity which he bought from Silvester son of Henry, and the same Silvester acquired that by gift of Henry, his father, which same Henry acquired that by hereditary succession through the death of Agnes the midwife, his mother, and the aforesaid Agnes acquired that by ancient succession of her parents, and he pays in respect thereof per annum 3s. 6d. to the almoner of Ely, and to the aforesaid Silvester 1 rose. By which warranty the almoner receives the said income they are unaware.

[870]   The same Walter holds 1 messuage in the parish of St Andrew's, which same messuage he bought from Jacob, son of William the miller, and that Jacob acquired that by hereditary succession through the death of William his father, and the aforesaid William bought that from Radulph Paulyn, and the same Radulph acquired it through ancient ancestral succession, and he pays in respect thereof per annum to the aforesaid almoner of Ely 4s. By which warranty the almoner receives the said income they are unaware.

[871]   Margaret daughter of Gregory holds 1 messuage in the same parish which she bought from Thomas de Cottenham and Margaret his wife, which same Margaret acquired that by hereditary right through the death of Hugo de Newton, her father, and the said Hugo bought that from Matthew Marshall, and the said Matthew bought it from Cecilia Seger, and the same Cecilia acquired that by descent of her ancestors, and she pays in respect thereof per annum to the aforesaid Thomas and Margaret his wife ½d., and to Richard Bateman junior 1 lb. pepper.

[872]   Walter le Rus of Waledene and Alice Dru his wife hold 1 messuage in the same parish which same messuage the aforesaid Dru of St Edmunds and Alice his wife bought at one time from the prioress and convent of St Radegund's, which same messuage Robert of Trumpington gave to the aforesaid prioress and convent and asked that the said Robert should not bear the burden on the said messuage of maintaining the watch, for which he pays per annum to the aforesaid prioress and convent of St Radegund's 5s. 6d.

[873]   Walter Ardwyne holds 1 curtilage in the same parish which same he bought from Matilda wife of Bartholomew le Taylur and from Robert his heir, which same curtilage Geoffrey Potekyne gave to the aforesaid Bartholomew and Matilda his daughter in marriage, and the said Geoffrey acquired that by ancient succession of his parents, and he pays in respect thereof to the bailiffs of Cambridge who hold the same town in fee farm from the lord King as is stated above for their farm 1d.

[874]   Sir Alan of Little Bradley, chaplain and warden of the Hospital of Balsham holds 3 shops in the parish of St Edward's, Cambridge, which the lord bishop of Ely gave to the said hospital for the maintenance of its brothers, which same shops the lord Bishop Hugh who no longer is, bought from Isabella former wife of Nicholas Wombe, and the said Isabella acquired those by gift of Nicholas Wombe, her son, and the said Nicholas acquired those by gift of Michael Bernard, and the said Michael bought those from Margeret Perle, and the said shops descended to the said Margaret by ancient succession of her parents, for which he pays per annum to the bailiffs of Cambridge who hold the same town in fee farm from the lord King as is stated above to their farm for hawgable 1d.

[875]   The same Alan holds 2 messuages in the parish of St Andrew's which same messuages the said Bishop Hugh gave to the said Hospital of Balsham when it was newly founded for their maintenance, which same Lord Bishop Hugo bought from Richard Payn of Balsham, chaplain, and the said Richard bought them from Stephen son of Thomas Le Rus, and the said Thomas bought them from Maurice de Eltisley, which same Maurice acquired those by gift of Radulph, former rector of the church of Eltisley, which Radulph rector of the aforesaid church bought from Hugo Newton, and the said Hugo bought those from the prior and convent of Barnwell, and he pays in respect thereof per annum to the prior of Barnwell 6s. as tenant-in-chief of the fee, and to the bailiffs of Cambridge who hold the same town in fee farm from the lord King as is stated above to their farm for hawgable 6d.

[876]   Cecilia sister of William Godsone holds 1 messuage in the same parish which she acquired by gift of Elena Alsope, and the said Elena bought that from Henry Galion, and the said Henry inherited that by ancestral succession through the death of his father, and she pays in respect thereof per annum to the heirs of Robert Seman 2s. as lord of the fee.

[877] Robert Godsone holds 1 messuage in the same parish which he bought from Roger le Farmere, which same Roger acquired the said messuage by gift and enfeoffment of Margaret Doy, and the said Margaret acquired that by ancient succession of her ancestors, and he pays in respect thereof per annum to Nicholas Doy and his heirs 4s. and 1 rose.

[878] The same Robert holds 1 shop in the same parish [St Andrew's] which he bought from Robert, chaplain of Ely, which same Robert acquired the said shop by gift and enfeoffment of Lord John de Stalar, which same Lord John acquired that by ancient acquisition, and he pays in respect thereof per annum to Richard son of John 18d. by assignment of the said Lord John de Stalar.

[879] John son of Paul Wombe holds 1 messuage in the parish of St Andrew's which same messuage descended to him by hereditary right through the death of Cassandria, his mother, which same Cassandria acquired that by hereditary succession through the death of Gregory Edward, her father, and the said Gregory bought that from Thomas Godrike, and the said Thomas acquired that by ancient succession of his ancestors, and he pays in respect thereof per annum to the heirs of the said Thomas ½d.

[880] The same John holds 1 messuage in the parish of Holy Trinity by hereditary succession through the death of Cassandria, his mother, and the said Cassandria acquired that by hereditary succession through the death of Gregory, her father, and the said Gregory acquired that by purchase from the ancestors of John Segyn, and he pays in respect thereof per annum to Alan Segyn, son and heir of the aforesaid John Segyn, 2s. 6d.

[881] The same John holds 1 messuage in the same parish which he acquired by hereditary succession through the death of Simon, his brother, which same Simon acquired that by hereditary succession through the death of Cassandria, his mother, and the said Cassandria acquired that by hereditary right through the death of Gregory Edward, her father, and the said Gregory acquired that and held it from Adam Gerlond, and he pays in respect thereof per annum to the heirs of Adam 9d.

[882] The same John holds 1 messuage in the parish of St John's which he acquired by hereditary succession through the death of William, his brother, and the said William acquired and held that from Alice Gregory, and the said Alice acquired and held that by ancient succession of her ancestors, and he pays in respect thereof per annum to St Andrew's Church 2s.

[883]   John Brodeye holds in fee a certain messuage in the parish of Holy Trinity, which same messuage he bought from Henry le Cuvere and Emma his wife, which said Emma acquired that by gift of Roger, her father, and that Roger acquired the said messuage by gift of Matilda Aleyns, and the said Matilda acquired that messuage by ancestral succession, and he pays in respect thereof per annum to the nuns of Swaffham 4d., by which warranty the said nuns receive the said income they are unaware. And to the aforesaid Henry and Emma 1 root of ginger.

[884]   Robert de Bunstede holds 1 messuage in the parish of St Andrew's in the fee farm of Mariota, widow of the late Richard of Barton, which same messuage the said Mariota acquired by gift of John, her son, and that messuage descended to the said John by hereditary right through the death of Richard of Barton, his father, and that messuage descended to the said Richard by hereditary right through the death of Simon of Barton, his brother, and the said Simon bought that messuage from Fulk Sutor, for which he pays per annum to the aforesaid Mariota and her heirs 5s.

[885]   John Godsone holds 1 messuage in the parish of St Andrew's which same he bought from Walter Edward, which same messuage descended to the said Walter by inheritance through the death of Robert Edward, his father, which same Walter acquired that by inheritance through the death of William Edward, his father, and the said William acquired that by ancient purchase, and he pays in respect thereof per annum to the said Walter and his heirs 1 rose, and for the maintenance of a lamp for the Lord in the aforesaid church 21d.

[886]   The same John holds 1 messuage in the same parish [St Andrew's] which he bought from Richard le Coffrer, and the said Richard bought that from William Carpenter, and the said William from John le Watersmith, and the said John acquired that through ancient purchase, and he pays in respect thereof per annum to the heirs of the said Richard 1 rose, and to Walter Tailor and his heirs 6d., and to the sacrist of Ely 4s. By which warranty the said sacrist receives the said income they do not know.

BARNWELL, SUBURB BELONGING TO THE TOWN OF CAMBRIDGE

[887]   Richard Pet holds 1 messuage in the town of Barnwell and a ½ acre of land belonging to the said messuage, which same messuage with the said land he bought from the prior and

convent of the same town, for which he pays per annum to the aforesaid prior and convent 4s., in which manner the said prior and convent do not know how they came by the said messuage and land.

[888] Item the same Richard holds 1 messuage in the same town which he bought from Master Robert Ong' and the same Robert bought that from Walter Werret, and the same Walter bought that from John of the Infirmary, and the same John held that by hereditary succession from his father, for which the aforesaid Richard pays per annum to the aforesaid Robert Ong' 12d. And the same Robert acquits the aforesaid Richard to the prior and convent of Barnwell; by which warranty they receive the said rent they do not know.

[889] Item the same Richard holds 3 acres of land in the fields of the same town, which he bought from Luke of St Edmund's, and the same Luke held that by inheritance from Master Thomas, his brother, and the same Thomas held that by gift of Walter, his father, and the same Walter held that by hereditary succession, for which the aforesaid Richard pays per annum to the aforesaid Luke 12d.

[890] Item the same Richard holds a ½ acre of land in the aforesaid fields in fee from Luke of St Edmund's, which he bought from Oliver le Porter, and the same Oliver bought that from Henry Gut. And the same Henry held that by hereditary succession, for which the aforesaid Richard pays per annum to the aforesaid Luke 6d. as tenant-in-chief of the lord's fief, by assignment of the aforesaid Oliver, and to the said Oliver 1 rose.

[891] Item the same Richard holds in the aforesaid fields 3 acres of land in fee from Leon Dunning, which he bought from Richard son of Ivo. And the same Richard bought those from the aforesaid Leon. And the same Leon held those by hereditary succession, for which the aforesaid Richard pays per annum to Andrew, son of the aforesaid Richard, 4d. And Richard to Luke 7d. And the aforesaid Andrew acquits the aforesaid Richard to the aforesaid Leon as tenant-in-chief of the lord's fee.

[892] Geoffrey Paie holds 1 messuage in the town of Barnwell and 3 half acres of land in the fields of the same town, which same messuages and said land descended to the aforesaid Geoffrey by inheritance through the death of Robert, his father, and the same Robert bought those from John Seliman, and the same John bought those from John Timpon. And the same John held those by hereditary succession of his father, for which the aforesaid

Geoffrey pays per annum to the aforesaid John Seliman 3s., and 1 ounce of cumin. And the aforesaid John acquits the aforesaid Geoffrey to the prior of Barnwell as tenant-in-chief of the lord's fee; by which warranty they receive the said rent they do not know.

[893]   Henry Merchant holds 1 messuage in the town of Barnwell which he bought from the prior and convent of the same town, for which he pays per annum to the aforesaid prior and convent 18d., in which manner the prior and convent do not know how they came by the said messuage and land.

[894]   Osbert Carter holds 1 messuage in the town of Barnwell from the prior and convent of the same town, which same messuage he received with Agnes, his wife, in frank marriage from Beatrice, mother of the aforesaid Agnes. And the same Beatrice bought that from Simon Feisond. And the same Simon bought that from the prior and convent of Barnwell, for which the aforesaid Osbert pays per annum to the aforesaid prior and convent 12d., in which manner the prior and convent do not know how they came by the said messuage and income.

[895]   Item Hugo Mainer holds 1 messuage and 1 rood of land in the town of Barnwell in fee from the prior and convent of the same town, which same he bought from the aforesaid prior and convent, for which he pays per annum to the aforesaid prior and convent 10½d., by which warranty they do not know.

[896]   Item the same Hugo holds 1 messuage in the same town which he bought from Adam le Maiden. And the same Adam bought that from William le Noreis, and the same William bought that from Andrew, clerk. And the same Andrew held that by inheritance through the death of Andrew, his father, for which the aforesaid Hugh pays per annum to the aforesaid Adam 1 peppercorn. And to William le Noreis 5d. And the same William pays per annum for the said messuage to the hospital of Stourbridge for perpetual alms 2d., and to the bailiffs of Cambridge who hold the said town in fee farm from the lord King, for their farm ½d.

[897]   Item the same Hugo holds 1 messuage in the aforesaid town which same he bought from Adam Carbunel, and the same Adam held that by gift of Matilda, his mother, and the said Matilda held that by hereditary succession through the death of her father, for which the aforesaid Hugo pays per annum to the prior and convent of Barnwell 20½d. as tenant-in-chief of the lord's fee by assignment of the aforesaid Adam, by which warranty they receive the said rent they do not know.

[898] Item the same Hugo holds 1 messuage in the said town, which same descended to the aforesaid Hugh by inheritance through the death of Geoffrey, his father, and the same Geoffrey bought that from Andrew, son of Edriz. And the same Andrew held that from Alan de Deresle. And the same Alan held that by ancient heritage, for which the aforesaid Hugo pays per annum to Eleanor, former wife of Nicholas Childman, and the heirs of the aforesaid Nicholas, 10d. And the aforesaid Nicholas bought the said income of 10d. from John de Deresle, heir of the aforesaid Alan de Deresle.

[899] Item the same Hugo holds 1 messuage in the said town and a ½ acre of land in the fields of the same town pertaining to the said messuage, which same messuage with aforesaid ½ acre of land he bought from Alicia, daughter of Richard at the head of the town. And the said Alicia held that by inheritance through the death of Richard, her father. And the same Richard bought that from Andrew son of Edriz. And the same Andrew held that from Alan de Deresle, and the same Alan held that by ancient heritage, for which the aforesaid Hugo pays per annum to the aforesaid Alicia 1½d.

[900] The same Hugo holds a ½ acre in the aforesaid fields, which he bought from Isabella, daughter of Alan de Teversham and the said Isabella held that by inheritance through the death of Alan, her father. And the same Alan bought that from Nicholas Doi, and the same Nicholas held that by hereditary succession, for which the aforesaid Hugo pays per annum to the aforesaid Isabella 1d.

[901] The same Hugo holds 1 acre of land in the aforesaid fields which he bought from Luke of St Edmund's. And the same Luke held that by inheritance through the death of Master Thomas, his brother. And the same Thomas held that by gift of Walter, his father, and the same Walter held that by succession, for which the aforesaid Hugo pays per annum to the aforesaid Luke 4d.

[902] The same Hugo holds a ½ acre of land in the aforesaid fields, which he bought from Margaret, former wife of John of the Infirmary. And the said Margaret held that by gift of Agnes, her mother, and the said Agnes held that by inheritance through the death of Martin, her father, for which the aforesaid Hugo pays per annum to the aforesaid Margaret 6d. And the same Margaret pays the said 6d. to the aforesaid Agnes, her mother, and the same Agnes acquits the aforesaid Hugo and Margaret to Luke of St Edmund's, as tenant-in-chief of the lord's fee.

[903]   Item Isabella, daughter of William Paie holds 1 messuage in the town of Barnwell, which same descended to the aforesaid Isabella by inheritance through the death of Dionisia, her sister. And the said Dionisia bought that from Robert, son of Silvester. And the same Robert held that by inheritance through the death of Silvester, his father, and the same Silvester held that by ancient heritage, for which the aforesaid Isabella pays per annum to the aforesaid Robert 1 rose. And to Luke of St Edmund's 6d. as tenant-in-chief of the lord's fee, by assignment of the aforesaid Robert.

[904]   Richard Hastinges holds 1 messuage in the town of Barnwell which same he bought from Margaret, former wife of John of the Infirmary. And the said Margaret held that by gift of Hugo, her father, and Agnes, her mother. And the aforesaid Hugo and Agnes owed that by inheritance through the death of Martin, father of the aforesaid Agnes, for which the aforesaid Richard pays per annum to the aforesaid Margaret 6d., and the said Margaret pays the aforesaid 6d. to Hugo and Agnes, his wife, and the aforesaid Hugo and Agnes, his wife acquit the aforesaid Richard and Margaret to Luke of St Edmund's as tenant-in-chief of the lord's fee.

[905]   Item Hugo le Noreis and Agnes, his wife, hold 1 messuage in the town of Barnwell, which same descended to the aforesaid Agnes, his wife, by inheritance through the death of Martin, her father. And the same Martin bought that from Walter of St Edmund's. And the same Walter held that by hereditary succession of his father, for which the aforesaid Hugo and Agnes pay per annum to Luke of St Edmund's 10d. as tenant-in-chief of the lord's fee.

[906]   The same Hugo and Agnes, his wife, hold 1 acre of land in the fields of the same town, which they bought from John of the Infirmary and the same John held that by inheritance through the death of Roger, his father, for which the aforesaid Hugo and Agnes pay per annum to Luke of St Edmund's 7d. as tenant-in-chief of the lord's fee.

[907]   The same Hugo and Agnes, his wife, hold 1 rood in the aforesaid fields, which descended to the aforesaid Agnes by inheritance through the death of Martin, her father, and the same Martin bought that from Geoffrey Melt, and the same Geoffrey held that by hereditary succession through the death of Walter, his father, for which the aforesaid Hugo and Agnes pay per annum to Luke of St Edmund's 6d. as tenant-in-chief of the lord's fee.

[908]   The same Hugo and Agnes, his wife, hold ½ acre of land in the aforesaid fields, in fee from William de Novacurt, which

descended to the aforesaid Agnes by inheritance through the death of Martin, her father. And the same Martin bought that from William Novacurt. And that William held that by hereditary succession of his father, for which the aforesaid Hugo and Agnes, his wife, pay per annum to the aforesaid William Novacurt 6d. as tenant-in-chief of the lord's fee.

[909]   The same Hugo and Agnes, his wife, hold in the aforesaid fields 5 roods of land, which descended to the aforesaid Agnes, his wife, through the death of Martin, her father, and the same Martin bought those from the prior and convent of Barnwell, for which the aforesaid Hugh and Agnes pay per annum to the aforesaid prior and convent 2s. 6d. as tenant-in-chief of the lord's fee; by which warranty they receive the said rent they do not know.

[910]   Richard Jado holds 1 messuage in the town of Barnwell, which same messuage he holds by donation in frank marriage with Agnes, his wife, from William le Noreis, and the same Wiliam held that by gift of Hugo, his father, and Agnes, his mother, which same Agnes held that by inheritance of Martin, her father, for which the aforesaid Richard pays per annum to the aforesaid William 12d., and the same William acquits the aforesaid Richard to Luke of St Edmund's as tenant-in-chief of the lord's fee.

[911]   Item the same Richard holds 1 messuage in the same town which same he bought from John Crul, and the same John bought that from Luke of St Edmund's, and the same Luke held that by inheritance through the death of Master Thomas, his brother, and the same Thomas held that by gift of Walter, his father. And the same Walter held that by hereditary succession, for which the aforesaid Richard pays per annum to the aforesaid John 10d. And the same John acquits the aforesaid Richard to Luke of St Edmund's as tenant-in-chief of the lord's fee.

[912]   The same Richard holds 3 half acres of land in the fields of the same town which he bought from Luke of St Edmund's, and the same Luke held those by inheritance through the death of Master Thomas, his brother, and the same Thomas held those by gift of Walter, his father, and the same Walter held those by hereditary succession, for which the aforesaid Richard pays per annum to the aforesaid Luke 4d.

[913]   Isabella, former wife of William Paie holds 1 messuage in the town of Barnwell and 1 acre of land in the fields of the same town, which same messuage with said acre of land, the prior and convent of Barnwell formerly gave and confirmed by charter to the aforesaid William Paie and Isabella, his wife, and the aforesaid

prior and convent held that by donation of Geoffrey, chaplain. And the same Geoffrey held the said messuage with aforesaid land by hereditary succession from the part of his father, for which the aforesaid Isabella pays per annum to Luke of St Edmund's 14d. as tenant-in-chief of the lord's fee, by assignment of the aforesaid prior and convent.

[914]　The same Isabella holds 2 acres of land and ½ acre in the fields of the same town in fee from William Novacurt, which the aforesaid prior and convent gave to the aforesaid William and Isabella, his wife. And the aforesaid prior and convent held those by gift of the aforesaid Geoffrey, chaplain. And the same Geoffrey bought those from William Smith, and the same William held that from the ancestors of the aforesaid William Novacurt, for which the aforesaid Isabella pays per annum to Deonisius de Huntingdon 21d. And the same Deonisius acquits the aforesaid Isabella to William de Novacurt as tenant-in-chief of the lord's fee.

[915]　The same Isabella holds ½ acre of land in the aforesaid fields, which aforesaid prior and convent gave to the aforesaid William Paie and Isabella, his wife. And the aforesaid prior and convent held that by gift of the aforesaid Geoffrey. And the same Geoffrey bought that from William son of Ivo, and the same William held that by paternal inheritance, for which the aforesaid Isabella pays per annum to William Eliot 2d., by assignment of the aforesaid prior and convent.

[916]　The same Isabella holds ½ acre of land in the aforesaid fields, which the aforesaid prior and convent gave to the aforesaid William Paie and Isabella, his wife. And the aforesaid prior and convent held that by gift of the aforesaid Geoffrey, chaplain. And the same Geoffrey bought that from Richard son of Ivo, and the same Richard held that by inquest, for which the aforesaid Isabella pays per annum to Agnes of Barton 2d., by assignment of the aforesaid prior and convent.

[917]　The same Isabella holds ½ acre of land in the aforesaid fields, which the aforesaid prior and convent gave to the aforesaid William Paie and Isabella, his wife, and the aforesaid prior and convent held that by gift of the aforesaid Geoffrey, chaplain. And the same Geoffrey held that by hereditary paternal succession, for which the aforesaid Isabella pays per annum to John But 2d., by assignment of the aforesaid prior and convent; moreover the aforesaid Isabella pays per annum to the aforesaid prior and convent for the aforesaid messuage and for the 5 afore-named acres of land 1 mark.

[918]   Roger de Huntingfield and Agnes, his wife, hold 1 messuage in the town of Barnwell, which same Hugh de Brunner gave to the aforesaid Agnes, and the same Hugo held that by gift of Walter Carter, and the same Walter bought that from Thomas Oliver. And the same Thomas bought that from the aforesaid Roger de Huntingfield. And the same Roger held that from Radulph de Mordon, for which the aforesaid Roger and Agnes, his wife, pay per annum to Thomas Oliver 2s. ½d., and for a light for the Blessed Mary in St Giles's Church of Barnwell, 16d. And the aforesaid Thomas pays per annum to John Crul 8d., and the same John acquits the aforesaid Roger and Agnes and Thomas to Luke of St Edmund's as tenant-in-chief of the lord's fee.

[919]   The same Roger holds 1 messuage in the same town until the end of his life from Hugh Mainer, which same Hugh bought that from Henry Feikin, and the same Henry held that by inheritance through the death of Simon, his father, for which the aforesaid Roger pays per annum to the aforesaid Hugh 14½d., and the same Hugh pays the aforesaid 14½d. to John, heir of the aforesaid Henry, and the same John acquits the aforesaid Roger and Hugh to the prior and convent of Barnwell as tenant-in-chief of the lord's fee; by which warranty they do not know.

[920]   Thomas Oliver holds 1 messuage in the town of Barnwell, which same messuage he holds by gift of William Oliver, his father and Margaret, his mother, which same aforesaid William and Margaret, his wife, bought that from Agnes Morel, and the said Agnes held that by inheritance through the death of her mother, for which the aforesaid Thomas pays per annum to Richard Lincke 1d. And to Agnes wife of Alan the Stabler 1d. And the said Agnes acquits the aforesaid Thomas to Luke of St Edmund's as tenant-in-chief of the lord's fee.

[921]   The same Thomas holds 1 rood of land in the fields of the same town, which he bought from Silvester Lincke and Matilda, his wife. And the said Matilda held that by hereditary succession through the death of Johanna, her mother, for which the aforesaid Thomas pays per annum to Richard Lincke 3d., and the aforesaid Richard acquits the aforesaid Thomas to Leon Dunning as tenant-in-chief of the lord's fee.

[922]   Radulph de Winepol holds 1 messuage in the town of Barnwell, which same messuage he holds by gift of the prior and convent of the same town, for which he pays per annum to the aforesaid prior and convent 12d. as tenant-in-chief of the lord's fee, in

which manner the prior and convent are unaware of how they came to the messuage and income.

[923] Sarra daughter of Thomas le Mason holds 1 messuage in the town of Barnwell, which same she holds by gift of Thomas, her father, and the same Thomas held that by gift of Richard, his brother, and the same Richard held that from the prior and convent of Barnwell, for which the aforesaid Sarra pays per annum to the aforesaid prior and convent 2d. as tenant-in-chief of the lord's fee; by which warranty they came to the said income they do not know.

[924] Lecia, former wife of Peter Stote, holds 1 messuage in the town of Barnwell, which same Peter, former husband of the aforesaid Lecia bought from Reginald le Noreis, and the aforesaid Reginald bought that from Henry Dinggel and the same Henry held that with Helewisa, his wife, in frank marriage, for which the aforesaid Lecia pays per annum to Margaret daughter of Aubrin' 2s. ½d. And the said Margaret acquits the aforesaid Lecia to Luke of St Edmund's as tenant-in-chief of the lord's fee.

[925] Item Oliver Prat holds 1 messuage in fee in the town of Barnwell, which same descended to the aforesaid Oliver by inheritance through the death of Nicholas, his father, and the same Nicholas held that by inheritance of Roger, his father. And the same Roger held that from Robert Novacurt, for which the aforesaid Oliver pays per annum to William de Novacurt 3s. as tenant-in-chief of the lord's fee.

[926] The same Oliver holds 1 messuage in the same town which same he bought from William Caim, and the same William held that by inheritance through the death of Matilda, his mother, for which the aforesaid Oliver pays per annum to Alan the Stabler 1d., by assignment of the aforesaid William, and the aforesaid Alan acquits the aforesaid Oliver to the prior and convent of Barnwell as tenant-in-chief of the lord's fee, by which warranty they came to the said income they do not know.

[927] The same Oliver holds 1 half acre of land in the fields of the same town, which descended to the aforesaid Oliver by inheritance through the death of Nicholas, his father, and the same Nicholas bought that from Agnes Tuffe, and the said Agnes held that by gift of Winfrid, her father, and the same Winfrid bought that from Stephen King. And the same Stephen held that by hereditary succession, for which the aforesaid Oliver pays per annum to Hugh son of Geoffrey Faber 4d. as the heir of the

aforesaid Stephen King, and the aforesaid Hugh acquits the said Oliver to Luke of St Edmund's as tenant-in-chief of the lord's fee.

[928] Item William de Teversham holds 1 messuage in the town of Barnwell which he bought from Beatrice Potion, which same Beatrice bought that from the prior of Barnwell, which same prior bought that from William son of John Mason, which same John held that by ancient hereditary succession through the death of Andrew, his father, for which the aforesaid William pays per annum to the said prior 12d.

[929] Item the same William holds 2 roods of land in the fields of Barnwell, which he bought from Matilda Crul, and the said Matilda bought those from Geoffrey Melt, which same said Geoffrey held those from Henry Melt, his father, by hereditary right and pays in respect thereof per annum to Lord Philip of Coleville 6d. for the aforesaid land, which same pays 6d. to William Melt, son and heir of Geoffrey Melt, who sold it to Lord Henry de Coleville, father of the aforesaid Philip.

[930] Matilda Jun holds 1 messuage in the town of Barnwell, which same messuage she holds by gift of Alberta, her mother, and the said Alberta held that by gift of Warin, her father, and the same Warin held that by hereditary succession, for which the aforesaid Matilda pays per annum to Agnes, heiress of the aforesaid Alberta, 3d. And the said Agnes acquits the aforesaid Matilda to Luke of St Edmund's as tenant-in-chief of the lord's fee.

[931] Robert le Neve and Florencia his wife, hold 1 messuage in the town of Barnwell, which same messuage Master Nicholas, doctor, father of the aforesaid Florencia gave to the aforesaid Florencia, which same aforesaid Master Nicholas held that by gift of the prior and convent of Barnwell, for which the aforesaid Robert and Florencia, his wife, pay per annum to the said prior and convent 2s. And to the bailiffs of Cambridge who hold the said town in fee farm from the lord King, namely to their farm 4½d., in which manner the prior and convent came to the said income they do not know.

[932] Isondia Salandin holds 1 messuage in the town of Barnwell, which same she has by gift of John, her father, which same John bought that from Geoffrey de Sartrino, which same Geoffrey bought that from Isabella Ace, which same Isabella held that by hereditary succession, for which the aforesaid Isondia pays per annum to William de Novacurt 12d. And to Geoffrey Salandin, son and heir of the aforesaid John Saladin, 1 pair of gloves at the price of ½d.

[933]   Item the same Isondia holds ½ acre of land in the fields of the same town, which she bought from Roger de Huntingfield, which Roger bought from Thomas of St Edmund's and the same Thomas held that by gift of Walter, his father, and the same Walter held that by hereditary succession, for which the aforesaid Isondia pays per annum to Luke of St Edmund's 4d. as tenant-in-chief of the lord's fee and to the aforesaid Roger ½d.

[934]   Matilda Tele holds 1 messuage in the town of Barnwell and a ½ acre of land in the fields of the same town in fee from William Novacurt, which same messuage with said ½ acre of land descended to the aforesaid Matilda by inheritance through the death of Martin, her father, and the same Martin held that from feoffment of Adam de Cokefeld. And the same Adam held that by ancient inheritance, for which the aforesaid Matilda pays per annum to the aforesaid William de Novacurt 14d. as tenant-in-chief of the lord.

[935]   The same Matilda holds 5 roods of land in the aforesaid fields in fee from the prior and convent of Barnwell, which same descended to the aforesaid Matilda by inheritance through the death of Martin, her father, and the same Martin held those by ancient inheritance, for which the aforesaid Matilda pays per annum to the aforesaid prior and convent 3s. as tenant-in-chief of the lord; by which warranty they receive the said income they are unaware.

[936]   Item the same Matilda holds in the aforesaid fields a ½ acre of land which William, former husband of the aforesaid Matilda bought for himself and Matilda, his wife, from William Castelein, and the same William held that by ancient inheritance, for which the aforesaid Matilda pays per annum Luke of St Edmund's 2d. as tenant-in-chief of the lord's fee by assignment of the aforesaid William.

[937]   Peter Long holds 1 messuage in the town of Barnwell in fee, which same messuage descended to the aforesaid Peter by inheritance through the death of Simon, his father, which same Simon held that by inheritance through the death of Radulph, his father, and the same Radulph held that by inheritance, for which the aforesaid Peter pays per annum to Michael de Huntingdon ½ lb. of cumin, and the same Michael acquits the aforesaid Peter to William de Novacurt as tenant-in-chief of the lord's fee.

[938]   William de Celar holds 1 messuage in fee in the town of Barnwell, which same messuage descended to the aforesaid William by inheritance through the death of Alicia, his mother, which same

Alicia held that by gift of Roger, her father. And the same Roger bought that from Simon Lungis, and the same Simon held that by inheritance from his father, for which the aforesaid William pays per annum to William de Novacurt 12d. And to the almoner of Barnwell in perpetual alms 12d.; by which warranty they are unaware.

[939] Item the same William holds 1 acre of land which he bought from Luke of St Edmund's and the same Luke held that by inheritance through the death of Master Thomas, his brother. And the same Thomas held that by gift of Walter, his father. And the same Walter held that by hereditary succession, for which William pays per annum to the aforesaid Luke 4d.

[940] Item the same William holds ½ acre of land in the aforesaid fields, which descended to the aforesaid William by inheritance through the death of Alicia, his mother, and the said Alicia bought that from John Infirmarer. And the same John held that by inheritance through the death of Roger, his father. And the same Roger held that by paternal inheritance, for which the aforesaid William pays per annum to Agnes, daughter and heiress of the aforesaid John 2½d. And the said Agnes acquits the aforesaid William to William de Novacurt as tenant-in-chief of the lord's fee.

[941] Item the same William holds ½ acre of land in the aforesaid fields which he received in frank marriage with Alicia, his wife, from Richard Pet, and the same Richard bought that from William son of Ivo. And the same William held that by hereditary succession, for which the aforesaid William pays per annum to the aforesaid Richard 4d., and the same Richard acquits the aforesaid William to the heirs of Cristiana Astines as tenant-in-chief of the lord's fee.

[942] The same William holds ½ acre of land in the aforesaid fields which he received in frank marriage with Alicia, his wife, from Richard Pet, and the same Richard bought that from Oliver le Porter, and the same Oliver bought that from Henry Gut, and the same Henry held that by hereditary succession from Henry, his father, for which the aforesaid William pays per annum to the aforesaid Richard 6d., and the same Richard acquits the aforesaid William to Luke of St Edmund's as tenant-in-chief of the lord's fee.

[943] John son of John Crul holds 1 messuage in fee in the town of Barnwell, which descended to the aforesaid John by inheritance through the death of Muriella, his mother, which same Muriella held by gift of Osbert King, her father. And the same Osbert

bought that from Isabella Gerard, and the said Isabella held that by hereditary succession, for which the aforesaid John pays per annum to the prior and convent of Barnwell 4d. as tenant-in-chief of the lord's fee, by which warranty they are unaware.

[944] Item the same John holds ½ acre of land in the fields of the same town, which descended to the aforesaid John by inheritance through the death of Muriella, his mother, which aforesaid Muriella held by gift of Osbert King, her father. And the same Osbert bought that from Walter at the Church of St Edmund's, for which the aforesaid John pays per annum to Luke of St Edmund's 3d. as tenant-in-chief of the lord's fee.

[945] John Crul holds 1 messuage in the town of Barnwell until the end of his life from Adam Oliver and Dionisia, his wife, which same messuage descended to the said Dionisia by inheritance through the death of William, her father, and the same William bought that from Nicholas Lungis, and the same Nicholas held by hereditary succession, for which the aforesaid John pays per annum to the aforesaid Adam and Dionisia 1d. And the aforesaid Adam and Dionisia pay the said 1d. for a light for the Blessed Mary in the chapel of Barnwell.

[946] The same John holds 1 messuage in the same town which he bought from Felicia Gerard, and the said Felicia held that by hereditary succession through the death of William, her father. And the same William bought that from the prior and convent of Barnwell, for which the aforesaid John pays per annum to the aforesaid prior and convent 6d. by assignment of the aforesaid Felicia. And to the aforesaid Felicia 1 rose; the prior and convent are unaware of the manner by which they came to the said messuage.

[947] The same John holds a piece of vacant land in the same town which he bought from Simon Smith, and the same Simon bought that from Henry Faukes, and the same Henry held that by hereditary succession, for which the aforesaid John pays per annum to the aforesaid prior and convent 6d. by assignment of the aforesaid Simon.

[948] The same John holds ½ acre of land in the fields of the same town which he bought from Stephen King, and the same Stephen held that through the death of Osbert, his father, for which the aforesaid John pays per annum to Hugh son of Geoffrey Smith 3d., and the same Hugh acquits the aforesaid John to Luke of St Edmund's as tenant-in-chief of the lord's fee.

[949]   The same John owns a ½ acre of land in the aforesaid fields, which he bought from William Caim, and the same William held that by hereditary succession of Matilda, his mother, for which the aforesaid John pays per annum to Luke of St Edmund's 6d. as tenant-in-chief of the lord's fee, by assignment of the aforesaid William.

[950]   Item Adam Mason, holds 1 messuage in the town of Barnwell, which same he holds by gift of Richard, his father, which same Richard held that by purchase from Agnes le Suein, which same Agnes held that by hereditary succession, for which the aforesaid Adam pays per annum to William de Novacurt 4d. as tenant-in-chief of the lord's fee.

[951]   Item John of the Infirmary holds 1 messuage in the town of Barnwell, which same descended to the aforesaid John by inheritance through the death of John his father, which said John bought from Nicholas Pappe, which same descended to the aforesaid Nicholas by inheritance through the death of Hugh, his father, and the same Hugh held that from the prior and convent of Barnwell, for which the aforesaid John pays per annum to the said prior and convent 2s. as tenant-in-chief of the lord's fee, by which warranty they are unaware.

[952]   Item the same John holds ½ acre of land in the fields of the same town, which descended to the aforesaid John by inheritance through the death of John, his father, which same John held that by inheritance through the death of Radulph, his brother, which Radulph bought that from Geoffrey de Borvell, and the same Geoffrey held that in exchange for the same amount of land from Robert Maniaunt. And the same Robert bought that from Cassandria, daughter of Warin Astin. And the said Cassandria held that by hereditary succession, for which the aforesaid John pays per annum to the aforesaid Geoffrey de Borvell 1d. And the same Geoffrey acquits the aforesaid John to the aforesaid Cassandria Astin.

[953]   Item the same John holds ½ acre of land in the aforesaid fields, which descended to the aforesaid John by inheritance through the death of John, his father, and the said John held that by inheritance from Radulph, his brother. And the same Radulph bought that from Simon Lungis. And the same Simon held that by hereditary succession, for which the aforesaid John pays per annum to Leon Dunning 4d., and the same Leon bought the said income from the Lord of Rushden.

[954] Adam Oliver holds 1 messuage in the town of Barnwell, which same descended to the aforesaid Adam by inheritance through the death of William, his father, which same William bought that from Radulph de Mordone. And the same Radulph held that by hereditary succession, for which the aforesaid Adam pays per annum to the prior and convent of Barnwell 2s. as tenant-in-chief of the lord's fee; by which warranty they came to the said income they do not know.

[955] Item the said Adam holds 1 messuage in the same town which he bought from Thomas Stebing. And the same Thomas held that by inheritance through the death of Walter, his father, which same Walter bought that from Godfrey de Dunham. And the same Godfrey bought that from Nicholas Pappe, and the same Nicholas held that by hereditary succession, for which the aforesaid Adam pays per annum to John of the Infirmary 7d. And the same John acquits the aforesaid Adam to the prior and convent of Barnwell as tenant-in-chief of the lord's fee; by which warranty they came to the said income they are unaware.

[956] Item the same Adam holds ½ acre of land in the same fields of the town, which descended to Deonisia, his wife, by inheritance through the death of William, her father, which same William bought that from Walter of St Edmund's. And the same Walter held that by ancient inheritance, for which the aforesaid Adam pays per annum to Geoffrey Salandin 8d., and the same Geoffrey acquits the aforesaid Adam to Luke of St Edmund's as tenant-in-chief of the lord's fee.

[957] Item Richard Lincke holds 1 messuage in the town of Barnwell, which same descended to the aforesaid Richard by inheritance through the death of Silvester, his father, which same Silvester held that by inheritance through the death of Alicia, his mother, and the same Alicia held that by inheritance of Robert, her father, which same Robert held by hereditary succession, for which the aforesaid Richard pays per annum to the prior and convent of Barnwell 2s., by which warranty they came to the said income they are unaware.

[958] Item the same Richard holds 1 messuage in the same town, which descended to the aforesaid Richard by inheritance through the death of Matilda, his mother, which same Matilda held by inheritance of Jona, her mother, which same Jona held by inheritance from Mabilia, her mother. And the same Mabilia bought that from William Smith, and the same William held that by hereditary succession, for which the aforesaid Richard pays

per annum to the said prior and convent 13d., by which warranty they came to the said income they are unaware.

[959] Item the same Richard holds 3 roods of land in the fields of the same town, which descended to the aforesaid Richard by inheritance through the death of Matilda, his mother, which said Matilda held by inheritance from Jona, her mother, and the said Jona held those by inheritance from Mabilia, her mother, and the said Mabilia held those by hereditary succession, for which the aforesaid Richard pays per annum to Leon Dunning 6d., which same income the said Leon bought from the Lord of Rushden.

[960] Hugh son of Geoffrey Smith holds 1 messuage in the town of Barnwell, which descended to the aforesaid Hugh by inheritance through the death of Geoffrey, his father, which same Geoffrey held that in exchange for another from John Russel, which same John bought that from John de Toft, which same John bought that from William, his brother, which same William held that from the prior and convent of Barnwell, and in respect thereof the aforesaid Hugh pays to the aforesaid prior and convent 5s. by assignment of the aforesaid John, in which manner, the said prior and convent are unaware of how they received the said messuage.

[961] Item the same Hugh holds 1 messuage in the same town which descended to the aforesaid Hugh by inheritance through the death of Agnes, his mother, which same Agnes held that by inheritance through the death of Alicia, her mother. And the same Alicia held that from the prior and convent of Barnwell, and in respect thereof the aforesaid Hugh pays per annum to the aforesaid prior and convent 7d.; in which manner the prior and convent received the said income they are unaware.

[962] Item the same Hugh holds half of 1 messuage in the said town and a half acre of land in the fields of the same town, which same messuage with said land descended to the aforesaid Hugh by inheritance through the death of Agnes, his mother, which same Agnes held that by inheritance from Alicia, her mother, which same Alicia held from the prior and convent of Barnwell. And in respect thereof the aforesaid Hugh pays per annum to the aforesaid prior and convent 12d., by which warranty they are unaware.

[963] Item the same Hugh holds 1 messuage in the same town, which same messuage descended to the aforesaid Hugh by inheritance through the death of Geoffrey, his father, which same Geoffrey held that by inheritance from Osbert, his father, which same Osbert held that from Robert Novacurt, and in respect thereof

the aforesaid Hugh pays per annum to William de Novacurt 8d. as tenant-in-chief of the lord's fee.

[964] Item the same Hugh holds ½ virgate in the fields of the same town in fee from Luke of St Edmund's, which descended to the aforesaid Hugh by inheritance through the death of Geoffrey, his father, which same Geoffrey held that by inheritance from Matilda, his mother, which same Matilda held that from Walter of St Edmund's, and in respect thereof the aforesaid Hugh pays per annum to Luke of St Edmund's 5s. as tenant-in-chief of the lord's fee.

[965] Item the same Hugh holds 1 acre of land in the fields of the same town which descended to the aforesaid Hugh by inheritance through the death of Geoffrey, his father, which same Geoffrey held that by inheritance from Matilda, his mother, which said Matilda held that from the prior and convent of Barnwell. And in respect thereof the aforesaid Hugh pays per annum to the aforesaid prior and convent 20d.; by which warranty they received the said income they are unaware.

[966] Item the same Hugh holds 1 rood of land in the aforesaid fields, which descended to the aforesaid Hugh by inheritance through the death of Geoffrey, his father, which same Geoffrey bought that from Geoffrey Melt, which same Geoffrey held that through the death of Henry, his father. And in respect thereof the aforesaid Hugh pays per annum to the Lord Philip de Coleville 2d.

[967] Item the same Hugh holds 1 rood in the aforesaid fields, which descended to the aforesaid Hugh by inheritance through the death of Agnes, his mother, which same Agnes held that by inheritance through the death of Henry, her father, which same Henry bought from Adam Dunning, and in respect thereof he pays per annum to Leon Dunning 4d. as tenant-in-chief of the lord's fee.

[968] Item the same Hugh holds ½ acre of land in the aforesaid fields which descended to the aforesaid Hugh by inheritance through the death of Agnes, his mother, which same Agnes held that by inheritance through the death of Alicia, her mother, which same Alicia bought that from Andrew, clerk, which same Andrew held by hereditary succession. And in respect thereof the aforesaid Hugh pays per annum to Luke of St Edmund's 4½d. as tenant-in-chief of the lord's fee.

[969] Beatrice, former wife of Geoffrey Smith, holds 1 messuage in the town of Barnwell, and 3 roods of land in the fields of the same town, which same messuage with said land Beatrice holds by gift

of Geoffrey, her former husband, which same Geoffrey held that by inheritance from Matilda, his mother, for which she pays per annum to Leon Dunning 16d.

[970] Item the same Beatrice holds 1 messuage in the same town which she has by gift of Hugh, her brother, which same Hugh held that by inheritance through the death of Robert, his father, which same Robert held from the prior and convent of Barnwell, for which the said Beatrice pays per annum to the aforesaid Hugh 6½d. And the aforesaid Hugh acquits the aforesaid Beatrice to the prior and convent of Barnwell as tenant-in-chief of the lord's fee; by which warranty they received the said income they are unaware.

[971] John Stokin holds 1 messuage in the town of Barnwell, and a ½ acre of land in the fields of the same town, which same messuage with said land descended to the aforesaid John by inheritance through the death of Henry, his father, which same Henry held that by inheritance from Simon, his father, which same Simon held from the prior and convent of Barnwell, for which the aforesaid John pays per annum to the aforesaid prior and convent 3s. 4d.; by which warranty they received the said income they are unaware.

[972] Walter de Bornell holds 1 messuage in the town of Barnwell, which same he bought from Walter son of Henry Smith, which same Walter held that by inheritance through the death of Juliana, his mother, which same Juliana held that by inheritance from Jona, her mother, which same Jona held by hereditary succession, for which the aforesaid Walter pays per annum to the prior and convent of Barnwell 7d., by assignment of the aforesaid Walter.

[973] John Tail holds a certain house in the town of Barnwell, which he bought from Henry Cardun, which same Henry bought from the prior and convent of Barnwell, and in respect thereof he pays per annum to the aforesaid Henry 6d., and the same Henry acquits the aforesaid Henry to the prior and convent of Barnwell as tenant-in-chief of the lord's fee; by which warranty they received the said income they are unaware.

[974] Henry Cardun holds 1 messuage in the town of Barnwell, which he bought from the prior and convent of the same town and he pays in respect thereof per annum to the aforesaid prior and convent 18d., in which manner the said prior and convent are unaware of how they received the said messuage.

[975] Item the same Henry holds 1 messuage in the same town until the end of his life, which same messuage he holds through

Matilda, his former wife, which same Matilda bought that from Robert Cook, which same Robert bought that from Robert le Poleter, of which Robert we do not know, and in respect thereof he pays per annum to Geoffrey de Bornell 10½d., and the same Henry arranged for a burning light in St Andrew's Church at Barnwell.

[976] Agnes of the Infirmary holds 1 messuage in the town of Barnwell, which same descended to the aforesaid Agnes by inheritance through the death of John her brother, which same John held that by inheritance from John, his father, which same John held that by hereditary succession from Robert, his father which same Roger held that from the prior and convent of Barnwell, and she pays in respect thereof per annum to the aforesaid prior and convent 5½d.; by which warranty they received the said income they are unaware.

[977] Odo Cook holds 1 messuage in the town of Barnwell and 3 half acres of land in the fields of the same town, which same messuage and 3 half acres of land he bought from John Infirmarer, which same John held that by inheritance from Roger, his father, for which the aforesaid Odo pays per annum to Robert, clerk of Teversham 16d., and the same Robert acquits the aforesaid Odo to the prior of Barnwell as tenant-in-chief of the lord's fee.

[978] The same Odo holds ½ acre of land in the fields of the same town which he bought from Luke of St Edmund's, which same Luke held that by inheritance through the death of Master Thomas, his brother, which same Thomas held that by gift of Walter, his father, which same Walter held by hereditary succession and in respect thereof he pays per annum to the aforesaid Luke 1d.

[979] Laurence Dixi holds 1 messuage in the town of Barnwell which descended to the aforesaid Laurence by inheritance through the death of Sabina, his mother, which same Sabina held that by gift of Margaret, her mother, which same Margaret bought that from the prior and convent of Barnwell, and in respect thereof he pays per annum to the said prior and convent 12d.; by which warranty they received the said income they are unaware.

[980] Nicholas of the Infirmary and Margaret, his wife, hold half of 1 messuage in the town of Barnwell, which descended to the aforesaid Margaret by inheritance through the death of Henry, her father, which same Henry bought that from Robert of Hinton, which same Robert held from the prior of Barnwell, for which they pay per annum to the aforesaid prior 6d.; by which warranty they received the said income they are unaware.

[981] Item Nicholas and Margaret, his wife, hold ½ acre of land in the fields of the same town, which descended to the aforesaid Margaret by inheritance through the death of Alicia, her mother, which same Alicia bought that from Andrew, clerk, which same Andrew held that by gift of Andrew, his father, which same Andrew bought that from the prior of Barnwell. And in respect thereof they pay per annum to the aforesaid prior 6d.; by which warranty they received the said income they are unaware.

[982] Item Nicholas and Margaret, his wife, hold 1 rood of land in the aforesaid fields, which descended to the aforesaid Margaret by inheritance through the death of Henry, her father, which same Henry bought that from Adam Dunning, which same Adam held that by acquisition, and in respect thereof they pay per annum to Leon Dunning 4d.

[983] Item Nicholas and Margaret, his wife, hold 3 roods of land in the aforesaid fields, which descended to the aforesaid Margaret by inheritance through the death of Alicia, her mother, which same Alicia bought that from Henry Gut, which same Henry held by inheritance from Henry Mole, his father, for which they pay per annum to Luke of St Edmund's 3d. as tenant-in-chief of the lord's fee.

[984] Item Nicholas and Margaret, his wife, hold ½ acre of land in the aforesaid fields, which descended to the aforesaid Margaret by inheritance through the death of Alicia, her mother, which same Alicia bought that from Andrew, clerk, which same Andrew held that by gift of Andrew, his father, which same Andrew bought that from Walter at the church of St Edmund's, for which they pay per annum to Luke of St Edmund's 3d. as tenant-in-chief of the lord's fee.

[985] Item Nicholas and Margaret, his wife, hold ½ rood of land in the aforesaid fields which descended to the aforesaid Margaret by inheritance through the death of Alicia, her mother, which same Alicia bought that from John Infirmarer, which same John held that by hereditary succession from Roger, his father, and in respect thereof they pay per annum to Agnes, daughter of the aforesaid John and his heir, 1d.

[986] Item Nicholas and Margaret, his wife, hold in the aforesaid fields 5 roods of land which they bought from Luke of St Edmund's, which same Luke held those by inheritance through the death of Thomas, his brother, which same Thomas held those by gift of Walter, his father, which same Walter held by hereditary succession, for which they pay per annum to the aforesaid Luke 7½d.

[987] Item Nicholas holds 1 rood of land in the aforesaid fields from Alicia daughter of Jula until the end of the life of the aforesaid Alicia, which same Alicia regained that from Geoffrey de Bornell for her dower 3 roods, which same Geoffrey bought those from Henry Gut, former husband of the aforesaid Alicia, which same Henry held those by inheritance from Henry, his father, for which he pays per annum to the aforesaid Geoffrey de Bornell 4d.

[988] Geoffrey son of Thomas Dalt holds 1 messuage in the town of Barnwell, which same descended to the aforesaid Geoffrey by inheritance through the death of Thomas, his father, which same Thomas bought that from Reginald son of Richard, which same Reginald held that by inheritance from Richard, his father, which same Richard held that from Walter at the church of St Edmund's and he pays in respect thereof per annum to Luke of St Edmund's 6d. as tenant-in-chief of the lord's fee.

[989] Item the same Geoffrey holds 1 messuage in the same town which descended to him by inheritance through the death of Thomas, his father, which same Thomas held that by inheritance from Alan, his father, which same Alan bought from Andrew son of Edriz, for which the said Geoffrey pays per annum to Isabella Paie 4d., and the said Isabella acquits the aforesaid Geoffrey to Luke of St Edmund's as tenant-in-chief of the lord's fee.

[990] Item Geoffrey holds 4 acres of land in the fields of the same town, which descended to the aforesaid Geoffrey by inheritance through the death of Thomas, his father, which same Thomas held that by inheritance from Alan, his father, which same Alan held that from feoffment of Walter at the church of St Edmund's, and in respect thereof the aforesaid Geoffrey pays per annum to Luke of St Edmund's 4s. 2d.

[991] Item Geoffrey holds in the fields 1 acre of land which descended to him by inheritance through the death of Thomas, his father, which same Thomas held that by inheritance from Alan, his father, which same Alan held by feoffment of the prior of Barnwell and in respect thereof the said Geoffrey pays per annum to the aforesaid prior 2s., by which warranty they are unaware.

[992] Item Geoffrey holds in the aforesaid fields a ½ acre of land, which descended to him by inheritance through the death of Thomas, his father, which same Thomas held that by purchase from Andrew Leufene, which same Andrew held that by inheritance from Hugh, his father, which same Hugh held that by gift of Andrew, his brother, and in respect thereof the aforesaid Geoffrey

pays per annum to the prior and convent of Barnwell 5d. by assignment of the aforesaid Andrew, by which warranty they are unaware.

[993] Item Geoffrey holds 1 acre in the aforesaid fields by inheritance through the death of Thomas, his father, which same Thomas bought that from Robert son of Silvester, which same Robert held that by inheritance from Silvester, his father. And in respect thereof he pays per annum to Dionisa de Huntingdon 6d. by assignment of the aforesaid Robert. And the same Dionisia acquits the aforesaid Geoffrey to William de Novacurt as tenant-in-chief of the lord's fee.

[994] Item Geoffrey holds in the aforesaid fields a ½ acre of land by inheritance through the death of Thomas, his father, which same Thomas bought that from Robert son of Silvester, which same Robert held that by inheritance from Silvester, his father, and in respect thereof he pays per annum to the aforesaid Robert 1 pair of white gloves at the price of ½d. And to William de Novacurt as tenant-in-chief of the lord's fee 5d.

[995] Item Geoffrey holds in the aforesaid fields a ½ acre of land by inheritance through the death of Thomas, his father, which same Thomas held that by inheritance from Alan, his father, which same Alan held that by feoffment of Robert de Novacurt, and in respect thereof the said Geoffrey pays per annum to William de Novacurt 5d.

[996] Hugh de Brunner holds 1 messuage in the town of Barnwell, which same messuage descended to the aforesaid Hugh by inheritance through the death of Robert, his father, which same Robert bought that from Geoffrey son of Dera Robins, and the same Geoffrey held that by inheritance from Dera, his mother, which same Dera held that from the prior and convent of Barnwell, for which the aforesaid Hugh pays per annum to the aforesaid prior and convent 9d., by which warranty they are unaware, and to the aforesaid Geoffrey ½d.

[997] Item Hugh holds 1 messuage in the same town which he bought from Robert son of John Cook, and the same John held that by gift of the prior and convent of Barnwell and in respect thereof the aforesaid Hugh pays per annum to the aforesaid Robert ½d., and to the prior and convent 12d.; by which warranty they received the said income they are unaware.

[998] The same Hugh holds 1 messuage in the town of Cambridge in the parish of Holy Trinity, which same messuage descended to the aforesaid Hugh by inheritance through the death of William,

his uncle, and the same William bought that from Robert Edward, and the same Robert held that by inheritance from Robert, his father. And in respect thereof the aforesaid Hugh pays per annum to Walter le Bedel 12d., and to the prioress of St Radegund's 2s., by assignment of the aforesaid Robert.

[999] The same Hugh holds 1 messuage in the same town outside Trumpington Gate, which same messuage he received in frank marriage with Scolicia, his wife, from Richard Pet, and the same Richard bought that from Walter of St Edmund's and the same Walter held that by ancient inheritance, and in respect thereof the aforesaid Hugh pays per annum to Luke of St Edmund's 2s. as tenant-in-chief of the lord's fee.

[1000] The same Hugh holds 1 acre of land in the fields of Barnwell, which descended to the aforesaid Hugh by inheritance through the death of Robert, his father. And the same Robert bought that from John Paie. And the same John held that by inheritance of Robert, his father. And in respect thereof he pays per annum to Luke of St Edmund's 2d. as tenant-in-chief of the lord's fee.

[1001] The same Hugh holds 1 acre of land in the aforesaid fields, which he bought from Luke of St Edmund's, and the same Luke held that by inheritance through the death of Master Thomas, his brother, and the same Thomas held that by gift of Walter, his father, and the same Walter held that by hereditary succession, and in respect thereof the aforesaid Hugh pays per annum to the aforesaid Luke 6d.

[1002] The same Hugh holds ½ acre of land in the aforesaid fields, which he received in frank marriage with Scolicia, his wife, from Richard Pet, and the same Richard bought that from Thomas Plote, and the same Thomas bought that from Robert Edward. And the same Robert held that by inheritance of Robert, his father, and the same Hugh in respect thereof pays per annum to the aforesaid Richard 1d., and the same Richard acquits the aforesaid Hugh to Lord Philip de Coleville as tenant-in-chief of the lord's fee.

[1003] The same Hugh holds ½ acre of land in the aforesaid fields which he received in frank marriage with Scolicia, his wife, from Richard Pet, and the same Richard bought that from Richard Wombe. And the same Richard held that by inheritance through the death of John, his brother. And the same John held that by inheritance of Bartholomew, his father. And in respect thereof the aforesaid Hugh pays per annum to the aforesaid Richard 1d.

[1004] The same Hugh holds ½ acre of land in the aforesaid fields, which he bought from John Ace, and the same John held that by inheritance through the death of Elena, his mother, and the same Elena held that by inheritance of William, her father. And in respect thereof the aforesaid Hugh pays per annum to the aforesaid John 1d.

[1005] The same Hugh holds ½ acre of land in the aforesaid fields which descended to the aforesaid Hugh by inheritance through the death of Robert, his father. And the same Robert bought that from William, clerk. And the same William held that by hereditary paternal succession, and in respect thereof the aforesaid Hugh pays per annum to the aforesaid prior and convent of Barnwell 7d.; by which warranty they received the said income they are unaware.

[1006] Thomas Stebing holds 1 messuage in the town of Barnwell which he bought from the prior and convent of Barnwell, and in respect thereof he pays per annum to the aforesaid prior and convent 3s., in which manner the prior and convent are unaware how they received the said messuage.

[1007] Item the same Thomas Miet holds 1 acre of land in the fields of the same town, which he bought from Isabella Paie. And the same Isabella bought that from Luke of St Edmund's, and the same Luke held that by inheritance through the death of Thomas, his brother. And the same Thomas held that by gift of Walter, his father, and the same Walter held that through hereditary succession. And in respect thereof he pays per annum to the aforesaid Isabella 8d., and the aforesaid Isabella acquits the aforesaid Thomas to Luke of St Edmund's as tenant-in-chief of the lord's fee.

[1008] Dionisia, former wife of William de Huntingdon, holds 1 messuage in the town of Barnwell, which same descended to Dionisia by inheritance through the death of William, her father, and the same William held that by inheritance through the death of Robert, his brother. And the same Robert held that through the death of Kenevi, his father, and in respect thereof the said Dionisia pays per annum to William de Novacurt 9d. as tenant-in-chief of the lord's fee.

[1009] Item the same Dionisia holds 1 messuage in the same town which same messuage Geoffrey, former husband of the aforesaid Dionisia bought from Isabella de Wilburham, which same Isabella held that by inheritance through the death of Geoffrey, her father. And the same Geoffrey held with Matilda, his wife, from Richard of Bishops Stortford and in respect thereof the aforesaid Dionisia pays per annum to the aforesaid William de Novacurt 6d. as tenant-in-chief of the lord's fee.

[1010] Item the same Dionisia holds 3 acres of land in the fields of the same town, which descended to the aforesaid Dionisia by inheritance through the death of William, her father, and the same William held those by inheritance of Robert Kenewi, his father, and the same Robert held those by inheritance of Kenewi, his father, for which the said Dionisia pays per annum to the aforesaid William de Novacurt 10d.

[1011] Item the same Dionisia holds 2 acres of land in the aforesaid fields which descended to the aforesaid Dionisia by inheritance through the death of William, her father, and the same William held those by inheritance of Robert, his father, and the same Robert held those by inheritance of Kenewi, his father, for which the aforesaid Dionisia pays per annum to the prior of Barnwell and the convent at the same place 18d.; by which warranty they received the said income they are unaware.

[1012] Item the same Dionisia holds 1 acre of land in the aforesaid fields, which John de Teversham, former husband of the aforesaid Dionisia formerly bought for himself and Dionisia, his wife, from the aforesaid prior and convent. And in respect thereof she pays per annum to the aforesaid prior and convent 3s. 2d.; by which warranty they received the said income they are unaware.

[1013] Item the same Dionisia holds in the aforesaid fields 3 half acres of land which the aforesaid John, her former husband bought for himself and Dionisia, his wife, from John le Rus, and the same John held that by inheritance through the death of Maurice, his father, for which she pays per annum to the almoner of Barnwell 8d. in perpetual alms, by assignment of the aforesaid John.

[1014] Item the same Dionisia holds ½ acre of land in the aforesaid fields, which William de Huntingdon, her former husband, bought for himself and the aforesaid Dionisia, his wife, from William Brodeie, and the same William bought that from Henry Gut, and the same Henry held that by inheritance of Henry, his father. And in respect thereof she pays per annum to the aforesaid William 1d. And the same William acquits the aforesaid Dionisia to Luke of St Edmund's as tenant-in-chief of the lord's fee.

[1015] Item the same Dionisia holds in the aforesaid fields 3 acres of land and a ½ acre, which same descended to the aforesaid Dionisia by inheritance through the death of William, her father, and the same William held that by inheritance of Robert, his father, and the same Robert held that by inheritance of Kenewi, his father, for which she pays per annum to Luke of St Edmund's 2⁷⁸s. 6d. as tenant-in-chief of the lord's fee.

[1016] Michael, son of Dionisia de Huntingdon, holds 1 messuage in the town of Barnwell, which same messuage he bought from Nicholas Lungis, and the same Nicholas held that by inheritance of Radulph, his father, and the same Radulph held that from Robert de Novacurt, and in respect thereof he pays per annum to William de Novacurt 12d. as tenant-in-chief of the lord's fee.

[1017] John Russel holds 1 messuage in the town of Barnwell, which he bought from Matilda Tele, which same Matilda held that by inheritance through the death of Martin, her father. And the same Martin bought that from the prior of Barnwell, and in respect thereof he pays the aforesaid Matilda 1 clove gillyflower and to the aforesaid prior 2s. as tenant-in-chief of the lord's fee; by which warranty they received the said revenue they are unaware.

[1018] Item the same John holds 1 messuage in the same town and a ½ acre of land belonging to the said messuage, which same messuage with said land he held in exchange for 1 messuage from Geoffrey Smith. And the same Geoffrey held that by inheritance of Matilda, his mother, and the same Matilda held that from the prior of Barnwell, and in respect thereof the aforesaid John pays to the aforesaid prior 20d. by assignment of the said Geoffrey.

[1019] Item John holds 1 acre in the fields of the same town which he bought from Odo, son of Winfrid Brewer, and the same Winfrid bought that from Nicholas Pappe, and the same Nicholas held that by inheritance of Hugh, his brother, and in respect thereof he pays per annum to the aforesaid Odo 1 clove gillyflower, and to the aforesaid prior of Barnwell 4d.; by which warranty they received the said revenue they are unaware.

[1020] Item John holds 2 acres in the aforesaid fields, which he bought from John Infirmarer, and the same John held that by inheritance through the death of John, his father, and the same John held that by inheritance of Robert, his father, and in respect thereof he pays per annum to the aforesaid John 1 rose and to Leon Dunning 2s. as tenant-in-chief of the lord's fee.

[1021] Item John holds 3 half acres of land in the aforesaid fields which he bought from Emma Brodeie, which same Emma bought that from Leon Dunning and the same Leon held that by hereditary succession from Adam, his father, and in respect thereof he pays per annum to the aforesaid Leon 4d.

[1022] Item John holds in the aforesaid fields 3 half acres of land which he bought from Simon Scan and Cassandria, his wife, which same 3 half acres of land descended to the aforesaid Cassandria by inheritance through the death of Gold, her brother. And the same Gold bought that from Cristiana Astines, and in respect thereof the aforesaid John pays per annum to the aforesaid Simon and Cassandria 2d., and the aforesaid Simon and Cassandria acquit the aforesaid John to the heirs of Cristiana Astine.

[1023] William Brodeie holds 1 messuage in the town of Barnwell which he bought from Roger Attehel, and the same Roger held that by inheritance of Mabilia, his mother, which same Mabilia held that from Adam de Cokefeld, for which he pays per annum to Robert son of the aforesaid Roger 1d. And to William de Novacurt 14d. as tenant-in-chief of the lord's fee.

[1024] Michael Albus holds 1 messuage in the town of Barnwell which descended to him by inheritance through the death of Richard, his father, and the same Richard bought that from William Smith, and the same William held that by inheritance through the death of Robert, his father. And the same Robert held that by inheritance of Kenewi, his father, and the same pays per annum to Dionisia de Huntingdon, heir of the aforesaid William Smith 2s., and the said Dionisia acquits the aforesaid Michael to the prior of Barnwell as tenant-in-chief of the lord's fee.

[1025] William Paie holds 1 messuage in the town of Barnwell which descended to him by inheritance through the death of Sabina, his mother. Which same Sabina bought that from the prior of Barnwell, and in respect thereof he pays per annum to the aforesaid prior 2s. 6d., by which manner the prior and convent received the said messuage they are unaware.

[1026] Isabella daughter of John de Eia holds 1 messuage in the town of Barnwell which same she bought from Lord Geoffrey, chaplain, and the same Geoffrey bought that from Henry Gut, and the same Henry held that by inheritance through the death of Henry, his father, and in respect thereof she pays per annum to the prior of Barnwell 10d. by assignment of the aforesaid Geoffrey.

[1027] Geoffrey, son of Geoffrey of Barnwell, holds a certain house in the town of Barnwell, which he bought from Agnes Cokelin, which same Agnes held that by inheritance through the death of Margaret, her mother, which same Margaret held that by inheritance of Geoffrey, her father, and the same Geoffrey bought that from the prior and convent of Barnwell, and the same pays per annum to the aforesaid prior and convent 4d. by assignment of the aforesaid Agnes.

[1028] Item Joachim Salandin holds 1 messuage in the town of Barnwell, which same messuage he bought from Simon Mundi, and the same Simon held that by inheritance through the death of Radulph, his father, and the same Radulph bought that from William Smith, and the same William bought that from Robert de Novacurt, and the same Robert held that by hereditary succession. And in respect thereof the aforesaid Joachim pays per annum to Isabella Paie 9d., which same Isabella pays the said 9d. to Dionisia de Huntingdon, and the aforesaid Dionisia acquits the aforesaid Joachim and Isabella to William de Novacurt as tenant-in-chief of the lord's fee.

[1029] Item Joachim holds 1 messuage in the same town which he bought from Robert de Teversham, and the same Robert held that by gift of Alicia Mamaunt, which same Alicia held that by inheritance of Robert, her father, and the same Robert bought that from Simon Mundi, and the same Simon held that by inheritance from Radulph, his father, for which the aforesaid Joachim pays per annum to the said Robert 1 farthing, and the aforesaid Isabella Paie 9d., by assignment of the aforesaid Robert.

[1030] Item Joachim holds ½ acre of land in the fields of the same town, which he bought from Luke of St Edmund's and the same Luke held that by inheritance through the death of Thomas, his brother, and the same Thomas held that by gift of Walter, his father, and the same Walter held that by hereditary succession and in respect thereof he pays per annum to the aforesaid Luke 2d.

[1031] Walter Merchant holds 1 messuage in the town of Barnwell which same he bought from the prior and convent of the same town and in respect thereof he pays per annum to the aforesaid prior and convent 12d.; by which manner the prior and convent received the said messuage they are unaware.

[1032] Aldus Waveloc holds 1 messuage in the town of Barnwell, which he bought from Richard Pet and Margaret, his wife, which same messuage the aforesaid Margaret bought from William son of Wulveva, and the same William held that by inheritance from Wulveva, his mother, and in respect thereof he pays per annum to the aforesaid Richard and Margaret 4d., and the aforesaid Richard and Margaret pay the aforesaid 4d. to Margaret Sped, which same Margaret acquits the aforesaid Aldus and Richard and Margaret to the prior and convent of Barnwell as tenant-in-chief of the lord's fee. By which warranty they received the income they are unaware.

[1033]   Robert de Teversham holds 1 messuage in the town of Barnwell, which he bought from William de Wilbraham. And the same William bought that from Stephen King, and the same Stephen held that by inheritance from Osbert, his father, and the same Osbert bought that from the prior and convent of Barnwell for which the aforesaid Robert pays per annum to Muriella, daughter and heir of the aforesaid William, 10d. and 1 farthing[79]. And the said Muriella pays the said 10d. to Michael Carter, heir of the aforesaid Stephen. And the aforesaid Michael acquits the aforesaid Robert and Muriella to the prior and convent of Barnwell as tenant-in-chief of the lord's fee. By which warranty they received the income they are unaware.

[1034]   The same Robert holds a piece of land in the said town which he bought from Imainia, daughter of Radulph Cokelin, which same Imainia held that by inheritance through the death of Margaret, her mother, which same Margaret held that by inheritance from Geoffrey, her father, and the same Geoffrey bought that from the prior and convent of Barnwell. And in respect thereof the aforesaid Robert pays per annum to the aforesaid Imainia 1 farthing, and to the aforesaid prior and convent 8d.; by which warranty they received the income they are unaware.

[1035]   Item Robert and Catherine, his wife, hold 1 messuage in the aforesaid town, which same messuage Robert Mamaunt, former husband of the aforesaid Catherine, bought for himself and the aforesaid Catherine, then his wife, from Richard Pet and from Margaret, his wife, which same messuage the aforesaid Margaret bought from William son of Wulveva, and the same William held that by inheritance from Wulveva, his mother, for which they pay per annum to the aforesaid Richard and Margaret 10d., and the aforesaid Richard and Margaret pay the said 10d. to Margaret Sped, and the aforesaid Margaret acquits the aforesaid Robert and Catherine and Richard and Margaret to the prior and convent of Barnwell as tenant-in-chief of the lord's fee; by which warranty they received the income they are unaware.

[1036]   Item Robert and Catherine his wife hold 1 acre of land in the fields of the same town, which Robert Mainaunt, former husband of the aforesaid Catherine at one time bought from Stephen King, and the same Stephen held that by inheritance through the death of Osbert King, his father, and the same Osbert bought that from Walter at the church of St Edmund's, and in respect thereof they pay per annum to Hugh son of Geoffrey Smith, heir of the aforesaid Stephen 8d. And the said Hugh acquits the aforesaid Robert and Catherine to Luke of St Edmund's as tenant-in-chief of the lord's fee.

[1037] Item Robert and Catherine his wife hold in the aforesaid fields a ½ acre of land which the aforesaid Robert Maniaunt, former husband of the aforesaid Catherine bought from John King, and the same John held that by gift of Osbert, his father, and the same Osbert held that in exchange for the same amount of land from John le Winur' of Chesterton, and the same John held that through inquisition, and in respect thereof they pay per annum to the aforesaid John and his heirs 1 rose, and to the church of Chesterton 2d.

[1038] Item Robert and Catherine, his wife, hold in the aforesaid fields a ½ acre of land which the aforesaid Robert Maniaunt, former husband of the aforesaid Catherine bought for himself and Catherine his wife, from Geoffrey de Bornell. And the same Geoffrey bought that from Henry Gut, and the same Henry held that by inheritance from Henry Molle, his father, and in respect thereof they pay per annum to the aforesaid Geoffrey 3d., and the same acquits the aforesaid Robert and Catherine to Luke of St Edmund's as tenant-in-chief of the lord's fee.

[1039] Item Robert and Catherine hold ½ acre of land in the aforesaid fields, which Robert Maniaunt, former husband of the aforesaid Catherine bought for himself and the aforesaid Catherine, his wife, from Geoffrey de Bornvell' and the same Geoffrey bought that from Mariota Melt, which same Mariota held the same by inheritance from Geoffrey Melt, her father. And the same Geoffrey held that by inheritance from Henry Melt, his father, and in respect thereof they pay per annum to the aforesaid Geoffrey 2½d.

[1040] Item Robert and Catherine hold a third part of 1 acre of land in the aforesaid fields, which Alicia Maniaunt formerly gave to the aforesaid Robert and Catherine, his wife, which same Alicia held that by inheritance through the death of Robert, her father, and the same Robert bought that from Leon Dunning. And the same Leon held that by inheritance of Adam, his father, and the same Adam held that by ancient acquisition, and in respect thereof they pay per annum to the heirs of the aforesaid Alicia Maniaunt 1 rose.

[1041] Michael Carter holds 1 messuage in the town of Barnwell, which he bought from Adam son of Jelion', and the same Adam held that by purchase from John Glide, and the same John held that by inheritance from Stephen King, and the same Stephen held that by inheritance of Osbert, his father, and in respect thereof he pays per annum to the prior and convent of Barnwell 2s. By which warranty they received the income they are unaware.

[1042] Robert the Fuller and Mabilia his wife hold 1 messuage in the town of Barnwell, which same messuage descended to the aforesaid Mabilia by inheritance through the death of Matilda, her mother, which same Matilda held that by gift of John Salandin, her brother. And the same John held that by inheritance of Richard, his father, and the same Richard held by inheritance of Sirith, his father, and in respect thereof they pay per annum to Geoffrey Salandin 9d., and the same Geoffrey acquits the aforesaid Robert and Mabilia to the prior of Barnwell as tenant-in-chief of the lord's fee; by which warranty they received the income they are unaware.

[1043] Item Robert and Mabilia, his wife, hold in the fields of the same town a ½ acre of land which descended to the aforesaid Mabilia by inheritance through the death of Matilda, her mother, which same Matilda bought that from Stephen King, and the same Stephen held that by inheritance of Osbert, his father, and the same Osbert held that from Walter at the church of St Edmund's, for which they pay per annum to Hugh son of Geoffrey, heir of the aforesaid Stephen King, 4d., and the same Hugh acquits the aforesaid Robert and Mabilia to Luke of St Edmund's as tenant-in-chief of the lord's fee.

[1044] Geoffrey Salandin holds 1 messuage in the town of Barnwell, and 3 roods of land in the fields of the same town belonging to the said messuage, which same messuage with said land descended to himself by inheritance through the death of John, his father, and the same John held that by inheritance of Richard, his father, and the same Richard held that from the Lord of Rushden, for which he pays per annum to Leon Dunning 2s., and the same Leon bought the said income from the heir of the Lord of Rushden.

[1045] Item Geoffrey holds ½ acre of land in the fields of the same town which descended to him by inheritance through the death of John, his father, and the same John bought that from John Infirmarer, and the same John held that by inheritance of Roger, his father, and the same Roger held that from Walter at the church of St Edmund's, and in respect thereof he pays per annum to Luke of St Edmund's 3d. as tenant-in-chief of the lord's fee.

[1046] Hugh de Nedham holds 1 messuage in the town of Barnwell, which he bought from Geoffrey Carvar', and the same Geoffrey bought that from Radulph de Teversham, and the same Radulph bought that from Matilda, daughter of Peter Stote, which same Matilda held that by inheritance of Peter Stote, her father, and the same Peter bought that from William, clerk, and the same William held that from the prior and convent of Barnwell, and in respect thereof the said Hugh pays per annum to the aforesaid Radulph de Teversham 8½d., and the same Radulph pays per annum to the aforesaid Matilda daughter of the aforesaid Peter Stote 1 farthing, and to the prior and convent of Barnwell 8d.; by which warranty they received the income they are unaware.

[1047] Radulph de Teversham holds 1 messuage in the town of Barnwell, with 1 rood of land belonging to the said messuage, which same messuage with rood of land he bought from William Brodeie, and the same William held that in exchange for 1 messuage from Geoffrey de Burnell', and the same Geoffrey held that from the prior and convent of Barnwell and in respect thereof he pays per annum to the aforesaid William 1 pair of gloves at the price of ½d., and to the aforesaid prior and convent 3s., by assignment of the aforesaid William.

[1048] Item Radulph holds 1 acre of land in the fields of the same town which he bought from Alan Culling, and the same Alan bought that from the Lord Roger, vicar of Hinton, and that Roger bought that from Luke of St Edmund's, and that Luke held that by inheritance through the death of Thomas, his brother, and the same Thomas held that by gift of Walter, his father, and the same Walter held that by hereditary succession, and in respect thereof Radulph pays per annum to the aforesaid Alan 1 clove gillyflower, and the same Alan acquits the same Radulph to Luke of St Edmund's as tenant-in-chief of the lord's fee.

[1049] Item Radulph holds in the aforesaid fields a ½ acre of land which he bought from Luke of St Edmund's and the same Luke held that by inheritance through the death of Thomas, his brother, and the same Thomas held that by gift of Walter, his father, and the same Walter held that by hereditary succession, and in respect thereof he pays per annum to the aforesaid Luke 2d.

[1050] Item Radulph holds in the aforesaid fields a ½ acre of land which he bought from William and from Alicia Maniaunt, his wife, which same Alicia held that by inheritance through the death of Robert, her father, and the same Robert bought that from John Salandin, and the same John bought that from John Infirmarer, and the same John held that by inheritance of Roger, his father, and in respect thereof he pays per annum to the aforesaid William and his heirs 3d. and 1 farthing, and the heirs of the aforesaid William pay the said 3d. to Geoffrey Salandin, and the same Geoffrey acquits the aforesaid Radulph and William to Luke of St Edmund's as tenant-in-chief of the lord's fee.

[1051] John Net and Avicia, his wife, hold 1 messuage in the town of Barnwell, which same messuage they bought from John de Dunton, and the same John held that by gift of Radulph de Kingseton, and the same Radulph bought that from William Bloue, and that William bought that from Henry Blowe, his brother, and the same Henry held that by inheritance from Martin, his father, and in respect thereof they pay per annum to the aforesaid John 1 rose, and to Hugh de Brunner 1 lb. of cumin, and to Luke of St Edmund's 7d. as tenant-in-chief of the lord's fee.

[1052] Item John and Avicia, his wife, hold 1 acre of land in the fields of the same town which Radulph former husband of the aforesaid Avicia bought for himself and the aforesaid Avicia, his wife, from William Brodeie, and the same William held from purchase from Henry Blowe, and the same Henry held that by inheritance from Martin, his father, and in respect thereof they pay per annum to the aforesaid William 12d. and 1 rose, and the same William acquits the aforesaid John and Avicia to Luke of St Edmund's as tenant-in-chief of the lord's fee.

[1053] Alan le Stabler holds 1 messuage in the town of Barnwell which descended to him by inheritance through the death of Martin, his father, and the same Martin held that by inheritance from John, his father. And the same John held that from the prior of Barnwell, and in respect thereof he pays per annum to the aforesaid prior 6d., by which warranty they are unaware.

[1054] Item Alan holds 1 rood of land in the fields of the same town which he bought from Henry Gut, and the same Henry held that by inheritance of Henry Molle, his father, and the same Henry held that from Walter at the church of St Edmund's, and in respect thereof he pays per annum to Luke of St Edmund's 3d.

[1055] Item Alan holds in the town of Barnwell 1 messuage which descended to Agnes his wife by inheritance through the death of Aubrina, her mother, which same Aubrina held by inheritance from Warin, her father, and the same Warin held that from Walter at the church of St Edmund's, and in respect thereof he pays per annum to Luke of St Edmund's 10d. as tenant-in-chief of the lord's fee.

232

[1056] Item Alan holds 1 rood in the fields of the same town, which he received in exchange for an income of 16d. from Robert de Madingley, and the same Robert held that by inquisition, and in respect thereof he pays per annum to the aforesaid Robert and his heirs 1d.

[1057] Margaret Sped holds 1 messuage in the town of Barnwell and a ½ acre of land belonging to the said messuage, which same messuage with said land she bought from Matilda, daughter of William Wulvewe, which same Matilda held that by inheritance from William, her father, and the same William held that from the prior of Barnwell and in respect thereof she pays per annum to the aforesaid prior 3s.; by which warranty they received the income they are unaware.

[1058] Item the same Margaret holds in the fields of the same town 3 half acres of land which she bought from Luke of St Edmund's, and the same Luke held that by inheritance through the death of Thomas, his brother, and the same Thomas held that by gift of Walter, his father, and that Walter held by ancient inheritance and in respect thereof she pays per annum to the aforesaid Luke 9d.

[1059] Item the same Margaret holds in the aforesaid fields 3 half acres of land which she bought from Geoffrey Smith, and the same Geoffrey held that by inheritance through the death of Matilda, his mother, which same Matilda held those from Walter at the church of St Edmund's, and in respect thereof she pays per annum to Hugh son of Geoffrey Smith 8d., and the said Hugh acquits the aforesaid Margaret to Luke of St Edmund's as tenant-in-chief of the lord's fee.

[1060] Item the same Margaret holds in the aforesaid fields a ½ acre of land which she bought from John King, and the same John held that by gift of Osbert King, his father, and the same Osbert held that from Walter at the church of St Edmund's, and in respect thereof she pays per annum to Hugh son of Geoffrey Smith, heir of the aforesaid John, 3d., and the aforesaid Hugh acquits the aforesaid Margaret to Luke of St Edmund's as tenant-in-chief of the lord's fee.

[1061] John le Man holds 1 messuage in the town of Barnwell which descended to him by inheritance through the death of Adam, his father, and the same Adam held that by gift of the prior and convent of Barnwell. And in respect thereof he pays per annum to Hugh Mainer 6d., and to the aforesaid prior and convent 7d.; by which warranty they received the income they are unaware.

[1062] Gilbert Bernard holds 1 messuage in the town of Barnwell with 3 acres of land in the fields of the same town in the fee of William de Novacurt, which same messuage with said land Dionisia, widow of William de Huntingdon, gave to Margaret, wife of the said Gilbert. Which same messuage with said land descended to the said Dionisia by inheritance through the death of William Smith, her father, which same William held that from Robert Novacurt, for which messuage and said land the said Gilbert pays per annum to the said Dionisia and her heirs 3s. 6d., and the said Dionisia acquits the aforesaid Gilbert to William de Novacurt as tenant-in-chief of the lord's fee.

[1063] Item Gilbert holds 1 messuage with its appurtenances in the town of Cambridge in the parish of St Edward's, which same messuage descended to the aforesaid Gilbert by inheritance through the death of Michael Bernard, his father. And the same Michael bought that from William Wulsi. And the same William held that by hereditary succession and in respect thereof the aforesaid Gilbert pays per annum on behalf of the heirs of the said William, to the prioress of Swaffham 8s.; by which warranty they received the income they are unaware.

[1064] Item Gilbert holds 1 messuage with its appurtenances in the parish of St Edward's in the town of Cambridge, which messuage descended to the aforesaid Gilbert by inheritance through the death of Michael, his father, and the same Michael bought that from William Wulsi, and the same William held that by ancient hereditary succession and in respect thereof the said Gilbert pays per annum on behalf of the heirs of the said William, to Lord Simon de Panton 1d., and to the bailiffs of Cambridge who hold the said town in fee farm, to their farm 1d.

[1065] Item Gilbert holds 2 messuages with their appurtenances in the town of Cambridge in the said parish of St Edward's, with 1 acre of land in fields of the same town. Which same messuages with said land descended to the aforesaid Gilbert by inheritance through the death of Michael Bernard, his father. And the same Michael bought that from John Cokerel, and the same John held that by ancient hereditary succession, for which the aforesaid Gilbert pays per annum to Agnes Fiyion and her heirs 12s. 8d., and to the heirs of the said John Cokerel 3d., and to the bailiffs of Cambridge who hold the said town in fee farm for their farm 1d.

[1066] Item Gilbert holds 1 messuage with its appurtenances in the parish of St Benedict's in the town of Cambridge, which same messuage he bought from Michael son of John Michael, which messuage descended to the aforesaid Michael by inheritance through the death of John, his father, and the same John held that by inheritance through the death of Michael, his father, for which the aforesaid Gilbert pays per annum on behalf of the said Michael and his heirs, to the prioress of St Radegund's 3½d., by which warranty they received the income they are unaware.

[1067] Item Gilbert holds 1 messuage and 2 shops with their appurtenances in the parish of St Mary's, Cambridge, which same messuage with 2 shops descended to the aforesaid Gilbert by inheritance through the death of Margaret, daughter of John Bernard. Which same Margaret held those by inheritance through the death of John, her father, and the same John held those by inheritance through the death of Bernard Orgar, and the same Bernard held those by inheritance of Orgar, his father, and in respect thereof the aforesaid Gilbert pays per annum to the prior and convent of Barnwell 20d. And for the said shops to St Mary's Church's 8d.; by which warranty the prior and convent received the said income they are unaware.

[1068] Item Gilbert holds 1 piece of vacant land in the parish of St Edward's, Cambridge, which same piece of land descended to the aforesaid Gilbert by inheritance through the death of Alicia, his mother. And the said Alicia held that by inheritance through the death of William Wulsi, her father, and the same William held that by ancient hereditary succession, for which he pays per annum to Robert Seman and his heirs 1 lb. of cumin.

[1069] Item Gilbert holds 1 piece of vacant land in the parish of St Benedict's, Cambridge, in Lorteburne Lane, which descended to the aforesaid Gilbert by inheritance through the death of Alicia, his mother, which same Alicia held that by inheritance through the death of William Wulsi, her father and the same William held that by ancient inheritance, for which he pays per annum to Luke of St Edmund's 10d.

[1070] Item Gilbert holds 2 acres of land in the fields of Barnwell, which he bought from Michael Pilat, which same Michael held those by inheritance through the death of Reginald, his father, and the same Reginald bought those from Nicholas Malerbe, and the same Nicholas held those by inheritance through the death of Michael Malerbe, his father, and the same Michael held those by ancient inheritance, for which the aforesaid Gilbert pays per annum to the aforesaid Michael and his heirs ½d., and to the bailiffs of Cambridge who hold the said town in fee farm for their farm 1 farthing.

[1071] Item Gilbert holds ½ acre of land in the aforesaid fields, which he bought from William de Huntingdon, which same William bought those from John Salandin, and the same John held those by purchase from John Infirmarer, and in respect thereof the aforesaid Gilbert pays per annum to Geoffrey Salandin 4d.

[1072] Item Gilbert holds 2 acres of land in the fields of Barnwell, which he bought from William de Huntingdon, and that William bought those from Leon Dunning, and the same Leon held those by inheritance from Adam, his father, for which he pays per annum to the aforesaid Leon 2d. by assignment of the aforesaid William.

[1073] Item Gilbert holds 4 acres of land in the aforesaid fields which he bought from William Brodeie, for which he pays per annum to the aforesaid William and his heirs 15[80], and to the heirs of John Salandin 4d., and to Leon Dunning 2d., and to Luke of St Edmund's 6d.

[1074] Item Gilbert holds 1 acre of land in the aforesaid fields, which he bought from Stephen King, and the same Stephen held that by inheritance through the death of Osbert King, his father, and in respect thereof he pays per annum to the heirs of the aforesaid Stephen 2d.

[1075] Item Gilbert holds 3 half acres of land in the aforesaid fields which he bought from Alicia Maniaunt, which same Alicia held that by inheritance through the death of Robert, her father, for which he pays per annum to Geoffrey de Burnell 8d., and to Leon Dunning 2d.

[1076] Item Gilbert holds ½ acre of land in the aforesaid fields which he bought from John of Thurlow and the same John held that by inheritance through the death of Radulph, his brother, and in respect thereof he pays per annum to Luke of St Edmund's 6d., by assignment of the aforesaid John.

[1077] Item Gilbert holds 1 rood of land in the aforesaid fields, which he bought from William de Huntingdon, and the said William bought that from Alexander son of Hugelina and the said Alexander held that by inheritance through the death of Hugelina, his mother, and in respect thereof he pays per annum to Luke of St Edmund's 2d.

[1078] Item Gilbert holds 1 acre of land in the aforesaid fields which he bought from Osbert son of Nicholas Wombe, and the said Osbert held that by gift of Michael Bernard, and the same Michael bought that from Peter Makeston, and in respect thereof he pays per annum to the heirs of the aforesaid Peter Makeston 1d.

[1079] Item Gilbert holds 3 half acres of land in the aforesaid fields which descended to the aforesaid Gilbert by inheritance through the death of Michael, his father, and the same Michael bought those from Cassandria Astin, which same Cassandria held that by inheritance through the death of Godfrey, her brother, and in respect thereof he pays per annum to the heirs of the said Cassandria 1½d.

[1080] Item Gilbert holds ½ acre of land in the aforesaid fields which he bought from Matilda Tele, which same Matilda held that by inheritance through the death of Martin, her father, and in respect thereof he pays per annum to William de Novacurt 1d., by assignment of the aforesaid Matilda.

[1081] Oliver le Porter holds 1 messuage in the town of Barnwell, which he bought from the prior and convent of the same town, and in respect thereof he pays per annum to the aforesaid prior and convent 3s., in which manner the prior and convent are unaware of how they received the said messuage.

[1082] Item Oliver holds 1 messuage in the same town which he bought from Master Radulph of Nottingham, and the same Radulph bought that from Alexander de Impington, and the same Alexander bought that from Godfrey, clerk, and the same Godfrey bought that from William Melt, and the same William held that by inheritance of Geoffrey Melt, and in respect thereof he pays per annum to the aforesaid prior and convent 12d.; by which warranty they received the said income they are unaware.

[1083] Item Oliver holds 1 rood of land in the fields of the same town which he bought from Matilda Tele, which same Matilda held that by inheritance through the death of Martin, her father, and in respect thereof he pays per annum to Luke of St Edmund's 6d. by assignment of the aforesaid Matilda.

[1084] Item Oliver holds ½ acre of land in the aforesaid fields until the end of his life, which he formerly received in frank marriage with Agnes, his wife, from Matilda Tele, which same Matilda held that by purchase from Geoffrey Melt, and the same Geoffrey held that by inheritance from Henry Melt, his father, and in respect thereof he pays per annum to Lord Philip de Coleville 2d.

[1085] Geoffrey de Barnwell holds 1 messuage in the town of Barnwell, which same messuage he received in exchange for another from William Brodeie, and the same William held that by inheritance through the death of William, his father and in respect thereof he pays per annum to the prior and convent of Barnwell 4s. 2d., by assignment of the aforesaid William.

[1086] Item Geoffrey holds 4 acres of land in the fields of the same town which he bought from Lord Henry de Coleville, which same Henry bought those from William Melt, and the same William held those by inheritance through the death of Geoffrey, his father, and in respect thereof he pays per annum to the aforesaid Lord Henry de Coleville 8s. 6d., and to the prior and convent of Barnwell 22d.; by which warranty they received the said income they are unaware.

[1087] William Jado holds 1 messuage in the town of Barnwell, which he bought from Simon de Bedford and from Margaret, his wife. Which said Margaret held the said messuage by inheritance through the death of Aubrina, her mother, and the same Aubrina held that by inheritance through the death of Warin Mason, her father, and in respect thereof he pays per annum to the aforesaid Simon and Margaret 10d., and the aforesaid Simon and Margaret acquit the aforesaid William to Luke of St Edmund's as tenant-in-chief of the lord's fee.

[1088] Odo son of Winfrid holds 1 messuage in Barnwell, which descended to him by inheritance through the death of the said Winfrid, his father, which same Winfrid held that by hereditary right through the death of Hamo Messor, his father, which same Hamo held that by ancient purchase, and in respect thereof he pays per annum to the prior of Barnwell 20d.; by which warranty the said prior does not know how they received the said income.

[END OF THE BARNWELL ROLL]

Notes

[1] J; StR.
[2] TNA Special Collections, 'Hundred Rolls and Eyre Veredicta', available at http://discovery.nationalarchives.gov.uk/details/r/C13523 (accessed 30 July 2017). See also Sheffield Hundred Rolls Project, available at http://www.roffe.co.uk/shrp.htm (accessed 2 April 2017).
[3] TNA, 'Hundred Rolls and Eyre Veredicta'.
[4] Diana E. Greenway, 'A Newly Discovered Fragment of the Hundred Rolls of 1279–80', *Journal of Society of Archivists* 7 (2) (1982): 73–7, p 73.
[5] Sandra Raban, *A Second Domesday: The Hundred Rolls of 1279–80* (Oxford, 2004), p 121.
[6] Helen M. Cam, *The Hundred and the Hundred Rolls: An Outline of Local Government in Medieval England* (London, 1930).
[7] Raban, *Second Domesday*.
[8] Greenway, 'Fragment', p 73.
[9] TNA SC5/CAMBS/TOWER/2 Barnwell Hundred Roll; TNA SC5/CAMBS/TOWER/1/Parts1–3 Cambridge Borough Hundred Rolls.

[10] Raban, *Second Domesday*, pp 48–50.

[11] Helen M. Cam, *Liberties and Communities in Medieval England* (Cambridge, 1944), p 40; VCH 2 Huntingdon, pp 198–9; Sheriff of Cambridgeshire and Huntingdonshire, available at https://en.wikipedia.org/wiki/Sheriff_of_Cambridgeshire_and_Huntingdonshire (accessed 29 October 2018). Sir William was succeeded by Baldwin St George in 1278, who could also have been involved; he too had been sheriff earlier, but little is known about him.

[12] *Rotuli Hundredorum Temp. Henry III and Edward I., in Turr' Lond' et in Curia Receptæ Scaccarij Westm. Asservati* (2 vols) (London, 1812 and 1818).

[13] TNA, 'Hundred Rolls and Eyre Veredicta'.

[14] M, pp 142–58.

[15] Raban, *Second Domesday*, p 154.

[16] EB; SP.

[17] B. Dodwell, 'The Free Tenantry of the Hundred Rolls', *Economic History Review* 14 (2) (1944): 163–71; Junichi Kanzaka, 'Villein Rents in Thirteenth-Century England: An Analysis of the Hundred Rolls of 1279–1280', *Economic History Review* 55 (4) (2002): 593–619; E. Kosminsky, 'The Hundred Rolls of 1279–80 as a Source for English Agrarian History', *Economic History Review* 3(1) (1931): 16–44.

[18] Howell's unpublished research particularly focused on East Cambridgeshire settlements about 5–10 miles east of Cambridge and clustered in an arc around Fulbourn Fen, namely Fulbourn, Teversham, Stow-cum-Quy, Little Wilbraham and Great Wilbraham. She examined the relationship between land use, the size of landholdings, the spatial distribution of smallholdings, inheritance strategies and family composition. The paper presented a range of statistical evidence derived from family landholdings recorded in the Hundred Rolls and identified by a shared surname. Cicely A. H. Howell, *Land, Family and Inheritance in Transition; Kibworth Harcourt 1280–1700* (Cambridge, 1983); Cicely A. H. Howell, 'Contrasting Communities: Arable and Marshland' (unpublished draft, 1979); Cicely A. H. Howell, 'Peasant Inheritance Customs in the Midlands, 1280–1700', *Land and Inheritance: Rural Society in Western Europe, 1200–1800*, ed. Jack Goody, Joan Thirsk and E. P. Thompson (Cambridge, 1978), pp 112–55; Cicely A. H. Howell, 'Stability and Change 1300–1700: The Socio-Economic Context of the Self-Perpetuating Family Farm in England', *Journal of Peasant Studies* 2(4) (1975): 468–82; Cicely A. H. Howell, 'The Economic and Social Condition of the Peasantry in South East Leicestershire, A.D. 1300–1700' (DPhil thesis, University of Oxford, 1974).

[19] The survey was a precursor to the mortmain legislation of 1290. Sandra Raban, 'Mortmain in Medieval England', *Past and Present* 62 (1974): 3–26. The Cambridgeshire Ragman Rolls have also been examined, but they provide little information on the town. Leonard E. Scales, 'The Cambridgeshire Ragman Rolls', *English Historical Review* 113 (452) (1998): 553–7.

[20] H. C. Darby, *The Domesday Geography of Cambridgeshire* (Cambridge, 1936), pp 264, 313; Ann Williams and G. H. Martin (eds), *Domesday Book: A Complete Translation* (London, 2002).

[21] W. M. Palmer (ed.), *The Assizes Held at Cambridge 1260: Being a Condensed Translation of Assize Roll 82 in the Public Record Office with an Introduction* (Linton, 1930); TNA JUST 1/81 Cambridgeshire Eyre of 1247 Foreign pleas roll, including essoins, 31 Henry III; TNA JUST 1/82 Cambridgeshire Eyre of 1261, Roll of civil, foreign and crown pleas, jury calendar, essoins and attorneys 45 Henry III; TNA JUST 1/83 Cambridgeshire Eyre of 1268 General oyer and terminer, lands

given away as a result of the Barons' War, roll of pleas, presentments, amercements and jury calendar 53 Henry III; TNA JUST 1/84 Cambridgeshire Eyre of 1272 Roll of civil and foreign pleas 56 Henry III; TNA JUST 1/85 Cambridgeshire Eyre of 1272 Roll of crown pleas, 56 Henry III; TNA JUST 1/86 Cambridgeshire Eyre of 1286 Rex roll of civil, foreign and crown pleas, gaol delivery, plaints, amercements and fines, jury calendar, essoins and attorneys, 14 Edward I; TNA JUST 1/96 Cambridgeshire Eyre of 1299 Berwick's roll of civil, foreign, king's and crown pleas, gaol delivery, plaints, jury calendar, essoins and attorneys, 27 Edward I. C. A. F. Meekings, *Crown Pleas of the Wiltshire Eyre, 1249* (Devizes, 1961), p 3; TNA, 'General Eyres', available at http://www.nationalarchives.gov.uk/help-with-your-research/research-guides/general-eyres-1194-1348/#sevenpointthree (accessed 30 July 2017);

22 Meekings, *Crown Pleas*, p 3; TNA, 'General Eyres'.

23 TNA, 'Pipe Rolls', available at http://www.nationalarchives.gov.uk/help-with-your-research/research-guides/medieval-financial-records-pipe-rolls-1130-1300/ (accessed 30 July 2017); Eilert Ekwall (ed.), *Two Early London Subsidy Rolls* (London, 1951), pp vii–xiii.; TNA, 'Taxation Before 1689', available at http://www.nationalarchives.gov.uk/help-with-your-research/research-guides/taxation-before-1689/ (accessed 30 July 2017); TNA E179 Database http://www.nationalarchives.gov.uk/e179/default.asp (accessed 30 July 2017); William M. Palmer, *Cambridgeshire Subsidy Rolls 1250–1695* (London, 1912).

24 PR (London, 1884–2016), especially the published rolls for the years 1130–1224, 1230 and 1242 vols 1–9, 11–19, 21–58, 50, 52–8, 60, 62, 64, 66, 68, 73, 75, 77, 80, 85, 86, 89, 91, 93, 94; TNA E 372/70 Tallage of 1225; TNA, 'Pipe Rolls'.

25 Anthony Musson and W. M. Ormrod, *The Evolution of English Justice: Law, Politics and Society in the Fourteenth Century* (Basingstoke, 1999), pp 14–15.

26 C. T. Flower, David Crook and Paul Brand (eds), *Rotuli Curiae Regis/Curia Regis Rolls* (10 vols) (London and Woodbridge, 1922–2006); Doris Mary Stenton (ed.), *Pleas before the King and His Justices 1198–1202 I: Introduction with Appendix Containing Essoins 1199–1201, A King's Roll of 1200 and Writs 1190–1200* (4 vols) (London, 1952–67); Doris Mary Stenton (ed.), *Pleas before the King and His Justices 1198–1202 II: Fragments of Rolls from the Years 1198, 1201 and 1202* (4 vols) (London, 1952–67); Doris Mary Stenton (ed.), *Pleas before the King and His Justices 1198–1202 III: Rolls or Fragments of Rolls from the Years 1199, 1201 and 1203–6* (4 vols) (London, 1952–67); Doris Mary Stenton (ed.), *Pleas before the King and His Justices 1198–1202 IV: Rolls or Fragments of Rolls from the Years 1207–1212* (4 vols) (London, 1952–67).

27 CPR; CCR; The Gen Guide, Patent Rolls, available at https://www.genguide.co.uk/source/patent-rolls-medieval-courts/5/ (accessed 9 January 2018); University of Nottingham Manuscripts and Special Collections Guide, 'Letters Patent', available at https://www.nottingham.ac.uk/manuscriptsandspecialcollections/researchguidance/deedsindepth/freehold/letterspatent.aspx (accessed 9 January 2018).

28 P. Brand (ed.), *Plea Rolls of the Exchequer of the Jews, VI: Edward I, 1279–81* (6 vols) (London, 2005); S. Cohen (ed.), *Plea Rolls of the Exchequer of the Jews, V: Edward I, 1277–1279* (6 vols) (London, 1992); H. Jenkinson (ed.), *Calendar of the Plea Rolls of the Exchequer of the Jews, III: Edward I, 1275–1277* (6 vols) (London, 1925); H. G. Richardson (ed.), *Calendar of the Plea Rolls of the Exchequer of the Jews, IV: Henry III, 1272; Edward I, 1275–1277* (6 vols) (London, 1972); J. M. Rigg (ed.), *Calendar of the Plea Rolls of the Exchequer of the Jews, I: Henry III, 1218–1272* (6 vols), I

(London, 1905); J. M. Rigg (ed.), *Calendar of the Plea Rolls of the Exchequer of the Jews, II: Edward I, 1273–1275* (6 vols) (Edinburgh, 1910); TNA, 'Exchequer of the Jews Plea Rolls', available at http://discovery.nationalarchives.gov.uk/details/r/C6509 (accessed 9 January 2017).

29 PDC; PDH; PDR; TNA, 'Land Conveyances by Feet of Fines 1182–1833', available at http://www.nationalarchives.gov.uk/help-with-your-research/research-guides/land-conveyance-feet-of- s-1182-1833/ (accessed 9 January 2017).

30 British Library Cole MS5833, pp 112, 127–34.

31 BT.

32 British Library MS Harley 5813 Excerpt comprising transcription of Corpus Christi Deeds; Robert Willis and John Willis Clark, *The Architectural History of the University of Cambridge and the Colleges of Cambridge and Eton* (2 vols) I (Cambridge, 1886); British Library Cole Add. MS 5809, Friars of the Sack, fol. 85; British Library Cole Add. MS 5809, History of Barnwell Priory, fols 87–9; British Library Cole Add. MS 5810, Number of Houses and Inhabitants in Cambridge in 1728, fol. 190; British Library Cole Add. MS 5810, Index to Lyne's Map of Cambridge, 1574, fols 193–5; British Library Cole Add. MS 5813, History of St Clement's Church, fol. 38; British Library Cole Add. MS 5813, Various Deeds, fols 32, 42, 43, 60–2; British Library Cole Add. MS 5813, Benefactors of the Guild of Our Lady (1315), fols 137–42; British Library Cole Add. MS 5821 History of Barton Manor and deeds, fols 229–33; British Library Cole Add. MS 5821 Benjamin's House at the Tolbooth, fols 229–33; British Library Cole Add. MS 5826 Taxation and Advowsons Documents of 1291 from Bishop Grey's Register, fols 171–88; British Library Cole Add. MS 5826 Account of the School of Pythagoras at Cambridge, fols 46–50; British Library Cole Add. MS 5832 Ancient Places in Cambridge, fols 214–15; British Library Cole Add. MS 5833 Mayors and Bailiffs of Cambridge to 1380; W. M. Palmer, 'The Stokes and Hailstone MSS', *Proceedings of the Cambridge Antiquarian Society* 33 (1933): 169–70; Willis and Willis Clark, *Architectural History*, pp xcv–xcvi.

33 LB. This manuscript was later used by a number of antiquaries and extracts from it were printed in Anon, *The History and Antiquities of Barnwell Abbey and of Sturbridge Fair* (London, 1786).

34 Bodleian MS Gough Cambridgeshire 1 General collections for the county and University of Cambridge with the Isle and Bishopric of Ely, extracted from the Charters, Registers, etc by Francis Blomefield, Clerk, late of Caius College and afterwards Rector of Fersfield in Norfolk: I Prior of Barnwell's Register (2 vols) I.

35 StR.

36 StJ.

37 StJ; Miri Rubin, *Charity and Community in Medieval Cambridge* (Cambridge, 1987).

38 Merton College Archives, University of Oxford, *Liber Ruber*; S.

39 Online catalogue of Corpus Christi Deeds, available at https://janus.lib.cam.ac.uk/db/node.xsp?id=EAD%2FGBR%2F2938%2FCCCC09 (accessed 1 August 2017); Catherine P. Hall, 'The Gild of Corpus Christi and the Foundation of Corpus Christi College: An Investigation of the Documents', *Medieval Cambridge: Essays on the Pre-Reformation University* ed. Patrick Zutshi (Woodbridge, 1993), pp 65–91.

40 Peterhouse, St Peter's College A1–3 and the Site of the College A1–29.

41 M. B. Hackett, *The Original Statutes of Cambridge University. The Text and its History* (Cambridge, 1970); E. Leedham-Green, *A Concise History of the University of Cambridge* (London, 1975), p 6.

42 Catherine Casson, Mark Casson, John S. Lee and Katie Phillips, *Compassionate Capitalism: Business and Community in Medieval England* (Bristol, 2020).

43 The statistical information in the Hundred Rolls is entered in an Excel spreadsheet. Individual properties are listed in row sequence on this spreadsheet. The reference number in the row relates to the row numbers on the Excel spreadsheet. The numbers begin at 2 because row 1 is the column heading on the spreadsheet.

44 Photograph of this paragraph very dark and difficult to read.

45 Photograph very dark and impossible to read.

46 Photograph very dark and impossible to read.

47 The words 'each year for all of their lives 8s. and the corrodies of 2' are missing from the photo; this translation taken from the Record Commission transcription.

48 MS damaged.

49 MS damaged.

50 MS folded over in photo – cannot read name properly.

51 Word missing.

52 MS folded over in photo between the words 'which same land…' and '… Robert acquired that by'. This translation taken from Record Commission transcription.

53 Illegible on photograph.

54 Illegible on photograph.

55 The words 'Walter acquired that messuage by gift of Baldwin Blancgernun, for which he' are in a fold in the MS in the photograph. This translation taken from the Record Commission transcription.

56 MS folded over in places for this paragraph – text cannot be read properly. This translation made from the Record Commission transcription.

57 MS folded over in places for this paragraph – text cannot be read properly. This translation made from the Record Commission transcription.

58 Name in fold in MS in the photo. 'William' taken from the Record Commission transcription.

59 The words 'he pays in respect thereof per annum to the said' are in a fold in the MS in the photo.

60 Number in fold in MS. '2d' taken from the Record Commission transcription.

61 The words 'in the town and in the' are in a fold in the MS in the photo. This taken from the Record Commission transcription.

62 The words 'by inheritance' are in a fold in the MS in the photo. This taken from the Record Commission transcription.

63 The word 'Radegund's' is in a fold in the MS in the photo. This taken from the Record Commission transcription.

64 The words 'until the' are in a fold in the MS in the photo. This taken from the Record Commission transcription.

65 Words missing from MS – 'fields of' assumed.

66 MS damaged.

67 MS damaged.

68 *unam.*

69 MS damaged.

70 MS damaged – number not legible.

71 Thomas his brother, who inherited it from Walter his father.

72 Word missing: probably 'acre'.

73 The words 'lord Roger of the Exchequer 2s., and to the' have been missed out between photos. This translation taken from the Record Commission transcription.

74 Word missing.

[75] Word missing.

[76] Payee unspecified.

[77] Name missing.

[78] MS damaged – number not clear. This amount taken from the Record Commission transcription.

[79] '1 farthing' inserted above the line in the MS, but not inserted against the next mention of the '10d.'.

[80] Word missing after '15'.

Appendix 1

Amercements in Cambridge 1176–7: List of people, many from Cambridge, who were amerced for carrying corn by water without a licence

Name	Sum (pence)
Hildebrand of Cambridge	480
John of Lynn (*Lenna*)	80
Robert son of Anketil'	80
Edric of Lynn (*Len*)	800
Eustace son of Bernard	320
Godland	40 jointly assessed
Radulph brother of Godland	40 jointly assessed
Absolon	200 jointly assessed. Pardoned by writ of Geoffrey, Bishop of Ely
Walter, father of Absolon	200 jointly assessed. Pardoned by writ of Geoffrey, Bishop of Ely
Richard of Ditton	80 pardoned by writ of Geoffrey, Bishop of Ely
Reginald de Moneia	80
Turketell' of the Bridge	80
Osbert Crane	160
Aluric Huchepain	80
Robert of Newport	80
Osgot brother of Alfgar	80
William Brown (*le Brun*)*	240 pro recto
William Lof*	80 pardoned by writ of Geoffrey, Bishop of Ely

(continued)

Name	Sum (pence)
Robert son of Selede*	80 pardoned by writ of Geoffrey, Bishop of Ely
Everard of Powis*	80 pardoned by writ of Geoffrey, Bishop of Ely
Tiedric*	80 pardoned by writ of Geoffrey, Bishop of Ely
Eliza (*Aelizia*) of Chesterton*	1,600
Alan le Bret*	240
William de Frusselak	80
Radulph Wastel	80 jointly assessed
Stephen Nichtwat	80 jointly assessed
Albric Ruffus	160
Geoffrey Murdac	80
Serlone the cellarer (*sellario*)	80
Lefwin, brother of Serlone	80
William Stramar'	80 jointly assessed
Serlone, brother of William	80 jointly assessed
Absalon Stramar'	320
Walter Eare	80
Geoffrey Scutland	80
Daiman of Cambridge	80
Godric Eare	80
Geoffrey Boigris	40 jointly assessed
Edmundo	40 jointly assessed
Radulph of Bradley (*Bradelega*)	80
William Finch	1,200
William of Well(es)	80
Richard the plumber (*plumbario*)	80
Henry Frostulf	160
Godland	40 jointly assessed
Osbert	40 jointly assessed
Hawan	40 jointly assessed
Hawan's brother	40 jointly assessed
Aszio carnifax/macecrer'	80
Godard le Scipre	240
Radulph son of Alfgar	80
Ingelmar of Cambridge	80
Estmund	80
Godard le Trottere	80

(continued)

Name	Sum (pence)
Wulward of the Bridge	80
Alfelin of the Bridge	320
Alfgar Blund	80
Richard of Barnwell	40 jointly assessed
Eustace of Barnwell	40 jointly assessed
Ailwin brother of Wulward	480
Spileman Salnar	80
Walter son of Gilbert	80
John of Chesterton	80
Alfgar of Exning	160
William of Swavesey	40 jointly assessed
Andrew of Swavesey	40 jointly assessed
TOTAL	£24 6s 8d fully paid in 39 tallies

Notes: * Entry is annotated '*pro recto*'. The list also includes: Turstin of Hemingford for disseisin (80); William de Miniach' for having no pledge; and Edward of Godmanchester *quia non habuit quandam feminam ad rectum*. The total owed, including these fines, is given as £24 6s 8d, fully paid in 39 tallies.

This table also appears in M, pp 171–2, but his spelling of the names is different and his amounts are in £ s d. The table has been reformatted to facilitate cross reference to the main text.

Source: PR *23 Henry II: 1176–1177* (98 vols) 26, pp 183–5

Appendix 2

Cambridge tallage of 1211:
analysis of payments 1211–25

Name	Tallage 1211	Debt remaining in 1219	Total paid by 1225	Percentage paid	Last date of payment	Date fully paid off
Hildebrand Punch	320	164	320	100	1221	1221
Adam le Wanter	480	264	408	85	1222	
John son of Alvred/Helene	160	88	72	45	1214	
Robert le Wanter	160	82	72	45	1214	
John Crocheman	800	464	336	42	1214	
Jordan Niker	480	388	260	54.17	1224	
Radulph feltrarius/le Feutrer	160	112	48	30	1211	
Robert Faber	480	324	156	32.5	1211	
William Doy	320	152	320	100	1221	1221
Benedict feltrarius/Feutrer	160	82	78	48.75	1214	1214
Edward son of Edward	1,200	680	628	52.33	1224	
William son of Edward	240	132	240	100	1222	1222
Simon the Tailor	320	152	168	52.5	1214	
Absolon son of Segar	160		160	100	1214	1214
Radulph Prudfot	1,200	672	528	44	1214	
Simon Niger	480	268	212	44.17	1214	
Reginald of Fordham	240	120	220	91.67	1224	
Fulco Crocheman	1,200	660	540	45	1214	
Radulph Wombe	640	340	640	100	1221	1221

(continued)

Name	Tallage 1211	Debt remaining in 1219	Total paid by 1225	Percentage paid	Last date of payment	Date fully paid off
Ivo Pipestraw	160	124	36	22.5	1211	
John son of Selede	560	308	418	74.64	1224	
Bernard son of Edric	480	80	320	66.67	1222	1222
John Lane	320	152	168	52.5	1214	
Harvey son of Selede	640	324	312	48.75	1214	
William Wulsi	640	336	324	50.63	1220	
Geoffrey son of Robert	240	168	72	30	1211	
William Macecren/carnifax	1,200	640	560	46.67	1214	
Gregory son of Hugo	320	152	336	105	1224	1224
Ivo Macecren/carnifax	320	158	266	83.13	1224	
Richard Gudred/Guthier	720	408	490	68.06	1220	
Serlo le Wanter	160	120	48	30	1211	
Walter Sissard [Cissor]	240	132	108	45	1214	
Alan telarius	160		60	37.5	1211	
Richeman	160	88	164	102.5	1222	1222
Henry telarius	160	88	72	45	1214	
Richard Gibelot	720	408	312	43.33	1214	
Harvey Gogging	480	100	320	66.67	1224	1224
Richard at the Gate	2,400	1,280	2,160	90	1224	

(continued)

Name	Tallage 1211	Debt remaining in 1219	Total paid by 1225	Percentage paid	Last date of payment	Date fully paid off
Reginald of Abinton	480	276	282	58.75	1224	
Reginald of Abinton: his wife	480	360	120	25	1211	
Simon Bagge	1,200	680	1,036	86.33	1224	
Thomas Doy	320	176	180	56.25	1224	
Selede Pinberd	480		132	27.5	1211	
Roger Doy	160	82	160	100	1222	1222
Adam telarius	480	282	414	86.25	1224	
Richard le Peiner [Parmenter?]	160	82	78	48.75	1214	
John nephew of Hugo	400		120	30	1211	
Kaily tannur	1,200	640	840	70	1224	
William of Selford [Shelford]	480	256	416	86.67	1224	
Osbert le Combere	160	76	156	97.5	1221	1221
Alex le Fittere	240	132	198	82.5	1224	
Elias son of Osbert	160	94	166	103.75	1221	1221
Richard le Geliner	640	348	504	78.75	1224	
Walter son of Escolice	240	132	156	65	1224	
Richard of Barnwell	2,400	920	1,160	48.33	1214	
Algar of Welles	320		320	100	1214	1214
Walter son of Absolon	640		160	25	1211	

(continued)

Name	Tallage 1211	Debt remaining in 1219	Total paid by 1225	Percentage paid	Last date of payment	Date fully paid off
Geoffrey son/brother of Ivo	160	88	160	100	1221	1221
Matthew son of Geoffrey	160	100	60	37.5	1211	
Godric le Haur	240	112	128	53.33	1214	
Simon son of the same/Godric	320	296	142	44.38	1214	
Sumer	160	88	72	45	1214	
Michael son of Orgar	640	320	640	100	1223	1223
Reginald Godso [Godsone]	1,200	608	592	49.33	1214	
Ivo son of Matilda	240	124	182	75.83	1224	
Walter Eare	480	288	192	40	1214	
Martin Wulward	960	512	460	47.92	1223	
Radulph brother of Ivo	160		48	30	1211	
Henry son of Elye	480	240	408	85	1224	
Ivo son of Absolon	1,200	792	968	80.67	1224	
Reginald Mulloc	160		48	30	1211	
Hugo de Kertlinge	160	76	160	100	1223	1223
William Billing	800	464	336	42	1214	
Reginald S(c)ortenicht	240	132	198	82.5	1224	
John of Estfleet	800	360	360	45	1214	
Reginald son of Alvred	1,280	640	856	66.88	1224	

(continued)

Name	Tallage 1211	Debt remaining in 1219	Total paid by 1225	Percentage paid	Last date of payment	Date fully paid off
Bartholomew/Brithnod the tannur	1,600	800	800	50	1214	
Geoffrey Clait	320	180	290	90.63	1224	
Warin son of Anketil	240	144	96	40	1214	
Richard Curteis	320	296	144	45	1214	
Giles Curteis	320	180	140	43.75	1214	
Hugh Piscator [Fisher]	240	132	174	72.5	1223	
Radulph son of Geoffrey	480	276	300	62.5	1224	
Richard Billing	160	88	132	82.5	1224	
William Prest	160	94	66	41.25	1214	
Peter Criket	160	76	120	75	1224	
Radulph Pirle	160	94	66	41.25	1214	
Geoffrey Wulward	160	94	166	103.75	1224	1224
Childman	320	172	290	90.63	1224	
Adam Werial	160	76	160	100	1223	1223
Geoffrey Sibert	160	112	48	30	1211	
John faber	240	132	210	87.5	1224	
Ketel the Merchant	320	156	234	73.13	1223	
Absolon Frost	240	168	72	30	1211	
Aldred gener Ketel	400	156	304	76	1224	

(continued)

254

Name	Tallage 1211	Debt remaining in 1219	Total paid by 1225	Percentage paid	Last date of payment	Date fully paid off
Warin son of Norman	240	132	228	95	1224	
Frere	640	328	564	88.13	1224	
Roger Blund	160	112	48	30	1211	
William Sciper/Sliper	480	348	132	27.5	1211	
William Pandevant	240	192	48	20	1211	
Baldwin Blancgernun	1,600	480	1,480	92.5	1224	
Harvey son of Eustace	800	480	800	100	1224	1224
Robert Seman	160	88	72	45	1214	
Geoffrey Hareng	240	124	196	81.67	1224	
Reiner de Winebodesham	240	132	162	67.5	1220	
Robert Custance	240	132	108	45	1214	
Richard Pottere	240	156	84	35	1211	
Robert Vivien	960	552	408	42.5	1211	
Richard son of Richard	320	164	312	97.5	1224	
Henry Vivien	240	132	204	85	1221	
Richard Wulward	960	520	502	52.29	1220	
Walter Blund	320	176	144	45	1214	
Thomas Pupelot	240	138	210	87.5	1224	
William Hitti	160	76	160	100	1223	1223

(continued)

Name	Tallage 1211	Debt remaining in 1219	Total paid by 1225	Percentage paid	Last date of payment	Date fully paid off
Godfrey Pie	160	112	48	30	1211	
Absalon of Newnham	160	124	36	22.5	1211	
Richard of Stortford/forestarius	480	264	216	45	1214	
Robert Cocus	240	180	60	25	1211	
Ketel Cag	160		160	100	1214	1214
TOTAL	55,600	29,978	34,790			

Notes: The information above for 1211 and 1219 is also provided by M, pp 169–70 and pp 167–8. However, M interprets the 1219 data as a second tallage whereas close examination reveals this second 'tallge' to be simply the unpaid balances from the tallage of 1211. This explains why the 'tallage' of 1219 is lower than the tallage of 1211, is applied to only a subset of the original people, and not to additional people, and why the amounts are often odd rather than rounded amounts, as in 1211.

Reinterpretation of the table along these lines provides interesting information on the amount of tallage that was actually paid by different people.

The table summarizes detailed calculations based on annual payments. Numerous adjustments were made for errors of arithmetic or translation of debts in the original source. A positive adjustment to the amount paid indicates a benefit of the citizen as it is, in effect, a payment made by mistake on their behalf, whilst a negative adjustment is to the benefit of the King and to the detriment of the citizen, as it increases the citizen's debt carried forward to the next year.

Robert le Wanter's debt at the end of 1214 was overstated by 6d but the error was corrected in 1219. In 1214 he paid off 2s 6d of his outstanding debt of 9s 4d, and the balance due was wrongly entered as 7s 4d when it was actually 6s 10d.

Jordan Niker was overcharged 10s by translation error when his 1215 debt of 22s 4d was converted into a 1219 debt of 32s 4d. The error does not seem to have been corrected later.

John son of Selede was overcharged 4d by arithmetical error in 1214 when 2.5 marks less 8s was recorded as a debt of 308d. The error does not seem to have been corrected later.

Bernard son of Edric gained one mark from an error of translation in 1214. He owed 2 marks from 1211 but this appeared as a debt of only one mark in 1214.

Harvey son of Selede gained 4d in 1214 due to translation error. He owed 37s 4d from 1211 but this was reduced to an opening debt of only 37s in 1214.

William Wulsi gained the same amount in the same way. He owed 38s 4d from 1211 and this was reduced to 38s in 1214.

Harvey Gogging gained one mark from an error of translation in 1214. He owed 2 marks from 1211 but this was shown as only one mark in 1214.

Osbert le Combere was undercharged 4d by arithmetical error in 1214 when his payment of 2s 8d was treated as a payment of 3s. This left him with a debt of 76d instead of 80d, which he eventually paid off in full.

Elias son of Osbert was overcharged 6d by translation error when his debt of 7s 4d at the end of 1214 was converted into a debt of 7s 10d in 1219.

Richard le Geliner gained 4d from an error of translation in 1214. He owed 37s 4d from 1211 but had a debt of only 37s at the beginning of 1214.

Richard of Barnwell gained 2 marks from an error of translation in 1211. He owed 10 marks at the end of 1211, but only 8 marks at the beginning of 1214.

Algar of Welles appears to have paid in full his 1214 debt of one mark, but the record is unclear.

Simon son of Godric suffered both arithmetical and translation errors which partially cancelled out leaving him on balance worse off. Arithmetical error in 1214 meant that his remaining debt (18s 8d less 4s) was recorded as 10s 8d instead of 14s 8d. In translation to 1219 this debt was inflated by 10s to 24s 8d. He had paid off none of this debt by 1225.

Martin Wulward owed 42s 8d in 1214 and again in 1223, but does not appear during the intervening years. The debt of 42s 8d has been imputed to the intervening years.

Ivo son of Absalon gained 6s from arithmetical error in 1219 when his payment of 3s reduced his debt carried forward to 1220 by 9s.

John of Estfleet gained half a mark by arithmetical error in 1214 when his debt of 3.5 marks less payment of 10s was recorded as leaving only 20s unpaid.

Richard Curteis suffered both arithmetic and translation errors from which, on balance, he lost considerably. In 1214 he gained 8d, when his debt outstanding from 1211 was reduced by 8d from 18s 8d to 18s. After he paid 4s in 1214, however, his debt outstanding was increased to 24s 8d instead of being reduced to 14s. He therefore lost 10s 8d to offset against the 8d he had earlier gained, giving a net loss of 10s. After 1214 neither he nor Gilbert Curteis is mentioned again.

Hugh Fisher was reported as owing 14 marks at the beginning of 1214, whereas he clearly owed only 14s. 'Mark' had been substituted for 'shilling'. Correcting this explains why his payment of 3s left him with a debt of only 11s.

Geoffrey Wulward lost 6d through error of translation in 1219. He owed 7s 4d at the end of 1214 but 7s 10d at the beginning of 1219.

Childman gained 4d from a translation error in 1214. He owed 18s 8d from 1211 but this was reported as 18s 4d in 1214.

Ketel the merchant gained 8d from an error of translation. He owed 18s 8d at the end of 1211 but only 18s at the beginning of 1214.

Aldred gener Ketel suffered both arithmetical and translation errors which partially cancelled out, leaving him better off by 76d. He gained 7s by arithmetical error in 1211 when a payment of 9s reduced 2.5 marks assessed for tallage to 17s 4d instead of 24s 6d. Translation error in 1219 then increased this debt by 8d to 18s.

Richard son of Richard lost 6s by arithmetic error in 1214. He owed 17s 8d at the beginning of 1214, paid 10s into the treasury but only reduced his debt by 4s to 13s 8d.

Richard Wulward has a major discrepancy in his entry which suggests the existence of a serious error that was later corrected. He owed 4 marks at the end of 1211 and at the beginning of 1214. It is stated that in 1214 he paid off only 3s 4d and left only 11s owing. At the beginning of 1219, however, he owed 43s 4d which is the sum that he would have owed had he paid 10s in 1215. In 1219 he paid half a mark; thus it is reasonable to suggest that he may have paid 10s in 1214 rather that the quoted 3s 4d. The figures in the table have been adjusted to show this.

Ketel Cag appears to have paid his debt of half a mark in full in 1214, but the record is not entirely clear.

Most of the arithmetic errors relate to 1214. Several of the discrepancies involve the sum of 10s, which corresponds to single 'x' in roman numerals; such discrepancies could result from a simple scribal error. All the discrepancies occur in 1214–19, at the end of King John's reign and the beginning of the minority of Henry III that followed. There are no errors or discrepancies after 1220; this suggests that administrative problems in the Exchequer had been resolved by then.

Source: All surviving PR 13 John Michaelmas 1211 66 NS 28; 14 John Michaelmas 1212 68 NS 30; 16 John Michaelmas 1214 73 NS 35; 17 John 75 NS 37; 2 Henry III Michaelmas 1218 77 NS 39; 3 Henry III Michaelmas 1219 80 NS 42; 4 Henry III Michaelmas 1220 85 NS 47; 5 Henry III Michaelmas 1221 86 NS 48; 6 Henry III Michaelmas 1222 89 NS 51; Norman Pipe Rolls Henry III 91 NS 35; 8 Henry III Michaelmas 1224 92 NS 54; 7 Henry III Michelmas 1223 94 NS 56

.

Appendix 3

Amercements of the Abbot of Ramsey and William de Kantilup and their associates in Cambridge in 1219

The sheriff renders account for £53 3s 10d for the mercy of the men of the town and hundred [of Cambridge] whose names and debts and the causes of their debts are given in the following roll and how much they have delivered to the treasury.

Name	Offence	Fine	Paid	Balance
Everard son of Eustace	Disseisin	80	24	56
William Talemasche	Pro convincendis xij	640	240	400
Henry son of Godfrey and Agnes	Pro licencia concordandi	80	40	40
Thomas son of Godwin	Did not have the person he pledged	80	48	32
Harvey de Burgat' and William	Pro licencia concordandi	80	40	40
Henry son of Albric and Rohesia and Mabilia	Pro licencia concordandi	80	40	40
Alan of Orwell	Did not have the person he pledged	80	24	56
Twelve knights of Chavel'	For foolish talk	960	320	640
Hugo Biendeu	Did not have the person he pledged	80	24	56
The village of Cunington	Pro fuga of William the Scribe	120	60	60
Alan son of Leving	To escape prosecution	80	30	50
Radulph son of Ivo	For encroachment	80	30	50
Ivo son of Absalon	For selling wine contrary to the assize	160	80	80
Martin Wulward	For selling wine contrary to the assize	80	12	68
Ivo son of Matilda	For selling wine contrary to the assize	80	40	40
Salomon Frost	For selling wine contrary to the assize	120	60	60
Reginald of Fordham	Pro fuga	80	36	44
Simon Niger	Pro fuga	80	24	56
Childman	Pro fuga	160	48	112
Richard Bulling	Pro fuga	80	40	40
Elias son of Robert	Pro fuga	120	40	80
Geoffrey son of Joscelin	To escape prosecution	80	24	56
Peter of Luton	To escape prosecution	80	40	40

(continued)

Name	Offence	Fine	Paid	Balance
William of Ripton	Did not have the person he pledged	80	40	40
Eudo of Swineshead	For mercy	80	40	40
Radulph of Swineshead	Disseisin	240	120	120
Men of Cambridge	De decana Sawal' marineri	80	80	0
Men of Cambridge	De decana Baldewini bercarii	80	80	0
Alexander fittere	To escape prosecution	80	30	50
Martin son of Geoffrey	To escape prosecution	80	48	32
Algar son of Robert	Pro fuga	80	40	40
Geoffrey son of Wulward	Pro fuga	240	24	216
Radulph Wombe	Pro fuga	240	80	160
Rener of Wimboldham	Pro fuga	80	40	40
Thomas Frusselake	Pro fuga	80	24	56
Simon Blund	Pro fuga	80	24	56
Robert Nadun	Pro fuga	80	40	40
Geoffrey son of Ivo	Pro fuga	80	40	40
Thomas mercurius	Pro fuga	80	40	40
John Marescall	Pro fuga	160	80	80
William Cobon	For a pledge for Juliane	80	12	68
Decana Nicholas Blanchard	Pro fuga	80	40	40
Elias son of Andrew	For encroachment	80	60	20
Adam Change	Did not have the person he pledged	80	80	0

Notes: The table excludes cases pertaining explicitly to towns and villages outside Cambridge.

Pro fuga means literally 'for fleeing [the town]' but in practice probably means evading a tax or a regulation and specifically one concerning the sale of wine.

Source: PR 3 Henry III: Michaelmas 1219 (92 vols.) 80 (NS 42), pp 70–3

Appendix 4

Gifts (oblata), representing fines for offences made by Cambridge people in 1221

Name	Offence	Fine	Paid	Balance
John son of Henry son of Harvey	Not specified	320		
Robert son of Robert	Not specified	80		
Robert son of Ivo	Not specified	80		
William son of Simon	Not specified	80		
William son of Harold	Not specified	80		
Osbert of Stivichele	Not specified	80		
William Caval	Not specified	56		
Simon son of Beatrice	Not specified	40		
Geoffrey *cementario*	Not specified	40		
Richard son of Agnes	Not specified	32		
Thomas son of Humphry	Not specified	40		
Martin son of Geoffrey	Not specified	32		
Decenna William Ulf	Not specified	80		
Not stated	For the chattels of William le taffur	18		
Robert Franc	Not specified	160		
Radulph son of Fulk	Not specified	36		
Radulph son of Fulk	For the chattels of Alan	96		
Radulph son of Fulk son of Theobald	For chattels	204	72	132
Matilda wife of William textor	Not specified	80		
Decenna Arnulf	*Pro fuga* Geoffrey	80		
William Bedell'	Not specified	80		
Decenna Roger Renchene	Not specified	80		

(continued)

Name	Offence	Fine	Paid	Balance
William Marisco	Not specified	80		
William of Crawden	Not specified	80		
William le Newemen	Not specified	80		
Geoffrey of Edlington	Not specified	80		
Alicia de Amundsville and Thomas son of Thomas	Not specified	80		
Decenna Thomas son of Geoffrey	Not specified	80		
Decenna William Baker	Not specified	80		
Walter son of Robert	Not specified	120		
Harvey Lutte	Not specified	80		
Henry of Fukeworde	*Pro licencia concordandi*	240	80	160
Roger of Torpel	For his relief	800	800	0
Radulph son of Geoffrey*	For encroachment	[56]	24	32
Thomas de Pupelot	For encroachment	56	12	44
Hugo of Kirtling and William son of John	*Pro licencia concordandi*	40		
Algar of Wells	For selling wine contrary to the assize	40	20	20
Roger Wellifedd	For not having [a witness]	80	20	60
Basilia wife of Godwin	Disseisin	80	40	40
William son of Guido	For not having [a witness]	80	24	56
William de Bello Campo	For summoning Oliver	480		
Hugo Gloverer	Disseisin	56		
Margaret de Sparraguz	*Pro habendo pone*	80		
Godfrey son of Godfrey	For a writ	80		
Hugo of Elm	For a writ	80		
Richard of Wales	For a writ	80		
John de Hudobovill'	For his fine	80		
Walter de Saillum	For escaping prosecution	80		
Robert Twiselet	For selling wine	160		
Philip and Alan, brothers	*Pro fuga*	80		
Richard Wulward	*Pro fuga*	240		
Hugo Helde	*Pro fuga*	80		
Andrew of Winepol	For selling wine	80		
Richard of Winepol	For a false claim	80		

(continued)

Name	Offence	Fine	Paid	Balance
Andrew son of Philip	For selling wine	320		
Roger Raseman	For not having [a witness]	80		
Laurence of Burwell	For escaping prosecution	80		
Andrew of Cockfiled	For unjust detention	80		
Edelina widow of William Arnold	For escaping prosecution	80		
Roscelin of Hellinton'	*Que retraxit se*	80		
Decenna Guido Hundewrichte	*Pro fuga* Roger	80		
Sybil daughter of Alan of Childerley	For escaping prosecution	80		
Hugo son of William	For not having [a witness]	80		
Henry Brown (*le Brun*)	For default	80		
William son of the master	For default	80		
William of Cancia	For not having [a witness]	80		
Saher son of William	Disseisin	80		
Henry son of Robert	Disseisin	80		
Roger son of Baldric	Disseisin	80		
Decenna Henry le Caggere	*Pro fuga*	80		

Notes: The enrolments in which these gifts are recorded also contain unpaid debts arising from 1219 amercements. These have been excluded, together with new payments due from people, towns or villages unconnected with Cambridge.

On *pro fuga* see Appendix 1.

Some of the reported offences may be just pretexts for levying a fine.

Blanks in the two right-hand columns indicate that no information is available. This may in turn indicate that the fine was paid in full.

Radulph son of Geoffrey paid 2s and owed another 2s 8d. The record states that he owed only 2s to begin with. This has been adjusted to 4s 8d.

Source: PR 5 Henry III 1221, pp 174–6

Appendix 5

Summary of information in published editions of the Pipe Rolls relating to people and places in Cambridge, 1130, 1158–1224, 1230 and 1242

Date	Summary of relevant contents
31 Henry I, 1130, pp 34–7	Richard Bassett and Aubrey de Vere account for the farm of Surrey, Cambridgeshire and Huntingdonshire. Fulk who was the sheriff owes £280 and 117s 5d blanche of the old farm. He also owes £80 of the premium for having the farm. He owes £9 5s 3d for previous danegeld.
	He owes 20s for the previous aid of the borough of Cambridge.
	The aid of the borough of Cambridge was £12, of which there was pardoned to William of Ely 5s, Richard the marshall, 7s, (both being dead), Adam the clerk 6s and Saretus the sarjeant 15d [Farrer, p 285]
	William Gernun and his brother Ralph owe 13 silver marks for a breach of the peace.
	Richard the constable [of Cambridge castle?] owes one mark of gold.
	In pardon by the king's writ [selected entries]: Ruald son of Wigan 8s; Payn Peverel £4; Alur' gern' 8s.
2 Henry II, 1155–6 FC, p 285	The farm of the county is 80 marks.
	The sheriff claims allowance of £4 from his farm of the borough and mill of Cambridge
	Richard son of William accounts of 20s for a Jew who was slain.
	The burgesses of Cambridge owe 10 marks for pleas of Henry de Pomeri.
	The sheriff accounts for 60 marks [of an amercement] for the Jews of Cambridge, 40 marks of which were paid to the Queen.
	William the archdeacon [of Ely] was pardoned 3s 6d.
3 Henry II, 1156–7 FC, p 286	The farm of the county is £235 blanche

(continued)

Date	Summary of relevant contents
4 Henry II, 1157–8 FC, p 285	Salomon the king's goldsmith was granted the previous year 60s per annum out from the mill at Cambridge.
5 Henry II, 1158–9, pp 53–4	Burgesses of Cambridge owe £20. There was pardoned to the Bishop of Ely 4s 10d, and to Roger the Usher 2s 8d [FC, p 286] Jews of Cambridge owe 50 marks. The Knights Templar are in charity for one mark. Bonenfant the Jew owes 100s. Miles of Cambridge owes £20. Salomon the goldsmith pays 60s for the mill at Cambridge. Repair of the King's house in Cambridge castle 3s.
6 Henry II, 1159–60, pp 33–4	David son of the Jewish countess renders 100s for Bonenfant the Jew. Bonenfant the Jew owes 40s for a false claim.
7 Henry II, 1160–1, pp 44–6	[As above] Burgesses of Cambridge owe £20. Fulk son of Warin is pardoned by royal writ. The borough of Cambridge gives £20 [for the livery of knights in the army], of which there is pardoned to the Earl of Leicester 9s 10d, the sheriff 6s 10d and Roger the usher of the Treasury 3s 4d [FC, p 286]
8 Henry II, 1161–2, pp 47–9	Burgesses of Cambridge pay £12, of which there is pardoned to the Earl of Leicester one mark, the sheriff 4s 6d and Roger the usher 2s 2d [FC, p 286].
9 Henry II, 1162–3, pp 62–5	[Sheriff:] Pain of Hemmingford leaves the office of sheriff of Surrey, Cambridgeshire and Huntingdonshire after at least nine years [FC, p 286] Nicholas de Chenet owes 40s *per defectu*. Adam of Barnwell owes 10s by royal writ. Paid by Saher de Quincy.
10 Henry II, 1162–3, pp 16–7	[Sheriff:] Hamo Pecche pays £190 19s 2d. Salomon the goldsmith pays 60s for the mill.
11 Henry II, 1164–5, pp 60–3	[Sheriff:] Hamo Pecche pays £190 19s 2d. Salomon the goldsmith pays 60s for the mill. Gilbert son of Dunning amerced 10 marks for a dispute with Saher de Quincy [FC, p 286]
12 Henry II, 1165–6, pp 84–7	[Sheriff:] Old farm: £14 17s 4d blanche. *In soltis*: Isaac the Jew: £15 12s 2d and £6 8s 10d; Aaron the Jew £30. In mercy: Vivo the Jew: £4 9s 4d. New pleas: Seman of Trumpington 4s 1d; John Estling 3s; William son of Radulph 4s 8d; Roger Dunning and his wife 8s 5d.
13 Henry II, 1166–7, pp 164–8	[Sheriff:] Philip of Daventry. County farm: £325 0s 7d blanche. Salomon the goldsmith pays 60s for the mill.

(continued)

Date	Summary of relevant contents
14 Henry II, 1167–8, pp 99–108	[Sheriff:] Philip of Daventry. New farm: £325 0s 7d blanche. Old farm: 14s 5d.
	Salomon the goldsmith pays 60s for the mill.
	Adam Ruffus of Branton owes half a mark and 40d [two separate entries]
	Burgesses of Cambridge owe 50 marks for aid for the marriage of Matilda the king's daughter
	William of Chesterton owes 6s 8d *per defectu*.
15 Henry II, 1168–9, pp 143–9	[Sheriff:] Philip of Daventry. New farm: £322 14s 1d blanche. Old farm: 59s 10d blanche.
	Salomon the goldsmith pays 60s for the mill.
	Gilbert son of Dunning owes 20s for mercy for speaking [an argument] between him and Saher de Quincy
	For encroachments: Burgesses of Cambridge owe 25 marks.
16 Henry II, 1169–70, pp 91–5	[Sheriff:] Ebrard de Beche and Warin de Bassingbourne pay the farm.
	Salomon the goldsmith pays 30s for the mill [for half-year?]
	Philip of Daventry owes arrears of the previous farm. He also owes 66s 8d for the chattels of Roger Maresc' *q hoiem intfec.*
	Estate of Ely: The Hospital and Infirmary of Barnwell owe 20s per annum; the Infirm of the Bridge of Barnwell owe 8s 8d; the Nuns of Grenecroft owe 2s in Cambridge.
17 Henry II, 1170–1, pp 112–15	[Sheriff:] Ebrard de Beche and Warin de Bassingbourn pay the farm.
	Salomon the goldsmith pays 60s for the mill.
	The sheriffs receive credit for £26 13s 4d for 200 quarters of breadcorn sent to the army in Ireland, 3s for six hand-mills, 7s 6d for hire of vessels from Cambridge to Lenn [Lynn], 49s for allowance to a steersman and 19 sailors for one month, 3s 2d for allowance of a serjeant sent to the king with the munitions, 2s for reed mats placed beneath the corn, and 2s for loading and unloading the same [FC, p 287]
18 Henry II, 1171–2, pp 112–17	[Sheriff:] Ebrard de Beche and Warin de Bassingbourn pay the farm.
	Salomon the goldsmith pays 60s for the mill.
	To repair Cambridge gaol 60s by royal writ.
	Jews of Cambridge owe half a mark of gold for making an agreement between themselves.
	Estate of Ely: The Hospital and Infirmary of Barnwell owe 20s per annum; the Nuns of Grenecroft owe 2s for lands and a mill in Cambridgeshire; William son of Absolon owes 11s 4d.

(continued)

Date	Summary of relevant contents
19 Henry II, 1172–3, pp 156–62	[Sheriff:] Ebrard de Beche and Warin de Bassingbourn pay the farm.
	Salomon the goldmith pays 60s for the mill in Cambridge.
	For works at Cambridge castle £31 by writ of Richard de Lucy and by view of Aelfelmi and Seman of the Bridge.
	Jews of Cambridge owe half a mark of gold for making an agreement between themselves. They pay 60s to discharge the debt.
	Burgesses of Cambridge owe £40 to the assize [or tallage].
20 Henry II, 1173–4, FC, pp 287–8	[Sheriff:] Ebrard de Beche and Warin de Bassingbourn pay instalments on the old and new farms.
	Salomon the goldsmith pays 60s for the mill.
	For works at the new castle of Huntingdon and hiring carpenters and *crossis* and security and other minor works £21 9s 7d by royal writ by view of Baldwin Blancgernun.
	The sheriffs obtain credit for a loan of 60s upon their livery made to three knights residing in Cambridge castle; £40 in the livery of 20 knights who were retained in the castle when the Flemings last plied there, namely for 40 days from the day next before the feast of St Botolph to the feast of St James. [FC, pp 287–8]
	The Hospitallers are pardoned 40s of their assize of the borough of Cambridge for Godard their man, according to the liberty of having one man quit in every borough of the king [FC, p 288]
	Assizes of the town of Cambridge pay £16.
21 Henry II, 1174–5, pp 138–43	[Sheriff:] Ebrard de Beche and Warin de Bassingbourn pay instalments on the old and new farms.
	[As above] Salomon Goldsmith pays 60s for the mill in Cambridge.
	Assizes of the town of Cambridge pay 52s 8d.
22 Henry II, 1175–6, pp 70–6	[Sheriff:] Ebrard de Beche and Warin de Bassingbourn pay instalments on the old and new farms.
	Salomon the goldsmith pays 60s for the mill.
	Assizes of the town of Cambridge pay 47s 8d.
	The sheriffs take credit for 35s in the expenses of the gaol by view of Edward and Langlif [FC, p 288]
	William Ruffus is pardoned by royal writ for half a mark in Huntingdonshire.
	Sturmi of Cambridge owes one mark for a false claim.
	Alard the tanner of Cambridge owes 2 marks for receiving enemies of the King.
	The town of Cambridge owes 40 marks amercement for the fore St Ivo Quarrel owes 20 marks for the same.
	William of Chesterton owes 2 marks for default.
	William Wulward owes 2s 6d.

(continued)

Date	Summary of relevant contents
23 Henry II, 1176–7, pp 178–87	[Sheriff:] Ebrard de Beche and Warin de Bassingbourn pay instalments on the farms.
	Walter son of Hugo renders the farm for the half-year. In the treasury £140 3s 1d blanche.
	In soltis by royal writ the jews Benedict, Deodato, Josce and Vivo for £14 8s 6d.
	Assize of the town of Cambridge pays 40s.
	William son of Ordmar and Walter his brother owe half a mark for pledges for Ordgar.
	The sheriff owes 3s for mercy for Hildebrand of Cambridge who carried corn by water without licence from the justices. Many others are also amerced (see Appendix 1).
	The aid of boroughs and towns: Cambridge owes £20.
24 Henry II, 1177–8, pp 113–16	[Sheriff:] Walter son of Hugo renders the farm. £321 19s 10d blanche in the treasury.
	William Ruffus is pardoned by royal writ of 16s 3.5d of the town farm of Cambridge. Robert de Hou, man of William Ruffus, is pardoned 11s 8d which was taken from him at the assizes [He is also pardoned 15s in a separate entry concerning the assizes.]
	The Assize of Cambridge yields 16s 8d.
	Robert son of Ordmar owes 17s 6d for unjust disseisin.
25 Henry II, 1178–9, pp 31–4	[Sheriff:] Walter son of Hugo renders the farm. £309 3s blanche in the treasury.
	William Ruffus has quittance of land in Cambridge for 16s 3.5d.
	William de Argentin owes half a mark for not having William the man his fugitive.
	There are many entries concerning part-payment of debts incurred the previous year.
26 Henry II, 1179–80, pp 33–8	[Sheriff:] Walter son of Hugo renders the farm. £225 8s 1d blanche in the treasury.
	William Ruffus has quittance of land in Cambridge for 16s 3.5d.
	The sheriff owes 2s 8d *de exitu terre* [for land relinquished by] Anger in Cambridge.
	Wulward of Cambridge owes 20s for detaining rent from Anger's house.
	William of Chesterton owes half a mark *pro olla inventa* [for a pot that was found]
27 Henry II, 1180–1, pp 97–101	[Sheriff:] Walter son of Hugo renders the farm. £240 14s 5d blanche in the treasury.
	[William Ruffus has quittance of land in Cambridge for 16s 3.5d.
28 Henry II, 1181–2, pp 4–5, 74–6	[Sheriff:] Walter son of Hugo renders the farm. £324 3s 8d blanche in the treasury.
	William Ruffus has quittance of land in Cambridge for 16s 3.5d.
	The sheriff owes 2s 8d *de exitu terre* Anger in Cambridge.

(continued)

Date	Summary of relevant contents
29 Henry II, 1182–3, pp 41–5	[Sheriff:] Radulph Bardulf renders the farm. £283 4s 9d blanche in the treasury.
	William Ruffus has quittance of land in Cambridge for 16s 3.5d.
	John Mercator owes one mark for exchanging money (*quia cambivit*) contrary to the assize. Gilbert the plumber, Hugo Maurus, Robert Mercator of Norwich and William son of Emme owe half a mark for the same.
	Bernard Grim owes half a mark for a false claim.
	The town of Cambridge owes 10 marks for the liberty to hold all its assizes.
	Hildebrand Gambard owes one mark for the export of corn contrary to prohibition (*quia asportavit bladum contra prohibitionem*).
	The sheriff owes 3s 10d *de exitu terre* Anger in Cambridge.
30 Henry II, 1183–4, pp 10–13	[Sheriff:] Radulph Bardulf renders the farm. £280 9s 5d blanche in the treasury.
	William Ruffus has quittance of land in Cambridge for 16s 3.5d.
	The sheriff owes 3s 6d (corrected in the text from 3s 10d) *de exitu terre* Anger in Cambridge [see above].
31 Henry II, 1184–5, pp 54–60; FC, p 288	[Sheriff:] Radulph Bardulf renders the farm. Old farm: 104s 1d blanche in the treasury; New farm £308 9s 10d blanche in the treasury.
	William Ruffus has quittance of land in Cambridge for 16s 3.5d.
	The town of Cambridge owes £30 blanche for the half-year farm.
	In Stowe hundred William Ruffus pays 8d.
	The township of Cambridge proffers 10 marks that their complaints may be diligently dealt with, saving the king's right [FC, p 288]
	The town of Cambridge pays 10 marks and must speak carefully and without prejudice about the King's law (*ut loquela sue diligenter tractentur salvo jure regis.*)
	The burgesses of Cambridge owe 300 marks [of silver] and one mark of gold to have their town at farm and no interference from the sheriff.
32 Henry II, 1185–6, pp 32–6	[Sheriff:] Nicholas son of Robert renders the farm: £263 17s 1d blanche in the treasury.
	William Ruffus has quittance of land in Cambridge for 16s 3.5d.
	The town of Cambridge owes £60 blanche for its farm.
	The sheriff owes 3s 4d *de exitu terre* Anger in Cambridge.
33 Henry II, 1186–7, pp 78–82	[Sheriff:] Nicholas son of Robert renders the farm: £264 11s 4d blanche in the treasury.
	William Ruffus has quittance of land in Cambridge for 16s 3.5d.
	The town of Cambridge owes £60 blanche for its farm.
	The sheriff pays 6s 4d for land of Anger in Cambridge.

(continued)

Date	Summary of relevant contents
34 Henry II, 1187–8, pp 40–6	[Sheriff:] Nicholas son of Robert renders the farm: £265 0s 2d blanche in the treasury. The burgesses of Cambridge owes £60 blanche for their farm. Gerard Hareng owes 3 marks for disseisin. Robert Blund owes half a mark for pledge of Andrew. William Niger owes half a mark for avoiding prosecution. The sheriff pays 6s 4d for land of Anger in Cambridge. He also pays 2s consideration (*gersuma*) to have a certain portion of that land at farm. Tallage of properties and lands of the King: the town of Cambridge owes £73 10s.
35 Henry II/1 Richard I, 1188–9 FC, p 289	The sheriff claims credit for 25s 6d for the cost of carrying the treasury of Geoffrey, Bishop of Ely, from Cambridge to London, 10s 5d cost of carrying his wine to Selveston, and 3s 11d in the livery of John 'Austurcarius', his horses and his birds.
2 Richard I, 1190, pp 112–17	[Sheriff:] William Muschet. [County farm not specified] Cambridge farm: £41 15s 3d blanche William Ruffus has quittance of land in Cambridge for 16s 3.5d. William owes 200 marks to become sheriff of Buckinghamshire and Bedfordshire and for his daughters to marry as they wish. Tallage dominiorum [Tallage of ownership]: Burgesses of Cambridge owe £55 4s 2d. Burgesses of Cambridge owe 10 marks because they did not do as they were told and exempt Barnwell.
3–4 Richard I, 1191–2, pp 112–17	[Sheriff:] William Muschet Cambridge farm: £41 15s 3d blanche William Ruffus has quittance of land in Cambridge for 16s 3.5d. For works at Cambridge castle £9 8s 8d, by view of Henry of the Cemetery and Gerard the parmenter. For arrows, engines and munitions for the castle 2s by the same writ. Judas the Jew of Cambridge owes 100s for retracting his appeal. Osbert of Cambridge owes half a mark for the pledge of Nicholas of Coventry. Vives son of Josce owes half a mark for the pledge of Judas of Cambridge. Vives brother of David owes 40s for the same; Bonevie owes 10 marks for the same; and David son of Cypora owes 5 marks for the same. Leo son of Josce owes 18s for justice (*pro recto*) v. William of Chesterton.
5 Richard I, 1193, pp 9–13	[Sheriff:] Richard Anglicus owes 20s blanche for the old farm. Reginald de Argentin owes for the new farm. William Ruffus has quittance of land in Cambridge for 16s 3.5d. Escheats (selected): 3s 2d for land which was of Anger in Cambridge. Albric of Madingley owes half a mark for the pledge of William de Burdelais. Bailiffs of Cambridge owe 5 marks for false measurement.

(continued)

Date	Summary of relevant contents
6 Richard I, 1194, pp 22, 76–80	[Sheriff:] Reginald de Argentin owes for the new farm.
	William Ruffus has quittance of land in Cambridge for 16s 3.5d.
	3s 2d escheat for land which was of Anger in Cambridge.
	Harvey son of Eustace owes 20s for having recognition v. William Ruffus for 50 acres and 3s rent in Cambridge and Newnham of which Willliam dispossessed Eustace his father in the king's prison as he says.
	Gerard the parmenter and Dera his wife owe one mark for summons and recognition of novel disseisin at Westminster between themselves and Robert son of Walter.
7 Richard I, 1195, pp 49, 61, 119–25	[Sheriff:] Reginald de Argentin owes for the farm.
	William Ruffus has quittance of land in Cambridge for 16s 3.5d.
	In default of stocking (*defalta instauramenti*) 2 carrucates in Chesterton 40s; for 10 sheep 20s; for 10 *scrophis* and one *verre* 10s; to carry prisoners for the sheriff from Huntingdon to Cambridge 5s; for irons for the prisoners 3s 6d.
	Escheats (selected): Thomas of Huntingdon owes 2s for a messuage in Cambridge that was of Anger of Cambridge. Also 2s for some land of Anger which he held as security for Simon of Holme. Also 8d and 12d for other lands of Anger in Cambridge. Also 2s for a waste messuage of Anger which by tradition belonged to Thomas of Huntingdon, clerk to the court of the Exchequer.
8 Richard I, 1196, pp 208, 274–81	[Sheriff:] Werrisc de Marinnes owes £180 0s 4d blanche [for half-year?].
	William Ruffus has quittance of land in Cambridge for 16s 3.5d.
	Repairs to Cambridge castle: 52s 3d by royal writ and view of Curteis of the Bridge, Robert son of Geoffrey and Hugh the Provost (*prepositi*).
	Thomas of Barton owes half a mark for novel disseisin; Robert de Marisco for the same.
	Debts of the Jews are still outstanding. Hervey Judas owes 5s 3. for false claim and half a mark for novel disseisin.
9 Richard I, 1197, pp 77–82	[Sheriff:] Werric de Marinnes owes £373 9s d for the current farm, and has £10 outstanding from the previous year.
	William Ruffus has quittance of land in Cambridge for 16s 3.5d. William owes £40 7s 2d from the old farm of Buckinghamshire and Bedfordshire for 4 Richard I; and 117s 9d from 5 Richard I outstanding from various liberties and quittances; £4 for 4 hawks; also £42 for 42 hawks from 10 and a half preceding years. The total is £34 4s 10d.
	Repairs to Cambridge castle: 33s 4d by royal writ.
	Joachim son of Simon owes 10 marks to have a messuage in Cambridge which his father mortgaged to (*invadiauerat*) Anger of Cambridge, which was forfeited by Anger to the King.

(continued)

Date	Summary of relevant contents
10 Richard I, 1198, pp 153–62	[Sheriff:] Robert de Insula. County farm: £373 9s 4d blanche
	[William Ruffus has quittance of land in Cambridge for 16s 3.5d.
	For stocking 2 carrucates at Chesterton (*instauramento 2 carrucarum*) 48s by royal writ. For 10 boars (*scrophis*) 10s by the same writ 10s; for 20 palfreys bought for the work of the king at the feast of St Ivo £54 18s 4d; to carry rags (*pannis*) to Westminster, which were detained for not paying the assize (*qui arestati fuerunt quia non fuerunt de assisa*) 3s 4d. To carry one approver (*probatori*) from Cambridge to Westminster 20d. To keep custody of the said palfreys for 4 days 19s 5d; to carry prisoners from Cambridge to Westminster 5s.
	Moses of Cambridge owes half a mark for having justice regarding 60s v. Robert del Sap.
	William of Chesterton owes one mark for having dogs contrary to the assize.
	Simon de Insula owes half a mark to have enrolled in the Great Roll that he has a concession from Geoffrey son of Peter, the King's Justices and Barons of the Exchequer that he holds, by the service of 2s per annum which he (and his heirs) pay to the King, a vacant messuage over the water in Cambridge between the house of Robert son of Geoffrey, fisherman, and the house of Turstin Grennart, concerning which inquiry was made by the Justices which proved that there was no loss to the King (*quod nullum commodum R. inde provenire solebat*).
	Documents relating to the Justices of the Jews are recorded.
1 John, 1199, pp 153–62	[Sheriff:] Robert de Insula. County farm: £373 9s 4d blanche
	Cambridge farm: £41 15s 3d blanche
	William Ruffus has quittance of land in Cambridge for 16s 3d. He still owes £54 4s 10d for the farm of Buckinghamshire and Bedfordshire.
	William Uncle, constable of Cambridge, is paid £8 9s 9d to provision the castle and provide armed men to guard it and maintain peace [in response to the threat of disturbances following the sudden death of King Richard I].
	Escheats: Simon de Insula owes 2s 8d for a house previously held by Anger of Cambridge; and 2s for a waste messuage held by Anger, and 8d for the land of the same. Also 2s owed for the previous year. Also 12d for other land of Anger.
	Benedict of Talemunt pays the debt of Moses of Cambridge, who still owes half a mark for justice against Robert del Sap.
	The town of Cambridge owes 100 marks. The town also owes 250 marks for having its farm, together with such freedoms as other of the King's towns possess.
	Baldwin the man of Alberic Ruffus owes half a mark for selling wine contrary to the assize.
	Thomas del Ho and Matilda his wife, once the wife of Matthew, and Matilda daughter of the said Mathew and Felicia his wife owe half a mark for assize of novel disseisin at Westminster v. Alberic pincernam and Fulk his son concerning a free tenement in East Hatley.
	The Lepers of Steresbregg' (Stourbridge) owe half a mark for a writ of novel disseisin at Westminster v. Walter of Branford. The same Walter owes one mark for disseisin.
	Curteis of Cambridge is amerced half a mark for default.

(continued)

Date	Summary of relevant contents
2 John, 1200, pp 163–9	[Sheriff:] Robert de Insula. County farm: £373 9s 4d blanche
	Cambridge farm: £41 15s 3d blanche
	New escheats: Simon Ruffus owes half a mark for an agreement (*pro licentia concordandi*); Walter Eare 20s for a false claim; and Robert son of Selede for the same.
	Peter of Makeston owes half a mark for writ of novel disseisin concerning a free tenement in Cambridge.
	The Prior of Barnwell owes 50 marks for having the manor of Chesterton at fee farm for £30 per annum, and possession of ten rental books which he was promised.
	The Canons of Barnwell owe £15 for their farm of Chesterton for the half-year.
3 John, 1201, pp 119–27	[Sheriff:] Hamo de Valoignes and Ruelent de Valoignes. County farm: £186 14s 8d blanche for half-year
	Cambridge farm: £20 blanche for half-year.
	William Ruffus has quittance of land in Cambridge 16s 4d for the whole year
	The town of Cambridge still has 100 marks outstanding for their charter.
	The Canons of Barnwell owe £30 for their farm of Chesterton for the year.
	Simon de Insula owes one palfrey for confirmation of a charter which Simon son of Eve made concerning land with appurtenances in Impington.
4 John, 1202, pp 131–8	[Sheriff:] Walter de Stivechele. County farm: £35 4s 7d blanche for the remainder of the previous year.
	Cambridge farm: £40 blanche
	William Ruffus has quittance of land in Cambridge for 16s 4d. He also owes £54 4s 10d for the farm of Buckinghamshire and Bedfordshire.
	Repair of the King's house in Cambridge castle 37s 2d by royal writ. For carrying two prisoners from Lynn to London 3s 2d by the same writ. For a gift of clothing for them 2s 10d. For irons for the prisoners 14d by royal writ.
	For 500 loads of corn sent to Norway, namely 100 loads of wheat and 400 of barley, £67 12s 10.5d blanche.
	Hamo de Valoignes owes £25 8s blanche for the remainder of his farm of the county from the previous year. Robert de Insula owes £45 0s 5d blanche from two years ago.
	The town of Cambridge is amerced 100 marks for receiving additional frankpledge.

(continued)

Date	Summary of relevant contents
5 John, 1203, pp 1–6	[Sheriff:] (1) Walter de Stivechele; (2) Warin son of Gerald and Henry of Codham. County farm: £186 14s 8d blanche for half-year.
	Cambridge farm: £40 blanche per annum
	William Ruffus has quittance of land in Cambridge for 8s 2d (half-year).
	Walter de Stivechele, Hamo de Valoignes and Robert de Insula all have debts outstanding from previous county farms.
	Simon Ruffus pays for Anger's properties.
	Repairs to Cambridge castle: 5 marks by writ of Geoffrey son of Peter and 3 marks by royal writ.
	New offerings involving Jewish money lenders:
	Master Benjamin, Jacob son of Manasses, Abraham, Manasses son of Benjamin, Samuel son of David and Santo de Gurnei pay 20 marks that William of Shelford and Matthew his brother are distrained for payment of £42 by chattels and money.
	Reinfrid son of Roger pays four palfreys to allow him to borrow 400 marks which have been subscribed by the Jews Jacob of Northampton, Meriane son of Isaac, Simon of Oxford, Moses of Spain, Mer' and Mosse nephew of Merien', to be repaid over four years.
6 John, 1204, pp 113–20	[Sheriff:] Warin son of Gerald and Henry of Codham. County farm: £373 9s 4d blanche
	Cambridge farm: £40 blanche.
	[William of Ruffus has died.] William Ruffus has quittance of land in Cambridge for 16s 4d. He still owes £54 4s 10d from the farm of Buckinghamshire and Bedfordshire [see above]. The debt is to be paid in Norfolk. Radulph de Trublevill has his son and heir.
	The sheriff owes 2s 8d rent for a house previously held by Anger of Cambridge; and 8d for other land and also 12d for other land.
	Simon de Insula still owes 2s for a waste messuage in Cambridge.
	The town of Cambridge still owes 100 marks for receiving additional frankpledge.
	William of Trumpington owes half a mark for permission to hold some unspecified property (*ut convention facta teneatur*).
	Robert son of Richard of Newnham owes one mark for mercy.
	New offerings (selected):
	Hugh son of Walter owes half a mark to have recognition by mort d'ancestor at Holy Trinity in fifteen days at Westminster concerning one virgate of land in Witham v. William Ruffus [deceased].
	Walter son of Gerald of Chesterton owes one mark to have a royal order at Holy Trinity in fifteen days at Westminster v. Prior of Barnwell concerning six acres of land in Chesterton.
	Anketil son of Herbert and Juliana his wife owe half a mark to recognise novel disseisin and summon the itinerant royal justices between themselves and Baldwin Blancgernun who has been summoned to the royal court on the morrow of the Assumption.
	Henry of Cobham [joint sheriff] owes 2 marks to distrain the men of Cambridge by someone other than himself to pay 100 marks for which they are in mercy [see above].

(continued)

Date	Summary of relevant contents
7 John, 1205, pp 81–7	[Sheriff:] Robert of Tatteshall and Master Aristotiles. County farm: £186 14s 7d blanche for half-year
	Cambridge farm: £40 blanche.
	William Ruffus [the heir?] has quittance of land in Cambridge for 8s 2d (half-year presumably)
	Repair of the King's house in Cambridge castle, 66s 8d by royal writ.
	Simon de Insula owes 2s for a waste messuage in Cambridge and 4s 4d owed for the lands of Anger.
	Canons of Barnwell owe £30 blanche for the farm of Chesterton.
	Simon de Insula owes one palfrey (valued at 5 marks) for a confirmation [of a charter?].
	The town of Cambridge still owes 100 marks (see above)
	Pleas of the court (selected):
	Absolon son of Absolon owes half a mark for an inquiry. Alan of Barton owes 20s for disseisin.
8 John, 1206, pp 160–70	[Sheriff:] Joscelin of Stivechele. County farm: £373 9s 4d blanche
	Cambridge farm: £40 blanche
	Repair of the King's house in the castle of Cambridge £4 15s by royal writ. Alard Flanders [of Fordham] and Robert de Percy and associates are paid 5s for acting for the king in respect of Cambridge castle.
	Simon de Insula owes 2s for a waste messuage in Cambridge. He owes 4s 4d for the lands of Anger.
	Simon de Insula owes 200 marks and 2 palfreys for the wardship of Robert de Furnell.
	Prior of Barnwell owes 10 marks for encroachment.
	Amercements: Henry Ruffus amerced half a mark for a false claim; Hereward [Henry?] Wombe half a mark; William de Novacurt 10s; Richard Wulward half a mark; Alan of Barton half a mark *pro disseisin*. Roger Eare, the same; Walter Eare the same; Reginald of Fordham the same.
9 John, 1207, pp 102–13	[Sheriff:] Joscelin of Stivechele
	County farm: £186 (1) 4s 8d blanche for half-year. Fulk son of Theobald owes the same amount for the other half-year. He pays 120 marks and 3 palfreys to hold the farm of Cambridgeshire and Huntingdonshire, with custody of Cambridge castle, from Easter 8 John for seven years, to be paid annually, the purchase price to be paid in instalments of 100 marks.
	Cambridge farm: £40 blanche.
	Repair of the gate and the King's house in the castle of Cambridge £10 19s 4d by royal writ, with a view by Robert Custance and Frere.
	William Ruffus acquitted of land in Cambridge 8s 2d (for half-year, presumably).
	The burgesses of Cambridge owe 100 marks to hold the town at fee farm for £40, paid in two annual instalments of £20.

(continued)

Date	Summary of relevant contents
10 John, 1208, pp 183–9	[Sheriff:] Fulk son of Theobald. County farm: £373 9s 4d blanche Cambridge farm: £40 blanche Repairs to the house at Cambridge castle 45s 2d by royal writ. To escort prisoners from Cambridge to London 5s by the same writ, In quittance of lands of William Ruffus 16s 4d.
11 John, 1209, pp 156–62	[Sheriff:] Fulk son of Theobald County farm: £373 9s 4d blanche Cambridge farm: £40 blanche In quittance of lands of William Ruffus 16s 4d. Repairs to the King's house in Cambridge castle: 78s 8d by royal writ. Four casks of red wine and one cask of wine from Auxerre and their carriage from London to Cambridge, £7 17s 3d by royal writ. Amercements: Robert Blund, one mark; Burgesses of Cambridge, 40 marks; Robert son of Alvred one mark; Richard at the Gate 20s; Walter Sissard half mark; William Eare 2 marks; Harvey Gogging and his associates 6 marks; and Simon telarius half a mark.
12 John, 1210, pp 38, 111–17	[Sheriff:] Fulk son of Theobald. County farm: £373 9s 4d blanche Cambridge farm: £40 blanche Repairs to Cambridge castle: 86s 5d by royal writ In quittance of lands of William Ruffus 16s 8d. William de Mortimer owes 100s for lands in Newnham which the King gave his father and which the Brothers of the Hospital [of Jerusalem] in Cambridge hold. Amercements of the Itinerant Justices in Autumn: Josceline of Stivechele is fined 40 marks for transgression. William of Trumpington is fined 60 marks, but pardoned 20.
13 John, 1211, pp 94–103	[Sheriff:] Fulk son of Theobald. County farm: £373 9s 4d blanche Cambridge farm: £40 blanche Repairs to Cambridge castle: 86s 5d by royal writ In quittance of lands of William Ruffus 16s 8d. Amercement of the men of Cambridge: see Appendix 2.
14 John, 1212, pp 76–82	[Sheriff:] Fulk son of Theobald. County farm: £186 14s 7d blanche for a half-year Cambridge farm: £20 blanche for a half-year. Repairs to a house in Cambridge castle: 57s by royal writ In quittance of lands of William Ruffus 16s 8d. Osbert Ruffus is amerced for 8 marks. Prior of Barnwell owes one palfrey for having possession of a fulling mill at *Suggebi* which Gilbert Peche gave to the church of Barnwell

(continued)

Date	Summary of relevant contents
16 John, 1214, pp 71–8	[Sheriff:] William, Earl of Salisbury, and Werric de Marignes. County farm: £373 9s 4d blanche
	Cambridge farm: £40 blanche
	Repairs to a house in Cambridge castle: 32s 5d.
	Fulk son of Theobald [former sheriff] owes £137 and three palfeys for multiple debts enrolled previously.
	William of Trumpington owes 4 marks for transgression.
	Prior of Barnwell owes one mark for an agreement.
	Tallage Maneriorum: Town of Cambridge owes £100.
17 John, 1215, pp 66, 74, 87	[Sheriff:] William, Earl of Salisbury. County farm: £186 14s 8d blanche for a half-year
	Cambridge farm: £20 blanche for half-year
	Repairs to a house in Cambridge castle: 45s 3d. Repairs to a fracture in the tower 24s 6d.
2 Henry III, 1218, pp 78–82	[Sheriff:] Fulk de Breautee and Radulph de Bray. County farm: £373 9s 4d blanche
	Cambridge farm: £40 blanche
	Repairs to Cambridge gaol £4 10s 10d by view of Geoffrey Hareng' and Aldred Chapmann.
	In quittance of lands of William Ruffus 16s 8d.
	Town of Cambridge owes £30 of the new tallage.
3 Henry III, 1219, pp 62–73	[Sheriff:] Fulk de Breautee and Radulph de Bray. County farm: £373 9s 4d blanche
	Cambridge farm: £40 blanche
	In quittance of lands of William Ruffus 16s 8d.
	Radulph son of Fulk son of Theobald owes £137 6s 6d and 3 palfreys for many debts from previous years.
	The men of Cambridge have paid £4 14s 7d of the old tallage, and £18 17s of the total tallage.
	Liecia of Cambridge owes one mark for an agreement; the Prior of Barnwell owes half a mark for the same; Robert son of Robert owes half a mark to have a representative in court (*pro habendo pone*) v. Seman of Newnham and Gunilda his wife concerning land in Newnham; Margaret daughter of Eustace Sparaguz owes half a mark for the same v. Roger of Fordham concerning a messuage in Cambridge, and v. Julian widow of Astini of Cambridge and Godfrey son of Warin concerning another messuage in Cambridge.
	Amercements of the Abbot of Ramsey and William de Kantilup and their associates are imposed on many men of Cambridge (see Appendix 3)

(continued)

Date	Summary of relevant contents
4 Henry III, 1220, pp 137–48	[Sheriff:] Fulk de Breautee and John de Ulecot. County farm: £373 9s 4d blanche
	Cambridge farm: £40 blanche
	In quittance of lands of William Ruffus 16s 8d.
	The men of Cambridge pay half a mark for Ivo son of Absolon; 40d for Ivo son of Matilda; 5s for Salomon Frost; 40d for Richard Bulling; 40d for Algar son of Robert; 40d for Reiner of Wimboldsham; 40d for Robert Nadun; 40d for Geoffrey son of Ivo and half a mark for John Marescallo.
	Martin Wulward owes 5s 8d for selling wine; Robert Toylet owes half a mark for the same; Andrew brother of Richard of Winepol half a mark for the same.
	Simon Niger owes half a mark (or 4s 8d) *pro fuga*; Richard Wombe half a mark for the same; Richard Wulward 20s for the same; Thomas de Frusselak' 4s 8d for the same; Decana Wulward half a mark *pro fuga* Richard Wulward; Decana William Hulf' half a mark *pro fuga* William de taffur, and the sheriff 18d for William's chattels.
	Radulph son of Fulk son of Theobald owes 3s for the chattels of a fugitive that has fled abroad; 17s for the chattels of Richard, fugitive; and 8s for the chattels of Alan son of Arnold; half a mark for the chattels of Wulward fugitive.
	Richard of Winepol owes half a mark for false claim.
	William de Marisco owes half a mark which he does not have (*quia non habuit*).
5 Henry III, 1221, pp 170–80	[Sheriff:] Fulk de Breautee and John de Ulecot. County farm: £373 9s 4d blanche
	Cambridge farm: £40 blanche
	Repairing a gaol and a house at Cambridge castle 21s 1d.
	In quittance of lands of William Ruffus 16s 8d.
	Offerings (*De Oblatis*) (selected): Childman 6d; Alexander Fittere 10d; Thomas the mercer 28d; Geoffrey Wulward 16s *pro fuga*; Radulph Wombe half a mark *pro fuga*; Martin Wulward 5s 8d for selling wine; Thomas de Frusselak 4s 8d *pro fuga*; Richard Wombe half a mark *pro fuga*; and Andrew de Winepol half a mark for selling wine.
	Tallage of Cambridge (see Appendix 2)
6 Henry III, 1222, pp 22–32	[Sheriff:] Fulk de Breautee and John de Ulecot. County farm: £373 9s 4d blanche
	Cambridge farm: £40 blanche
	Expenses of Henry of Hauvill' staying in Cambridge with falcons from Norway, 40s by royal writ. By the same writ he has expenses for keeping the birds quiet and secure in the park, 16s 6d.
	To repair Cambridge castle 6s 6d.
	In quittance of lands of William Ruffus 16s 8d.
	Radulph son of Fulk owes £127 6s 6d and 3 palfreys for the many debts of his father in continuation of roll 15 John (£5 less than last year), and £37 16s 4d for debts to the Jews
	Amercements (selected): Radulph son of Fulk, 11s; Thomas Pupelot, 3s 8d for encroachment
	Various debtors from earlier years are listed

(continued)

Date	Summary of relevant contents
7 Henry III, 1223, pp 192–201	[Sheriff:] Fulk de Breautee and John de Ulecot. County farm: £373 9s 4d blanche
	Cambridge farm: £40 blanche
	Osgood, messenger of the King of Norway, who carries one goshawk is paid 20s expenses, and Askero his colleague 1 mark expenses. Also Henry de Hauvill is paid for the journey he made from Lynn to London with a goshawk sent by the King of Norway to the King of England.
	Robert Toylet fined 1 mark for selling wine contrary to the assize
	Offerings (*De Oblatis*) (selected): Robert de Hasting' fined one mark for a false claim.
8 Henry III, 1224, pp 70–81	[Sheriff:] Fulk de Breautee and John de Ulecot. County farm: £33 7s 4d blanche for a quarter-year
	Cambridge farm: £10 blanche for quarter-year.
	The Prior of Barnwell owes 20s for having several places in the town of Cambridge which are of the Prior's fee and which Jacob Chimmoc, Jew, held before the war and which were destroyed in the war and were in the King's hands, which fine the justices received and enrolled through Thomas de Chimelli.
	Many amercements from 1221 remain unpaid.
15 Henry III, 1230, pp 55–65	[Sheriff:] Geoffrey of Hatfield. County farm: £373 9s 4d blanche
	Cambridge farm: £40 blanche
	Geoffrey de Scalaris owes £144 7s 11d for many debts previously recorded. Hamo Pecche owes £23 8s 1d similarly.
	The men of Cambridge owe one mark of their farm for a house which was of Benjamin, Jew.
	Geoffrey son of Simon de Turri owes £18 6s on account of his debts to the Jews. William de Bordelais £27 similarly. Roger de Quency owes £180 18s 11d similarly.
	The town of Cambridge renders £22 8s 6d for tallage.
	Robert Wulward owes 5s for an agreement.
	The sheriff owes 22s from the sale of old houses in Cambridge castle.
	William Ruffus holds half a fee of the Honour of Boulogne for which he owes 40s scutage for avoiding military service. He also owes half a mark for withdrawal from the assizes.

(continued)

Date	Summary of relevant contents
26 Henry III, 1242	[Sheriff:] Henry de Colne. County farm: £373 9s 4d blanche
	Cambridge farm: £40 blanche
	The Friars Preachers for timber for repairs by gift of the king 5 marks by royal writ
	Richard Wombe owes 2s 3d for tallage; William Carnifax owes 2s tallage;
	William Kailly owes 5s 8d for transgression; Fulk son of Warin owes de pluribus prestitis 7 marks and for default 5 marks.
	William Ruffus owes £20 for scutage
	Gilbert Crocheman owes £20 1s 6d for debts to the Jews
	Hervey Dunning owes 100s for disseisin regarding pledges of Robert Seman, Adam Dunning and John Selede
	The sheriff owes half a mark for an agreement with Stephen Hawkeston
	Harvey Parleben owes 5s for many transgressions
	Adam son of Eustace owes 30 marks for many transgressions regarding pledges of Eustace son of Harvey, Radulph Wombe and others
	Robert de Stivichele owes 10 marks for fines for many transgressions
	Henry de Colevill owes 20s for respite and 20s for an agreement.

Notes: The Roll for 8 Richard I, 1196, is missing and for that year the information has been taken from the Chancellor's Roll. The Roll for 15 John, 1213, is also missing, and no replacement is available. The rolls for 1225–9 have not been transcribed.

The same sheriff administered both Cambridgeshire and Huntingdonshire throughout this period. Apart from the farm paid by the sheriff, all the information relates to people or properties in the town of Cambridge and not to Cambridgeshire as a whole.

Many entries in the original rolls represent previous debts carried forward. Debts are normally recorded in the table above only in the year in which they were incurred; the only exception is very long-standing debts, which are sometimes noted for the reader's interest Rents and other recurrent items are included selectively, depending on whether they concern persons of particular interest (see Chapter 4 in Casson, Casson, Lee and Phillips, *Compassionate Capitalism*).

The very first Pipe Roll, of 1130, was recently published in a new English translation, with the original Latin text for comparison. The entries for the remaining rolls have been translated by the editors.

To economize on space, a relatively free style of translation has been used. Some common phrases have been shortened; in particular, 'renders account', which appears in very many entries, has been abbreviated to 'owes'. Money 'owed' represents new debt incurred or still outstanding from the previous year; money owing at the end of any year appears as the mount owing at the beginning of the following year.

Money is expressed mainly in £, s and d, although marks (160d) are also used. Pipe Roll information is unsuitable for statistical analysis, and so money has not been expressed in pence alone.

Sources: Published editions of PR 1130–1224, 1230 and 1242. For other years: FC

Appendix 6

Selected excerpts from *Rotuli Curiae Regis* I–XX, relating to people and places in Cambridge

Date	Page	Summary
	Vol. I	
1194	9	William Brown (*Brun*) petitioner and Godard son of Stohard tenant agree that William gave 3 roods of land in Fordham to Godard and his heirs in perpetuity for … pence per annum for all service excluding foreign service
1194	97	Reginald de Argentin who is on the King's service at Cambridge v. Thomas de Bassingbourn concerning a plea of homage through Turstan le Violur. Thomas essoins himself.
1194	106, 107	Reginald de Argentin in person v. Thomas de Bassingbourn concerning a plea of homage through William Arbelastar. To be heard on the morrow of St Leonard one month in Westminster. See also p 134.
1194	110–11	Joscelin of All Saints in person v. Simon son of Eve concerning a plea of land through Elia de Ket. To be heard on the feast of St Michael 15 days in Westminster
1198	235	Everard of Barton (*B'ton*) v. Alice of Grantchester concerning a plea of dower through William of Barton. Affidavit.
1199	243	Simon of Sexton v. Gundred of Madingley concerning a plea of land through Richard son of Bigan. On the octave of St Michael in 15 days affidavit. On the day given Harvey son of Eustace asked to see Gundred's essoin, which he did not have. Gundred appointed Simon his son in his place …
1199	253	Adam son of Savary v. Alice wife of Elie concerning a plea of dower through Hugo son of Richard for himself. Alice wife of the same Adam v. the same through Geoffrey son of William. William Clicus de Witewudeha' concerning the same through Walter de Cotes. Everard the chaplain v. the same Alice concerning a plea of land through Geoffrey of Madingley. Henry son of William concerning the same through William of Burthop. Cecil his mother concerning the same through Richard. Affidavit for all. Continued in several further entries.

(continued)

Date	Page	Summary
1199	266	Ivo Quarrel … Radulph Sanzaveir concerning a plea of land through Richard son of William. Affidavit.
1199	276	Adam of Barton v. Alice of Grantchester concerning a plea of land through Alan of Barton. Affidavit.
1199	278	Goding' essoins Robert Seman through Gilbert son of John
1199	280	Curteis and Gilbert his son v. Walter son of Algar concerning a plea of horses through Robert son of William and Alex ….
1199	281	William Frisselak (*Frisselu*) v. Hugo de Ullington concerning a plea of land through Philip son of Ivo. Octave of Trinity
1199	284	Gundred (*Gunware*) v. Harvey son of Eustace and Simon Sexton concerning a plea of dower through Pagan son of Hamo … Affidavit
1199	285	Richard of Mountfichet in the service of the Duke [of Normandy] v. Jews of Cambridge concerning a plea of debt through William de la Hague
1199	287	Prior of Barnwell v. Laurence son of William regarding a plea of homage through John Cardun. Octave of Trinity. Affidavit.
1199	304	Edua Blancgernun [who was the wife of Gilbert Blancgernun] v. Eva wife of Segar concerning a plea of land through Warin son of Gilbert; see FC, p 289
1199	308	Radulph de Grafham and Isobel his wife in a plea of land v. Ivo Quarrel. Continued on p 427.
1199	308, 321	William des Bauues, William le Moine, Thomas of Trumpington and Alex Mangant are sent to view the infirmity of Geoffrey Picot, essoined against Harvey son of Eustace. They say he is not ill and a date is set for Easter 15 days at Westminster for him to come. Geoffrey says that not all four men were knights and that some are his mortal enemies. Harvey sends his armed champion and asks for this to be recorded. Geoffrey says that his champion is in gaol. Geoffrey asks to make a pledge instead. A date of the feast of St John the Baptist 15 days is set for a duel. [A final concord is made.]
1199	323	John de Pattishall (*Perteshall*) having been in possession of a false or forged writ, takes refuge in St Clement's church, Cambridge, and abjures the land of John, Lord of England
1199	324	Richard of Crauden and Geoffrey of Adersley are sent to hear and view the P|rior of Barnwell who is ill and to see who would speak on his behalf between him and Harvey son of Eustace about 4 messuages which Harvey claims v. the Prior.
1199	326–7	Reginald son of Alured and Michael son of Orgar are sent with writs from the sheriff to get testimony from Absolon son of Absolon concerning land which Absolon Cholle, father of Absolon, held of Bernard Grim in fee. Continued on p 422.
1199	336–7	Harvey son of Eustace petitioner v. Prior of Barnwell concerning 3 messuages with appurtenances in Cambridge … William Suppior came to defend his right and ask for a view. A date is given on the feast of St John 15 days.

(continued)

Date	Page	Summary
1199	404	Gilbert de Derefield, Reginald de Trumpington, William son of Humphrey and Walter de la Haia are sent to the Prior of Barnwell to ask if he wishes to appoint someone to speak for him on a plea of homage v. Laurence of Crauden ....
1199	404–5	Harvey son of Eustace v. Gervase Wrench concerning one virgate of land with appurtenances in Gransden .... Continued on II, p 98.
1199	421	Grand assize between Robert Ruffus petitioner and Stephen Ragedal defendant concerning half a hide of land with appurtenances in Wratting ....
1199	431–2	Assize of morte d'ancestor between Absolon son of Absolon, petitioner, concerning one acre of land with appurtenances in Keneboc and Martin Wulward, tenant, on the feast of St Michael one month. Martin calls to warrant Baldwin Blancgernun. A day is given for them to appear before the bench.
1199	435–6	Harvey son of Eustace petitioner v. Prior of Barnwell concerning 3 messuages in Cambridge which he inherited. The prior comes as defendant. A day is set for the feast of St Michael one month. Harvey has a writ and four knights and has chosen twelve to hold an assize.
	Vol. II	
1199–1200	53	Aug' of Cambridge must appear on the fourth day v. William le Burdelais concerning a plea of 42 acres of land and 5 acres of meadow with appurtenances in Madingley. He does not come but essoins himself. The land is placed in the hands of the King. He is summoned for the feast of St Martin 15 days. Harvey son of Eustace seeks to replevy the land.
1199–1200	97	Hugo son of Petronilla appeals Harvey son of Eustace concerning the King's peace, that on the Nativity of the Blessed Mary Harvey with others came armed to Hugo's house, entered it, broke his mother's arms and carried off the building ....
1199–1200	98	Harvey son of Eustace v. Gervase Wrench concerning one virgate of land with appurtenances in Gransden which he had inherited from Gilbert son of Dunning ....Harvey offers proof by Jordan of Riseburgh and by his body. A duel is arranged.
1199–1200	110	Harvey son of Eustace appoints William of Buckingham the elder his attorney
1199–1200	109–10	William le Burdelais petitions v. Aug'm of Cambridge concerning land in Madingley which is in the hands of the King [see p 53 above]. At the same time Harvey son of Eustace seeks to replevin the land [i.e. recover possession as the person with the strongest claim].
1199–1200	143	Precept by the sheriff to make inquiry concerning a messuage in Gamlingay claimed by Hugo son of Peter de Capella and Petronilla his mother and Hugo's sisters against Harvey son of Eustace. The jury finds in favour of Harvey.
1199–1200	147	Harvey son of Eustace who essoined himself for illness asks for a licence to come to court

(continued)

Date	Page	Summary
1199–1200	179	Walter de Insula stakes a claim to land in Babraham (*Braha*) which Harvey son of Eustace claims against Jordan the Goldsmith (*aurifaber*)
1199–1200	253	Adam de Falesha', attorney for Gilbert Peche, petitioner v. Simon Sexton concerning three virgates of land with appurtenances in Cheveley. Simon calls to warrant Harvey son of Eustace to be heard on the morrow of St John.
	Vol. V	
1207	39	A jury inquires whether the church of St Peter in the town was given by the king or by Herbert, chaplain, Reginald son of Alfred, William of Caldecot and Ivo Pipestraw. They say that neither the king nor his ancestors gave the church. But they know well that Langlinus, who held the church and was parson too, gave the church a second time, as was the custom in Cambridge, to his kinsman Sigar, who held it for 60 years or more, and was parson too. He gave it to his son Henry, who also held it for 60 years, and then gave it outright by charter to the Hospital of St John. [See Maitland, 1898, p 175, who notes that Absolon son of Sigar was tallaged in 1177]
	Vol. VII	
1214	105	Lecia, widow of Robert Fabro, and Thomas and Robert her sons, are attached to explain why they prosecuted in an ecclesiastical court a plea regarding a lay fee of John Fabro of Cambridge, contrary to the prohibition of the king. They come and explain themselves; they pay the king one mark for *licencia concordandi* and agree to plead only in a lay court.
	Vol. VII Appendix	
1199	343	Martin of Gamlingay appoints Geoffrey Picot his son in his place v. Harvey son of Eustace in a plea of land to win or lose
1199	349	Michael son of Orgar v. Harvey son of Eustace on Wednesday after the feast of St Bartholomew concerning his land in Cambridge which, as surety, is in the king's hands for default.
	Vol. VIII	
1220	70–1	The Lepers of St Mary Magdalene of Cambridge by their attorney v. Everard of Trumpington concerning a messuage and 20 acres of land with appurtenances in Howes, to which others have no entry except by William their father because the term of lease has expired. Everard comes and defends his right of entry, and says that he holds the land by inheritance, and that his father held in fee for 40 years. The lepers can produce no evidence and put themselves on the country. Everard wins the case. The lepers can seek more evidence if they wish.
1220	275	Prior of Barnwell on the fourth day v. Leticia of Trumpington in a plea concerning the right of presentation of a suitable parson to the church of St John which is vacant. She does not come and is summoned. Judgement: to appear at Easter 15 days.
1220	282	Mabilia de Marenny puts in place John de Marenny v. Prior of Barnwell in a plea of advowson.

(continued)

Date	Page	Summary
1220	287	The assize come to inquire who presented the last parson, who is now dead, to the church of St John, which is vacant. John Marenny claims v. the Prior of Barnwell. The Prior says that the inquiry should not proceed because William son of Absolon presented the last parson and the late William handed down the right of appointment to Hugo his brother, who after he died with seisin of the land and no heirs gave the church to the priory by charter, to which he testifies. John says that the advowson descended to Mabilia his mother from the aforesaid Hugo and she demised her land and so the advowson belongs to her heirs. Because his mother is still alive and is not present and is not named in the writ, judgement is for the prior. John is in mercy and cannot proceed without his mother, but is pardoned.
1220	288	Mabilia de Marenny is summoned to explain why she did not allow the prior of Barnwell to present a suitable parson to the church of St John. Adam son of Philip is summoned in the same way, and he concedes that Hugo son of Absalon gave the church to the priory by charter. But to complicate matters, William son of Absolon, brother of Mabilia and uncle of the said Adam on his mother's side, presented the clerk who was the last parson, now deceased, and the said William passed the advowson to the aforesaid Hugo his brother, and the said Hugo, through lack of heirs, gave the same to Mabilia, mother of the said Adam, and her sisters, and he therefore seeks seisin. The prior concedes that William made the last presentation and that the advowson descended to Hugo his brother, but insists that Hugo gave the advowson by charter to the priory. Adam says that the charter was not intended to do harm [to the family], and was made when William faced terminal illness, sickness of death, and a crisis where he was unable to see. The prior says that he had full powers, was acting according to religion, that he lived for a long time and that the charter was made in the Cambridge court and witnessed by many men of the town. Agreement is made by *licencia justiciariorum* with cirograph. [See M, p 176]
	Vol. IX	
1220	60–1	The sheriff orders the bailiffs of Cambridge to make a record in the court of the exchanges between Mabilia de Novacurt, petitioner, and Adam of Cokefield, defendant, regarding a third part of 72 acres and 2.5 marks of rent with appurtenances in Cambridge, which she claimed in dowry. On the feast of Holy Trinity 15 days Harvey son of Martin, John Crocheman, Walter son of Walter and Walter son of Ernest come to record what she demands.... After all essoins have been made and a view taken as requested, Adam comes and says that he will not respond to the writ … as all the land and rent are held freely, and not in desmesne or by rent, which those present know, namely his tenants William Faber, Henry son of Elie, Harvey son of Eustace, William cementarius, Andrew Molle and Osbert le Rey. As Mabilia cannot answer, the judgement is that Adam can go, and she can seek another writ if she wishes.
		Mabilia comes and says that the record in only partly correct and suggests a compromise. The four men maintain that, saving the liberty of the town, Adam did not hold the land at the time of the writ. They will defend their judgment through the body of a free man in the court, namely John [their champion]. As Adam is absent on a journey, the case is adjourned to the morrow of St Peter and St Paul 15 days. [Bracton, case 1393; M, pp 184–5]

(continued)

Date	Page	Summary
1220	178	Mabilia de Novacurt v. Adam of Cokefield continued. The four men say that Wiliam Faber holds 4 acres and one rood annually and more in fee by charter from Adam; Henry son of Elie holds one acre in the same way; Harvey son of Eustace holds 26.5 acres and another 2.5 acres annually for 15 years; Andrew Molle half an acre in the same way; and Osbert le Rey 3 acres in the same way. They all say that they held this land annually in over forty transactions.
1220	325	Mabilia de Novacurt v. Adam of Cokefield continued. On the feast of St Hilary three weeks a chirograph is made by which Mabilia renounces all claims in return for one mark rent for her life. Adam appoints Robert le Poher in his place.
	Vol. XII	
1225	165	Letitia daughter of John on the fourth day v. Richard de Argentin concerning a plea of who holds a messuage in Cambridge outside the Trumpington Gate which Richard claimed v. William of St Edmunds and Alice his wife and which Master Geoffrey, grandfather of the aforesaid Letitia, held. Richard did not come and was summoned. Judgement: he is attached for the feast of St Martin 15 days. On this day William is at the bench and Alice essoins herself.
	Vol. XIII	
1227	19	William, cantor of Barnwell, William, Dean of Cambridge and John, prior of the Hospital of Cambridge, are attached to respond to Adam son of Walter and Silvester of Salfleteby concerning why they pleaded concerning chattels in an ecclesiastical court. Philip, parson of the church of St Clement, is attached to explain why he followed the same mode, contrary to prohibition. They all come and say that they hold no pleas of any kind. Adam and Silvester produce no suit, and the four go free. Adam and Silvester are in mercy for false claims by pledge of Peter of Fulebek.
1228	187	John of Stowe by his attorney on the fourth day v. William Blancgernun concerning rent of 3.5 marks which he owed. William does not come. The sheriff is ordered to attach him. The sheriff instructs the bailiffs of Cambridge, but they do nothing. The sheriff is further instructed for the octave of St Martin.
1229	312	Harvey son of Martin for himself and Alice his wife, whom he represents v. Richard de Argentin, who calls to warrant John de Gravele, concerning a messuage with appurtenances in Cambridge. Harvey claims that Alice through Alice her aunt on her mother's side holds a fee in law and domain from the time of King Henry and takes a profit of 5s and more. The said aunt passed on this land to Margaret her daughter, sister of the said Alice …He offers half a mark for an inquiry. Richard comes and defends his seisin by words and by body through his free man [champion] John son of Radulph. Harvey repeats his offer. Agreement is made by *licencia justiciariorum*.

(continued)

Date	Page	Summary
1229	316	Walter Ambechese is attached to respond to Alice daughter of Stephen of Trumpington concerning why he withholds rent to be paid by charter. Walter comes to say that the charter is invalid *in Judaismo* and he cannot acquit it. A day is given in Easter three weeks to produce the charter, but the charter is not offered to the bench and so Alice has the messuage and the charter is returned. [The sheriff later enforces this decision, p 410]
1230	538	William de Burdeleys v. Harvey son of Eustace regarding 40 acres of land with appurtenances in Madingley. Harvey comes and requests a view. A date is set for Holy Trinity 15 days …
1230	558	Robert son and heir of Nicholas le Moyne v. Harvey son of Eustace concerning a quarter of a knight's fee with appurtenances. Harvey is attached to explain why he has failed to pay a fine of 10s annually by chirograph before the justices in eyre in Huntingdon. Harvey comes and says that he has offered the payment many times but Robert would not take it. The fine is paid.
	Vol. XIV	
1231	270	The assize comes to determine the advowson in time past by which the parson, who is dead, was presented to the church of St Michael, which is vacant. John son of Isanti claims it v. Walter son of Apsolon. Walter says that the assize should not be taken because Ivo Pipestraw appointed William son of Apsolon, now deceased, to the church, and he was the last parson. Ivo died without heirs and had four sisters, namely Alice, first-born, grandmother of the aforesaid John; Dera, the second-born, mother of Walter; Matilda, the third-born; and Albreda, who died without heirs. After the death of Ivo, Alice and Matilda confirmed Master William son of Apsolon, brother of Walter, who is his heir, to the church by charter, to which they testify. Walter seeks judgement before John can respond. John, who is a minor, concedes that Ivo had four sisters and died without an heir, but says that nothing shows that the advowson should go to Walter. When he comes of age and recovers his charters he can become a clerk and be presented by the bishop, and so the entire advowson should come to him. [See Maitland, 1898, pp 175–6]
	Vol. XV	
1233	21	Richard Faber and Alice his wife v. William Basset, whom the Prior of Hatfield called to warrant concerning half a messuage with appurtenances in Cambridge. Richard and Alice say they have entrance through Mabilia, daughter of Robert and sister of Alice, who released the property to Alice, who was her heir. William says that Alice never had seisin because her father gave the messuage in marriage to Elie and Mabilia, and after the death of Elie Mabilia gave the messuage to him and he released it to the prior. [Mabilia is presumably dead.] The sheriff is to arrange for 12 men to determine on oath which account is true and to report to the county court on the octave of Holy Trinity. After the inquiry reported, the two parties made concord by chirograph.

(continued)

Date	Page	Summary
1233–4	87	Prior of Ely on the fourth day v. Richard, Dean of Cambridge, Adam, Dean of Chesterton, and William, precentor of Barnwell, questioning why they held a plea of the advowson of Alington chapel in an ecclesiastical court contrary to prohibition. They do not come. The sheriff is to inquire why they do not use a lay court. Mandate for the Bishop of Ely to come on the feast of St Hilary 15 days.
1233–4	97	Mabilia widow of Roger Parleben on the fourth day v. Andrew of Wigenhale concerning a plea of portions of two messuages with appurtenances in Cambridge; *and* v. Anthony, Master of the Hospital of St John, concerning a portion of a messuage with appurtenances in the same town; *and* v. Richard son of Wylle and Humanam his wife and Peter son of Radulph and Eleanor his wife concerning a portion of 30d rent with appurtenances in the same town; *and* v. Harvey of Hinton concerning a portion of 2 acres with appurtenances in the same town; *and* v. Roger son of Godard concerning a third of an acre with appurtenances in Madingley. All claimed in dower. No-one comes, and so they are summoned. Judgement: the portions are placed in the king's hands and the case adjourned to the feast of St Hilary 15 days.
1234–5	129	Elota widow of Isanti son of Lefwyn v. John Absolon concerning a third part of 4 acres of land with appurtenances in Cambridge for dower. John comes and says that the summons is unreasonable as he has next Monday (the first after All Souls) as his day. John appoints Thomas of Therlton' in his place.
1234–5	148	Elota widow of Isanti son of Lefwyn v. John Absolon continued. John comes and says that she [Elota] does not have dowry because Isanti never held the land, neither before or after he was married, and he puts himself on the country; and Elota similarly. The sheriff is ordered to have 12 men appear on the feast of Hilary one month and swear on oath whether Isanti held the land either on the day he was married or afterwards. The jurors report that Isanti did not have the land on the day of his marriage and that dowry is not possible. John goes free; Elota pauper.

(continued)

Date	Page	Summary
1235	358–9	Alexander de Bancis and Elicia his wife, with Margaret and Cecilia her sisters, complain to the king that, when possessed of a house which descended to them in law through Richard Burghard', uncle of Elicia and her sisters, in the king's peace, on the Sunday before the Purification in the 19th year of the king's reign, there came Paul Wombe, John Potekin, Henry Potekin, John Gogging, Michael Gogging, Simon Godelot [Godso], Richard of Ditton, Geoffrey the Fichgoer', Simon of Newnham, Harvey Wombe, Nicholas Wombe, William Goldsmith [Aurifaber], Walter Crocheman, Osbert Goldsmith, Gregory Edward', Alan brother of Henry Pikerell', Dru the chaplain, Peter Beket, William Brodie, Nigel [Nicholas?] beyond the Market, Robert Tobbin [Toylet?], Thomas Eliot and many others. They broke into the house and assaulted, wounded and shamefully treated them, and rang the bells to attract others. It is claimed that Paul Wombe struck Andrew of Balsham, who was in the house at the time, with a hatchet and pike in the loin, endangering his life; Simon Godelot wounded William le Paumer twice in the head; and Michael Bernard wounded Radulph le Bole horribly in the head; Nicholas Wombe wounded Richard son of Simon with a stick; and Simon of Newnham knifed Stephen Coco in the left arm; and others similarly.
		Harvey son of Eustace, mayor, and Geoffrey Potekin, coroner and provost, are required to explain why they did not use force to impede the delinquents, nor attach them. The mayor and coroner did not respond, nor produce any record. The mayor and bailiffs made no inquiry, and so the liberties of the town are taken into the king's hands. It cannot be denied that the bells were rung.
		Radulph le Thanur of Newnham, John Alvenechild', Warin Grim, Michael Bernard, Reginald Enfut, and Richard of Newnham, transgressors, did not come. The coroner is in custody as he did not make inquiry nor keep a record. It is not known whether Andrew of Balsham has escaped. All the others are attached and held at Northampton [where the king would be 24–27 March 1235]. The petitioners have seisin of the house. The question of whether Richard of Burghard died seized of the messuage is unresolved.
	Vol. XVI	
1239	188	Wiliam Blodles is summoned to respond to Michael Malerbe regarding a plea of customary service in villeinage on a messuage, a croft and 9 acres of land in Newnham, namely 3s 6d rent, and 6 fowls, two days reaping, two days hoeing, a *merchetum* [fine] for giving his daughter in marriage, and a tallage at will. William has withheld service amounting to 10 marks to the damage of Michael. Michael says that Hamo le Butillier and Eleanor his wife, whose villein William is, gave by charter, which Michael produces, fully and without reservation, the customary services of Christiana of Newnham and William her son, held from Isabella of Neddingworth, chief lord. This seisin was given 10 years ago.
		William comes and defends himself. He says that he is a free man and is not Michael's tenant. He does not owe service, and puts himself on the country; and Michael similarly. The sheriff is ordered to make inquiry through a jury of 12 men.

(continued)

Date	Page	Summary
	Vol. XVII	
1242–3	178	John [son of] Isaud' by his attorney v. John Absolon concerning 7 acres with appurtenances in a suburb of Cambridge, involving two writs. John comes and requests a view, which he has. A date is set for the octave of the Purification.
1242–3	407	Alicia, widow of Geoffrey Potekin v. Roger of Fulbourn concerning a third part of a messuage with appurtenances in Cambridge in dowry. Roger comes and warrants John Potekin. He has him with the arrival of the justices.
1242–3	412	John son of Isanti v. John son of Absolon concerning 3 acres of land with appurtenances in a suburb of Cambridge. Alicia, grandmother of John, held the land in fee in the time of King John for her profit ... Alicia passed on the land to Isanti her son and heir, and so on... John son of Absolon then comes and defends his right. He recognises that Alice had seisin of the land in fee. Alice enfeoffed William son of Absolon, John's father, whose heir he is, by charter to which he testifies, and he puts himself before a jury of the town of Cambridge as to whether he has the greater right to the land. A day is set on the arrival of the justices, and 12 jurors are convened.
1242–3	417	John son of Isanti v. John son of Absolon continued. John son of Isanti asserts that his ancestor Ivo Pipestraw died in the reign of King John seized of a half-mark rent from the land in question. Ivo died without heirs and the land descended to Matilda and Alice his sisters, and when Matilda also died without heirs it descended to Isanti, Alice's son, and thence to his son John. John son of Absolon concedes that Ivo died seized of the land, but says that Ivo had three sisters, not two, the third being Dera, his mother. Therefore let things stand and John son of Isanti can sue with another writ if he wishes.
1243	485	[The heirs of William Ruffus in court at Huntingdon concerning property held in Cambridge and elsewhere.] Reginald le Moyne on the fourth day v. Emma de Legh' concerning who holds a fine made in the king's court at Westminster between Beringerus le Moyne and Isabella his wife, mother of the said Reginald, whose heir he is, and Radulph de Trubevil' and Alice his wife, sister of Emma, whose heir she is, concerning a reasonable portion [of property] which Beringerus and Isabella claimed through inheritance from William Ruffus, father of both Isabella and Alice, in Armeston, Kingham and Eggel, and also a reasonable portion which they claimed as heirs of Nicola, mother of Isabella and Alice, in Hemmingford', Gilling' and Cambridge by chirograph ... Emma does not come, and many of the others default. The sheriff is orderd to distrain the lands in question and to have the litigants present at Holy Trinity one month.
	Vol. XVIII	
1242	21	A day is set for Matthew Cristien' v. Nicholas le Vavasur and Agnes his wife concerning 23 messuages with appurtenences in Cambridge to be made by chirograph on the feast of St John the Baptist three weeks. Matthew appoints Richard of Abinton or Herbert of Hawkeston [Hauxton] in his place, and Nicholas and Agnes appoint Laurence del Brok'.

(continued)

Date	Page	Summary
1242	83	Matilda widow of John son of the Dean on the fourth day v. Thomas Miller (*Molend'*) concerning a plea of a third part of 2s rent with appurtenances in Newnham, and the same v. the Hospital of St John concerning a third part of a messuage with appurtenances in Cambridge, both of which she claims as dowry. They do not come and are summoned. The third parts are placed in the hands of the king. The defendants are summoned for the morrow of All Souls.
1243	128–9	The bailiffs of Cambridge are attached to respond to Baldwin de Akeny that they take toll and passage at Whittlesford [*Wicleford'*] bridge to the great detriment of Baldwin's market at Whittlesford. They infringe his liberty by charging 2d for every cart that crosses the bridge, 1d for a horse and 0.5d for a pedestrian to a total damage of £60. The bailiffs say that it is not possible for them to respond without the king because they hold the right of toll at farm from the king. The king holds toll and passage in remote parts of the county, at Reach, 9 leagues distant, and Swavesey, 6 leagues distant. From the time of King Henry II the bailiffs have held seisin. Furthermore neither the bridge in question nor the water is in the fee of Baldwin, but in the fee of Saher of St Andrea. The bailiffs claim that they can take custom from all carts, unless they come from a liberty of the king (such as Cambridge) or of the Knights Templar or some other liberty. A record of the discussion is considered at the king's court at Westminster. The consensus is that the sheriff should summon 12 men on the morrow of the Purification to decide between the two claims. [For Baldwin's initial complaint see Close Rolls, 1242–7, pp 6–7, which states that he is overseas on the king's service. VCH Cambridgeshire, vol. 6, p 270 suggests that the outcome is that Baldwin takes the toll only on his market day. Also see below.]
1244	344	William Bleuet essoins Eustace son of Harvey on the fourth day v. Leon son of Adam concerning a plea that he had an agreement with Eustace regarding two parts of a mill at Newnham. Leon does not come and is summoned. He is attached for the octave of St Michael.
1243	374	Baldwin de Akeny v. bailiffs of Cambridge continued. Essoin. A day at Easter five weeks is set for hearing a plea of liberty through Robert le Waleys. Affidavit.
1243	383	Bailiffs of Cambridge v. Baldwin de Akeny concerning a plea of transgression by Albredus le Messager. Essoin. A day is set for St Michael one month.
	Vol. XIX	
1249	43	Constantia widow of Alan of Bassingbourn v. The Prior of Mount Carmel on the fourth day, concerning a plea of a portion of a messuage with appurtenances in Newnham as dowry. The prior does not come, and is summoned. Judgement: the portion is in the hands of the king. Summons for the feast of St Hilary 15 days.
1249	45	Alicia wife of Nicholas Malerbe appoints Nicholas her man or John Crocheman as her attorney v. John de Sumery in a plea of land (see below).

(continued)

Date	Page	Summary
1249	68	Margaret widow of Michael Parleben v. William son of Ivo concerning a third part of 4 acres of land with appurtenances in Cambridge as dowry. William comes and calls to warrant John of Barton, who warrants that William is Michael's son and heir, and is a minor in the custody of Margaret [by charter of enfeoffment from Michael, which he produces]. A day is set for Easter 15 days. Margaret presents a charter of enfeoffment. [See below.] [The William who is warranted appears to be William son of Michael Parleben.]
1249	68	Emma de Meauton by attorney on the fourth day v. Simon Prat concerning a plea of 40s rent which he owes as a fine made between them in the court of the itinerant justices at Cambridge. Simon did not come and the sheriff was ordered to seize his lands and chattels, take the money, and give it to Emma. But the sheriff did nothing except mandate the bailiffs, who also did nothing. The sheriff is ordered to implement the order he was given and to have the money at the court at Westminster on the feast of St Hilary 15 days.
1249	68	Nicholas Malerbe and Alicia his wife, petitioners v. John de Sumery concerning one messuage and 5 acres of land with appurtenances in Haslingfield, of which Robert Skyleman, a relative of Alice, whose heir she is, died seized in desmesne and fee. John came and warranted Traer a Poel and Matilda his wife, Ernald de Munteny and Amabilia his wife, Hubert de Monte Caniso and Ela his wife and Peter son and heir of Thomas Picot, who is a minor in the custody of J. de Plesseto, Earl of Warwick. They have a day St Hilary 15 days in Hertfordshire. Alicia appoints Nicholas her man as her attorney.
1250	236	Alvred son of Disaud' v. Cecilia de Gedesho [Godso] and Amicia her sister concerning 7 acres of land with appurtenances in a suburb of Cambridge. Cecilia and Amicia come before this the bailiffs of Cambridge and petition the court with a charter for the land which they offered, and they have it.
1250	362	A day is given for Matilda, widow of Baldwin Blancgernun, to petition Harvey the Serjeant, Roger son of Warin and all others named in the writ of tenancy concerning a plea of dower in Cambridge on the feast of St John the Baptist 15 days. The bailiffs of Cambridge come and petition the court. The decision is that the bailiffs hold the tenancy in the meantime.
	Vol. XX	
1250	100	Margaret widow of Michael Parleben v. John of Barton concerning one third of a quarter acre of land with appurtenances in Cambridge as her dowry. [A continuation of a previous case but with a different defendant.] John comes and says that he does not need to respond as he pleaded this case before the itinerant court of Henry de Bathon and his associates at Cambridge [see above] where he warranted Hugo the son and heir of Michael Parleben, Margaret's man, who was a minor and in Margaret's custody. Afterwards Margaret came and withdrew all claim and John went free. [According to the original case John warranted William as the son rather than Hugo (see above); William son of Michael Parleben is well documented elsewhere but there is no other record of Hugo.]

Note: Volumes in the sequence I–XX that are not listed contain no entries directly relevant to Cambridge people or places. In the early rolls several items are repeated from year to year.

Source: *Rotuli Curiae Regis/Curia Regis Rolls*, Vols. I–XX

Appendix 7

Selected excerpts from *Calendar of Fine Rolls* I–III, relating to people and places in Cambridge

Date	Page	Summary
	Vol. I	
1222–3	300	Cambridge is tallaged for 25 marks [25m], and its neighbour Chesterton for 6m. By comparison, York is tallaged for 400m, Oxford for 200m, Norwich for 100m and Ipswich for 35m.
1223–4	397–8	The men of Cambridge pay a fine of 40m for having the house formerly of Bonenfant the Jew, which is in the king's hands, to be used to make a gaol. Service of 1m to the king and 2s to the chief lord of the fee.
	Vol. II	
1226	155–6, fn.1	Tallage for Cambridge is pardoned up to 100m, which was the amount actually owed. For comparison, Huntingdon owed 30m, Godmanchester 50m, Southampton 100m and York at 500m [The amounts originally assessed are not given]
1230–1	382	The men of Cambridge can purchase a plot, formerly of Bonenfant the Jew near to the stone house, from the king, for the use of the Friars Minor, if they give the king surety for 5m. The friars will then have seisin.
	Vol. III	
1234–5	37	The men of Cambridge have been fined 100m because the king took the town into his hands following a recent trespass. The sheriff, together with Matthew Christian and Henry de Colevill, is to go to Cambridge to ensure that the fine is assessed in full in view of the mayor and 12 trustworthy men, so that the paupers of the town are less aggrieved, and are spared for longer. Once collected, the fine must be at the Exchequer on the close of Easter in the 19th year. Matthew and Henry are to hasten to Cambridge.

(continued)

Date	Page	Summary
1234–5	52	[Continuation of above] The men of Cambridge have agreed to hand over on bail until the first session of the court Geoffrey Wombe, Geoffrey le Fittere, Simon of Newnham and William Goldsmith, indicted for the death of Andrew of Balsham. They can be released from prison at Northampton once 12 trustworthy and law-worthy men have been found to mainpern them.
1240–1	433	Cambridge is tallaged 40m and Chesterton 15m.

Appendix 8

Cambridge debts: selected cases from the Exchequer of the Jews, 1219–81

Date	Reference	Summary
1219	I, p 12	*The Prior of Barnwell is accused of occupying land forfeited to the King through debts owing to the Jews.* The Prior of Barnwell appears to a summons to show by what warrant etc. he entered upon land in Brunn [Bourne?] that belonged to Simon de Turri. The land is the King's gage for a debt owing by Simon to the Jews. The Prior produces three charters touching 7 acres, which Simon gave him, to wit, 2 in frankalmoigne, and 5 after a loan. Simon appears and warrants the Prior the 7 acres and the charters. The Prior appoints Master Ralph his attorney to hear his judgement. On Easter quindene Geoffrey de Turri appears and quitclaims to the Prior and convent the 5 acres that his father gave them in frankalmoigne. So Geoffrey is in mercy. *Note*: See also p 13, concerning Ralph, serjeant, Everard son of Milo and Hamo Peche
1220	I, p 28	The Prior of Barnwell warrants Geoffrey son of Eustace a messuage with appurtenances in Cambridge
1220	I, p 31	*Maurice Ruffus is accused of occupying land forfeited to the King through debts owing to the Jews.* Mandate to the Sheriff to summon Maurice Ruffus, John Litlebir', Everard of Trumpington, Robert of Madingley, Henry the Tailor and William Bainard to be before the justices at Westminster on the octave of St John to show by what warrant they entered upon the lands late of Albric of Madingley which are gages of the King, and that he inquire how much each of them hold and for how long they have held it, and what it be worth by the year, and what and how much they have received thereof etc. [see also I, pp. 12, 35, 53]

(continued)

Date	Reference	Summary
	I, p 54	*Maurice Ruffus is acquitted*. Maurice Ruffus goes quit of the debt that is demanded of him on account of the debts of Albric de Madingley, for the inquest testifies that his 20 acres of land late of the said Albric ... have been held by him and his father for 28 years and the term of the loan is 15 years. [*Note*: Albric could not have included this land in his pledge because he had already sold it at the time of the loan. The other accused are also acquitted for similar reasons.]
1244	I, p 62	John of Shelford paid Samuel son of Isaac and the heirs of Moses, son of Isaac, 100s due Michaelmas 27 Hen III and 100s due in the Easter term on account of a fine of £40.
1244	I, p 70	Henry de Colville offered himself on the fourth day against Philip [of Stanton] touching a plea that he acquit him of £40 with interest against Aaron de Blund. Philip defaulting on appearance, order that he be attached etc. on the quindene of St John to answer... [*Note*: See also I, pp 91–2.]
1253	I, p 119	John le Rus offered himself on the fourth day against Isaac son of Moses of Cambridge touching a plea of account. Isaac failing to appear, ... let him come on the octave of Holy Trinity ... Isaac of Senlis, Josce of Wyleton and Aaron le Blund, Isaac's mainpernors, are in mercy. The sheriff is Simon de Hochton.
1270	I, p 269	*Distraint of a debtor to the King on Jewish account*. Mandate to the sheriff that he distrain Philip de Colville, son and heir of Henry de Colville, to pay him for the use of the King £50 owing on Jewish account, so that he may have the money on the quindene of St John the Baptist to deliver to the Justices. The sheriff made no return and sent no word, so, as before, on the octave of St Hilary. *Note*: See also II, p 61
1272	I, p 282	*Abraham Motun accused of cheating*. Nicholas Hereward, tenant of part of the lands of William de Burgo, offered himself by his attorney etc. against Abraham Motun, touching a plea that, whereas he discharged a debt of 5 marks owing by the said William to the said Jew and has in his possession the sealed part of the charter withdrawn from the chirograph chest, the said Jew unlawfully detains the moiety of the charter that remains in his possession, and will not give it up ... The Jew failing to appear, and being already under distraint, mandate to the sheriff that ... he distrain him more ... The sheriff sends word that he has the chattels in safe keeping and that the Jew has no more chattels. And Karolo son of Jacob, and Isaac of York, his mainpernors, do not have him. Wherefore they are in mercy for the feast of St John Baptist month.

(continued)

Date	Reference	Summary
1272	I, p 282	*Abraham Motun accused of violence*. Geoffrey de Sawston, by his attorney, offered himself on the fourth day against Abraham Motun touching a plea that, with William Leverer and John Page, Abraham came with force and arms to Geoffrey's house in Sawston and broke his doors and drove away his beasts, valued at 60s, against the King's peace. Abraham failing to appear, and being already under distraint, mandate to the sheriff to distrain him more, etc. The sheriff sends word (as above) … *Note*: See also I pp 304–5, II p 5. Abraham cannot be found and has nothing in his bailiwick by which he can be distrained.
1272	I, p 305	*Dispute over ownership of land*. Writ of the King under the great seal to Roger Seyton and his fellow Justices in Eyre in the County of Cambridge, whereto the said Justices return, that Hugh Vivien and others were attached to answer Robert son of Robert de Houston touching a plea of novel disseisin … concerning a messuage, 55 acres of land, 5 acres of meadow and 3s rent, with appurtenances in Houston and Wychton. Hugh and the others come by Richard of Tuleslonde, their bailiff, and say that … Hugh has seisin of the lands and tenements by gage of a fee-debt of £12 which Hugh bought from Aaron son of Vives according to the Custom of Jewry. They admit that they till the land. Robert denies any debts. He says that Hugh and the others ejected him and took away his corn. Day assigned Michaelmas three weeks for judgement. *Note*: See also II, p 28
1273	II, p 29	*Allegation of unlawful distraint and violence*. Aaron son of Vives offered himself on the fourth day against Geoffrey, Dean of Cambridge, touching a plea that Geoffrey unlawfully demands more rent than is owed, and distrains him and his tenants in Cambridge, …. and causes them to be flayed, against the King's Peace. The Dean fails to appear. Mandate to the sheriff that he compel his appearance. The sheriff sends word that the Dean has no lay fee by which he may be attached. Therefore mandate the Bishop of Ely that he distrain him by his ecclesiastical chattels, so that he have his body etc. on the morrow of the feast of St Margaret. On which day the Bishop sent no word but returned the King's writ under his own seal. Therefore as before, Michaelmas month. On which day the Bishop neither sent word nor returned the writ. Therefore, as before, Hilary octave.

(continued)

Date	Reference	Summary
1273	II, p 43	*Humphrey of St Edmunds serves on an inquisition concerning Jewish property.* And whereas it is said that Belecote [a woman] has also the moiety of a house in Cambridge, therefore mandate to the sheriff that he inquire etc. and return the inquest on Michaelmas octave. On which day came the inquest by Nicholas Goldsmith, Abraham le Chapeler, Humphrey of St Edmunds, John Warin, Adam Scot. Jacob of Newmarket, Benedict of Newport, Salomon son of Aaron and others, who say upon their oath that the said Samuel had nothing in the county of Cambridge but two houses which are worth by the year, saving the lord's service, 5s 2d. For one of these houses Belecote gives the King 20d, which she pays to the King's receipt. Mandate to the sheriff that he give her administration thereof.
1273	II, p 74	*A Jew pleads sickness.* Robert son of Robert de Hoghton, offered himself on the fourth day against Aaron son of Vives touching a plea that he come to hear the inquest into the cause between him and the said Aaron and Andrew Bolstan (or Bocstan) touching unlawful distraint. Upon Aaron's default of appearance, mandate the constable to compel it. The constable sends word that Aaron is sick and keeps to his bed. Order as before, Michaelmas octave; on which day the constable sends word that Aaron is sick; wherefore Hilary octave. *Note:* Continued on pp 74–5.
1273	II, p 74	Robert son of Robert de Hoghton, offered himself on the fourth day against Hugh Vivien, Henry de Caysho and William Saumplus touching a plea that they come to hear the record and judgement in a case of novel disseisin (as above). The sheriff sends word that Hugh Vivien is not found, that Henry de Caysho has nought by which he may be attached and that William Saumplus has neither. Wherefore Michaelmas octave. *Note:* Continued on pp 74–5.
1273	II, p 112	*Payment of a debt to the King on Jewish account.* Be it remembered that Alexander de Stivichele came and acknowledged obligation to pay the King for Fulk son of Richard £6 which the said Fulk owes the King on account of Manser, son of Josce, to wit on the morrow of St Lucy 40s (which he paid in the King's Receipt), on Hilary quindene 40s and on Easter quindene 40s. The sheriff sends word that Richard de Hetot, James son of Hugh de Weston, Walter son of Martin and William de Gosholm mainperned for Alexander. On Hilary quindene Alexander came and paid 40s.

(continued)

Date	Reference	Summary
1273	II, p 117	*The House of Merton clears debts to the Jews on property it has acquired.* Acknowledgement by Saunte son of Ursell, for himself and his assigns, in favour of the Warden of the House of Scholars of Merton … of quittance of all right … that he had … in all the lands and tenements which they hold in Grantchester … by sale and demise of William of Appelford, late debtor to the said Jew, or elsewhere, on account of any debt of the said William … by charter, tally, or other instrument, within the chirograph chest or without, from the creation to the end of the world. Executed on the quindene of St John the Baptist, 1 Edward I.
1274	II, p 142	*Debts of Ralph le Rus.* William of Middleton offered himself on the fourth day against Ralph le Rus touching a plea of debt. Mandate to the sheriff that he distrain Ralph by lands etc. and have his body before etc. on this day. The sheriff neither sends nor return the writ; wherefore as before, for Michaelmas quindene. Payment made.
1274	II, p 134	*Dispute over who is to settle a debt to the King on Jewish account.* Master Luke of Ely, tenant of part of the lands of William de Wendlinge, being distrained for the quota for which he is answerable of a debt of £28 in which William was bound to the King … warrants John Wygerns as bound to acquit him. Geoffrey de Byteringe, tenant of part of the said lands … vouches to warranty William de Haulus'. Robert de Stuteville, tenant of part of the said lands, comes and …. vouches to warranty the Abbot of Wendlinge. Therefore mandate to the sheriff of Norfolk and Suffolk that he cause the said John and William and the Abbot of Wendlinge to come … on Michaelmas quindene to answer etc. And Stephen de Oxecroft came and vouched to warranty the Abbot of Laungle and has the same day.
1274	II, p 179	*Robert Hubert and Agnes Barton accused of concealing Jewish goods and chattels forfeit to the King.* Mandate to the sheriff that he cause the Prior of Royston, Geoffrey Spartegrave, Robert Hubert, Agnes of Barton, Abraham Biscop and Muriel, widow of Saulot Motun, to come before, etc. to answer the King touching diverse goods and chattels late of the said Saulot, which should have come to the King's hands by reason of Saulot's death, and which they have received against the peace, etc. On their default of appearance, mandate to the sheriff that he compel their appearance. The sheriff sends word that the mainpernors of the Prior and Agnes of Barton do not have them (wherefore they are in mercy), that Robert Hubert is dead, and that Abraham Biscop and Muriel are not found. Order, that he distrain all the aforesaid and the heirs of the said Robert and have their bodies before etc. on Martinmas octave, to answer etc. and hear etc. John Porthors, who was present, has the same day. Afterward John Porthors came and paid in the Kings Receipt 32s, as did also Geoffrey Spartegrave 5s and Agnes of Barton 2s 6d. The sheriff did not return the writ, wherefore, as before, for Hilary octave. Note: See II, p 265 below for continuation.

(continued)

Date	Reference	Summary
3 Edw I, 1274–5	IV, p 17	*Royal inquiry into Jewish chirographers.* The chirographers of Cambridge produced six bonds: Bonenfant son of the Rabbi (magister) (4), Samuel son of Isaac (1), and Richard son of Benedict (1). The following had no bonds in the chest: Jacob son of Abraham Crespin, Josce son of Deulesant, Abraham son of Isaac, Manser son of Abraham, Isaac son of Samuel, Josce son of Benedict, Sampson son of Bela, Solomon son of Isaac, Duce daughter of Benedict, Precieuse le Veuve and Abraham Mutiun [Motun] de Salomon. The chirographers appeared a week late and were in mercy. *Margin*: Let them be excused.
3 Edw I, 1274–5	IV, p 49	*The sheriff settles his account with the King.* The sheriff, Walter of Shelfanger, appeared by his clerk Walter de Spartegrave and proffered 8.5 marks which he had paid into the Receipt for diverse debts. He owes 100 marks which he is to pay a fortnight after Easter, when he is to render his account.
1275	II, p 265	*Robert Hubert and Agnes Barton: continuation.* Mandate of the sheriff that he cause twelve honest men of Cambridge, and six lawful Jews to come before etc. to recognize whether Sabina, widow of Robert Hubert, or her husband, Robert, received of the goods and chattels of the said Saulot £10 worth, and whether John Porthors received of the said goods and chattels £14 worth, which should have come into the King's hand by reason of the Jew's death; or whether the said Sabina, Agnes and John received nought of the said chattels which, by mandate of the King, were delivered to Robert of Fulham, then Justice of King Henry assigned to the custody of the Jews, for the said King's use, as the said Sabina, Agnes and John aver.
		The said Sabina and John then came and gave the King 20s that the inquest might be held before Hamo Hauteyn or Robert of Lydham at Cambridge. Whereof, mandate to the sheriff that he cause so many and such etc. to come before etc., to recognise as above; and that he distrain the Prior of Royston [Geoffrey Spartegrave], Abraham Biscop, and Muriel, widow of the said Saulot, by land etc. and have their bodies etc. on this day, to answer the King ... The sheriff sends word that the mainpernors of the Prior of Royston do not have him, whereof they are in mercy, that Abraham Biscop is not found, and that Muriel .... resides in Lincoln. Order, that he have in safekeeping the lands etc. and have their bodies before etc. on the feast of St John the Baptist three weeks to answer etc. and hear etc.
		Afterwards the Prior had Michaelmas octave whereon to answer the King... Amercement remitted.

(continued)

Date	Reference	Summary
1275	II, p 307	Mandate to the sheriff that he cause twelve etc. to recognise whether the Abbot of Sawtry holds any lands and tenements late of William Perrot, John de Scalaris and William Cross, who are bound to the King in diverse debts of Jewry. The sheriff sends word that the jurors made default on appearance and that their mainpernors do not have them, wherefore they are in mercy. And whereas the Abbot also made default of appearance, it is adjudged that the King have his recovery of the debts against the Abbot and that the Abbot is in mercy.
1276	III, pp 116–18	*Henry le Rus and other tenants of the lands of Robert de Hasting' owe the king a portion of the debt Robert incurred to Moses the Jew of Clare.* Tenants of the lands of Robert de Hasting' owe the King £16 on account of the debts of Moses of Clare the Jew. The debt is apportioned amongst the tenants, and the sheriff is ordered to distrain them so that he may have the money before the quindene of St John the Baptist. [The portion due is equal to approximately two-thirds of the valuation.] The tenants and the portions they owe are: Philip son of Robert £6 13s; Prior of Fordham £4 7s; Robert the Prior of Ixninge 4s 4d; Prior of Spinney 4s 4d; Prioress of Swaffham 6.8d; Richard of Ikelingham 16s; Peter son of Alexander 11s; Martin son of Alice 2s; Geoffrey le Lung 11s; Henry le Rus 2s; Henry le Akitur 2s; Alexander Mercator 4s 4d; Thomas son of Peter 2s; Richard Ingelot 16d. The Prior of Spinney and the Prioress of Swaffham come to court and consent to pay. [The Prioress of Swaffham, however, subsequently challenged the debt (III, p 118).] The Prior of Fordham came and warranted for Henry de Hasting' [presumably the heir] who is under-age and is a ward of Philip son of Robert de Northampton.
5 Edw I 1276–7	IV, p 99	*A Jew attempts to recover a debt.* Manser son of Aaron brings an action of debt against Henry Whaddon, brother and heir of Thomas of Whaddon. The defendant did not appear and the sheriff was ordered to produce him. His mainpernors are in mercy. Adjourned to three weeks after Easter. *Note:* See V, p 64 for continuation.
1277	III, p 255; also IV, p 99	*Another Jew attempts to recover a debt.* Benjamin son of Cok, a Jew, offered himself on the fourth day against Richard le Brus, tenant of … Robert de Herford', touching a plea of debt. Richard did not appear and the sheriff was ordered to distrain him. Four mainpernors were appointed but could not produce him and so are in mercy. Judgement … that he have his body before the court on the quindene of St John the Baptist.

(continued)

Date	Reference	Summary
1277	III, p 274	*The sheriff is accused of understating the value of the property held by Henry of Childerle who owes money to the King.* The sheriff was ordered to distrain Henry de Childerle and Stephen de Eye for 10 marks which they owe the King on account of a debt of Leo [son] of Preciosa, a Jew... The sheriff sends word that Henry has no goods or chattels in his bailiwick other than his crops, while Stephen cannot be found and has no lands or tenements. The Justices agree that Henry has land and chattels, including lands in which Aaron the Jew has a moiety for a term of years. Therefore the sheriff, to wit William le Moyne, is in mercy. An order is made *sicut alias* for the quindene of Trinity.
1277	III, p 277	*William Gogging is accused of forgery of goods supplied to Jewish merchants.* The sheriff was ordered to cause to be attached William son of Bartholomew [Gogging], mayor of Cambridge, so that he should have his body on this day to answer the King touching certain false plates made (*conflatis*) of other metals than of pure silver, lately seized upon Benjamin son of Isaac and Aaron son of Benjamin, being in the prison of London, which the same Jews had by the delivery of the said William. The sheriff sent word that he had returned the writ to the bailiffs of the liberty of Cambridge who answered that there is no-one of that name. Judgement is that he omit not, etc. and cause to be attached the said Bartholomew and his son, to the intent that he have their bodies before etc. on the quindene of Trinity.
		Note: William Gogging exists but he is not Bartholomew's son; see Chapter 4 in Casson, Casson, Lee and Phillips, *Compassionate Capitalism*.

(continued)

Date	Reference	Summary
1277	V, p 11	*Members of an inquest jury fail to appear.* The sheriff was ordered to distrain Robert Christien, Edmund de Abiton, Roger of Bassingbourne, John Hamelin, Henry de Lacy, Richard le Breton, John Martin, John the Porter, Thomas the Draper, John the Carpenter, Henry of Linton, and Simon the Baker by lands etc. so as to have their bodies before the court to inquire into the case of William of Middleton, clerk of the Exchequer of the Jews and John of Badburgham, clerk. They did not come. The sheriff appointed mainpernors. Richard Walterot, Radulph son of John and Richard son of Radulph [only three listed] for Robert Christien; William Godyn of Abiton, Richard the Provost of Abiton, Richard Walterot and Nicholas Aylmer for Edmund of Abiton; Henry Tristram, Andrew le Messer, Geoffrey Spayne and Hugo le Marchaund for John Hamely; Simon Cockel, Matthew le Rue, Richard But and Peter Albueton' for Henry de Lacy; Alfred Mauten, Walter Man', Henry Elys and John Biscop for Henry of Linton; Richard le Petyt, Peter son of John, John Ottewy and Henry Coteman for Richard le Breton; Henry le White, John Pye, Nicholas le Cloyer and John Underwood for John Martin [mistake corrected]; John Botterell', John Crispe, Peter the Provost and John Wymark for John the Porter; Alan Wyppe, Robert Safrey, John the Draper and Henry de Hamestall' for Thomas the Draper; William Cosin, William le Katur, William Bernard and Alan le Kenteys for John the Carpenter; and Alfred Maunt, Walter le Man', Henry Elys and John Biscop for Henry de Linton. Because Simon le Pestur has no land, John Wymark, Nicholas le Cleyer, Henry le White and John Scryppe are his mainpernors. They cannot produce the men. Therefore they are in mercy. Judgement is that their lands are distrained and that they appear in court on quindene of the feast of St Hilary. And because the sheriff, William le Moigne, did not respond he is in mercy too.
1278	V, p 55	*A debtor to a Jew fails to appear.* Bonenfant of the Rose Cross, a Jew, presented himself on the fourth day v. Mathew of Northampton concerning a portion of land of Roger Giffard on which he owes him 22s by cirograph for 6 marks. Matthew does not come. The sheriff appoints Roger Petyt of Hokiton [Oakington] and Roger of Berkewey as mainpernors, but they cannot produce him and are in mercy. Judgement is that they are distrained, and will have his body in court on the octave of Holy Trinity.
1278	V, p 55	*Another debtor to a Jew fails to appear.* Aaron son of Vives, Jew, on the fourth day, v. Richard de Brus concerning a plea of debt involving land of Richard de Hereford'. The defendant did not come. The sheriff appointed William the Provost of Toleslund and William Peronnel as mainpernors but they could not produce him. Judgement is to distrain their lands, and that they will bring his body to court on the octave of Holy Trinity. *Note:* See also V, p 116.

(continued)

Date	Reference	Summary
1278	V, p 55	*Another debtor to a Jew fails to appear.* Josce son of Saulot on the fourth day v. Simon le Waleys concerning a plea of debt regarding land of Walter Chapleyn of Cottenham. Simon does not come. The sheriff appoints Roger Dolle of Cottenham and John of Bradfield as mainpernors, but they cannot produce Simon and are in mercy. Judgement is that they are distrained and must have his body in court on the octave of Holy Trinity.
1278	V, p 56	*Another debtor to a Jew fails to appear.* Bonevye son of Vives, a Jew, on the fourth day, v. Adam de Rugg concerning a plea of debt regarding land of Adam of Somery. Adam does not appear. The sheriff appoints Simon the Stabler and William Catel of Bassingbourne as mainpernors. They cannot produce Adam and are in mercy. Judgement is that they are distrained and must bring his body to court on the octave of Holy Trinity.
1278	V, p 56	*Distraint for an outstanding debt to the King.* Mandate to the sheriff to distrain William Baldwin by goods and chattels to render the King £20 regarding a debt of Aaron son of Vives. Thomas Gode, Albredo, clerk, and others who endorsed the document have tendered 30s. William is distrained for the residual, namely £18 10s.
1278	V, p 62	*A debtor suspected of concealing his goods and chattels.* Mandate to the sheriff not to overlook anything in the bailiwick of John de Kameys, son and heir of Radulph de Kameys. His father Radulph borrowed £100 from Hag' son of Master [Rabbi?] Moses the Jew, which debt is now in the hands of the King. John does not appear. The sheriff appoints Joseph atte Ston of Crawell, Edward son of Odon of Crawell, Radulph Muryel of Henxton and Godfrey Joye of Henxton as mainpernors. They cannot produce John and are in mercy. They are distrained to bring his body to court on the octave of Holy Trinity.
1278	V, p 64	*A dispute concerning land which is possibly encumbered with a debt to the Jews.* William of Leyburn on the fourth day v. Roger de Nowers and Isabella his wife concerning a plea of debt regarding lands of Ivo Quarel. Roger does not appear. The sheriff distrains Roger by land and chattels to the value of 4s. He appoints Thomas Ingrit of Bouton', William Bovebrok' of Bouton', William Cok and Thomas Prudfot as mainpernors. They cannot produce him and are in mercy. Judgement is that they are distrained to produce his body in court on the quindene of the feast of St John the Baptist . *Note:* See also V, p 115
1278	V, p 77	*Recognition of a debt to a Jew.* Robert Crestyen, son and heir of John of Abiton, recognises his debt to Ben[jamin] de Wynton, Jew, of 30 quarters of corn, or for every quarter half a mark rent, due on the feast of St Martin, or in the near future. If he defaults his land and chattels will be forfeit. [This entry suggests a price of 80d, per quarter of corn; see Chapter 6 for a comparison.]

(continued)

Date	Reference	Summary
1278	V, p 89	*Appointment of attorney in a plea of debt.* Thomas Bacun appoints Stephen de Coghton or John of Leversham as his attorney v. Roger son of Fabri in a plea of debt to the Jews. *Note*: See also V, p 115.
1278	V, p 96	*Loss of a document involving William of Manefield, associate of Walter Merton.* Memorandum that Gam of Oxford, Jew, acknowledges that he lost his part of a debt of £20 which William of Manefield held.
1278	V, p 98	*Another debtor to a Jew fails to appear.* Bonenfant of the Rose Cross presented himself on the fourth day v. Robert son of Robert of Drayton concerning a portion of land of Roger Giffard. Robert does not come. The sheriff appoints John le Fevre of Dry Drayton and Reginald le Batcheler as mainpernors, but they cannot produce him and are in mercy. Judgement is that they are distrained, and will have his body in court on the quindene of St Michael.
1278	V, p 115	Thomas Bacun on the fourth day v. Roger son of le Fevre of Croxton, William le Lepere and Joanna his wife, Robert Aylewyn, Cristianam de Maun and William Gorge concerning a plea of debt regarding lands of Ivo Quarel. They do not appear. The sheriff appoints mainpernors: Andrew le Chareter of Croxton and Stephen Knyth of Croxton for Roger; Roger Gunyld and Robert Maggot for William le Lepere [spelled Kepere]; Andrew le Chareter of Croxton and Roger Gunyld for Joanna his wife; John Yeyte and Richard his son for Robert Aylewyn; Andrew le Chareter and Walter Luce for Cristian de Maun; and Stephen the Chaplain and Walter Luce for William Gorge. They cannot produce them and are in mercy. Judgement is that they are distrained and must bring their bodies before the court at the feast of All Souls. *Note*: See also V, p 64.
1278	V, p 130	*Inquest into the authenticity of a starr.* The sheriff ordered six Christians from Cambridge and six Jews from Huntingdon to attend court in Cambridge on the feast of St Jacob to determine the truth concerning a starr of John son of William of Orset made by Jacob Grubbe, Jew, as indicated by the writs now returned. The sheriff attached Robert Matefrey of Cambridge through John But and William Seman, Abraham le Chapeler through John Gerund and Richard Bateman junior, Robert of Shelford through Richard Bateman senior and Michael Pilat, John of Aylsham through Richard of Perham and John of Pickering, and Walter le Bercher through Richard Wombe and John Wombe. None of them appeared in court and they are all in mercy.

(continued)

Date	Reference	Summary
1279	V, p 179	*Inquiry into the date of a property transaction.* The sheriff ordered twelve honest and lawful men of no affinity to Simon Waleys to attend court to determine on what day and in what year Simon was enfeoffed of his land and tenements which he held from Walter the Chaplain. The twelve did not appear. The sheriff appointed two mainpernors for each juror. John de Bradfield was mainperned by Henry de Bradfield of Cottenham and John Austin of Cottenham; Roger atte Green by Henry Wyn and Roger Delle, also of Cottenham; John Thurgar by Stephen son of Robert of Cottenham and Henry Ting of Cottenham; Ben[jamin] of Cretton by Thomas Bogge of Impington and Thomas Amaunde; Henry de la Marche by by Geoffrey le Lathe of Impington and Alexander le Lathe of Impington; Robert the Knight of Beche by Thomas Amable of Beche and William of Staunton; William son of Robert of Madingley by Roger Blaunkpayn of Madingley and Roger Terry of Madingley; Jacob son of Warin by Robert Crungewell of Madingley and Nicholas le Charter of Madingley; Roger Wendout by Thomas Papelyun of Madingley and William le Bercher of Madingley; John son of William of Madingley by Robert le King of Madingley and Geoffrey de Tadelawe [Tadlow?] of Madingley; Robert Maupudre by John le Munz of Medelton [Middleton?] and Raduph le Gous of Medelton; and Robert de Borewell [Burwell?] by John son of William of Medelton and John de Borewell in Medelton. They did not appear and were therefore in mercy. Their bodies were to be present at Easter quindene. After several delays the jurors stated on oath that Simon was enfeoffed of his lands on the Nativity of the Blessed Mary 49 Hen III, which is before debts to the Jews were incurred in 1 Edward I. Simon is therefore quit of any liability.
1279	VI, p 77	*Acknowledgement of a payment to Queen Eleanor.* John de Whatel, guardian of the gold (*custos auri*) of Queen Eleanor mother of the King came to court and acknowledged that he had received from William Seman and his associates 40s owed to the Queen.
1280	VI, p 131	*Distraint on a debt to the King.* The sheriff orders that the land and chattels of John Auvrey [Aubrey?] are distrained to pay a debt of 100s to the King which was previously owing to Moses son of Jacob. The deadline is the octave of St Hilary.
1280	VI, p 131	*Distraint on the property of John le Rus, debtor to the Jews.* The sheriff orders that the land and chattels of John le Rus are distrained to pay a debt of £8 to the King which was previously owing to Moses son of Isaac. The deadline is the octave of St Hilary. *Note:* See below for the continuation of this case

(continued)

Date	Reference	Summary
1280	VI, pp 137–8	*The tenants of John le Rus are summoned.* The sheriff distrains the tenants of lands which were held by John le Rus for £4 which is owed to the King on account of debts to Moses son of Isaac. He summons the tenants of the lands in question, namely the Prior of Barnwell, the Master of the Hospital of St John, Richard son of Richard Laurence, Richard Wombe, Alicia Godeman, William of Wilbraham, Richard Bateman junior, the Friars of the Sack, John But, Nicholas Morice, Robert of Madingley, the Prioress of Swaffham, Guy of Mortuo Mari, Lucas Carettarius, Osbert le Ferrun, Cecilia of Over and Thomas of Clopton and asks them to provide documentary evidence. The Master of the Hospital of St John denies involvement, saying that his lands are from Richard, father of John. Richard son of Laurence says that he was enfeoffed before the debt to Moses was incurred. Richard Wombe says the same. More inquiries are made. William of Wilbraham, Richard Bateman junior and Nicholas Morice speak up to warrant Hugo son of John le Rus in order to help the court. John But warrants Thomas le Merveylyus. Robert of Madingley recognises that he is a tenant of half an acre. Osbert le Ferrun says that he has none of John's land, and offers verification. The others are mainperned. Andrew le Redere and Roger of Huntingfield mainpern the Prior of Barnwell; Thomas Godeman and Robert Lundr' mainpern Alicia Godeman; John Funtyngg' and Richard Peketo mainpern the Prioress of Swaffham; Richard Wombe and Henry Thoneye mainpern Lucas Carettarius; John le Bever and William de Lundr' mainpern Cecilia of Over; William Wilecok of Clopton and Robert Franklin mainpern Thomas of Clopton. The mainpernors do not have them and are in mercy. They will be distrained by their lands to appear at Easter one month. The sheriff reported that Guy de Mortuo Mari and the Friars of the Sack held part of the land.
1280	VI, p 148	*A plea of unjust detention of chattels.* The widow of Jacob, Jew of Cambridge, on the fourth day v. John le Maltere and Matilda his wife concerning a plea of unjust detention of chattels. They do not appear. The sheriff appoints four mainpernors: John le Malterer [John's son?], Poletere de Berkham, Henry son of Martin of Berkham, and Thomas de Parnes of Barkham. They still do not appear and all are in mercy. Their bodies are to come before the court on the feast of Holy Trinity quindene.

(continued)

Date	Reference	Summary
1280	VI, pp 168–9	*Recovery of debts to the King from tenants of the late John le Rus.* The sheriff reports on oath the result of an inquiry into the portions of land held from John le Rus by the Prior of Barnwell, the Brothers of the Hospital of St John, and other tenants, giving the values per annum over the period ending at the feast of St Hilary... The Friars of the Sack hold a capital messuage valued at 10s, which is held in dowry by Alicia the widow of John. [Alicia also holds in dowry 14 acres of arable land and half an acre of meadow value 10s.] [The following properties incur debts to the King equal to just under half their value:] Guy de Mortuo Mari, rector of the church of Kingston, holds one messuage value 33s 4d; John But holds one messuage value 15s; The Brothers of the Hospital of St John hold 15 acres of arable land value 15s and three acres of meadow value 10s 3d; Thomas of Clopton and his wife Agnes daughter of Andrew Treweman hold 4s rent and one cheese press 4d; the Prioress of Swaffham holds a half mark rent; Richard Wombe holds 20 acres of arable land value 12s; Richard Bateman junior holds 2 acres of arable land and one acre of meadow value 4s; William of Wilbraham, chaplain, holds 1 acre of arable land value 12d; Richard son of Richard Laurence holds 12d rent.; Hugo le Rus holds 5 acres of arable land value 3s; Lucas Carettarius holds three acres of arable land value 2s; William of Pickering hold a half mark of rent; Robert of Madingley holds half an acre of land value 6d; the Prior of Barnwell holds 60 acres of arable land value 30s 2d; Bartholomew Gogging holds 3 acres and 3 roods of arable land value 2s 8d; Robert son of Andrew Frede holds one acre of arable land value 12d; Simon son of Simon Godeman holds half an acre of arable land value 6d; Matilda de Walda holds 1.5 acres of arable land value 18d; Robert custodian of the chapel of St Edmunds holds 3.5 acres of arable land value 3s 6d; Cecilia widow of Peter de Welles holds 4 acres of arable land value 4s; Richard Pet holds half an acre of arable land value 6d; Nicholas Morice holds 3 acres of arable land and 3 acres of meadow value 8s 6d; Dyonisia widow of William of Huntingdon holds one acre of arable land value 12d; and Osbert le Ferrer holds one acre of arable land value 12d. *Note*: Arable land is valued at up to 12d per acre and meadow at up to 4s per acre. *Note*: For continuation see VI, p 203
1280	VI, pp 169–70	A complex starr concerning William son of Baldwin of Stowe and the jews Josce son of Saulot and Aaron son of Vives concerning payments of 80 marks (in four instalments) and 4 marks.

(continued)

Date	Reference	Summary
1280	VI, pp 198–9	*Inquiry involving twelve Cambridge Christians, six Huntingdon Jews and six London Jews.* John son and heir of John Avered of Cambridge and his tenants have been distrained to give back 100s which Master Elias son of Master Moses received from the King's Treasury in recompense for debts incurred by the Abbot of Stratford. John produces a royal charter with the great seal, dated 28 June 8 Edward I. The sheriff organises an inquiry by twelve honest and lawful men from Cambridge and six lawful Jews from Huntingdon to report on the feast of St Margaret. These comprise John of St Edmunds, Roger of Elmam [Elmham?] and other Christians from Cambridge, together with Josce son of Saulot and other Jews from Huntingdon. The constable of the Tower of London produces six Jews from London to certify the authenticity of the starr. These comprise Meyr nephew of Leon, Isaac of Everke and others. John is acquitted and the debt cancelled.
1281	VI, p 281	John Porthors v. Josce son of Saulot concerning a plea of debt by Thomas of Newnham.
1281	VI, p 281	John Lewyn v. Josce son of Saulot concerning a plea of debt by William of Kingston.
1281	VI, p 281	Henry of Barton v. Josce son of Saulet concerning a plea of debt by Andrew de Fluete

Sources: J. M. Rigg (ed.), *Calendar of the Plea Rolls of the Exchequer of the Jews, I: Henry III, 1218–1272* (6 vols) (London, 1905); J. M. Rigg (ed.), *Calendar of the Plea Rolls of the Exchequer of the Jews, II: Edward I, 1273–1275* (6 vols) (Edinburgh, 1910); H. Jenkinson (ed.), *Calendar of the Plea Rolls of the Exchequer of the Jews, III: Edward I, 1275–1277* (6 vols) (London, 1925); H. G. Richardson (ed.), *Calendar of the Plea Rolls of the Exchequer of the Jews, IV: Henry III, 1272; Edward I, 1275–1277* (6 vols) (London, 1972); S. Cohen (ed.), *Plea Rolls of the Exchequer of the Jews, V: Edward I, 1277–1279* (6 vols) (London, 1992); P. Brand (ed.), *Plea Rolls of the Exchequer of the Jews, VI: Edward I, 1279–81* (6 vols) (London, 2005)

Appendix 9

Cambridge: Jewish records of debts by people resident in or closely connected to Cambridge

Page	Details	Lender
	Debts recorded in the Cambridge Archa 8–24 Henry III	
252	Nigel le Seler and Eustace Elcorn 20s at the feast of St Eldrede 22 Henry III	Isaac son of Samuel and Jacob son of Deulesaut by chirograph
252	Henry son of Hugo the Merchant 5 marks: 2 marks at the feast of All Saints, 22 Henry III, and 3 marks at Pentecost following	Isaac son of Samuel and Jacob son of Deulesaut by chirograph
252–3	Peter le Hunt 40s at the feast of St Eldrede octave in 21 Henry III. 'Inde solvuntur' (in default) 16s at the end.	Isaac son of Samuel and Jacob son of Deulesaut by chirograph
253	John of Barton 12 marks at Hokeday, 21 Henry III, or 11 marks before the time limit	Isaac son of Samuel and Jacob son of Deulesaut by chirograph
253	John Hubert 10s at the feast of St Eldrede the Virgin 19 Henry III	Isaac son of Samuel and Jacob son of Deulesaut by chirograph
253	Alan Punch 6 marks in June 21 Henry III	Isaac son of Samuel and Jacob son of Deulesaut by chirograph
253–4	Alan son of Savary of Barton 8 marks; at the feast of St Andrew the Apostle 4 marks, and at Hokeday next 4 marks; also 2 quarters of corn at the feast of St Michael 22 Henry III, pledged by Radulph his son and heir.	Isaac son of Samuel and Jacob son of Deulesaut by chirograph
254	John Gogging 30s *ad capud* June 21 Henry III	Isaac son of Samuel and Jacob son of Deulesaut by chirograph

(continued)

Page	Details	Lender
254	Harvey Gogging 30s *ad incapite* June 20 Henry III	Isaac son of Samuel and Jacob son of Deulesaut by chirograph
254	Ivo Quarel of Buneton 12 marks and 2 quarters of corn at the feast of St Michael 23 Henry III	Isaac son of Samuel and Jacob son of Deulesaut by chirograph
255	Ivo Quarel 60s and 4 quarters of corn at Christmas 24 Henry III	Isaac son of Samuel and Jacob son of Deulesaut by chirograph
255	Ivo Quarel of Boneton £15 5s and 3 quarters of corn at the feast of All Saints 24 Henry III	Isaac son of Samuel and Jacob son of Deulesaut by chirograph
255	Radulph of Haverhill in Cambridge 17s in the middle of Lent 24 Henry III	Isaac son of Samuel and Jacob son of Deulesaut by chirograph
256	John of Cocheman [Crocheman?] 11.5 marks and one quarter of corn at the feast of All Saints 24 Henry III	Isaac son of Samuel and Jacob son of Deulesaut by chirograph
257	Peter of Barton 12s 6d and half a quarter of corn at the feast of All Saints 23 Henry III, and 18d before the end	Isaac son of Samuel and Jacob son of Deulesaut by chirograph
257	Robert of St Edmunds 2 marks on Ascension Day 20 Henry III	Isaac son of Samuel and Jacob son of Deulesaut and Aaron son of Isaac by chirograph
258	Alan son of Savary of Barton 22s 6d at the Purification of the Blessed Mary 24 Henry III	son of Deulesaut and Aaron son of Isaac by chirograph
258	John son of Adam of Barton 10s and one bushel of corn at the feast of St Michael 23 Henry III	Aaron son of Isaac
259	Richard son of Gregory 30s at the middle of the quindene after the feast of St Eldrede octave 21 Henry III, and otherwise at the centre of the quindene after the Purification of the Blessed Mary. If paid before the time limit 10s	Aaron son of Isaac
259	Simon de Kampes in Cambridge 2.5 marks at the feast of St Andrew the Apostle 20 Henry III. If paid before the time limit 13s 4d	Josce son of Isaac
259	Harvey of Cambridge one mark at Easter 15 Henry III	Duce son of Jabob
260	Harvey son of Eustace 6.5 marks at the Purification of the Blessed Mary 21 Henry III	Isaac son of Samuel
260	Adam son of Eustace 1s and one quarter of corn in the octave after the feast of St Michael 21 Henry III	Isaac son of Samuel

(continued)

Page	Details	Lender
261	Robert of St Edmunds 12 marks; 3.5 marks at Pentecost 21 Henry III; 8.5 marks at Christmas following, or 11 marks before the time limit	Isaac son of Samuel
261	Hugo son of Ernisius the Baker 6 marks: 1 mark at Christmas 23 Henry III, 10s at the following feast of St John the Baptist, 10s at the following Christmas and so on and in the third year following at the end 2 marks. 13s 4d before the time limit.	Isaac son of Samuel
262	Walter son of John son of Bernard 60s: 2 marks at the feast of All Saints 22 Henry III, 2 marks at the following Easter and half a mark at the following feast of St Michael	Isaac son of Samuel and Isaac le Blund
263	Michael Malerbe one mark at the feast of All Saints 23 Henry III, 0.5 mark at Easter following and 40d at Pentecost following.	Jacob son of Deulesaut by chirograph and by tally
263	Robert Seman 11s at the feast of St Michael 19 Henry III and one quarter of corn for the same term	Jacob son of Deulesaut by chirograph and by tally
265	Mabillie Doy of Cambridge 1.5 marks at the Purification of the Blessed Mary 21 Henry III	Avigay Vidue by chirograph
266	Simon Ding of Cambridge 20s and half a quarter of *sal' solvendis* [salt solution[; at the feast of St Peter ad Vincula 5s and the feast of St Nicholas following 15s	Deulesaut son of Isaac
267	Everard son of Fulco Crocheman 3.5 marks and one quarter of corn within a month after the feast of St Michael 22 Henry III	Jacon Crespin Jew of London by chirograph
267	Baldwin son of Baldwin Blancgernun 10 marks at the feast of St Michael 19 Henry III, 40d at Hokeday following, and so on from year to year until £16 has been paid	Jacon Crespin Jew of London by chirograph
267	Robert of St Edmund 100s at the feast of St Michael 19 Henry III, and then 5s year by year etc. …	Jacob Crespin Jew of London and Josce le Pestre by chirograph
267	Baldwin son of Baldwin Blancgernun £16 at Hokeday 19 Henry III, then 16s and so on year by year etc. …	Jacob Crespin Jew of London and Josce le Pestre by chirograph
268	John Aunre (Audre?) £4 10s 27d at the feast of St Michael 19 Henry III and 27d at Hokeday following and so on year by year [for 20 years]	Jacob Crespin Jew of London and Josce le Pestre by chirograph

(continued)

Page	Details	Lender
268	Auger (or Anger) son of Edric of Cambridge £22 4s: 13s 10d at the feast of St Michael 23 Hen III and 13s 10d at Hokeday following and so on from year to year until the sum is paid [note that the instalments cannot be equal]	Jacon Crespin Jew of London and Isaac son of Josce le Pestre by chirograph
268	Adam son of Eustace in Cambridge £15 10s at the feast of St Michael 24 Henry III and 10s at the following Hokeday and so on year by year [31 instalments]	Jacob Crespin Jew of London and Josce le Pestre by chirograph
268	John son of Maurice le Rus 1s at Easter 17 Henry III	Jacob Crespin Jew of London and Josce le Pestre by chirograph
270	John son of Alur' (Alured?) of Cambridge 15 marks: at the Purification 23 Hen III 4 marks, at the feast of St John following 4 marks, at the east of All Saints following 4 marks and at the Purification following 3 marks	Aaron son of Abraham Jew of London
271	John Gogging 60s at the Purification 24 Henry III	Aaron son of Abraham Jew of London
271	Michael Brithnod 10.5 marks at Hokeday 23 Henry III	Aaron son of Abraham Jew of London
274	Peter son of Richard of Barnwell 20s: 10s at the feast of St Ethelred 17 Henry III and 10s at Christmas following	Deulecres son of Dyaye of Norwich
274	Richard son of Osbert of Newnham 20s at the Purification 12 Henry III	Nakyn son of Samuel
275	Radulph son of Gilbert of Madingley 10s at the feast of St Edmund 18 Henry III	Florie son of Samuel
275	Radulph son of Gilbert of Madingley 8.5 marks and one quarter of corn at the feast of St Edmund 18 Henry III	Josce of Kent
	Other relevant debts in the Cambridge Archa 8–24 Henry III	
263	Robert a free man in Madingley 4 marks and one quarter of corn at the feast of St Ethelred octave 23 Henry III	Jacob son of Deulesant by chirograph and tally
272	Thomas Abbot of Walden (in Saffron Walden) and the convent there 600 marks: at the quindene of St John the Baptist 23 Henry III 25 marks, and at the quindene of St Andrew following 25 marks, and so on up to the end of 5 years, and in the four years following at the end £50 and in the year following 50 marks at the year end.	Leo Episcopus of York*

(continued)

Page	Details	Lender
	Debts recorded in the Cambridge Archa in 46 Henry III (1272) (Appendix V)	
276	William son of Robert le Rus, 5s by tally	Josce of Newport
276	Radulph son of Gilbert of Madingley 8 marks by tally	Josce of Cambridge
276	Walter son of John of Chesterton 40s by charter	Isaac son of Samuel and Jacob son of Deulesaut
276	Peter son of Richard of Bertiewell (Barnwell?) 20s by charter	Deulecres son of Dyaye
277	William Castell' of Cambridge 20s by charter	Abraham son of Mil'
278	Maurice Ruffus of Huningsheye 40s	Salomon son of Josce

Notes: J, p 146, provides a list of borrowers from the Jews whom he claims were residing in Cambridge. Several of the people he mentions cannot be identified from the other sources used in this book as being active in Cambridge, and so they have not been included in the list above.

* Leo Episcopus and his son-in-law Aaron of York were considered in 1219 to be amongst the six richest Jews in England.

Source: J; Appendices IV, V

Appendix 10

Feets of fines: selected cases relevant to the town of Cambridge

Date	Page	Summary translation
1194–5	KC, 16	Stephen son of Selede petitions v. Robert son of Sifred and the Templars of Jerusalem concerning two acres of land in the fields of Cambridge. ... [continued below]
1194–5	KC, 46	Stephen Cordubarius of Cambridge on the fourth day v. Robert son of Sofrei concerning two acres of land in the fields of Cambridge. Robert calls to warrant the Knights Templar ...
1195	FFHR, 46, p 40; PDC, 259–60	*William Ruffus buys land from Harvey son of Eustace.* Harvey son of Eustace petitions through William of Buckingham his attorney against the defendant William Ruffus through Philip son of Robert his attorney concerning 50 acres of land and 3s rent in perpetuity in the fields of Cambridge in Newnham. For this agreement William Ruffus gives Harvey son of Eustace 60 marks of silver.
1195	FFHR 65, p 53	Cristian, widow of Godard Ruffus, and Girard, and Irilda, Girard's wife, and Agnes daughter of the aforesaid Cristian, petition against William Brown (*le Brun*) concerning land in Little Landwathe.
1195	FFHR, 91, p 76	Ioelu de Creton petitions against Harvey son of Eustace concerning 50 acres of land and half ... a meadow in the fields of Creton.
1198–9	FFR, 238	Martina daughter of Richard came and demanded justice in the absence of Geoffrey Picot her son, concerning one hide of land in Gamlingay which she inherited and which the sheriff had taken into his possession. Harvey son of Eustace petitioned that a day be fixed for a hearing in the King's court at Westminster. [See PDC, p 278 below]

(continued)

Date	Page	Summary translation
1198	PDC, 264	*Harvey son of Eustace buys three messuages from Michael Malerbe.* Harvey son of Eustace petitioner against Michael Malerbe defendant in Cambridge through Thomas of Trumpington attorney for Michael. Michael recognises that three messuages and their appurtenances were inherited by Harvey ... and for this recognition Harvey gave the aforementioned Michael 60s 8d.
1198	PDC, 270	*William Pevel buys land from Simon Ruffus.* Simon Ruffus petitioner v. William Pevel defendant concerning two virgates of land with appurtenances in Mordon. A grand assize was summoned in which Simon set out his claim. By agreement the aforesaid William gave the aforesaid Simon 20s sterling.
1198	PDC, 272	Final concord between Urvei son of Emme petitioner v. Robert prior of Barnwell regarding one messuage with appurtenances in Barnwell. Urvei claimed that he had inherited the property in perpetuity from St Giles church. The prior agreed that Urvei could hold the house and receive one tale of bread for his life.
1198	PDC, 272	*Reginald son of Harvey buys land from Selone son of Nigel.* Selone son of Nigel petitioner v. Reginald son of Harvey defendant concerning 6 acres of land with appurtenances in Trumpington. Selone climed to have inherited the land. The aforesaid Reginald gave the aforesaid Serlon 20s sterling.
1198	PDC, 276	*Harvey son of Eustace buys 3 messuages from Harvey son of Edward.* Harvey son of Eustace petitioner v. Harvey son of Edward defendant concerning 3 messuages with appurtenances in Cambridge. Harvey son of Edward recognizes that the three messuages were inherited by Harvey son of Eustace in perpetuity. Harvey son of Eustace gave Harvey son of Edward 8s sterling.
1199	PDC, 278	*Harvey son of Eustace buys land from Geoffrey Picot.* Harvey son of Eustace petitioner and Geoffrey Picot defendant concerning one hide of land in Gamlingay. The aforesaid Harvey gave the aforesaid Geoffrey ...
1199	PDC, 280	*Absolon son of Absolon buys property from Martin Wulward.* Absolon son of Apsolon petitioner v. Martin Wulward defendant ... The aforesaid Martin gave the aforesaid Absolon one mark of silver
1199	PDC, 284	*Harvey son of Eustace buys property from Baldwin Blancgernun.* Harvey son of Eustace petitioner v. Baldwin Bl... defendant concerning one messuage and 9 acres of land with appurtenances in Cambridge. Baldwin recognises these as the property of Harvey and in return Harvey gives Baldwin the property [in the fields of Madingley?] in return for a service [rent] of 14d, paid in two [annual] instalments
1201	PDC, 288	Alex abbot of Sawtry petitioner through John the monk and [Harvey] son of Eustace defendant concerning one hide with appurtenances in Gamlingay. ...

(continued)

Date	Page	Summary translation
1201	PDC, 290	*Harvey son of Eustace buys land from Gilbert.* Gilbert ... petitioner v. [Harvey] son of Eustace concerning 3 virgates of land with appurtenances in Chauele [Cheveley]. ... Simon of Sexton gives evidence... The aforesaid Harvey gave the aforesaid Gilbert ...
1202	PDC, 298	*Laurence de Hotot purchases a property from Harvey son of Eustace for a lump-sum and annual rent.* Harvey son of Eustace petitioner v. Laurence de Hotot concerning half a virgate of land with appurtenances in Chauelay [Cheveley]. The aforesaid Laurence recognises the whole of the aforesaid land to belong to Harvey and the aforesaid Harvey concedes the land to Laurence and his heirs for 4s per annum for all service in two instalments, and Laurence gave Harvey 2 marks of silver and 2 bizants.
1203	PDC, 307	*Hugo son of Ernald buys land from Hugo Ruffus.* Hugo son of Ernald petitioner v. Hugo Ruffus and Philip son of Robert concerning a virgate of land with appurtenances in Eversden. Hugo Ruffus and Philip son of Robert Hugo son of Ernald paid an unknown amount in sterling silver to Hugo son of Ernald
1206	PDC, 315	William Ruffus petitioner v. Jordan of Horsee concerning a virgate of land and 5 acres with appurtenances in Horsee. ...
1206	PDC, 316	Emma Cholle petitioner v. Martin Wulward and Margery his wife and Ella the widow of William Cholle concerning a portion of a messuage with [appurtenances] in Cambridge. ... Marjory and Ella are sisters. ... Martin and his wife and Ella gave Emma 12s sterling.

Sources: PDC; KC; PR: FFHR; FFR

Appendix 11

Cambridgeshire subsidy rolls and eyres

Eyres 1247–99. The main eyres generated documents as as follows: TNA JUST 1/81, 1247, Foreign pleas, including essoins, 31 Hen III; TNA JUST 1/82, 1261, Civil, foreign and crown pleas, jury calendar, essoins and attorneys 45 Hen III; TNA JUST 1/83; 1268; General oyer and terminer, lands given away as a result of the Barons' War, roll of pleas, presentments, amercements and jury calendar, 53 Hen III; TNA JUST 1/84, 1272, Civil and foreign pleas, 56 Hen III; TNA JUST 1/85, 1272, Crown pleas, 56 Hen III; TNA JUST 1/86, 1286, Rex roll of civil, foreign and crown pleas, gaol delivery, plaints, amercements and fines, jury calendar, essoins and attorneys, 14 Edw I; TNA JUST 1/96, 1299, Berwick's roll of civil, foreign, king's and crown pleas, gaol delivery, plaints, jury calendar, essoins and attorneys, 27 Edw I.

Subsidy rolls. The earliest surviving subsidy roll for Cambridgeshire appears to be TNA E179/81/2 for 1225, but this applies only to Chesterton. Another early roll for Cambridgeshire is TNA E179/81/1, which Palmer (1912) dates to c.1250, but TNA tentatively attributes it to a thirtieth for 1283. Later rolls include an aid for marrying the king's daughter in 1302 (E179/81/3, E179/239/246) and a double scutage of 1305 (E179/242/65).

Translation of excerpts from TNA JUST 1/82 Cambridgeshire eyre of 1261, adapted from Palmer, W. M. (ed.), *The Assizes Held at Cambridge 1260: Being a Condensed Translation of Assize Roll 82 in the Public Record Office with an Introduction* (Linton, 1930).

The jury for the borough of Cambridge (Membranes 29d, 31d, 32d. Palmer, *Assizes*, pp 38–43)

The Borough of Cambridge comes by twelve.

Nicholas Childman, William Toylet, Reginald Sherewynd and Robert Huberd, chief bailiffs; Robert of St Edmunds, William son of Elye, John Martin, John Porthors, Walter Crocheman, Thomas Plote, Eustace

Eldcorn, William Seman, Peter son of William, Robert of Madingley, Ermesius Mercator, William of Cotes.

Simon son of John of Barton appeals in the county Thomas son of Reginald of Eadewald of mayhem, robbery and breaking the King's peace; and he appeals of force and aid Harvey of Wyneboldisham. Simon does not come; therefore let him be arrested and his pledges, John son of Robert of St Edmunds and John Porthors, put in mercy. Harvey is dead. Thomas comes and the jury agree that he is in mercy and keep him in custody.

Roger son of Cecily who appealed William de Staunton, Thomas his servant and William Alban his friend, John the parson and John his servant and Alan his friend, and Stephen le Cornewallleys, of robbery &c. does not come. Therefore let him be arrested and his pledges, Stephen Longstaff and Richard de Alderheth, put in mercy. William and others did not come, nor were attached, because Roger only proceeded against them for two county courts, because they were from Scotland. The jury cannot agree.

Two strange women lodged at the house of Walter de Malvern in Newnham, and during the night killed Margery his wife and Margery her daughter. The vill of Newnham is in mercy for not making suit.

Robert le Ver appealed William de Sanuton of blows, &c, and does not come; let him be arrested and his pledges put in mercy. William does not come, and the jury say that he is dead.

John the Vintner who appealed Henry Russell of felony, &c. does not comes, and therefore let him be arrested. Because Henry [Harvey?] Parleben the coroner did not take pledges for his presence, let judgment be had on him.

David de Boyton, of county Warwick, killed William de Boyton his friend between Cambridge and Newnham and fled immediately. Outlawed. No chattels, being a stranger clerk.

Robert son of Walter of Middlesex, Thomas de Lasham, and John Lowe wounded Gilbert Swain in the parish of All Saints so that he died. They fled and are outlawed, &c. They had no chattels, nor were in a tithing, because they were stranger clerks. The parish of All Saints is in mercy for not arresting them.

Malefactors unknown met John Swath in Bridge Street, Cambridge, and killed him. The hue and cry was raised by the whole town and the town did not arrest them, and is therefore in mercy. On the night when this happened, John with many others kept watch. Harvey Parleben, the coroner, did not attach the other watchmen (*vigilatores*), and so let judgment be had on him.

John de Aketon, Thomas Wyget and John Love were arrested for burglary of houses and were imprisoned in the town gaol, and Simon le Enveise was likewise imprisoned with them. They all escaped to the church of St Edward where they acknowledged their theft and abjured the realm before the coroner. No chattels; judgment of escape on the town of Cambridge.

Matilda Platfot, having one ear cut off, was arrested for theft and imprisoned in the town gaol, and escaped to the church of St Mary and abjured the realm.

Roger the son of Simon of Dullingham, aged seven years, was burnt in the house of Simon Cook in Barnwell. Emma Brodeghe, who was the first to find him, is not suspected. Judgement: misfortune.

Geoffrey de Rokesburgh placed himself in the church of St Peter outside the Trumpington Gate and acknowledged that he had killed a certain Roger le Veyll, and abjured the realm before the coroner.

Nicholas of Cornbury and Peter of Halesford placed themselves in the same church, acknowledged theft and abjured the realm. Chattels of Nicholas 6s, 6d, for which the town of Cambridge will answer.

A stranger was killed in Littlemore fields. It is not known who killed him. The first to find him has been hanged. No Englishry were presented within the liberty of Cambridge, nor murder adjudged … as the liberty claims to have of old … Henry [Harvey?] Parleben, the coroner, did not summon the neighbours for that death; therefore judgement on him.

Bartholomew the Sergeant, John and Hervey le Teynturer, bailiffs of Cambridge, are in mercy for contempt.

William of Belney, who appealed in the county Hugo le Batur of mayhem and breach of the peace, does not come. Therefore let him be arrested. He found no pledge or surety, being a poor man. Hugo did not come, nor is attached, since it is found by the coroner's roll that William began to appeal Hugo in the twenty-ninth year, and ever afterwards followed his appeal against him from court to court. And the coroner and bailiffs of Cambridge never afterwards attached Hugo, nor would send the said appeal to the county, to put Hugh in exigency from court to court, according to the law of England concerning outlawry. Therefore judgment on the liberty.

Malefactors unknown killed John Betun in St Mary's churchyard, in Cambridge. John Saleman and Simon son of Geoffrey of Ely were arrested for that death and imprisoned in the town gaol. Afterwards by the King's writ they were delivered on bail in the time of Roger de Wyz, then bailiff, who committed them. He returned the same writ in bail to twenty-four men, whose names they now have not. Therefore in mercy. And John and Simon come and defend that death, and for good or evil place themselves on their country. And the twelve jurymen say on their oaths that they are not guilty. Therefore quit. But they say that Bernard le Suur is guilty of that death; he has withdrawn himself and is suspected; therefore he is outlawed, &c. He had no chattels, nor was he in a tithing, and therefore the town is in mercy. Godfrey de Aqua, Robert of Teversham, Elyas de Teynturer, Nicholas son of Andrew of Wimpole, Henry Page, John of St Edmunds, Alan of Teversham and Walter son of Andrew, mainprised the aforesaid Simon and John but did not have them on the first day. Therefore in mercy.

Aunger son of Simon Baker and John the clerk of Magister Guy quarrelled together on the bridge of Cambridge: Aunger struck John in the belly with a knife, so that he died at once. Aunger fled straight-away to the church of St Clement and abjured the realm. He had no chattels, nor was he in a tithing, being a clerk, but he was received into the parish of St Clement without frank pledge. Therefore in mercy. Afterwards it was witnessed that Ralph le Bernicus, together with other clerics, by night … [incomplete].

Abraham le Chapeler appealed Paul Wombe [translated 'Pauline Wombe' by Palmer] of robbery and breaking the King's peace. Neither Abraham nor Paul appear. The jury say that they are agreed [that he is guilty]. Therefore let him be kept in custody.

Roger of Ely appealed Richard son of Hugh le Rus that when he was in the King's peace in his own house in Cambridge, on the eye of January 18th, 1257, about the hour of vespers, Richard came feloniously and gave him a blow with a knife on the left breast, three thumbs long and three thumbs deep, and also gave him another blow on the right arm, one thumb long. Roger offers to deraign [prove a claim] against Richard by his body as the court shall decree. Richard comes and says that he ought not to answer to the court as he is a clerk. The bishop's official, who is present, claims him as a clerk. But that it may be known how he is to be delivered to the bishop, whether guilty of the deed imputed to him, or not, let the truth of the matter be inquired into by the country. And the jury say that Richard insulted Roger in his own house and gave him the two blows. Therefore let him be delivered to the bishop as guilty.

Alice of Shelford, Matilda widow of John of Norton, Thomas of Basinges and Ralph the piper, placed themselves in church of St Clement, acknowledged themselves to be thieves and abjured the realm. No chattels, being strangers.

Robert son of Edith of Badburgham and John of Norton fled to the church of All Saints, acknowledged theft and abjured realm. John's chattels are valued at 6s, for which the town will answer. Robert had no chattels and neither was he in a tithing. The parish of All Saints amerced for not arresting them.

Henry the cheeseman of Burwell fled to the church of Holy Trinity, acknowledged theft and abjured the realm. Chattels valued at 12d. The parish is in mercy.

[Summary: Strangers took sanctuary, for theft, in the churches of St Mary's (three cases), St Sepulcre, St Peter by the Castle and St Edward. In each case, the parish was in mercy.]

John le Waleys fled to the church of the Friars Minors, and Seman de Badewe placed himself in the church of the Friars Preachers for theft and abjured the realm. No chattels, being strangers.

Thomas son of Robert le Mazun of Bumsted, fled to the church of St Giles of Barnwell, for the death of Walter Werry, and afterwards escaped from that church. He is outlawed. He was in the tithing of Peter Bird. Therefore he is in mercy. And judgement of escape on the vill of Barnwell.

An unknown man was found drowned in the mill dam of Alan la Zouch in Newnham. Richard de Herleton first found him and opened the sluice gates of the dam, and let the body float with the water to the dam of the King's mill. Afterwards the said Richard, Stephen son of Godwin of Hawkeston and John Mayfry came and took the dead body and buried it in the marsh near the dam, without view of the coroner. Therefore let them be arrested. No one is suspected of that death. Judgement: misfortune. Afterwards it was witnessed that Philip the miller of Alan la Zouch was with the said Richard and others when the body was buried. He himself, with the others, dug up the body on the second day after and put it back in the dam. Therefore let Philip also be arrested.

Richard Pope appealed Michael son of Andrew of Comberton that when he was in the King's peace in Cambridge, on the highway outside the house of Peter Curteis against the bridge of Cambridge, on St John the Baptist's day, 1258, between the dog and the wolf, the said Michael came evilly and feloniously and made a premeditated assault on him with a knife, giving him a puncture wound between the forearm and the hand, two thumbs long and down to the bone. … He offers to deraign with his body as the court shall decide. He appeals of force and aid Nicholas son of Gilbert of Comberton. Michael and Nicholas come. Nicholas seeks judgment as to whether he ought to answer the accusation of force and aid until the deed is proved. Michael asks for it to be allowed him that when the deed was supposed to have been done, if the deed was done, he was at Ely and not at Cambridge. And likewise that directly the deed was done hue and cry was not raised. And these things being allowed him, he puts himself upon his country excepting the town of Cambridge. Since it is found by the coroner's roll that he at once made his suit, &c., and by the twelve jurymen that he at once raised the hue and cry, and that he in no way varies in his appeal, and the said Michael is prepared to defend by his body, the judgment is that a duel shall be held between them; Michael shall give a pledge of defending and Richard of deraigning. Pledges of Michael: John Warry, Richard the Chaun, Robert the Tailor, John Sweyn. Pledges of Richard: Gregory of Balsham, John Godfrey, Raymond Bede, Adam the carter, John Pell of Shelford and Richard Curteis of Balsham. Afterwards the duel was fought between them and Michael was overcome. Therefore he is committed to gaol. His chattels are valued at 18s 7d.

Afterwards came Richard Pope ... A day is given to them, Wednesday, and then they shall come armed.

Ralph de Burdeleis, who appealed William Muschet of blows and robbery, does not come, and therefore his pledges are in mercy, namely Augustus de Burdelys of Drayton and William de Burdeleis of Hokinton. William Muschet does not come, nor was he attached, because it was not followed against him for three county courts.

Thomas of Andely, having been imprisoned for stealing a horse at Bury St Edmund's, escaped to church of the Brothers of Mount Carmel and abjured the realm. He was a vagrant with no chattels.

The jury present that the church of St Mary is in the gift of the King and that Symon de Wycomb now holds it of the King's gift; it is worth £10 a year. They also say that the Hospital of St John and the Hospital of Stourbridge used to be in the King's gift and now belong to the town of Cambridge, and that Hugh, formerly Bishop of Ely, removed Geoffrey the Chaplain, Keeper of the Hospital of Stourbridge and placed there another keeper, though it is not known by what warrant.

Concerning cloth sold against the Assize. They say that William son of Elye, Bartholomew Gogging, Henry Page and John son of John are drapers.

Concerning wines sold against the Assize. They say that Richard the Vintner, Simon son of Robert of Royse's Cross, Stephen of Hawkeston and William his friend dwelling in the city of London, Adam de Half and Richard of Barton sell wine in Cambridge contrary to the assize. Therefore in mercy.

Concerning encroachments. They say that Thomas Toylet, who is dead, obstructed a lane called Alwines lane, which was a common thoroughfare for the whole town. Also, since the last iter of the justices, Henry of the Castle encroached on the King's ditch, by erecting a wall on the ditch that was thirty feet long. Therefore he is in mercy, and the encroachment is ordered to be amended.

They also say that William le Breton made an encroachment on the great riverbank, near the great bridge. He planted willows where ships were accustomed to be steered, so that no ship or boat can sail there. Whereas ships used to pass by the arm of the river in the castle ward, the said William has built a bridge beyond the said … so that no ship can pass, to the great damage of the whole town, and he did this since the last iter. Let William be in mercy and let him amend the encroachment.

The jury also present that Golda of Ditton made a quay on the river of Heneye, so that whereas the water of the river used to run through the gutters of the town of Cambridge for the pleasure of the inhabitants, the water is obstructed by that encroachment, so that it cannot run through the gutters. Golda is in mercy, and the encroachment is to be amended by the sheriff.

Remarks about the borough from juries for other parts of Cambridgeshire

Membrane 33, Palmer, Assizes, p 14

The jury of the hundred of Flemeditch [which includes Barnwell], say that the burgesses of Cambridge have recently, within the last four years, begun to take toll of the tenants of the Bishop of Ely, and also take common toll which they call 'updrove' of each person leading or driving beasts through the middle of their town, whether they sell any or not. Therefore let it be spoken of elsewhere.

Membrane 25, Palmer, Assizes, p 33

The jury of the hundred of Whittlesford say that the men of Cambridge bought malt with one measure and sold by another. Therefore let it be spoken of.

Membrane 29, Palmer, Assizes, p 38

The jury of the hundred of Wetherley say that the burgesses of Cambridge when they buy malt make their measure before they buy to be heaped up, pressed with the hands and again heaped up; and they sell by rased [levelled] measure; and they take fresh toll now, for four years past, of all beasts passing through their town whether sold or not. Therefore let it be spoken of elsewhere.

People and events with Cambridge connections

Jury of Chesterton; Membrane 30, Palmer, Assizes, *p 5*

To the castle of Cambridge belongs a yearly rent of of 32d; namely Henry of the castle 4d; Peter Wulward 4d; Alice Seman 12d; Leon Dunning 6d; Nicholas Warin 6d; in addition the herbage of the castle, 5s, for which the sheriff will answer.

Jury of Northstow; Membrane 31, Palmer, Assizes, *p 17*

Concerning encroachments, they say that Master Guy of Barnard Castle ploughed part of the King's highway from Cambridge to St Neots so that it was obstructed for 4 perches. The sheriff is ordered to amend the same and Master Guy is in mercy.

Jury of Wetherley; Membrane 35, Palmer, Assizes, *p 34*

Henry Attepond sought from Simon de Mateshale 3s which Simon owed to Annice wife of Henry, but Simon was unwilling to repay. William de Childerley, a friend of Henry, struck Simon with a plough rod and after Simon retaliated with sword and blows, Henry took Simon's horse, which he kept for a long time before Simon recovered it under a royal writ. Simon fined one mark on the pledge of Ernisius the merchant of Cambridge and Robert of Madingley. Simon paid Henry one mark by the same pledges. Henry paid a fine of one mark by the pledges of Geoffrey Attepond and Adam the Rolier of Wimpole.

Appendix 12

Mayors and bailiffs of Cambridge, 1263–1300, as listed by the antiquary William Cole

(continued)

Date	Mayor	Bailiffs			
1263	Richard Laurence	Simon ad Aquam	Nicholas Morice	Robert of Madingley	Thomas Dunning
	Roger of Wyke	Peter of Wilbraham	Walter Em	William Eliot	John Porthors
	John Martin	John of Aylsham	Henry Toylet	Henry Nadun	
	Bartholomew Gogging	John Porthors	Gerard le Vyver	John of Aylsham	
	Guy le Spicer	Simon of Stockton	Robert Culling	John Prentice	Richard Dunning
	John But	John Gerund	William Seman	Richard of Hokele	Richard Bateman junior
1270	John Martin	Henry Toylet	John of Aylsham	Robert Wymund	Henry Nadon
	John Martin	Reginald of Comberton	Simon ad Aquam	John Feron	Roger of Withersfield
1272	John Martin				
1273	Bartholomew Gogging	John Porthors	Robert Wymund	John of Aylsham	Gerard de Stagno
	John Martin	John Gerund	Geoffrey le Ferrur	Robert Wymund	Robert Toylet
	John Martin	Roger of Withersfield	John Perrin	Simon of Bradley	Roger of Comberton
	John Martin	John of Aylsham	Gerard de Vivario	Michael Pylat	Robert of Madingley
	John Martin	John Porthors	William Goldring	Simon Godeman	Harvey Tinctor
	John Martin	John Porthors	William Elyot	Reginald Scherewind	Roger of Wilbraham
	Roger of Wykes	Peter of Wilbraham	Walter Em	William Elyot	John Porthors
	Bartholomew Gogging	John Porthors	Gerard de Vivario	John of Aylsham	
	Bartholomew Gogging	John Porthors	Robert Wymund	John of Aylsham	Gerard ad Stagnum
	Bartholomew Gogging	John Porthors	Robert Wymund	John of Aylsham	Simon of Bradley
	Guy le Spencer [Spicer]	Simon of Stockton	Robert Culling	John Prentice	Richard Dunning
	Guy le Spicer	Thomas of Snailwell	John of Trumpington		

Date	Mayor	Bailiffs			
1278	John But	John Gerund	Richard son of Richard Bateman	William Seman	Rochard of Hokele
	Robert Toylet				
	Richard Laurence	William Elyot	Simon ad Aquam	Gerard ad Stagnum	
	William Elyot	Henry Toylet	Henry Nadon	John Butt	John the Palfreyman
	William le Rus				
1281	John Martin				
1282	John Martin	John Porthors	Michael Pylat	Robert of Madingley	John Perrin
1283	John But	William Seman	John Porthors	Richard Laurence	Richard son of Richard Bateman
	John But	John Gerund	Richard son of Richard Bateman	William Seman	Richard of Hokele
	John Martin				
1284	John Martin	Robert Wymund	Robert Toylet	Geoffrey le Ferour	John Gerund
1285	John But	Roger of Withersfield	John the Palfreyman	Robert of Madingley	Simon of Bradley
1286	John But	John Porthors	Michael Pylat	Richard Bateman	John of Aylsham
1287	John But	John Martin	John Perrin	Humphrey of Costessye	Roger of Withersfield
1288	John Martin	Robert of Shelford	Reginald of Comberton	John Pawe	John of Branketre
1289	John Martin	John Perrin	John le Caumpes	Roger of Withersfield	Hunfrit the Draper

(continued)

Date	Mayor	Bailiffs			
1290	John Butt & Michael Pylat	Guardians			
1291	John But	John Porthors junior	Geoffrey le Ferur	John of Brankere	Robert Steresman
1292	John But	Master Thomas Toylet	Richard Crocheman	John Goldring	Stephen Hunne
1293	Michael Pylat	William of Holm	Alan of Welles	John Prentice	Thomas of Madingley
1294	Robert Toylet	Robert Malfrey	Michael Wulward	Michael son of John	Walter of Fulbourn
1295	John Gerund	Widone le Spicer	Peter the Baker	Simon Sephare	John Perin
1296	John But	William Pittock	John de Kynelrirle	Robert of Hinton	William of Bekiswelle
1297	John Dunning	John Gogging	Simon of Refham	Ralph of Comberton	Walter of Barking
1298	John Dunning	William de Ledes	Henry of Barton	Geoffrey of Costesseye	Auncell of Costesseye
1299	John Dunning	Simon Godeman	Geoffrey Knyvet	John Robilliard	John of Leek
1300	Guy le Spicer	Simon of Stockton	John Prentice	Robert Culling	Richard Dunning

Notes: It is sometimes unclear who were bailiffs at exactly what time because the information was collected by Cole mainly from deeds, some of which are not precisely dated. If different deeds of about the same time give conflicting accounts then each of the accounts appears in the table.

There is scattered earlier information too. Evidence from the *Curia Regis Rolls* suggests that Harvey son of Eustace was mayor in 1230 and 1235. Evidence from Merton deeds suggests that Richard Laurence was mayor 1269–70.

Roger de Wykes, mayor sometime 1263–8, is not discussed elsewhere in the text. He was a member of a jury investigating title to Thomas Toylet's land given to Barnwell Priory [LB, pp 115–17; BNM, p 5]; he witnessed a deed in 1263 in which John Frost sold land to Richard Laurence [StR365]. He was dead by 1279, leaving a widow Nicola [HR 327].

Source: BM Cole MS5833, pp 112, 127–34

Appendix 13

Ancient places in Cambridge

Ancient Place	Location
All Saints at the Castle	S of the corner of Castle Street and Shelley Row/Mount Pleasant, N of the river along the Huntingdon Road
All Saints in the Jewry	Memorial Garden on the E side of Trinity Street
Alwines Lane	Connects Conduit Street to Wallyslane
Austin Friars	Old Cavendish Laboratory, NE of Corpus Christ College, formerly the Old Mansion of the Austin Friars, and on the later site of the Old Physic Garden (before its removal to the present Botanical Garden)
Bede's House	North corner house at the end of St Johns Lane on Bridge Street (Magdalen Street)
Barnwell Causey	Maids Causeway
Barnwell Gate	Junction of Conduit Street and St Andrews Street between Christ's College and St Andrew's Church
Black Friars	Emmanuel College
Blackfriars Lane	Emmanuel Lane, off St Andrews Street
Bridge Street	Bridge Street
Butchery	Butcher's Row in the Market
Bynnebroc	Land on the bank of Bin Brook, W of the Bridge, now part of St John's College
Conduit Street	Sidney Sussex Street
Carmelite Friary	Kings College, near Provost's Garden
Castle	Castle Mound and the site of Cambridgeshire County Council Offices on the E side of Castle Street/Huntingdon Road, N of the river.
Cholles Lane	Also known as Whitefriars Lane. From Milne Street to the river, with the Carmelite Friary to the S
Conduit Street	Sidney Sussex Street
Cornhythelane	From High Street (Trinity Street) W to Cornhythe on the E bank of the river, with Trinity College to the S and St John's College to the N

(continued)

Ancient Place	Location
Cutler's Row	Also known as Shearer's Lane. St Mary's Lane from the N side of Great St Mary's Church to the NW corner of Market Hill
Dorodivers Lane	See Langrithes Lane. Leads from Emmanuel College, St Andrews Street, to Pembroke College, Trumpington Street
Druse Mere	Gray & Stubbings identify Druse Mere with the modern Drummer Street, near the bus station, and suggest that the name means 'muddy pool'. Millicent Essex identifies it with an easterly channel of the River Cam along the back of Trinity College
Faireyardlane	Slaughterhouse Lane, S of the Guildhall
Fayr Yard	Hog Hill or Beast Market, on N side of Pembroke Lane
Findsilver Lane	Lane between Trinity College and Caius College, W of High Street (Trinity Street); later known as Piss Pot Lane
Flax Hythe	On the E bank of a small channel from the River Cam that separates Garret Hostel Green from the town. Road access was by a lane running W from Milne Street
Friars of the Sack (Friars of the Penance of Jesus Christ)	Former house of John le Rus on the W side of Trumpington Street, now part of Peterhouse
Foulelane	From Kings Childer Lane S to Findsilver Lane through Trinity College
Garlicfayrelane	N from a junction with Jesus Lane along the route of the King's Ditch
Garret Hostel Green	Island in the River Cam, W of Trinity College. Named after a former student hostel. (The present Garret Hostel Lane was built by Henry VIII to compensate for the loss of other thoroughfares across the river caused by the building of new colleges)
Glomery Lane	From Trumpington Street (opposite St Mary's Passage) towards Milne Street
Granta	River Cam
Grenecroft	On the N side of Nun's Lane (Jesus Lane); now part of Jesus Green
Grey Friars	Sidney Sussex College
Hangmanslane	See Hintonway
Harlestone Lane	Thompson's Lane, from St Clement's Church on Bridge Street to Park Parade on the S bank of the river E of the bridge
Harleston's Hostel	On the S bank of the River Cam, E of the bridge, near St Clement's Church
Henny Lane/ Hennabby	From the High Street (Trinity Street) opposite St Michael's Church to the river, crossing Caius Lane. It ran S of Trinity College and through part of Trinity Hall, roughly parallel to Garret Hostel Lane

(continued)

Ancient Place	Location
High Street	Trinity Street
Hintonway	Also known as Hangmanslane. Christ's Lane off St Andrews Street
Holm	On the S bank of the River Cam, E of the Bridge
Honey Hill	Honey Hill (possibly an allusion to a muddy hill)
Hospital of St John the Baptist	St John's College
Howes	A hamlet on the Huntingdon road, N of the castle; the name suggests a slight rise or a barrow.
Kings Childer Lane	From High Street (Trinity Street) through Trinity College to Dame Nichol's Hythe on the E bank of the river
King's Hall	N side of Trinity College
Langrithes Lane.	Also known as Dorodivers Lane or Dowdewerslane or Dowdivers Lane. Pembroke Lane, connecting Trumpington Street to St Andrews Street. Formerly part of the route of the King's Ditch. Dowdewerslane is said to be derived from Deus Deners, which is in turn derived from Duzedeners, or 'Twelve Penny', which is said to be the name of a family, although this family does not appear in the Hundred Rolls
Lorimer's Row	Part of the market occupied by makers of metal harnesses
Lorteburne Lane	Free School Lane from St Benet Street to Pembroke Lane
Lyssheris Lane	Fisher's Lane
Market Street	Market Street. Known as Cordewanaria in 1332; it was where tradesmen worked on Cordovan leather, in particular making shoes
Michael House	Nevills Court, Trinity College, S of chapel
Milne Street	From Findsilver Lane and St Michael's Lane on the S side of Trinity College to the present Silver Street *via* the present Caius Lane, the W end of Kings College Chapel and the E front of Gibb's New Building, to Queens Lane and its junction with Silver Street
Nuns Lane	Jesus Lane
Nutts lane	See Segrimmeslane
Paschall Close	Near Tennis Court Road, E of Pembroke College
Peas Market	Peas Market
Pennyfarthing Lane	St Botolph's Lane from Trumpington Street, on the S side of St Botolph's Church, to Free School Lane
Petty Cury	From the SE corner of the Market to Barnwell Gate. The name may mean 'Little Cook's Row' to distinguish it from another Cook's Row elsewhere in the town.
Pilat's Lane	All Saints' Passage, formerly known as Jew's Street. Possibly named after the Pylat family who lived there.
Plotts Lane	See Segrimmeslane
Pound Hill	Near St Peter's Church, N of the river, near the former Pound Green

(continued)

Ancient Place	Location
Preachers Street	St Andrews Street, running SE from Barnwell Gate towards Linton
Priory of St Edmunds	E side of Trumpington Street, S of Pembroke College, on the site of Addenbrooks Hospital Old Building
Pyron Lane	From Trumpington Street (opposite St Edward's Church) to Milne Street, just S of King's College Chapel
Salthythe Lane	See Straw Lane
School of Pythagoras	Rear of St John's College, S of St Neot's road
Scolelane	Small lane running E and then S from Milne Street, passing to the rear of Senate House (which fronts onto Trumpington Street)
Sedge Hall	On the E side of Bridge Street, on the quay S of the bridge
Segrimmeslane	Also known as Plotts Lane and Nutts Lane. Kings Lane, from Trumpington Street, near St Benet's Church, to a junction with Queens Lane, formerly Milne Street, near the Provost's Garden, King's College
Shearer's Lane	See Cutler's Row
Shoemaker Lane	From the NE corner of Market Hill near Holy Trinity Church to Conduit Street
Slaughter Lane	From Market Hill to Fare Yard
Smallbridge Street	Mill Lane (route of the King's Ditch) from Trumpington Street, opposite St Botolph's Church, to the King's Mill and the Bishop's Mill near Newnham
Spittle End	S end of Trumpington Street, near the corner of Lensfield Road and the site of Conduit Head
St Austin's Hostel	King's College
St Austin's Lane	From Trumpington Street to Milne Street, just N of Kings Lane (Segrimmeslane)
St Benedict's Street	St Benet's Street from Trumpington Street to Peas Market
St Radegunds Priory	Jesus College
St Thomas Leys	Land bounded by Pembroke Lane (Langriths Lane) to the N, St Andrews Street (Preachers Street) to the E and Tennis Court Road to the S, now occupied partly by Downing College
Straw Lane	Also known as Salthythe Lane. From Milne Street to the river, close by and parallel to Segrimmeslane
Swinecroft	Large area of land, later known as the Marsh, between Trumpington Street to the W, Regent Street to the E and Lensfield Road to the S. In 1279 it lay behind the Priory of St Edmund on the E side of Trumpington Street
Trumpington Gate	On Trumpington road, by St Botolph's Church
Wallyslane	Wall's Lane

(continued)

Ancient Place	Location
Water Lane	From Milne Street to the river, close by and parallel to Straw Lane
White Friars	S of King's College, N of Queens' College, W of Milne Street, E of the river
Whitefriars Lane	See Cholles Lane

Sources: British Library Cole Add. MS 5810, Number of houses and inhabitants in Cambridge in 1728, fol. 190; British Library Cole Add. MS 5810, Index to Lyne's Map of Cambridge, 1574, fols 193–5; Daphne H. Brink, *The Parish of St Edward, King and Martyr, Cambridge: Survival of a Late Medieval Appropriation* (Cambridge, 1992); Peter Bryan, *Cambridge: The Shaping of the City*, new ed. (Cambridge, 2008); Ronald Gray and Derek Stubbings, *Cambridge Street Names: Their Origins and Associations* (Cambridge, 2000);) M. Lobel, *Historic Towns Atlas: Cambridge* (London, 1975)

Appendix 14

Family dynasties
of property owners

Medium-size families

The Bateman family

The driving forces in the Bateman family were the two Richards, father and son. Their reputation was such that both were jurors for the Hundred Rolls. The first recorded member of the family is Selede, who had two sons, Eustace and John. John had at least five sons: Richard senior, Geoffrey, Gilbert of Hardleston, John Tws and Wade.[1] Three of the five sons had different surnames, whilst the other two had no surname at all. Richard senior had a son Richard junior, his heir. In 1279 they both held significant amounts of property.[2]

Richard senior converted to Judaism. It is possible that other sons of John Selede converted too and adopted new names. Richard received a reward for his conversion from Barnwell Priory. In return he gave the Priory two fees worth 12s per annum.[3] Richard (probably senior) also gave 4s annual rent to Anglesey Priory.[4]

Both father and son acquired significant property portfolios through purchase. Richard senior's portfolio was centred around the market: it comprised a messuage in St Mary's which he bought from Adam of Lincoln; two shops in the Butchery bought from Richard Burs; and some vacant land in St Mary's, also bought from Richard Burs. He also inherited a shop in St Edward's from his father.[5] In 1295 Robert junior was paying 4s. rent on a shop in the Butchery to Barnwell priory.[6] It may be Richard senior who in c.1274 purchased from St Radegund's Priory a messuage formerly of William Novacurt (an aristocrat) in return for rents on various properties, namely a messuage in St Botolph's near the King's

Richard Bateman and his family

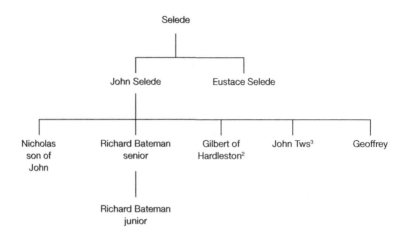

Notes:
[1] Wade is described as the uncle of Richard Bateman junior. The tree assumes that Wade, rather than his wife, is Richard senior's sibling.
[2] Gilbert of Hardleston is described as Richard junior's uncle. The tree assumes that Gilbert, rather than his wife, is Richard senior's sibling.
[3] John Tws is described as the brother of Richard Bateman. Given the context of the reference this is most likely to refer to Richard Bateman senior.

Ditch by Trumpington Gate and three shops in Pyron Lane, running from Trumpington Street towards Milne Street.[7]

Richard junior purchased a messuage in St Mary's bought from Humphrey of Clopton and Juliana his wife; four shops in St Mary's from Thomas of Cottenham; three shops in St Michael's and a messuage in St Edwards from Anglesey Priory, which they had been given by Richard Hubert; 3.5 acres in the Cambridge fields bought from John But; and 0.5 acres in the same fields bought from John above the market. Richard also acquired some property through his family: a messuage in St Mary's from his uncle Gilbert (who got it from Richard senior) on which he paid 10s rent to Barnwell Priory, and 3.5 acres in the Cambridge fields which he inherited from his father, who bought them from John Blodles.[8] Richard junior witnessed many deeds c.1270–90, including deeds of a gift to the Guild of St Mary.[9] He seems to have been more of an establishment figure than his father. He was bailiff in 1278 and 1283/4/6.[10]

In 1278 father and son stood surety for two of six Christian jurors inquiring, together with six Jewish jurors from Huntingdon, into the authenticity of a starr. None of the jurors appeared in court and their mainpernors were in mercy.[11] Richard senior may have died c.1285. It seems that after this Robert junior disposed of some property, though not, apparently, the property that he had inherited. In 1288 he sold a tenement in a lane off the High Street to Godfrey of Hauxton, merchant, and his wife Hawisia and in 1293 he sold another tenement in the same area to Matilda le Comber and her son John.[12] He died c.1316, leaving a widow Beatrix, who disposed of one of the properties in the market, namely a shop with a solar, to William Hayward, burgess, and Benedicta his wife.[13]

The Batemans, father and son, were self-made men who rose from relative obscurity to hold high civic office. They seem to have advanced through the butchery trade. Their accumulation of property is consistent with the reinvestment of trading profits into property in a part of the town – namely the Butchery – with which they were familiar. Richard senior provided the economic foundations for the civic esteem that his son later enjoyed. Richard junior may have become a property speculator. The family were involved with three religious institutions: Barnwell Priory, Anglesey Priory and St Radegund's, although how far their involvement with them was charitable rather than commercial is difficult to say.

Michael Bernard and his family

The Bernard family traces its origins back to Orgar, who had a son Bernard.[14] Bernard may have had brothers; there are references to Geoffrey and Alard, sons of Ordgar, but whether Ordgar is the same person as Orgar is debateable.[15] In any case Geoffrey and Alard left little legacy.

Bernard son of Orgar had three sons, John, Michael and Nicholas, and possibly a fourth, Simon.[16] John held a considerable amount of land from Barnwell Priory.[17] He also held a messuage in Bridge Street, and bought and resold land in Cambridge fields.[18] John had two sons, Walter and Nicholas, and a daughter Margaret.[19] In 1237 Walter owed 60s to Isaac son of Samuel and Isaac le Blund. Nicholas purchased a messuage in St Clement's from Queen Eleanor, mother of Edward I, which had been escheated from the Jews when they were expelled from the town.[20] Simon held a messuage in St Andrew's parish and land near the Hospital of St John in the parish of All Saints by the Jewry.[21] Some of this land appears to have been tenanted.[22]

Michael (d. by 1279) was the most important figure, witnessing many deeds in Cambridge.[23] He held various properties, including a messuage next to Lorterburlane in St Botolph's, a messuage near Pyron Lane, leading towards St John's, and land in Cambridge fields.[24] He had four

Bernard dynasty

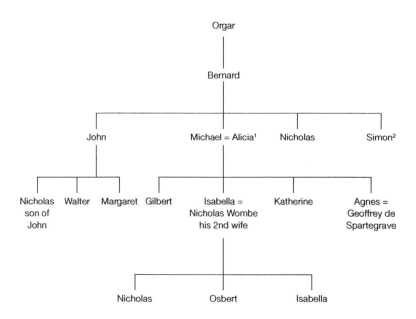

Notes:
[1] Daughter of William Wulsi.
[2] Conjectural relationship; could be Michael's nephew.
[3] No information is provided regarding Orgar, Bernard's father. It is possible that he may have been the man known as Ordgar, whose father was Roger and whose sons were probably Bartholomew, Geoffrey, Radulph and Adelard (StR, 2,12, 50/1,299]. No connection can be found between these people and Bernard's sons listed above, which suggests they are part of a different family, or a separate line of descent.

children, Gilbert, Isabella, Katherine and Agnes.[25] Gilbert was the son and heir and held various properties, including a tenement near to Glomery Lane.[26] He inherited a messuage and two shops on the death of his aunt, Margaret, daughter of John Bernard.[27] In 1279 he paid 9s rent to Geoffrey Spartegrave and Agnes his wife for various messuages.[28] Gilbert married Margaret, who may have been the daughter of William of Huntingdon and Dionysia his wife, who was in turn the daughter of William Fabro.[29] Michael's daughter Isabella married Nicholas Wombe, and they had two sons, Nicholas and Osbert, and a daughter, also called Isabella.

The Bernard family had a long pedigree in Cambridge and had links with the Wombe family, which was another of the old Cambridge families. They survived and prospered largely through Michael's efforts. Two of his three daughters made good marriages and his heir kept the family fortune intact.

Childman family

The founder of the family, as recorded in the Hundred Rolls, was Childman.[30] He was tallaged for 2 marks in 1211, amerced one mark *pro fuga* in 1219, and fined 6d in 1221.[31] Childman held extensive property in St Clement's parish, near the Hospital and the river. Some of this property was inherited, and it is unclear how much of it he acquired himself. The portfolio reveals an emphasis on retailing; it comprised two messuages and a shop in St Clement's, one shop in the market, 3 shops in an unspecified location and 13.5 acres in various plots in the Cambridge fields.

Childman had a son Nicholas Childman senior, who married Mariota, daughter of Michael Gogging, the son of Harvey Gogging. They had at least two children: Nicholas junior and his sister Cecilia, who married Peter de Welles and had a son, Peter de Welles junior; both Cecilia and her son were alive in 1279.[32] Mariota brought a dowry of a messuage in the parish of St Benedict together with 4 acres of land in the Cambridge fields, which Nicholas senior later used as dowry for his daughter Cecilia.

Nicholas junior inherited some of his father's messuages, shops and lands, all of which were sold by him. He was dead by 1279, but was survived by his widow, Eleanor.[33] Cecilia's marriage brought Peter de Welles, a successful entrepreneur, into the family. He purchased two messuages in St Mary's from Stephen son of Stephen Hauxton, a messuage in St Benedict's from Eustace Selede, a messuage in St Botolph's from Thomas Mulloc and 4 acres of land in two plots in Cambridge fields. He exchanged 20 acres of land in Barton for 20 acres in Cambridge fields held by Barnwell Priory.[34] He also bought a large piece of land in St Benedict's

Childman dynasty

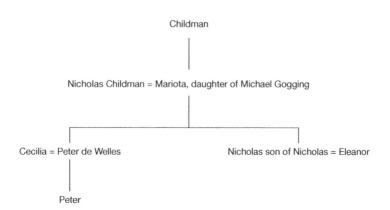

from Master William of Beeston (who had in turn bought it from Stephen above) which lay vacant and burned in 1279.[35]

The Childman story is one of steady decline. Childman himself seems to have inherited most of his extensive property portfolio. It constituted a small retail empire. His son Nicholas sold off quite a lot of the legacy, and his son Nicholas junior sold much of the rest, so that no Childman is recorded as a property owner in 1279. At that time Eleanor, Nicholas junior's widow, received a small amount of rent from a property that had been sold. There is no evidence of major benefactions, nor of borrowing from the Jews.

Decline was only mitigated by gains from marriage. Nicholas senior's marriage to Mariota bought a useful dowry, but Cecilia's marriage to Peter de Welles was key. Although Peter seems to have brought little in terms of inheritance, he was entrepreneurial, and had acquired substantial property by 1279. The declining retail empire was rescued by an advantageous marriage to an entrepreneur. But it was the Welles name that prospered, and not the Childman name.

Eliot/Elyot/Elyhot family

William Eliot figures prominently in the Hundred Rolls. He was the son of Henry Eliot senior.[36] William was bailiff in 1270 and c.1275–6, and mayor in 1278, and his name appears in the bede roll of St Mary's Guild.[37]

Henry Eliot senior, a member of the le Rus family (see above) seems to have been the first to take the name Eliot. He married Sabina, daughter of Oregar, brother of Geoffrey Oregar and aunt of Geoffrey's son Simon. It seems likely that Geoffrey died before Simon and that Simon died before Sabina, so that Sabina inherited from Simon.[38] Henry senior had a brother, Richard son of Hugo, who was the son of Hugo le Rus and his wife Margaret, daughter of Louis (see below).[39] Henry senior inherited a house and a curtilage in St John's through his father and other properties through his wife: a capital messuage, two curtilages with a house and 2.5 acres of land in St Andrew's; a messuage in the market; and 4.5 acres of land.[40] He bought a messuage in Mill Lane and two houses in St John's, one from Maurice le Rus and the other from Richard Bonney.[41]

Henry and Sabina had at least five sons: Nicholas, Master Thomas, William, Henry junior and John. The heir was Henry, who died early, leaving property to Nicholas, who also died early, leaving his brother Master Thomas to inherit.[42] Henry junior held land near Hinton Way, outside the Barnwell Gate in St Andrew's parish.[43] He may also have held the stone house that was occupied by Henry Eliot in 1295.[44] Master

William Eliot and his family

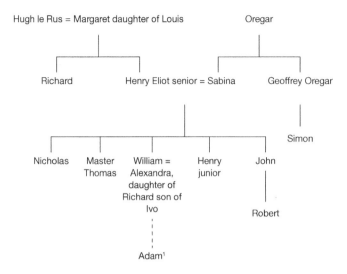

Note: [1] Adam does not appear in the Hundred Rolls, but he is almost certainly a member of a later generation of the family. In view of the large amount of property that he inherited he may have been William's heir (as shown) but this is not certain.

Thomas was involved in the riot of 1235, although he does not seem to have been a ring-leader (he was probably very young at the time). He inherited some of his property from his brother Nicholas, which may have descended to them through their mother.[45]

Master Thomas died next and his brother William inherited. He married Alexandra, daughter of Richard son of Ivo.[46] The fifth son John had a son named Robert and when Robert died Henry junior inherited some of his nephew's property which he gave to his brother William.[47] William eventually inherited all of Henry senior's properties through the death of his brothers; he also acquired two messuages, in St Michael's and in St John's, together with over 10 acres of land through dowry.[48] One of these messuages may have been a magnificent stone house with solar and cellar given by Richard son of Ivo.[49] He also inherited a messuage in St Mary's directly from his brothers; this messuage may have included a mill.[50] He bought another messuage in St Mary's from his uncle, Richard son of Hugo le Rus, and several plots of land from Eustace Dunning and Luke of St Edmunds.[51] The location of these properties, and the possession of a mill, suggest a link with the grain trade.[52]

The Eliots were not an 'old Cambridge family' although they were descended from one (the le Rus family). Henry senior seems to have been the first to take the name Eliot, but it was only with the rise of his son William to bailiff and then mayor that the family acquired prominence. Although Henry senior had five sons, the wealth was not dissipated but rather remained concentrated in the hands of the surviving son, William, who demonstrated competent management of the property portfolio and made a good marriage. William witnessed many deeds in Cambridge; he was often the first named witness, or the first-named after the mayor. The family continued to hold high civic offices into the fourteenth century.

Robert of Madingley and his family

Robert of Madingley (d. shortly before 1279) took his name from a village 3 miles west of Cambridge. He was probably descended, like the le Rus family, from Eustace of Madingley, but by what route is impossible to determine.[53] Robert senior married Eva and they had a son Robert junior and two daughters, Agnes and Margaret.[54] Agnes married Thomas, who seems to have been known variously as 'son of the priest', 'merchant' and 'mercer', while Margaret was unmarried in 1279.[55] Robert junior married Derota, daughter of Thomas of Tuddenham and his wife Matilda.[56] Robert junior was Robert's heir and may have had sons William and Thomas. William was appointed a juror of the Exchequer of the Jews in 1279, and John son of William of Madingley was also appointed at about the same time. Thomas was bailiff in 1293. He also held property in Cambridge; in 1317 he sold a messuage in St Edward's parish at the corner of the Butchery and the Oatmarket, close to the properties in St Mary's held by Robert junior, his father.

Robert senior had accumulated a lot of property by the time of his death. He held three messuages in St Mary's; one bought from Isabella Wombe, one obtained from Thomas son of Laurence and one obtained as dowry, together with over 12 acres of land in Cambridge fields and Newnham, mostly purchased in small lots from various sellers, including Barnwell Priory, Leon Dunning, William Waubert, Henry Nadon and Richard the tailor and Margaret his wife.[57] He also received 3s rent from St Mary's parish paid by Robert son of Robert of Hauxton.

Robert must have played an important role in the establishment of the Guild of St Mary. His name appears first in a list of deceased benefactors compiled c.1315.[58] His widow inherited a messuage occupied by Alexander the mason paying 4s rent, which rent she gave to the Guild, while his daughter Margaret was provided for by Matilda daughter of Isanti (see below).[59] Robert (probably senior) was a juror of the county

Robert of Madingley and his family

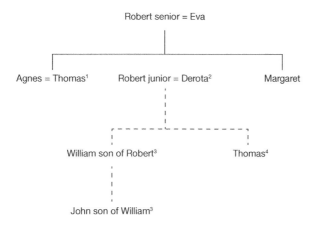

Notes:
[1] Thomas is variously named 'son of the priest', 'mercer', 'merchant'.
[2] Derota is the daughter of Thomas of Tuddenham and his wife Alice.
[3] William's relation to Robert and John's to William are inferred from their names, from the dates they were active and from the contexts in which their names appear.

assize of 1260 (Appendix 11) while his son was a juror for the Hundred Rolls. Robert senior was probably the bailiff who served in 1263 and sometime 1273–8, while his son was bailiff in 1282 and 1285.[60]

Robert of Madingley senior achieved only a modest degree of wealth in view of his probable connection to a wealthy family, possibly because he was a younger son. He concentrated his own legacy on a single son, who, like his father, achieved distinction in civic life. The family remained influential in the town into the 14th century.

Smaller families

Andrew family

Richard of Histon is the first recorded person in the Andrew family tree. He was a chaplain who held land in Tornecroft from St Radegund's Priory for a rent of 2s and two capons.[61] The deed was witnessed by Harvey son of Eustace and can be dated to c.1220–30. Richard had a son, Aldred and a grandson, John.[62] He held a couple of messuages which were inherited by his grandson John.[63]

Andrew family

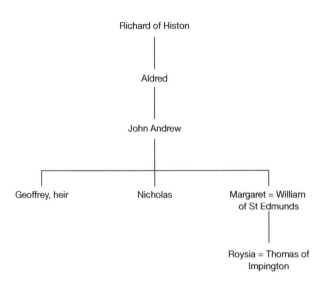

John purchased land from various people, including John Frost junior, John Finch, Radulph Bolle, Alicia daughter of Radulph, and Emma daughter of Ketel, He also held land in Chesterton; he died around the time that the rolls were being compiled. In Chesterton he held customary land from Barnwell Priory, as did his son Geoffrey. John's sub-tenants included Simon Draneland, Nicholas of Gretton (Girton) and Alice Hoseburn.[64]

John had three children: two sons, Geoffrey the heir, and Nicholas, and a daughter Margaret. Geoffrey was a major property owner in St Giles parish, where he owned nine properties.[65] Almost all of Geoffrey's properties were inherited from his father, John. Nicholas also held property in St Giles, which he was given by his father (as a younger son). Margaret married William of St Edmunds and the couple had a had a daughter Roysia who married Thomas of Impington.

John was not connected with elite families but seems to have been an industrious individual who invested his profits in property. The properties were all located within easy reach of the Barnwell fields in Chesterton. His daughter made a good marriage. After his death he was enrolled as a benefactor of the Guild of St Mary.

Aure/Auwre/Aured family

The Aure family tree begins with Aure the draper, whose had a son Reginald; this is probably the Reginald son of Aured who was tallaged for 8 marks in 1211.[66] Reginald had three children: two sons, John and Simon, and a daughter, Alicia. John senior had a son John junior and a daughter Alicia who married into the Godeman family.[67] John senior's sister Alicia married into the Potecar family and had a daughter Johanna.[68] Little is known about Simon except that he inherited a messuage that he gave to his sister.

In 1279 John junior held two messuages. The first, in St John's, was given to him by his sister Johanna before the royal justices at Woodstock; Johanna had been given this by her mother Alice, who had in turn been given it by her brother Simon, who got it from his father Reginald. The second messuage was in St Botolph's and was inherited from his father and grandfather. John Junior had a daughter Joanna.[69] She too held a messuage in St Botolph's, which by 1279 she had sold to Richard Desaxton and Matilda his wife. Alicia, John junior's sister, became a widow; she too held a messuage in St Botolph's which she had sold to Gerard de Vivar by 1279.[70]

The family traded no property at all; the dynamics of their portfolio was driven entirely by inheritance. If there was an entrepreneur, it was probably Aure the draper, the founder of the dynasty, although it is quite

Aure/Auwre dynasty

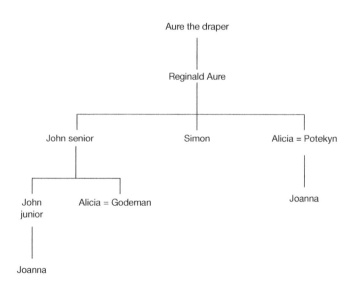

possible that he inherited his property too. The two daughters however, both named Alicia, made good marriages into other small but prosperous families: the Godeman family and the Potecar family.

John of Braintree and the Aubrey family

John of Braintree owned a substantial property portfolio in 1279, but little is known of his origins. There is no evidence of relatives in Cambridge, so it is possible that he came from Braintree in Essex and settled in Cambridge, where he married into the Aubrey family. The Aubrey family shared with the Bateman family a common ancestor in John Selede. This John had at least five sons, one of whom was Geoffrey. Geoffrey's heir, and most probably his son, was Aubrey, butcher. Aubrey had two children: a son and heir John, chaplain, and a daughter Matilda, who married John of Braintree. Both John and Matilda were alive in 1279, but there is no evidence on whether they had children.

John of Braintree accumulated a sizeable portfolio in which several of the properties carried a significant rent burden payable to religious institutions. There were four messuages, a shop and two pieces of vacant land. Much of the property was in St Benedict's parish and the neighbouring parish of St Edward, both of which are to the south of the market area. One messuage was bought from John son of Gervase the

John of Braintree and the Aubrey family

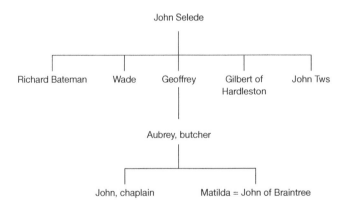

Note: For further details of the top of the tree see 'Richard Bateman and his family', p 344.

baker, which John had given his wife before she was bethrothed, another from Thomas, son of John Warin, and his sister Margaret, and a third from Andrew Pruet.[71]

The fourth messuage, in Newnham, together with the shop, and a piece of vacant land, was acquired as dowry from John Aubrey, his brother-in-law.[72] These were part of John Aubrey's inheritance from his late father. The shop paid rent of 6s to the Abbey of Chatteris and 4s to the Hospital of St John, while the vacant land paid 2s for the maintenance of a candle in St Mary's church. By comparison, the messuage in Newnham paid a mere 4d to the Hospital of St John. These three properties, taken together, constituted a generous dowry; but the high rents on two of the properties may have caused John Aubrey some difficulty paying them out of his income as a chaplain; giving them to his brother-in-law may not have been so great a sacrifice as it might appear.

John Aubrey gave the rest of his inheritance to Isabella Morin, daughter of Richard Morin. This comprised three messuages in St Edward's, one on a lease for life, paying 2s to St Radegund's; one paying 4s to St Radegund's and one paying 4s to Barnwell Priory.[73] He also gave her more than 3 acres of land.[74] Isabella also inherited property from her parents. Her father, Richard Morin, gave her a stall in St Edward's bearing a rent of 4s. 4d to Saer son of William Dencot, and her mother gave her 0.5 acres of land in Cambridge fields.[75] The stall may have been related to Richard's business, and might conceivably have been a butcher's stall. Nevertheless, the income from the stall, plus income from tenants, would have had to finance the sizeable rent payments on all of the properties. It is a mystery as to why John Aubrey left so much wealth to someone apparently outside the family. It is possible that Isabel's mother, Edwina, was also John's sister, so that Isabel was his niece. With John's sister Matilda married to a wealthy husband, and Isabella's siblings similarly well-provided for, it is possible that John decided to look after his unmarried niece. Furthermore, the Aubrey family and the Morin family held land in the same part of town and might well have been involved in the same line of business.

John of Braintree was probably an incomer like John of Aylsham mentioned above. He married into a family that had accumulated significant wealth through a single entrepreneur, Aubrey the butcher. John Aubrey, Aubrey's son and heir, did not add to the family fortune, but he did not dissipate it either; he simply gave it away, partly to his sister and partly to another female relative. John of Braintree was himself an entrepreneur, and as an incomer he probably helped to rejuvenate the family business.

Walter Em

Walter Em was a self-made man. His origins seem to have been quite humble, being the son of Robert Em, from whom he inherited only a small amount of property. This 'oft-mentioned' Walter, to quote the Hundred Rolls, amassed a considerable portfolio of property, all of which seems to have descended to his sole surviving daughter Margaret, who married into the powerful Seman dynasty.[76]

Walter seems to have been an only child and possibly to have had an only child; his father may have been an only child too. The Hundred Rolls documents seventeen properties that Walter purchased during his life. These purchases were financed, it would seem, out of the profits of the grain trade. His main properties were certainly located near the river. There were four messuages in St John's parish, two in Strawylane, one in Mill Lane and one in Milne Street, and a granary at Dame Nicholas Hythe previously owned by Leon Dunning. He held some vacant land in St Botolph's and about 12 acres of land in the Cambridge fields. Almost all of the properties were bought from different people; some, like John Porthors and Nicholas Childman, were well-known, but many seem to have been small property-holders such as Simon Furri and Henry Clay of Howes. Walter Em inherited just two properties: a messuage in Segrimslane in St Benedict's parish, and 2 acres in Cambridge fields, held from the heirs of Petronilla de Cotes.

Walter Em seems to have been a classic entrepreneur accumulating wealth through trade in order to enhance his inheritance. However, he did not create a lasting dynasty, as lack of a male heir caused his legacy to disappear from view. In contrast his daughter's marriage meant that his portfolio to helped sustain an existing dynasty, namely that of the Seman family.

Walter Em's family

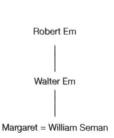

Robert Em

Walter Em

Margaret = William Seman

The Godeman family

The Godeman family had two branches, one descending through Simon Godeman senior and the other through Hugo Godeman.[77] The most probably explanation (if any) is that Hugh and Simon were brothers.

Simon Godeman senior had a son, Simon junior, who had a daughter Avicia. Simon junior and his daughter were both major landowners in 1279.[78] Simon Godeman senior bought property which Simon junior inherited and kept. Simon junior acquired additional property, buying even more than his father, and gave it all to his daughter Avicia, who had not married, it seems, by 1279. In 1279 Simon junior held a messuage in St Michael's from Richard Wombe and about 13 acres of land in the Cambridge and Barnwell fields. Avicia his daughter held several properties in All Saints in the Jewry; a messuage paying 2s rent to Thremhall Priory, a messuage in St John's held from Thomas Plote, a house with land near Dame Nicholas Hythe, and a shop; she also held over 16 acres of land in the Cambridge fields. Simon became bailiff in 1299 and witnessed a number of deeds at that time. Either he or his father was bailiff earlier, c.1273–8.

Hugh Godeman had a son Thomas who was a contemporary of Simon junior. Thomas also acquired considerable property. He lived above the water in St Clement's, paying 11s 6d rent to Master Robert Aunger.

Godeman family

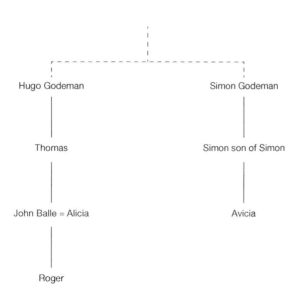

He also held a messuage in St Andrew's and another in St Peter's at the Castle, together with vacant land in St John's. Like Simon, however, much of his portfolio comprised land in the Cambridge fields. Thomas was a customary tenant in Chesterton in 1279 and witnessed deeds as late as 1285.

Thomas's daughter Alicia married John Balle and pre-deceased him.[79] Her dowry from her father was a messuage in St Mary's and was inherited by her son and heir Roger, who then sold back the messuage to his father. Alicia was recorded as a tenant of John le Rus in Newnham in 1280.[80]

The Godemans were clearly an entrepreneurial family. The location of their properties suggests that they were involved in the grain trade. They do not seem to have had dynastic ambitions, though. They had few children; indeed, neither Simon junior nor Thomas seem to have had male heirs. Simon gave a lot of his property to his daughter well before his death.

John Martin and his family

It is said that John Martin was mayor on no fewer than fifteen occasions, and in particular in 1270, 1281–2, 1284 and 1288–9.[81] His father was Martin, about whom little is known. John married Avicia, daughter of William Toylet. John inherited some property in the form of a messuage in St Botolph's which his father purchased from Alicia Segar and 4 acres of land which he acquired as dowry. However John acquired most of his property himself, purchasing three messuages with 5 acres of land in Newnham from John son of Geoffrey le Hose; one messuage with 1 acre of land in Newnham from Leon Dunning; and 6 acres of land in the fields of Cambridge held from Barnwell Priory.[82] In 1274 he purchased from Abraham son of Isaac, 'the king's Jew of Cambridge', the houses and rents in the parish of St Sepulchre which Isaac's father had acquired from the Prior of Barnwell some years previously.[83] The legacy of this purchase does not appear in the Hundred Rolls, however. John made another

John Martin and his family

Martin   Thomas Toylet

John Martin = Avicia

big transaction in 1285 when he purchased from St John's Hospital the estate of John le Hose in Newnham, comprising a tenement with a croft formerly of Thomas Corn, a courtyard formerly of Alice le Reder and half a tenement formerly of Stephen the butcher. He clearly had access to the finance required to undertake such large transactions, and it seems likely that there was a speculative element in them.

John was a self-made man who acquired not only wealth but also reputation in a relatively short space of time. He made an astute marriage and also developed useful contacts through which he was able to make large property transactions.[84]

Morin family

This low-profile family originated with Radulph Morin, who had two sons, Geoffrey and Richard. Geoffrey the heir married Matilda and they had a son John.[85] Radulph died, and Geoffrey inherited, and when Geoffrey died Richard inherited. Richard married Edwina, and they had two daughters, Agnes, the heir, and Isabella. Agnes married Roger of Wilburton. Isabella had not married by 1279, by which time she had inherited considerable property from John Aubrey (who may have been related to Edwina – see above).

Radulph Morin inherited a messuage in St Edward's and 0.5 acres of land in the fields of Cambridge. This may have been what Radulph's ancestors acquired when they first bought property in Cambridge. Geoffrey inherited from Radulph, and on Geoffrey's death this property passed to Richard, and on his death to Agnes, and thence to her husband Roger.[86] Roger seems to have had no property of his own; from this point of view it was not a good marriage.

Morin family

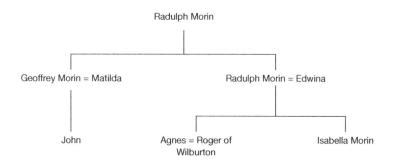

Geoffrey acquired another messuage in St Edward's as dowry through his marriage to Matilda, but then sold it to Simon Prat, son of Geoffrey of Ely.[87] Edwina brought a small dowry of 0.5 acres of land in Cambridge fields, while her husband Richard bought a stall in St Edward's from William Pruet.[88] This may be the property described, at the time it was acquired, as 'a shop between the shop of Henry Hubert and a shop of Nigel le Seller, both held of the nuns; rent 5s and 4s gersuma'.[89] Richard's and Edwina's properties descended to Isabella, who was fortunate to be able to supplement this inheritance with a substantial portfolio given by John Aubrey, chaplain (see above).[90] Geoffrey was one of a number of leading citizens who made an agreement with the burgesses in 1240 regarding a lane in St Clement's parish next to the Hospital.[91]

The Aubrey family held property in the same part of the town as the Mori family, in and around St Edward's parish. It is largely because of Isabella's good fortune in the form of her bequest from John Aubrey that the family appears prominently in the Hundred Rolls. With the possible exception of Richard, the family, and those who married into it, appear to have shown little enterprise themselves.

Potecar/Potekyn dynasty

The family name means apothecary. There were two distinct branches of the family. The first began with Roger of Fulbourn, baker, who had two sons, Geoffrey Potecar and Gregory.[92] Geoffrey married Matilda, daughter of Richard of Fulbourn and they had four children: three sons, John, Thomas and Nicholas, and a daughter, Matilda.[93] John had a son, Alexander Bozun, while Matilda married Bartholomew the Noble, a tailor and had two sons, Robert, the heir, and Henry.[94]

Geoffrey was the most ambitious member of the family. He was coroner and provost at the time of the 1235 riot. Neither he nor the mayor, Harvey son of Eustace, took action, or even recorded what happened. One reason may be that two of Geoffrey's relatives, John and Henry Potekin (possibly his son and grandson) were prominent among the rioters. It was largely because of this leniency towards the rioters that the king took the town into his own hands.[95] Geoffrey died about 1242, leaving a widow Alice, who was presumably his second wife. By 1279 his son Nicholas had become the wealthiest member of the family. He inherited a shop in Holy Trinity, a messuage in St Benedict's, and a messuage in St Mary's that was owned jointly with John son of Richard Goldring.[96] While Geoffrey purchased much of his property, Nicholas mainly inherited from Geoffrey.

Potecar/Potekyn family

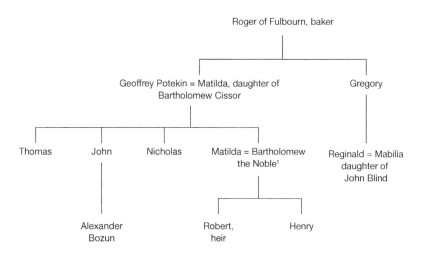

Note: [1] Also known as Bartholomew Cissor (the tailor).

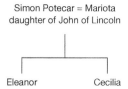

The second branch of the family was headed by Simon Potecar, who had no visible connection to the rest of the dynasty. He married Mariota, daughter of John of Lincoln, and had two daughters, Eleanor and Cecilia, neither of whom appears to have been married in 1279. Simon inherited very little.[97] He bought two messuages in Holy Trinity, one from Master John of Histon and the other from William Warderobe. He also acquired a third part of a messuage in the same parish from Mabilia, daughter of John Reyner. Simon also acquired some land through Mariota's dowry, a portion of which was settled on each daughter.[98]

The Potecar family did not achieve great wealth or distinction; the richest members alive in 1279 were Nicholas and Simon. Both held a couple of messuages in Holy Trinity, which seems to have been the centre of the apothecary trade, plus few other small properties. They may be more typical of the small traders and artisans in Cambridge than some of the families discussed above.

Notes

1. HR 567.
2. HR 505, 611, 772, 795.
3. HR P14/5.
4. HR P22.
5. HR 563-68.
6. LB, p 287.
7. StR, p 162.
8. HR 606-13.
9. CCCC09/05/2, 3.
10. Appendix 12.
11. EJ V; Appendix 8, p 130.
12. CCCC0908/76; CCCC09/2/5.
13. CCCC09/09/6. There is also reference to a Robert Bateman, whose wife Cecilia, daughter of Walter Corde, granted land to her son Adam c.1260–90 (CCCC0917/3/4).
14. HR 1067.
15. CCCC09/12/1.
16. There is also reference to Eustace son of Bernard who was amerced for 2 marks in 1176–7 for carrying corn by water without a licence, but he is too early to have been one of Bernard son of Orgar's sons [Appendix 1].
17. LB, p 322.
18. StR, p 334.
19. HR 182; HR 1067.
20. HR 182.
21. HR 555, StJ, pp 16, 18, 75.
22. StJ, p 18. Other possible members of the Bernard dynasty include Absolon, who witnessed an early deed concerning the Hospital of St John (StJ, p 5); Geoffrey, who served as a juror on a case involving Barnwell Priory in 1288 (LB, p 112); and Thomas, who served on jury regarding the property of Barnwell Priory in 1248 and he (or his son, perhaps) served again in 1289 (LB, pp 103, 178).
23. StJ, pp 20, 24-5.
24. StJ 208; StJ 87, 94; StR, p 309.
25. HR 117/8, R9; HR 632, 874; HR 1078; HR 833.
26. HR 1063; CCCC09/08.
27. HR 1067.
28. HR R9.
29. HR 1062; StR, p 308.
30. HR 154.
31. Appendixes 2, 3, 5; M, pp 168-9.
32. HR 311, 397-8.
33. HR 167, 183, 601, 898.
34. HR 397-404.
35. HR 397, P4. John son of Roger Childman, who witnessed a deed relating to a messuage in Milne Street 1220-60 appears to have no relationship to any of those mentioned above (CCCC09/16C/3).
36. HR 828.
37. Appendix 12; BNM, p 8.
38. HR 822.

[39] HR 827.

[40] HR 829; HR 822/3, 826, 834, 839.

[41] HR 828; HR 830/1.

[42] HR 825,826.

[43] StR, p 136a.

[44] LB, p 286.

[45] HR 824.

[46] HR 822.

[47] HR 825.

[48] HR 832/3, 839/40.

[49] CCCC09/12/4a.

[50] HR 825; CCCC09/08/104.

[51] HR 827; HR 838/840/841.

[52] There was also an Adam Eliot, who does not appear in the Hundred Rolls. He held a mill in the market place, which he may have inherited from William CCCC09/08/104. In 1293 he held a messuage near Dame Nicholas Hythe and St Michael's church CCCC09/12/3. In 1295 he held a stone house in St Andrew's, LB, p 286. He also paid 5s rent to the Hospital of St John for a tenement once of William Seman StJ, p 31. He may have been the son and heir of one of the brothers, possibly William, but it is difficult to say.

[53] In 1220 a Robert of Madingley was charged by the king with entering the lands of Albric of Madingley who had died indebted to the Jews, but it is difficult to connect this person with the Robert who was recently deceased at the time of the Hundred Rolls. It is just conceivable that he could be the same person; if so, he was probably a younger son, as he appears to have inherited very little.

[54] CCCC09/05/2.

[55] HR 481, 596, 801; HR 632.

[56] HR 624,631.

[57] HR 622-4.

[58] BT, p 19.

[59] HR 747; CCCC09/05/2; HR 632.

[60] Appendix 12.

[61] StR, p 25.

[62] HR 39/40.

[63] HR 57/8.

[64] See Chapter 4 Casson, Casson, Lee and Phillips, *Compassionate Capitalism*.

[65] HR 37-45.

[66] Appendix 2.

[67] HR 393 and HR 318.

[68] HR 502/3.

[69] HR 393.

[70] HR 318.

[71] HR 432, 433/5.

[72] HR 438.

[73] HR 505-7.

[74] HR 509/10.

[75] HR 508/11.

[76] See Chapter 4 Casson, Casson, Lee and Phillips, *Compassionate Capitalism*.

[77] HR 199, 679.

[78] HR 693-708.

[79] HR 554.
[80] Appendix 8; EJ, V, p 137.
[81] Appendix 12; BNM, pp 6–7.
[82] HR 378-84.
[83] CPR, 1274, 2 Edw I, p 42.
[84] Several people by the name of Martin were prominent in Cambridge life in the fourteenth century, but because the name is simply short for 'son of Martin' and there were many people with that name, it is difficult to determine whether or not they were related. It would be surprising, however, if John's descendants were not among them.
[85] HR 655.
[86] HR 533, 534.
[87] HR 655.
[88] HR 508/9.
[89] StR, p 195.
[90] HR 505-8, 509/10.
[91] StJ, p 38.
[92] HR 757.
[93] HR 757.
[94] HR 376, 686; HR 873.
[95] Appendix 6, p 358.
[96] HR 756/60.
[97] HR 787-92.
[98] There was also John son of Hugo Potecar and Gilbert nephew of Walter (HR 763-66) they also seem to have no connection with the main family.

References

Primary

Bodleian Library, Oxford

Bodleian MS Gough Cambridgeshire 1 General collections for the county and University of Cambridge with the Isle and Bishopric of Ely, extracted from the Charters, Registers, etc by Francis Blomefield, Clerk, late of Caius College and afterwards Rector of Fersfield in Norfolk: I Prior of Barnwell's Register (2 vols) I

British Library

MS Harley 5813, Excerpt Comprising Transcription of Corpus Christi Deeds

Cole MSS

Add. MS 5809, Friars of the Sack, fol. 85

Add. MS 5809, History of Barnwell Priory, fols 87–9

Add. MS 5810, Number of Houses and Inhabitants in Cambridge in 1728, fol. 190

Add. MS 5810, Index to Lyne's Map of Cambridge, 1574, fols 193–5

Add. MS 5813, History of St Clement's Church, fol. 38

Add. MS 5813, Various Deeds fols 32, 42, 43, 60–2

Add. MS 5813, Benefactors of the Guild of Our Lady (1315) fols 137–42

Add. MS 5821, History of Barton Manor and Deeds, fols 229–33

Add. MS 5821, Benjamin's House at the Tolbooth, fols 229–33

Add. MS 5826, Taxation and Advowsons Documents of 1291 from Bishop Grey's register, fols 171–88

Add. MS 5826, Account of the School of Pythagoras at Cambridge, fols 46–50

Add. MS 5832, Ancient Places in Cambridge, fols 214–15

Add. MS 5833, Mayors and Bailiffs of Cambridge to 1380

Cicely A. H. Howell Papers

Howell, Cicely A. H., 'Contrasting Communities: Arable and Marshland' (unpublished draft, 1979)

Corpus Christi College Archive, University of Cambridge

Online catalogue of Corpus Christi Deeds, available at https://janus. lib.cam.ac.uk/db/node.xsp?id=EAD%2FGBR%2F2938%2FCCCC09 (accessed 1 August 2017)

Merton College Archives, University of Oxford

Liber Ruber

Peterhouse Treasury, Peterhouse College, University of Cambridge

Peterhouse, St Peter's College A1–3 and the Site of the College A1–29

The National Archives

E179 Database, available at http://www.nationalarchives.gov.uk/e179/default.asp (accessed 30 July 2017)

Special Collections, 'Hundred Rolls and Eyre Veredicta', available at http://discovery.nationalarchives.gov.uk/details/r/C13523 (accessed 30 July 2017)

E 372/70 Tallage of 1225

JUST 1/81 Cambridgeshire Eyre of 1247, Foreign pleas roll, including essoins, 31 Henry III

JUST 1/82 Cambridgeshire Eyre of 1261, Roll of civil, foreign and crown pleas, jury calendar, essoins and attorneys 45 Henry III

JUST 1/83 Cambridgeshire Eyre of 1268, General oyer and terminer, lands given away as a result of the Barons' War, roll of pleas, presentments, amercements and jury calendar 53 Henry III

JUST 1/84 Cambridgeshire Eyre of 1272, Roll of civil and foreign pleas, 56 Henry III

JUST 1/85 Cambridgeshire Eyre of 1272, Roll of crown pleas, 56 Henry III

JUST 1/86 Cambridgeshire Eyre of 1286, Rex roll of civil, foreign and crown pleas, gaol delivery, plaints, amercements and fines, jury calendar, essoins and attorneys, 14 Edward I

JUST 1/96 Cambridgeshire Eyre of 1299, Berwick's roll of civil, foreign, king's and crown pleas, gaol delivery, plaints, jury calendar, essoins and attorneys, 27 Edward I

SC5/CAMBS/TOWER/2 Barnwell Hundred Roll

SC5/CAMBS/TOWER/1/Parts1–3 Cambridge Borough Hundred Rolls

Published sources

Primary

Bateson, Mary, *Cambridge Gild Records* (Cambridge, 1903)

Brand, P. (ed.), *Plea Rolls of the Exchequer of the Jews, VI: Edward I, 1279–81* (6 vols) (London, 2005)

Calendar of Close Rolls of Edward I (5 vols, 1272–1307) (London, 1970)

Calendar of Patent Rolls of Edward I (4 vols, 1272–1307) (London, 1893–1901)

Clark, John Willis (ed.), *Liber Memorandum Ecclesie de Bernewelle* (Cambridge, 1907)

Cohen, S. (ed.), *Plea Rolls of the Exchequer of the Jews, V: Edward I, 1277–1279* (6 vols) (London, 1992)

Ekwall, Eilert (ed.), *Two Early London Subsidy Rolls* (London, 1951)

Flower, C. T., David Crook and Paul Brand (eds), *Rotuli Curiae Regis/ Curia Regis Rolls* (10 vols) (London and Woodbridge, 1922–2006)

Hackett, M. B., *The Original Statutes of Cambridge University: The Text and Its History* (Cambridge, 1970)

Hunter, Joseph (ed.), *Fines, Sive, Pedes Finium: AD 1195–1214, I: Bedfordshire, Berkshire, Buckinghamshire, Cambridgeshire and Cornwall* (2 vols, 1835–44) (London, 1835)

Maitland, Frederic William (ed.), *Three Rolls of the King's Court in the Reign of King Richard I, AD 1194–5* (London, 1891)

Meekings, C. A. F., *Crown Pleas of the Wiltshire Eyre, 1249* (Devizes, 1961)

Palmer, W. M. (ed.), *The Assizes Held at Cambridge 1260: Being a Condensed Translation of Assize Roll 82 in the Public Record Office with an Introduction* (Linton, 1930)

Palmer, William M., *Cambridgeshire Subsidy Rolls 1250–1695* (London, 1912)

Jenkinson, H. (ed.), *Calendar of the Plea Rolls of the Exchequer of the Jews, III: Edward I, 1275–1277* (6 vols) (London, 1925)

Pipe Rolls, 98 vols (London, 1884–2016) especially the published rolls for the years 1130–1224, 1230 and 1242, vols 1–9, 11–19, 21–58, 50, 52–8, 60, 62, 64, 66, 68, 73, 75, 77, 80, 85, 86, 89, 91, 93, 94, 95, 98

Pipe Roll Society, *Feet of Fines of the Reign of Henry II and of the First Seven Years of the Reign of Richard I, AD 1182–1196* (London, 1894)

Pipe Roll Society, *Feet of Fines of the Tenth Year of the Reign of King Richard I and a Roll of the King's Court in the Reign of King Richard I, AD 1182–1196* (London, 1900)

Richardson, H. G. (ed.), *Calendar of the Plea Rolls of the Exchequer of the Jews, IV: Henry III, 1272; Edward I, 1275–1277* (6 vols) (London, 1972)

Rigg, J. M. (ed.), *Calendar of the Plea Rolls of the Exchequer of the Jews, I: Henry III, 1218–1272* (6 vols) (London, 1905)

Rigg, J. M. (ed.), *Calendar of the Plea Rolls of the Exchequer of the Jews, II: Edward I, 1273–1275* (6 vols) (Edinburgh, 1910)

Rotuli Hundredorum Temp. Henry III and Edward I., in Turr' Lond' et in Curia Receptæ Scaccarij Westm. Asservati (2 vols) (London, 1812 and 1818)

Rye, Walter, *Pedes Finium or Fines Relating to the County of Cambridge, Levied in the King's Court from the Seventh Year of the Reign of Richard I to the End of the Reign of Richard III* (Cambridge, 1891)

Sheffield Hundred Rolls Project, available at http://www.roffe.co.uk/ shrp.htm (accessed 2 April 2017)

Sheriff of Cambridgeshire and Huntingdonshire, available at https://en. wikipedia.org/wiki/Sheriff_of_Cambridgeshire_and_Huntingdonshire (accessed 29 October 2018)

Stenton, Doris Mary (ed.), *Pleas before the King and His Justices 1198–1202 I: Introduction with Appendix Containing Essoins 1199–1201, A King's Roll of 1200 and Writs 1190–1200* (4 vols) (London, 1952–67)

Stenton, Doris Mary (ed.), *Pleas before the King and His Justices 1198–1202 II: Fragments of Rolls from the Years 1198, 1201 and 1202* (4 vols) (London, 1952–67)

Stenton, Doris Mary (ed.), *Pleas before the King and His Justices 1198–1202 III: Rolls or Fragments of Rolls from the Years 1199, 1201 and 1203–6* (4 vols) (London, 1952–67)

Stenton, Doris Mary (ed.), *Pleas before the King and His Justices 1198–1202 IV: Rolls or Fragments of Rolls from the Years 1207–1212* (4 vols) (London, 1952–67)

Turner, G. J., *A Calendar of the Feet of Fines Relating to the County of Huntingdon Levied in the King's Court from the Fifth Year of Richard I to the End of the Reign of Elizabeth, 1194–1603* (Cambridge, 1913)

Underwood, Malcolm (ed.), *Cartulary of the Hospital of St. John the Evangelist* (Cambridge, 2008)

Williams, Ann and G. H. Martin (eds), *Domesday Book: A Complete Translation* (London, 2002)

Secondary sources

Anon, *The History and Antiquities of Barnwell Abbey and of Sturbridge Fair* (London, 1786)

Brink, Daphne H., *The Parish of St. Edward, King and Martyr, Cambridge: Survival of a Late Medieval Appropriation* (Cambridge, 1992)

Bryan, Peter, *Cambridge: The Shaping of the City*, new ed. (Cambridge, 2008)

Cam, Helen M., 'Cambridgeshire Sheriffs in the Thirteenth Century', *Proceedings of the Cambridge Antiquarian Society* 25 (1924): 78–102

Cam, Helen M., *The Hundred and the Hundred Rolls: An Outline of Local Government in Medieval England* (London, 1930)

Cam, Helen M., *Liberties and Communities in Medieval England* (Cambridge, 1944)

Casson, Catherine, Mark Casson, John S. Lee and Katie Phillips, *Compassionate Capitalism: Business and Community in Medieval England* (Bristol, 2020)

Darby, H. C., *The Domesday Geography of Cambridgeshire* (Cambridge, 1936)

Dodwell, B., 'The Free Tenantry of the Hundred Rolls,' *Economic History Review* 14 (2) (1944): 163–71

Farrer, William, *Feudal Cambridgeshire* (Cambridge, 1920)

Gray, Arthur, *The Priory of St Radegund, Cambridge* (London, 1892)

Gray, Ronald and Peter Stubbings, *Cambridge Street Names: Their Origins and Associations* (Cambridge, 2000)

Greenway, Diana E., 'A Newly Discovered Fragment of the Hundred Rolls of 1279–80', *Journal of Society of Archivists* 7 (2) (1982): 73–7

Hall, Catherine P., 'In Search of Sabina: A Study in Cambridge Topography', *Proceedings of the Cambridge Antiquarian Society* 65 (1973–4): 60–78

Howell, Cicely A. H., 'Stability and Change 1300–1700: The Socio-Economic Context of the Self-Perpetuating Family Farm in England', *Journal of Peasant Studies* 2 (4) (1975): 468–82

Howell, Cicely A. H., 'Peasant Inheritance Customs in the Midlands, 1280–1700', *Land and Inheritance: Rural Society in Western Europe, 1200–1800*, ed. Jack Goody, Joan Thirsk and E. P. Thompson (Cambridge, 1978), pp 112–55

Howell, Cicely A. H., *Land, Family and Inheritance in Transition; Kibworth Harcourt 1280–1700* (Cambridge, 1983)

Kanzaka, Junichi, 'Villein Rents in Thirteenth-Century England: An Analysis of the Hundred Rolls of 1279–1280', *Economic History Review* 55 (4) (2002): 593–619

Kosminsky, E., 'The Hundred Rolls of 1279–80 as a Source for English Agrarian History', *Economic History Review* 3 (1) (1931): 16–44

Leedham-Green, E., *A Concise History of the University of Cambridge* (Cambridge, 1996)

Lobel, Mary D., *Historic Towns Atlas: Cambridge* (London, 1975)

Musson, Anthony and Ormrod, W. M., *The Evolution of English Justice: Law, Politics and Society in the Fourteenth Century* (Basingstoke, 1999)

Muth, Richard F. and Allen C. Goodman, *The Economics of Housing Markets* (London, 1989)

National Archives, 'Exchequer of the Jews Plea Rolls', available at http://discovery.nationalarchives.gov.uk/details/r/C6509 (accessed 9 January 2017)

National Archives, 'General Eyres', available at http://www.national archives.gov.uk/help-with-your-research/research-guides/general-eyres-1194-1348/#sevenpointthree (accessed 30 July 2017)

National Archives, 'Land Conveyances by Feet of Fines 1182–1833', available at http://www.nationalarchives.gov.uk/help-with-your-research/research-guides/land-conveyance-feet-of-fines-1182-1833/ (accessed 9 January 2017)

National Archives, 'Pipe Rolls', available at http://www.nationalarchives.gov.uk/help-with-your-research/research-guides/medieval-financial-records-pipe-rolls-1130-1300/ (accessed 30 July 2017)

National Archives, 'Taxation before 1689', available at http://www.nationalarchives.gov.uk/help-with-your-research/research-guides/taxation-before-1689/ (accessed 30 July 2017)

Page, William (ed.), *The Victoria History of the County of Huntingdon, II* (3 vols) (London, 1932)

Palmer, W. M., 'The Stokes and Hailstone MSS.', *Proceedings of the Cambridge Antiquarian Society* 33 (1933): 169–70

Raban, Sandra, 'Mortmain in Medieval England', *Past and Present* 62 (1974): 3–26

Raban, Sandra, *A Second Domesday: The Hundred Rolls of 1279–80* (Oxford, 2004)

Rubin, Miri, *Charity and Community in Medieval Cambridge* (Cambridge, 1987)

Scales, Leonard E., 'The Cambridgeshire Ragman Rolls', *English Historical Review* 113 (452) (1998): 553–7

The Gen Guide, Patent Rolls, available at https://www.genguide.co.uk/ source/patent-rolls-medieval-courts/5/ (accessed 9 January 2018)

University of Nottingham Manuscripts and Special Collections Guide, 'Letters Patent', available at https://www.nottingham.ac.uk/ manuscriptsandspecialcollections/researchguidance/deedsindepth/ freehold/letterspatent.aspx (accessed 9 January 2018).

Willis, Robert and John Willis Clark, *The Architectural History of the University of Cambridge and the Colleges of Cambridge and Eton* (2 vols) I (Cambridge, 1886)

Theses

Howell, Cicely A. H., 'The Economic and Social Condition of the Peasantry in South East Leicestershire, A.D. 1300–1700' (DPhil thesis, University of Oxford, 1974)

Index

A

Abington, 13, 131
Abinton, Reginald of, 252
Absalon of Newnham, 256
Absolon, 245
Absolon son of Apsolon, 322
Absolon son of Segar, 250
Ace, John, 113, 117, 143, 223
Adam son, 23, 110, 149, 229
Adam telarius, 252
advowsons, 17, 24, 143, 165, 167,
 169–70
 of churches, 169–70
 and donation, 24, 167, 169–70
 of hospitals, 166–7
Ailwin brother of Wulward, 246, 247
Alan of Orwell, 260
Alan of Welles (bailiff), 336
Alan son of Leving, 260
Alan telarius, 251
Aldred gener Ketel, 254, 257
Alexander fittere, 261
Alexandria, 189–90
Aleyns, Matilda, 120, 178–9, 200
Alfelin of the Bridge, 246, 247
Alfgar of Exning, 246, 247
Algar of Welles, 252, 257, 264
Algar son of Robert, 261
Algold, Robert, 57
almoners
 of Barnwell, 13, 77, 134, 144–6, 171,
  193, 211, 224
 of Croyland, 101
 of Ely, 52, 74, 108, 121, 122, 135,
  154, 179, 193, 197
 of St Edmunds, 196
 of Tilty, 179
Alsope, William, 89, 177
Alwines Lane, 337

Ambrose, 8, 78–80, 84, 100
Amicia, 32, 80, 137, 143, 145, 172,
 186
Ampe, Richard, 32, 43, 47, 48
ancient acquisition, 34–5, 46–8, 69–70,
 80–6, 88–91, 93, 96, 123–4,
 127–8
Andre, John, 33–5, 37, 188
Andrew (and family), 351–2
Andrew of Cockfiled, 265
Andrew of Swavesey, 246, 247
Andrew of Winepol, 264
Andrew son of Philip, 265
Angelica Library, Rome, 6
Anglesey Priory, 25–6
Astin, Godfrey, 12
Aszio carnifax/macecrer, 246
Ategate/Attegate, Richard, 52, 72, 73,
 122
Attegrene, John, 41
attorneys, 239–40
Aubri/Abury/Aubrey, John, 106
Auger, Robert, 31–2
Auncell of Costesseye (bailiff), 336
Aunger, Robert, 16, 18, 35, 57,
 61–2, 79, 133, 135–6, 159, 161,
 171
Aure/Auwre/Aured (and family),
 353–4
Aured, John, 84, 97, 130, 173
Aure, John, 78, 125, 155–7
Austin Friars, 337
Auwre, John, 118–19

B

Bagge, Simon, 252
Baker, Decenna William, 264
Baker, Geoffrey, 86, 88

Baker, Gilbert, 23, 69, 142
Baker, Reverend Thomas, 5
Barnard Castle, 26, 34, 55, 70, 78, 87–8, 92, 331
Barnwell, 5, 11–17, 40–1, 47–52, 59, 61–6, 68–70, 94–5, 97–100, 116–18, 120–2, 127–9, 131, 140–1, 144–6, 155–6, 158–62, 171–2, 200–2, 204–5, 207–38
    Eustace of, 246
    Prior of, 5
    register, 5
    rental of 1295, 5
    Richard of, 246, 252
    Robert prior of, 322
    St Giles Church, 322
    suburb, 4
    Urvei son of Emme, 322
Barnwell Causey, 337
Barnwell Gate, 337
Barnwell Priory possessions, 11
Barnwell's register, 5
Barons' War, 325
Bartholomew/Brithnod the tannur, 254
Barton, 8, 29–32, 34, 49, 54, 68–72, 86–8, 144, 173, 175, 177–8, 180–1, 184–5, 192, 200
    Simon son of John, 326
Basilia in Cambridge and Barnwell, 14
Basilia wife of Godwin, 264
Bassat, Golde, 115–16
Bateman (and family), 343–5
Bateman, Richard, 9, 15, 25, 137, 139, 161, 178, 197
Bateman, Richard senior, 9, 106, 130, 138, 183
Bedell, William, 263
Bede's House, 337
Benedict feltrarius/Feutrer, 250
Bernard, John, 58, 235
Bernard, Michael, 47, 51, 122, 142, 190, 198, 234, 236, 345–6
Bernard, Simon, 128
Bernard son of Edric, 251, 256
Berwick's roll, 325
Biendeu, Hugo, 260
Billing, Richard, 254

Billing, William, 253
Bishop of Ely, 11, 165
Black Friars, 337
Blackfriars Lane, 337
Blancgernun, Baldwin, 22, 32, 55–6, 62–3, 132, 255, 322
Blancgernun, Walter, 35–7
Blancgernun, William, 12
Blanchard, Decana Nicholas, 261
Blodles, John, 93, 130, 138–9
Blodles, William, 130, 139
Blowe, Henry, 232
Blund, Alfgar, 246, 247
Blund, Roger, 255
Blund, Simon, 261
Blund, Walter, 255
Boigris, Geoffrey, 246
bondage tenant, 10
Bornell, 217–18, 220, 229
Botte, William, 32
Braci, William, 89–90, 109, 146
Bradele, 108–9, 113
Bradmore fields, 12
Bret, Alan le, 246
Bridge Street, 337
Brodeie, William, 224, 226, 231–2, 236–7
Brother Atius, 13–14, 50
Brown, Henry (le Brun), 265
Brown, William (le Brun), 245, 321
Bulling, Richard, 260
Burs, Richard, 58, 76, 130–1, 156
Butchery, 337
But/Butt, John (Mayor), 334, 335, 336
Bynnebroc, 337

C

Cag, Ketel, 256, 257
Caggere, Decenna Henry le, 265
Caim, William, 208, 213
Caldwell Priory, 26
Cambridge, 23, 110
    burgess of, by gift of Eustace
        Blancgernun, Baldwin, 322
    Ella the widow of William
        Cholle, 323
    Emma Cholle, 323

Harvey son of Edward, 322
Harvey son of Eustace, 322
Margery wife of Martin Wulward, 323
Martin Wulward, 323
borough Hundred Rolls, 2
churches and parishes
All Saints' Church, 169
All Saints at the Castle, 337
All Saints in the Jewry, 337
Holy Sepulchre, 16, 23, 35, 170, 172, 174, 192
Holy Trinity Church, 52, 178–9, 183, 194
Holy Trinity parish, 49, 52, 54, 58, 102, 124, 175, 178, 183–6, 199, 221
St Andrew's Church, 192–4, 199, 218
St Andrew parish, 21, 61, 62, 89, 123–4, 127–8, 169, 171, 186–8, 191–200
St Benedict's Church, 65, 83, 105–6, 133, 144
St Benedict parish, 72, 81, 86, 90–1, 98, 100–8, 110, 131, 133, 169, 175, 234–5
St Botolph's, 66, 80, 83, 85–6, 88–9, 91, 95–7, 99, 111, 117, 119, 121, 134–5
St Clement's, 18, 48, 52–3, 56–64, 68, 71, 73–4, 169, 171, 173–4, 183
St Edward parish, 102, 104, 106, 119–26, 130, 134–5, 138, 142, 146, 187, 193, 198, 234–5
St Giles's Church, 11, 19, 169, 207, 322
St Giles parish, 17, 22, 31, 40, 41, 42–7, 49, 51, 54
St John's Church, 87
St John parish, 17, 23, 25, 27–8, 61, 64–5, 87, 90, 98, 108–10, 112–16, 117–18, 167, 170, 189–90
St Mary's Church, 47, 64, 80, 106, 109, 112, 125–8, 130–1, 134–6, 139, 143
St Mary parish, 27–8, 30, 109, 112, 123–4, 127–40, 142, 144–7, 172, 175–6, 178, 180–1, 188–9
St Michael's Church, 25, 27, 110, 114, 128–9, 138, 143, 146, 150, 152–5, 169, 171, 182
St Peter's Church, 23, 50, 169–70
St Peter's parish, 25, 37–9, 43–4, 46, 50, 74–5, 79–80, 83, 86, 97, 101, 106
mayors and bailiffs (1263–1300), 334–6
Cambridge Colleges
Corpus Christi College, 6
Jesus, 6
King's Hall, 339
Peterhouse, 6
St John's, 6
Cambridge debts
Exchequer of the Jews (cases), 1219–81, 297–313
Jewish records of, 315–19
Cambridge rolls, 2
Cambridgeshire, 2–4, 9, 239, 239–40
eyres, 239–40, 325
grievances in, 2
and Huntingdonshire, 3
peasant landholding in, 4
subsidy rolls for, 325
canons, 11–17, 26, 60, 143, 162
Cardun, Henry, 217
Carmelite Friars, 29
Carmelite Friary, 337
Carpenter, Robert, 79, 140
Carpenter, William, 173, 200
Carter, Luke, 12, 98, 129
Castelein, William, 146, 156, 210
Casteleyn, William, 38–9
Caval, William, 263
Change, Adam, 261
Chapeler, Abraham le, 49, 74, 131–2, 156, 176, 182–3
Chauelay [Cheveley]
Harvey son of Eustace, 323
Laurence de Hotot, 323
Chesterton, 331
subsidy rolls for, 325

Childman, 53, 152, 254, 257, 260, 347–8
Childman, Nicholas, 325
Cholle, Emma, 323
Cholles Lane, 337
civil and foreign pleas, 325
Clait, Geoffrey, 254
Clark, John Willis, 241
Close Rolls, 5
Cobon, William, 261
Cocus, Robert, 256
Coleville, 44, 48, 209, 216, 222, 237–8
Combere, Osbert le, 252, 256
Conduit Street, 337
Cook, Geoffrey, 159, 174
Cook, Robert, 15, 122, 218
Cook, William, 104, 159
Copin, John, 147
Corde, Matilda, 56
Corde, Walter, 56
Cordubarius, Stephen, 321
Cornhythelane, 337
Coteler, William le 136–7, 194
Cotes
    William of, 325
Court of Common Pleas, 5; see also
        Curia Regis, sedentary court
Crane, Osbert, 245
Creton
    Harvey son of Eustace, 321
    Ioelu de Creton, 321
Criket, Peter, 254
criminal jurisdiction, 5
criminals' property, escheats of, 167
Cristiana, 117, 160–1, 192
Crocheman, Fulco, 250
Crocheman, John, 250
Crocheman, Richard (bailiff), 152, 336
Crocheman, Walter, 133, 152, 160, 325
Crocheman, William, 135, 152
crown pleas, 4, 164, 239–40, 325
Crul, John, 128, 205, 207, 211–12
Crutched Friars, 29
Culling, Robert (bailiff), 335, 336
Cunington, village, 260
Curia Regis Rolls, 5, 336
    sedentary court, 5
Curteis, Gilbert, 257
Curteis, Giles, 254

Curteis, Richard, 254, 257
Curteis, Robert, 52
Curteys, John, 127, 195
Custance, Robert, 255
Custancia, 137, 140
Cutler's Row, 338
Cyne, Reginald, 12

D

Daiman of Cambridge, 246
Dame Nichol's Hythe, 58, 65, 157
David, Count, 11
de Amundsville, Alicia, 264
de Argentin, Giles, 80
de Bello Campo, William, 264
Decenna Thomas son of Geoffrey, 264
de Creton, Ioelu, 321
de Eltisley, Maurice, 198
de Frusselak, William, 246
de Fulbourne, Maurice, 191
de Hauxton, Stephen, 12
de Henges, William, 12
de Hotot, Laurence, 323
de Hudobovill, John, 264
de Kertlinge, Hugo, 253
de Kynelrirle, John (bailiff), 336
de Ledes, William (bailiff), 336
de Mateshale, Simon, 331
de Moneia, Reginald, 245
de Mortimer, Guy, 28
de Mortimer, Lord William, 166
de Mortimer, Robert, 22, 162
de Novacurt, William, 27
Deonisia, 123, 133, 214
de Pupelot, Thomas, 264
de Saillum, Walter, 264
de Sparraguz, Margaret, 264
de Stagno, Gerard (bailiff), 335
de Stowe, Agnes, 137
de Stowe, Baldwin, 137
de Stowe, Matilda, 53
de Stowe, Richard, 113, 152
de Vivario, Gerard (bailiff), 335
de Winebodesham, Reiner, 255
de Wykes, Roger (Mayor), 336
Dionisia, 146, 204, 212, 223–7, 234
Domesday Book (1086), 2, 4
Dorodivers Lane, 338

Doy, Roger, 252
Doy, Thomas, 252
Doy, William, 250
Dreye, Stephen, 136
Druse Mere, 338
Dunning, Adam, 17–18, 38, 66, 69, 134, 137, 141, 155, 162, 216, 219
Dunning, Eustace, 23, 26, 38, 40–1, 45, 53–5, 60, 70–1, 73, 78, 87, 92–3, 113
Dunning family, 6
Dunning/Dunnyng, Harvey, 11, 26, 34, 37–8, 40, 67, 70–1, 73, 93, 156, 173
Dunning, John (Mayor), 45, 54, 336
Dunning, Leon, 38–9, 45–6, 49, 58, 93, 95, 110–11, 113–17, 129, 150, 166, 170, 172–3, 215–17, 225, 229–30, 236, 331
Dunning, Leonard, 181, 184
Dunning, Richard (bailiff), 181, 335, 336
Dunnyng, Leon, 35

E
Eare, Godric, 246
Eare, Walter, 246, 253
Edelina widow of William Arnold, 265
Edmundo, 246
Edric of Lynn (Len), 245
Edward I, 2, 163, 240–1
Edward, Gregory, 199, 293
Edward, Robert, 105, 178, 180, 193, 195, 200, 222
Edward son of Edward, 250
Edward, Walter, 195, 200
Edward, William, 193, 200
Eldcorn, Eustace, 63, 325
Eldcorn, Hugh, 63
Eleanor, 32, 58, 82, 88, 105, 193, 203
Elena, 38–9, 60, 65–6, 71, 73, 90, 144, 146, 184, 194, 196, 198, 223
Elesheved, William, 39, 61
Elias son of Andrew, 261
Elias son of Osbert, 252, 257
Elias son of Robert, 260

Eliot/Elyot/Elyhot (and family), 348–50
Eliot/Elyot/Elyhot, William, 40, 146, 158, 175, 187, 188, 206, 335
Eliza (Aelizia) of Chesterton, 246
Eltisley, 113, 198
Ely, 11–12, 18, 22, 25, 27, 52, 54, 133, 169, 171, 193–4, 196–7, 200
   almoner of, 52, 74, 108, 121–3, 135, 154, 179, 193, 197
   church of, 18
   former bishop of, 18, 24, 155
   Prior of, 27
Elyhot, Henry, 188–9
Elyhot, Thomas, 188
Elyot, Henry, 104
Elyoth, William, 64
Emma Cholle v. Martin Wulward, 323
Em, Robert, 65, 68
Em, Walter, 64–7, 118, 335, 356
encroachments, 163–4, 167
   on chases and warrens, 164
   on the king's dike, 167–8
   on market privileges, 164
Ere, Gregory, 98
escheats, 9, 58, 167–8
essoins, 239–40
Estmund, 246
Eudo of Swineshead, 261
Eustace of Barnwell, 246, 247
Eustace of Cambridge, 23
Eustace son of Bernard, 245
Everard of Powis, 246
Everard son of Eustace, 260
Eversden
   Hugo Ruffus, 323
   Hugo son of Ernald, 323
   Philip son of Robert, 323
Excel spreadsheet, 7, 242
Exchequer, 150, 164, 172, 240–2
Exchequer of the Jews, 5
   records of, 5

F
Faber, John, 254
Faber, Robert, 250
Faireyardlane, 338
Fayr Yard, 338

fee farm, 15–17, 21–7, 31–9, 43–4,
    48–52, 55–66, 68–9, 71–2, 74–7,
    81–4, 86–7, 89–92, 101–5,
    107–8, 111–13, 115–21, 123–8,
    147–8, 181–4, 186–96
feet of fines, 5, 321–3
    cases relevant to Cambridge, 321–3
Felicia, 41, 159, 162, 212
feoffment, 49, 53, 59, 145, 162, 175–6,
    183, 210, 220–1
Feron, John (bailiff), 335
fief, 9, 30–3, 39–40, 44–5, 47–8, 51–9,
    61–3, 83, 85, 91, 162, 165–6, 168
Finch, William, 246
Findsilver Lane, 338
Fisher, Hugh, 257
Fithion, Robert, 46
Fittere, Alex le, 252
Fiyion, Henry, 50
Flax Hythe, 338
Flemeditch, 331
Flinston, Simon, 128, 192–3
Florencia, 209
Foreign pleas, 325
Fot, Simon, 75, 83
Foulelane, 338
Franc, Robert, 263
Frere, 255
Friars Minor, 28–9
Friars of the Sack (Friars of the Penance
    of Jesus Christ), 29, 338
Friars Preacher, 28
Frost, Absolon, 254
Frost, John, 34–5, 53–4, 66, 72–3
Frost, Salomon, 260
Frostulf, Henry, 246
Froyslake, 44, 51
Frusselake, Thomas, 261
Fulk of Barnwell, 153, 160
Furri, Simon, 66, 83

G
Gamlingay, 322
Garlicfayrelane, 338
Garret Hostel Green, 338
Gaunter, 86, 195–6
Geliner, Richard le, 252, 257
Geoffrey *cementario*, 263

Geoffrey of Costesseye (bailiff), 336
Geoffrey of Edlington, 264
Geoffrey son, 146, 220–1
Geoffrey son/brother of Ivo, 253
Geoffrey son of Ivo, 261
Geoffrey son of Joscelin, 260
Geoffrey son of Robert, 251
Geoffrey son of Wulward, 261
Gerard, 83–4
Gerard ad Stagnum (bailiff), 335
Gerund, John, 335, 336
Gibelot, Richard, 251
Gilbert v. [Harvey] son of Eustace,
    323
Giles son of John Barton, 68–70
Glaseneye, Walter, 31
Glomery Lane, 338
Gloverer, Hugo, 264
Godelot, Simon, 177, 196
Godeman (and family), 357–8
Godeman, Simon, 115, 118, 155–7,
    335, 336
Godeman, Thomas, 61, 128, 151, 161,
    171
Godfrey, 109, 237, death of
Godfrey, 109, 145, 193, 214, 237
Godfrey son of Godfrey, 264
Godland, 245, 246
Godso, Cecilia, 75, 138, 143
Godso [Godsone], Reginald, 253
Godsone, John, 186, 195, 200
Godsone, William, 186, 194, 198
Gogging, Bartholomew (Mayor), 334
Gogging, Harvey, 91, 94, 100–1, 144,
    251, 256
Gogging, John (bailiff), 100, 102, 151,
    336
Gogging, Michael, 73, 83, 92, 96, 100,
    121–2, 151
Golde, Isabella, 144
Golde, John, 176, 184, 185, 194
Golde, Nicholas, 178
Golde, William, 176, 194
Goldring, John (bailiff), 336
Goldring, Richard, 9, 175–6
Goldring, William (bailiff), 335
Goldsmith, Nicholas, 126, 142
Goldsmith, Walter, 177, 181
Gough manuscripts, Bodleian, 6

granary, 25, 27, 65–6, 92, 113, 118, 150, 173
Granta, 338
Great Bridge of Cambridge, 168
Gregory, Richard, 108
Gregory son of Hugo, 251
Grenecroft, 338
Grey Friars, 338
grievances, 2
Grim, John, 20
Guardians (bailiff), 336
Gudred/Guthier, Richard, 251
guild records, 5
Gut, Henry, 201, 211, 219–20, 224, 226, 229, 232

H

Haliday, Walter, 96, 144, 177
Hamon, John, 43
Hampe, John, 47
Hangmanslane, 338
Hardy, Thomas, 85
Hareng, Geoffrey, 255
Harlestone Lane, 338
Harleston's Hostel, 338
Harvey, 43, 45, 53
Harvey de Burgat' and William, 260
Harvey son of Eustace, 255, 321, 322, 323, 336
Harvey son of Eustace petitioner v. Harvey son of Edward, 322
Harvey son of Eustace v. Laurence de Hotot, 323
Harvey son of Selede, 251, 256
Hatfield, 129, 135
Hauxton, 9, 12, 98–9, 103–4, 117, 137, 142, 144, 171, 174, 183
Hawan, 246
Hawan's brother, 246
Helde, Hugo, 264
Helewisa, 117–18, 170, 208
Henges, Margaret, 129–30
Henges, William, 129–30, 139
Henny Lane/Hennabby, 338
Henry, 44, 46, 49, 51, 57, 58, 182, 200, 207, 217
Henry, Master, 14, 68, 94
Henry II, King, 3

Henry III, King 239–40, 257
Henry of Barton (bailiff), 336
Henry of Fukeworde, 264
Henry son, 23, 42, 85, 134–5, 171, 186, 188, 196
Henry son of Albric and Rohesia and Mabilia, 260
Henry son of Elye, 253
Henry son of Godfrey and Agnes, 260
Henry son of Robert, 265
Henry telarius, 251
hereditary descent, 94, 176–8, 181, 196
hereditary paternal succession, 206, 223
hereditary succession, 30–3, 39–45, 47–8, 53, 55–6, 84, 127–8, 130–4, 143, 146, 148–9, 151, 179–80, 182–3, 185–6, 197, 199, 201–19, 222–3, 227
Herre, William, 27, 143–4
High Street, 338
Hildebrand of Cambridge, 245
Hinton, 31, 68, 94–5, 105, 180, 196, 218, 231
Hintonway, 339
Hirp, Henry, 48
Histon, 33, 42, 75, 120, 148, 160, 176, 181, 185
Hitti, John, 54, 61
Hitti, William, 255
Hockley, 112, 114
Holm, 339
Honey Hill, 339
Horsemonger, 37–8
Hospital of St John, Jerusalem, 28
Hospital of St John the Baptist, 339
Houghton, 42–3, 48, 51, 111, 124
Howes, 8, 34, 38, 40–1, 51, 67, 89, 151, 184, 339
Huberd, Robert, 25, 33, 59–60, 80, 112, 325
Huberd, Sabina, 45, 52, 59, 73, 136
Hubert, Henry, 132
Hubert, Robert, 73, 82, 93, 138, 143
Huchepain, Aluric, 245
Hugh son, 19–20, 208, 212, 215, 229–30, 233
Hugo, 175, 177, 184–6, 188–9, 197–8, 202–5, 207
Hugo of Elm, 264

Hugo of Kirtling and William son of John, 264
Hugo son of Ernald v. Hugo Ruffus and Philip son of Robert, 323
Hugo son of William, 265
Humphrey, 57, 73–4, 137, 157, 184
Hundewrichte, Decenna Guido, 265
Hundred Rolls, 1–2, 3–5, 8, 238–9, 242
   Cambridge, 1
   commission of 1255, 1
   enquiries of 1279–80, 2
   enquiry commissioners, 2
   geographical coverage, 1
   government enquiries, 1255, 1274–5 and 1279–80, 1
   liberties and landholding (1279–80), 2
   'liberties and the misdeeds of officials' (1274–5), 2
Hunne, Stephen (bailiff), 336
Hunte, 15, 107, 132–3, 161
Huntingdon, 23, 50, 153, 157–8, 162, 206, 210, 221, 223–7, 234, 236, 239
Huntingdonshire, 2–3
Huntingfield, 207, 210

I
income, 18, 27, 173
Infirmarer, John, 211, 218–19, 225, 230–1, 236
Ingelmar of Cambridge, 246
Isabella of Neddingworth, 293
Ismaina, 82, 174
Isondia, 209–10
Ivo Macecren/carnifax, 251
Ivo son of Absalon, 253, 257, 260
Ivo son of Matilda, 253, 260

J
Jews, 5, 58, 172, 240–1
John, Master, 26, 120, 181, 185
John nephew of Hugo, 252
John of Aylsham (bailiff), 334, 335
John of Braintree and the Aubrey (and family), 354–5
John of Brankere (bailiff), 336

John of Chesterton, 246, 247
John of Estfleet, 253, 257
John of Leek (bailiff), 336
John of Lynn (*Lenna*), 245
John of Trumpington (bailiff), 335
John son of Alvred/Helene, 250
John son of Henry son of Harvey, 263
John son of Selede, 251, 256
John the monk, 322
Jona, 214–15, 217
Jordan, 19–20, 40, 43, 127, 135, 145, 149, 174, 176, 184
Jordan of Horsee, 323
Juliana, 33, 36, 42, 48, 50, 57, 85, 126, 137, 139, 193–4, 217
jurors, 9
jury calendar, 239–40

K
Kaily tannur, 252
Karloc, Richard, 37
Kayly, Alan, 177, 187
Kenewi, by inheritance of, 224–6
Kenewy, William, 146
Kenilworth, Prior of, 27
Ketel, 33, 90, 173, 257
Ketel the Merchant, 254
Kew, 3
King John (reign of), 257
King, Osbert, 14, 211–12, 228, 233, 236
King's Childer Lane, 339
King, Stephen, 209, 230
knight's fee, 10, 162, 165
Knyvet, Geoffrey (bailiff), 336

L
Lady Alicia (former wife of Lord William of Buckworth), 44, 50–1
landholding, 2
   medieval, 4
   peasant, 4
   transfers, 5
Lane, John, 251
Langrithes Lane, 339
Lardario, 28, 118
Latin transcription, 5
Latin transcript, unpublished, 4

Laurence, 52
Laurence of Burwell, 265
Laurence, Richard (Mayor), 72–3, 139, 334, 335, 336
Laurence, Richard senior, 109, 139
Lecia, 208
le Ferrur, Geoffrey (bailiff), 335
Lefwin, brother of Serlone, 246
le Hanre, Matthew, 115
le Haur, Godric, 253
le Moyne, Sir William, 2
lepers, 24–5, 167
le Plowritte, William, 37–9
le Rus, John, 12
le Rus, Maurice, 148, 189, 224
le Rus, William (Mayor), 335
le Sanuer, Gregory, 12
le Sauver, Richemann, 108
le Savener, Gregory, 121
le Savener, Richemann, 122
le Spencer, Guy [Spicer] (Mayor), 334
le Spicer, Guy (Mayor), 334, 336
le Spicer, Widone (bailiff), 336
le Tailor, Maurice, 43
Leticia, 103, 107
le Vyver, Gerard (bailiff), 335
Liber Memorandum Ecclesie de Bernewelle, 5
    rental of 1295, 5
liberties and landholding (1279–80), 2
'liberties and the misdeeds of officials' (1274–5), 2
Lincke, Richard, 207, 214
Lincoln, 130, 182
Little Landwathe, 321
Lof, William, 245
Longis, Thomas, 36, 48, 85, 157
Longys, Thomas, 33, 36, 67
Lorimer's Row, 339
Lorteburne Lane, 339
Lucke, William, 117
Lungis, Nicholas, 212, 225
Lungis, Simon, 211, 213
Lutte, Harvey, 264
Lyssheris Lane, 339

M
Madingley, 9, 37–9, 47, 114, 136–7, 140–2, 174, 184, 233

Makeston, Peter, 123, 236
Malerbe, Michael, 29, 87–8, 116, 135, 141, 147, 192, 235, 322
Malerbe, Nicholas, 62, 70, 82, 90, 116, 135, 141, 235
Malfrey, Robert (bailiff), 336
Manefeld, 26, 34, 54–5, 70, 78, 92–3
Maniaunt, Robert, 213, 229
Marescall, John, 261
Margaret daughter of Gregory, 197
Margery wife of Martin Wulward, 323
Mariota, 82, 86–7, 92, 97, 99, 182, 200, 229
Mariote, John, 187
Marisco, William, 264
market privileges, 164
Market Street, 339
market town, 10, 163, 167
Marshall, Matthew, 197
Martin, John, 325, 334, 335
    and family, 358–9
Martina daughter of Richard, 321
Martin, Master, 96, 145, 176
Martin son of Geoffrey, 261, 263
Mason, John, 14–15, 209
Matelast, John, 135
Matilda wife of William textor, 263
Matthew son of Geoffrey, 253
mayors and bailiffs (1263–1300), 334–6
medium-size families
    Bateman, 343–5
    Bernard, Michael, 345–6
    Childman family, 347–8
    Eliot/Elyot/Elyhot family, 348–50
    Robert of Madingley, 350–1
Melt, Geoffrey, 13, 17, 204, 209, 216, 229, 237
Melt, Henry, 17, 150, 209, 229, 237
Melt, William, 209, 237–8
Mercator, Ermesius, 325
merchant guilds, 164
Merton College, Oxford, 5–6
    scholars of, 26, 34, 37–8, 42, 45, 55, 109, 113, 153, 156, 162
Michael House, 339
Michael son of John (bailiff), 336
Michael son of Orgar, 253
Miller, William, 96, 117, 191

Milne Street, 339
Molle, Henry, 229, 232
Mordon, 322
Morice, Nicholas, 35, 84, 88, 91, 97,
    107, 121, 136–7, 335
Morice, William, 91, 97
Morin (and family), 359–60
Morin, Geoffrey, 124, 146
Morin, Radulph, 124–5
Morin, Richard, 120, 124–5
Moryn, Richard, 70
Mulloc, Reginald, 253
Mun, Radulph, 109, 112
Mundi, Simon, 127, 227
Murdac, Geoffrey, 246

N

Nadon/Nado/Nadun, Henry, 67,
    127,135, 137, 140–1, 158, 160,
    335
Nadon, Robert, 135, 139–41
Nadun, Robert, 261
Newcome, Hugo, 184–5
Newemen, William le, 264
Newnham, 8, 23, 29, 72, 75, 77–80, 84,
    86, 88, 93, 95, 97, 98, 100, 106,
    151, 159, 321,
Nicholas, Master, 110, 117–18, 154,
    185
Nichtwat, Stephen, 246
Nigel, Master, 13, 85, 98, 107, 116–17,
    143
Niger, Simon, 250, 260
Niker, Jordan, 250, 256
Noreis, 202, 204–5, 208
Norman, 33, 41–2, 48, 54, 85, 167
Novacurt, William, 205–6
nuns, 171, 186
Nuns Lane, 339
Nutts lane, 339

O

Odo Cook, 218, 225, 238
Ong, Robert, 201
Oregar, Geoffrey, 188–9
Osbert of Stivichele, 263
Osgot brother of Alfgar, 245

P

Paie, William, 204–6, 226
Pandevant, William, 255
Pappe, Nicholas, 213–14, 225
Paris, Radulph, 174
Paris, William, 122
Parleben, John, 94, 191
Parleben, Robert, 13
Paschall Close, 339
pasture, common, 17, 165, 167
Patent Rolls, 5
Patent Rolls and Close Rolls, 5
paternal inheritance, 27, 141, 206, 211
Paternoster, John, 145
Paumer, 30, 103, 105, 107
peasant landholding, 3, 4
Peas Market, 339
Peiner, Richard le [Parmenter?], 252
Pennyfarthing Lane, 339
Perin, John (bailiff), 336
perpetual alms, 11–13, 15, 18–25, 28–9,
    79–80, 144, 154, 186, 192, 202,
    211
Perrin, John (bailiff), 335
Peter of Luton, 260
Peter of Wilbraham (bailiff), 334
Peter son, 23, 25, 87, 98–101, 110, 142,
    189
Peter son of William, 325
Peter the Baker (bailiff), 336
Pet, Richard, 200, 211, 222, 227–8
Petty Cury, 339
Peverel, Pagan, 11
Philip son of Robert, 321, 323
Picot, Geoffrey, 321, 322
Pie, Godfrey, 256
Pikerel, Henry, 76
Pikerel, John, 76
Pilat, Michael, 61, 171, 174, 235
Pilat's Lane, 339
Pilet, Michael, 61
Pinberd, Selede, 252
Pipe Rolls, 4, 4–5, 267–83
Pipestraw, Ivo, 251
Pirle, Radulph, 254
Piscator [Fisher], Hugh, 254
Pittock, William (bailiff), 336
Plea Rolls, 240–1
Plote, Thomas, 15, 157, 195, 222, 325

Plotts Lane, 339

Plumbe, Walter, 56

Podipol, Thomas, 140

Porthors/Portehors, John, 35, 41, 45, 53, 62, 67, 92–3, 107, 114, 128, 136, 157–9, 325, 334, 335

Porthors, John junior (bailiff), 336

Potecar, Gilbert, 177

Potecar/Potekyn dynasty, 360–1

Potecar, Simon, 181–2

Potekin, John, 94, 152

Pottere, Richard, 255

Pound Hill, 339

Prat, Geoffrey, 22, 97, 197

Prat, Simon, 49, 97, 146, 179, 197

Preachers Street, 340

Prentice, John (bailiff), 335, 336

prerogative rights, 4

Prest, William, 254

property market, 6

property portfolio, 6

Prudfot, Radulph, 250

Pruet, William, 106, 119–20

Punch, Hildebrand, 250

Pupelot, Thomas, 255

Purpresture, 165

Purs, Richard, 146

Pylat, Michael, 335, 336

Pyron Lane, 340

Q

Queye, Radulph de, 51, 159, 162

quitclaim, 16–17, 153, 180

R

Radulph brother of Godland, 245

Radulph brother of Ivo, 253

Radulph feltrarius/le Feutrer, 250

Radulph, Master, 155, 185, 192, 237

Radulph of Bradley (Bradelega), 246

Radulph of Swineshead, 261

Radulph son of Alfgar, 246

Radulph son of Fulk son of Theobald, 263

Radulph son of Geoffrey, 254, 264, 265

Radulph son of Ivo, 260

Ralph of Comberton (bailiff), 336

Ramsey Abbey, 2, 64, 176

Raseman, Roger, 265

Raveley, 2

Reginald of Abinton, 252

Reginald of Comberton (bailiff), 335

Reginald of Fordham, 250, 260

Reginald son of Alvred, 253

Reginald son of Gregory, 178

Reginald son of Harvey, 322

Renchene, Decenna Roger, 263

Rener of Wimboldham, 261

Richard at the Gate, 251

Richard of Barnwell, 246, 247, 252, 257

Richard of Ditton, 245

Richard of Hokele (bailiff), 335

Richard of Stortford/forestarius, 256

Richard of Wales, 264

Richard of Winepol, 264

Richard son of Agnes, 263

Richard son of Gregory, 43, 108, 122, 316

Richard son of Richard, 255, 257

Richard the plumber (plumbario), 246

Robert the painter, 12

Robert of Hinton (bailiff), 336

Robert of Madingley, 325, 350–1, 335

Robert of Newport, 245

Robert of St Edmunds, 325

Robert son of Anketil', 245

Robert son of Ivo, 263

Robert son of Robert, 263

Robert son of Selede, 246

Robert son of Sifred, 321

Robert son of Sofrei, 321

Robilliard, John (bailiff), 336

Roger of Comberton (bailiff), 335

Roger of Torpel, 264

Roger of Wilbraham (bailiff), 335

Roger of Withersfield (bailiff), 335

Roger of Wyke (Mayor), 334

Roger son of Baldric, 265

roll of pleas, 325

rolls

    Kew, 3

    missing roll, 3

    The National Archives Discovery catalogue, 3

    parishes properties, 3

Rome, 6
    Angelica Library, 6
rood of land, 15, 17, 39–41, 66–7,
        69–70, 77, 79, 141–2, 144,
        156–7, 209–10, 215–16, 219–20,
        230–2, 236–7
Roscelin of Hellinton', 265
Rotuli Curiae Regis, I–XX (excerpts),
        285–96
Rotuli Hundredorum, 1, 3, 362
royal inquiry, 2
royal itinerant justices, 4
royal rights, 2
    1274–5, 'liberties and the misdeeds of
        officials,' 2
    1279–80, liberties and landholding,
        2
    enquiry commissioners, 2
Ruffus, Albric, 246
Ruffus, Hugo, 323
Ruffus, William, 321, 323
Rushden, 213, 215, 230
Russel, John, 215, 225

S
Saher son of William, 265
St Austin's Hostel, 340
St Austin's Lane, 340
St Benedict's Street, 340
St Edmunds, 27, 37, 39, 50–1, 66,
        74–5, 79, 83–4, 95, 101–8,
        110, 160, 170, 195–7, 203–14,
        216, 218–20, 222–5, 227–33,
        235–8
    abbot of, 27, 46, 48, 50–1,
        56–7
St Edmund's Chapel, 130, 143
St Edmunds, Priory of, 340
St John's Hospital, 22–5, 54, 57, 78–9,
        84–6, 101, 107, 126, 130, 132–5,
        140, 158–61, 171, 178, 186
St Neots, 331
St Radegund's Priory, 18–22, 20–1,
        29–31, 34–5, 46, 60–1, 76,
        100–2, 110, 119, 126–8, 133–5,
        152–4, 156, 159–61, 169–71,
        173–4, 176–80, 184–7, 194–7,
        340

St Thomas Leys, 340
Salandin, Geoffrey, 209, 214, 230, 232,
        236
Salandin, John, 209, 230–1, 236
Salnar, Spileman, 246, 247
Salthythe Lane, 340
Saphir, William, 115
Sarand, Nicholas, 21
Scan, Simon, 115, 191, 226
Scherewind, Reginald (bailiff), 335
School of Pythagoras, 340
Sciper/Sliper, William, 255
Scipre, Godard le, 246
S(c)ortenicht, Reginald, 253
Scolelane, 340
Scolice, Alicia, 124
Scot, Adam, 38–9, 43
scutage, 9, 26, 162
Scutland, Geoffrey, 246
Sedge Hall, 340
Segrimmeslane, 340
Segyn, John, 32, 199
Selede, Eustace, 75, 77, 99, 134
Selede, John, 15, 119, 130, 138
Selede, Simon, 75, 77
Seliman, John, 155, 201, 202
Selone son of Nigel v. Reginald son of
        Harvey, 322
Seman, Alice, 331
Seman, Robert, 10, 12, 39–40, 43, 47,
        49–50, 52, 61, 63, 107–8, 121,
        126, 129, 255
Seman, William (bailiff), 9, 46, 59,
        64, 67, 73, 118, 133, 148, 325,
        335
Sephare, Simon (bailiff), 336
Serlone, brother of William, 246
Serlone the cellarer *(sellario)*, 246
Shearer's Lane, 340
Sherewynd, Reginald, 325
Shoemaker Lane, 340
Sibert, Geoffrey, 254
Simon ad Aquam (bailiff), 334, 335
Simon of Bradley (bailiff), 335
Simon of Refham (bailiff), 336
Simon of Stockton (bailiff), 334, 336
Simon Ruffus v. William Pevel, 322
Simon son of Beatrice, 263
Simon son of Godric, 257

Simon son of John, 326
Simon son of the same/Godric,
253
Simon the Tailor, 250
Sissard [Cissor], Walter, 251
Skin, Richard, 76
Slaughter Lane, 340
Smallbridge Street, 340
small families
Andrew, 351–2
Aure/Auwre/Aured, 353–4
Godeman, 357–8
John Martin, 358–9
John of Braintree and the Aubrey,
354–5
Morin, 359–60
Potecar/Potekyn dynasty, 360–1
Walter Em, 356
Smith, Geoffrey, 16, 212, 215–16, 225,
229, 233
Smith, Henry, 41, 48, 217
Smith, John, 88, 104, 191
Smith, William, 14, 16, 96, 206, 214,
226–7, 234
socage, 10
Sot, William, 91
Sped, Margaret, 227–8, 233
Spittle End, 340
Stanton, 37–8, 43, 107, 154
statistical information, of property rents,
1
Stebing, Thomas, 214, 223
Stephen Cordubarius of Cambridge v.
Robert son of Sofrei, 321
Stephen son, 9899, 198
Stephen son of Selede v. Robert son
of Sifred and the Templars of
Jerusalem, 321
Steresman, Robert (bailiff), 336
Stortford/forestarius
Richard of, 256
Stote, Peter, 208, 231
Stramar, Absalon, 246
Stramar, William, 246
Straw Lane, 340
subsidy rolls, 4, 325
Swaffham, Prior of, 27
Swaffham nuns of, 72, 90, 103, 150,
179, 186, 200

sworn juries, of knights, 2
Swyn, Harvey, 101
Sybil daughter of Alan of Childerley,
265

T
Talemasche, William, 260
tallage, 4–5
accounts, 4
of Cambridge, 1219, 4
rolls, 4
Tele, Matilda, 210, 225, 237
Thomas, Master, 190
Thomas mercurius, 261
Thomas of Madingley (bailiff),
336
Thomas of Snailwell (bailiff), 335
Thomas of Trumpington, 322
Thomas son of Godwin, 260
Thomas son of Humphry, 263
Thomas son of Thomas, 264
Thorel, Alicia, 115
Tinctor, Harvey (bailiff), 335
Toylet, Henry (bailiff), 58, 95, 150,
335
Toylet, Robert, 335, 336
Toylet, Thomas, 13, 93, 153, 155,
171–3, 336
Toylet, William, 23, 58, 95, 125, 150–1,
160, 172–3, 325
tracing transfers of land, 5
Trig, Robert, 56, 174
Trottere, Godard le, 246
Trumpington Gate, 23, 25, 74, 76,
79–80, 86, 101, 106, 117, 126,
131, 340
Turketell' of the Bridge, 245
Twiselet, Robert, 264

U
Ulf, Decenna William, 263
University archives, property market,
6
University of Cambridge, 6, 30, 132,
160, 163, 196, 241
University of Oxford, 6
Merton College archives, 6

university scholars, in writing rolls, 3
Urvei son of Emme petitioner v. Robert
    prior of Barnwell, 322

V

vacant land, 25, 34–6, 47–8, 98, 104–6,
    118, 121, 124, 131, 133, 144,
    146–7, 235
Vivien, Henry, 255
Vivien, Robert, 255

W

Waddon, 108, 158, 161
Wallyslane, 340
Walter, father of Absolon, 245
Walter of Barking (bailiff), 336
Walter of Fulbourn (bailiff), 336
Walter son of Absolon, 252
Walter son of Escolice, 252
Walter son of Gilbert, 246, 247
Walter son of Robert, 264
Wanter, Adam le, 250
Wanter, Robert le, 250, 256
Wanter, Serlo le, 251
Warin, John, 49
Warin, Nicholas, 331
Warin, Roger, 49
Warin son of Anketil, 254
Warin son of Norman, 255
Wastel, Radulph, 246
Water Lane, 340
Watermills, 11, 166
Waubert, John, 54, 151, 159
Waubert, William, 12, 141, 151, 159
Wellifedd, Roger, 264
Werial, Adam, 254
Weriel, Adam, 16
Werret, Walter, 16, 201
Wetherley, hundred of, 331
White Friars, 340
Whitefriars Lane, 340
Whittlesford, 331
Wilburham, 124, 127, 149, 187–8, 223
Wilicom, Picotus, 11
William Macecren/carnifax, 251
William of Bekiswelle (bailiff), 336
William of Buckingham, 321

William of Cancia, 265
William, of Cotes, 325
William of Crawden, 264
William of Holm (bailiff), 336
William of Ripton, 261
William of Selford [Shelford], 252
William of Swavesey, 246, 247
William of Well(es), 246
William Ruffus v. Jordan of Horsee,
    323
William son of Edward, 250
William son of Elye, 325
William son of Guido, 264
William son of Harold, 263
William son of Simon, 263
William son of the master, 265
Willis, Robert, 241
Wimund, Robert, 39–40, 73
Wimund, Walter, 40, 50, 126
Wisman, William, 41, 77, 112
Wombe, Bartholomew, 60, 94, 140,
    146–7, 149, 155, 158, 160, 170
Wombe, Isabella, 47
Wombe, John, 77, 84, 93, 99, 138,
    146–7
Wombe, Nicholas, 77, 93, 99, 107,
    137–8, 158–9, 198, 236
Wombe, Radulph, 60, 148–9, 250,
    261
Wombe, Richard, 64, 84, 89, 94, 104,
    146, 154–5, 160, 178, 222
Wulsi, William, 234–5, 251, 256
Wulward, Geoffrey, 254, 257
Wulward, Martin, 102, 114, 125, 253,
    257, 260, 322, 323
Wulward, Michael (bailiff), 44, 336
Wulward of the Bridge, 246, 247
Wulward, Peter, 44, 53–4, 56, 331
Wulward, Richard, 255, 257, 264
Wulward, Robert, 14, 44, 102, 114,
    125–6
Wulward, Roger, 114
Wulward, Thomas, 118, 127
Wymund, Robert (bailiff), 335

Y

Yde, William, 143, 177
Yve, John, 129, 187

Printed and bound by CPI Group (UK) Ltd, Croydon, CR0 4YY

23/04/2025

14661023-0004